THE TROPICS BITE BACK

THE TROPICS BITE BACK

Culinary Coups in Caribbean Literature

VALÉRIE LOICHOT

University of Minnesota Press
Minneapolis
London

The University of Minnesota Press gratefully acknowledges financial assistance provided for the publication of this book from the Emory College of Arts and Sciences and the Laney Graduate School.

A portion of chapter 1 was previously published as "Between Breadfruit and Masala: Food Politics in Glissant's Martinique," *Callaloo* 30, no. 1 (Winter 2007); copyright 2007 Charles H. Rowell; reprinted with permission from The Johns Hopkins University Press. A portion of chapter 3 was previously published as "Edwidge Danticat's Kitchen History," *Meridians: Feminism, Race, Transnationalism* 5, no. 1 (Fall 2004); reprinted courtesy of Indiana University Press. A portion of chapter 3 was previously published as "Reconstruire dans l'exil: La nourriture créatrice chez Gisèle Pineau," *Études Francophones* 17, no. 2 (Fall 2002).

Published by the University of Minnesota Press
111 Third Avenue South, Suite 290
Minneapolis, MN 55401-2520
http://www.upress.umn.edu

A Cataloging-in-Publication record for this book is available from the Library of Congress.
ISBN 978-0-8166-7983-6 (hc)
ISBN 978-0-8166-7984-3 (pb)

Printed in the United States of America on acid-free paper

20 19 18 17 16 15 14 13 10 9 8 7 6 5 4 3 2 1

CONTENTS

INTRODUCTION

The Cannibal and the Edible

> I am afraid we have eyes bigger than our stomachs, and more curiosity than capacity.
>
> —Michel de Montaigne, *Of Cannibals*

THE CARIBBEAN, IN THE CONQUEROR'S IMAGINATION, began with Columbus's mistake. *"Caríba,"* screamed by *Carib* Amerindians calling out their name, morphed, in Columbus's ears, into an explorer's warning: *caníbal.* The conqueror, so the story goes,[1] invested the strange sound with the image of the dog-headed anthropophagous ape of Greek and Roman mythology or cynocephalus. Instead of "carí," Columbus heard "cani," which he assimilated to the Latin *canis,* or dog, translated into the Greek *Cyno* carrying in its tow the suffix *-cephalus,* which invoked the monster imported from the ancient European myth. Thus, the 1492 encounter marks the simultaneous birth of the cannibal and the Caribbean in European lexicons and in European fantasies. The name of a people thus quickly dissolved into the figure of the savage man-eater. Columbus's mistake occurred during his first encounter with the archipelago as he stumbled upon the large island soon after christened Hispaniola, now hosting Haiti and the Dominican Republic. The land of Haiti has thus been inhabited, since the moment of Columbus's penetration, by the word "cannibal."

Metastazing from this linguistic error, Europeans and other Western colonizers, tourists, and readers have associated the Antilles with the primal act of eating, whether in the figure of the cannibal, or in that of its tamed counterpart, the Caribbean itself—its land, people, and language—all reduced to delectable objects: "Cannibal islands," "spice islands," "succulent women," "luscious beaches," "peppery language."[2]

I call this imperialist political and epistemological machine, which began with Columbus, and continued with Hegel and contemporary tourism, the "colonial mouth," which ingests, dissolves, and eliminates preexisting names such as Karukera, Madinina, Haïti, Caríba, Anacaona, to regurgitate upon them names and images that control them. Colonial and exotic discourses and practices have cooked, figuratively and at times literally, subjects of the Caribbean and the Black Atlantic. These gestures originate in the excessive hunger, curiosity, and greed of the colonial act, as Montaigne lucidly saw as early as 1580 in his essay "Des Cannibales," which can be identified as the founding theoretical critique of cannibalistic thinking. For Montaigne, the colonial greed—"we have eyes bigger than our stomachs"—exceeds in horror and in hubris the measured and ritualized custom of war cannibalism practiced by the Tupinambá Amerindians. European conquerors since their original contact with the "New World" have used the cannibalistic trope obsessively as the yardstick of savagery. In Montaigne's tour de force, the savagery resides not in the Brazilian cannibal but in the very hubris of the European fantasy, and stomach, that created or distorted it in order to cast its own evils onto the New World. What I call the "colonial food disease" is thus, first and foremost, that of the colonizer. The disease reduced Caribbean subjects to figures evoking pathological eating: the blood-thirsty cannibal, the glutton, the bulimic, the uncouth eater, the starved, the happy-to-be-starved, the selfless *da* or Antillean mammy, the wet nurse whose milk evades her own children, the cunning cook, the sugary *doudou,* the fruity octoroon, the grinning *Banania*-man or docile Uncle Ben served at our kitchen table.

Such controlling images inherited from colonial and racialist discourses persist in our contemporary daily lives.[3] In 2010, two events of a different scale, and thus of different globalized media visibility, marked the Caribbean: an earthquake in Haiti and a referendum in Martinique and French Guyana. The earthquake, which struck Haiti on January 12, 2010, has had the devastating consequences that we continue to witness and that Haitians continue to endure. On January 10, 2010, French president Nicolas Sarkozy proposed a referendum asking Martinicans whether they wanted more autonomy from the French government. Martinicans rejected the referendum by an overwhelming margin of 79 percent. At first glance, it would appear that these two events have nothing to do with each other. However, the media linked them by reducing them, I argue, to pathological eating, with starvation and overconsumption as the two sides of the same coin. In both cases, Haiti and Martinique were represented as being struck (at best) or cursed (at worst) by the food disease that I introduce in this chapter. Their respective states of hunger or overconsumption have been presented as a malediction in a vacuum not influenced by the political and historical circumstances that led these nations to such a state in the first place. In Western media representations, the default description of Haiti in the aftermath of the earthquake was "the poorest nation in the Western Hemisphere," ridden by illiteracy and hunger. Most disturbingly, this cliché presents Haiti as being simply "ridden by" a plight with no specification of the responsibility of nations such as France or the United States in the devastation of humans and soil, impoverishment and deforestation. As Britain-based critic Peter Hallward encapsulates: "This poverty is the direct legacy of perhaps the most brutal system of colonial exploitation in world history, compounded by decades of systematic postcolonial oppression."[4] Televangelist Pat Robertson's infamous commentary, presenting the earthquake as the result of a curse on Haitians who would have "signed a pact with the devil" to free themselves from French colonial power, is an acute case of this discourse. Mainstream critics and journalists, undoubtedly in a milder form, have described hunger in the Caribbean nation as a state severed from its historical contextualization. In so doing, they maintained Haiti in a discursive state of being a doomed victim of starvation. Hunger, thus, becomes the faceless subject that eclipses and absolves the responsible ones.[5]

In the wake of the Martinican referendum, writer Raphaël Confiant denounced his fellow Martinicans as "sub-humans," "foodstuff," and "below excremental."[6] Indeed, the Martinicans' response—especially after the 2009 generalized strikes demanding more autonomy[7]—is at best surprising, and at worst confirms what Confiant calls the Martinicans' fear of their "Papa Blanc" (White Daddy), who controls his "Martinican children" by the promise of keeping them fed through a politics of dependence.[8] However, Confiant, like the international press on Haiti, blames the victims without mentioning the oppressors' strategy of overfeeding to keep the colony intact, or without questioning the viability of the proposed referendum.[9] Confiant also perpetuates the colonial discourse by presenting his compatriots as food and excremental matter. In these two examples, whether starved or overconsumers, contemporary people of Haiti and Martinique are defined through their relationship to food, through a movement that repeats centuries of defining black slaves and their descendants as being controlled by their stomach.

Thus, the twofold goal of this book is to reflect on the overdetermination of Caribbean people through examining their relationship to food. More important, it also proposes to analyze food in the Caribbean not only as a basic need but also as a form of cultural expression, a form of political resistance, and a form of civilization.[10] Food, therefore, can be both the site of lost power and empowerment, depending on its source and its use. I will occasionally evoke Caribbean cooking and culinary art as discussed in cookbooks.[11] My central concern, however, is not to expose or analyze recipes but rather to acknowledge, through the literary works of Francophone, Anglophone, and Creolophone writers, the humanity reached by the cultural appropriation of food. This goal ultimately aims to substitute the controlling images of Caribbean people defined by food pathologies and transgressions by exposing acts of constructing humanity through literal, allegorical, or metaphorical acts of cooking and eating.

Caribbean subjects confront with teeth and discourse insidious images such as that of the fiery tropical cannibal to take center stage on the kitchen table of the literary scene. Guadeloupean writer Maryse Condé has termed this common strategy of resistance to colonialism an act of *mordre en retour* or "biting back."[12] Caribbean writers eat back at these representations by reclaiming images of pathological eating as culturally productive through actual gestures of cooking,[13] by turning food, often presented into a discursive mode of production, by entrapping Western readers in their own trap, by practicing literary cannibalism, and eventually, by establishing a literature in a postcannibalistic moment outside antagonistic or revengeful relations.

The geography of *The Tropics Bite Back* cannot be bound by clear spatial, political, or linguistic borders. It embraces multifarious sites such as the Caribbean communal yard or *lakou*; the slave quarters and its Creole gardens; the big-house kitchen cabin; the hills of free maroons; the beach for Sunday gatherings; the *potajé* or outdoor cooking structure; the tiny square kitchens of transnational urban spaces of immigration in the Bronx or in Parisian suburbs; the bodies of women and men "cooked" by historical violence and representation; the delirious fantasies of Europeans imagining the cannibal scene; the theoretical spaces of Glissant's creolization; or the cannibal writing that concocts preparations from shreds and ingredients of previously devoured texts.

The word "Tropics" is helpful in that it encompasses parts of the Americas outside the Caribbean per se, such as New Orleans, which nineteenth-century writer Lafcadio Hearn called "the gate of the Tropics" (*American Writings,* 669). The idea of the Tropics, otherwise called "torrid zone," was created to invent a "hot" zone—referring to climate, character, sexuality, and food—which would consolidate the borders of Europeanness and whiteness.[14] This fictional zone encompasses broadly the geographic zones located between the Tropic of Cancer and the Tropic of Capricorn. Thus, in this category can be included the Caribbean, Central America, part of South America, most of Africa, the Indian subcontinent, Southeast Asia, and part of Australia. Additionally, subtropical neighbors, such as the South of the United States, are often included in the Tropical zone. Very broadly, the tropical zone is marked by a common agriculture of cash crops, plantation economy, a history of slavery (as origin or destination), and colonial exploitation. From Buffon, to Hegel, to twenty-first-century representations, the Tropics have been reduced discursively to zones of tourism and leisure, disease, historical absence or stagnation, and acts of savagery such as incest and cannibalism.[15] However, like other controlling images, the idea of the Tropics has been reclaimed by Caribbean and Brazilian writers as a common zone of cultural and aesthetic construction. Examples of this reappropriation of the Tropics include the journal *Tropiques,* published under censorship in wartime Martinique (1941–45) through the leadership of Aimé Césaire, Suzanne Césaire, and René Ménil. The Brazilian cultural movement of *Tropicália* or *Tropicalísmo* that arose in the 1960s constitutes another instance in which a global art movement (concrete poetry, theater, music) reclaimed the Tropics to assert cultural specificity and audacity.[16]

Within this Tropical zone, the examples of Guadeloupe and Martinique will serve as our privileged examples. Independent Haiti will constitute a crucial point of comparison for the literature produced in the French territories. In 1946, the old French colonies of Guadeloupe and Martinique became "Overseas Departments." Sixty years later, they are still an integral part of the French Republic and the European Union in spite of their location in the Americas. By concentrating on food, this study displaces the focus from the struggle for national independence, which, in the current context, remains limited to survival tactics, to cultural resistance. I argue that it is through culture that Guadeloupe and Martinique cut the umbilical cord with the colonizing nation by asserting their particularity. The emphasis on culinary culture equates neither with surrender nor with refusal of politics, but rather with a political action played out in everyday and multifarious sites, a "food politics," as I elaborate in chapter 1, "From Gumbo to Masala."

This thorough examination of representations of food from the nineteenth to the twenty-first century replaces the islands in their immediate context of the Caribbean Black Atlantic.[17] The book thus severs Martinique and Guadeloupe from the political economic ensemble to which they belong, the European Union. Instead, it relocates them, through an analysis of their relationship to cooking and eating, in their Caribbean, American (in the continental sense), and African diasporic context. I will analyze the work of two Haitian writers, Edwidge Danticat and Dany Laferrière, living in Miami and Montreal, respectively, not only to highlight cultural commonalities between Guadeloupe and Haiti but also to consider their belonging to a wider American—and ultimately worldwide—contact zone. For Mary Louise Pratt, the term "contact zone . . . is an attempt to invoke the spatial and temporal copresence of subjects previously separated by geographic and historical disjunctures, and whose trajectories now intersect" (*Imperial Eyes,* 7). According to this logic, I put Suzanne Césaire into contact with the Brazilian modernist Oswald de Andrade, author of the *Manifesto anthropófago,* instead of presenting her as the inheritor of French surrealism,[18] thus exiting the trap of influence between French and Caribbean writers constructed as their secondary heirs. Instead of simply reversing the angle of influence, by showing, for instance, that Breton is Césaire's inheritor rather than the other way around, I shift the focus away from the European-American legacy by establishing an inter-American, and cross-Atlantic, discourse. Such a dialogue, like Pratt's "contact perspective," "treats the relation among colonizers and colonized, or travelers and 'travelees,' not in terms of separateness or Apartheid, but in terms of copresence, interaction, interlocking understandings and practices, often with radically asymmetrical relations of power" (ibid.).

I also situate food symbols used in the construction of national, cultural, or ethnic identities in relation to similar productions of the American contact zone. For instance, what I call "Our Common Creole Stew" (chapter 1) serves as a common denominator for the construction of a diasporic and Creole identity, in the sense of an encounter between disparate elements in a single space. Thus stews such as callaloo, gumbo, and *ajiaco* have the same structural function and relationship to memory and cultural performance in spite of their respective particularities. There is as well a repeating culinary trope traversing Brazil, Cuba, Martinique, Haiti, and the U.S. African diaspora, which links these zones otherwise separated politically. This is an example, on the culinary level, of what Kamau Brathwaite has done with rhythms and music, Benítez-Rojo with rhythms of capitalism and the plantation machine, Édouard Glissant with the repeating Plantation and what he calls the jazzing of the world, Anny Dominique Curtius with repeating tropes of religious iconography, and Derek Walcott with his submarine history.[19] "Our Common Creole Stew," then, connects disjointed American fragments while maintaining the difference necessarily contained in the very act of repetition.

In chapter 4, "Sexual Traps," I show how the violence imposed on Caribbean male and female bodies and the relationship between the sexually consumed body and tropes of reading are linked to the violence of slavery across the Americas. I incorporate, for instance, a comparison of male and female bodies reduced to consumable goods in Laferrière's and Pineau's novels to practices and representations of lynching in the United States. The chapters on Pineau and Condé situate the relationship to food in yet a different context of migration and exile. They thus extend the Creole zone to unlikely candidates such as North Africans in Paris or Chicanas in New York.

The primary texts I will analyze were produced between the late nineteenth century and the beginning of the twenty-first. The temporal length in consideration comprehends a series of stages of cultural resistance. In an initial phase (from the late nineteenth to the mid-twentieth century), values are inverted and the European colonizer is turned into the cannibal. For instance, folktales portray the sugarcane factories and their white owners as human-eating monsters. In the wake of Brazilian *antropófagismo,* propounded by Oswald de Andrade in 1928, Martinican authors such as Suzanne Césaire and Aimé Césaire reclaim the act of metaphorical literary cannibalism as an emancipating tool of cultural production. Beyond the "cannibalistic" phase, contemporary Caribbean authors such as Condé and Glissant use food metaphors to define the Caribbean in relation to a global world in which the colonizing nation ceases to function as an essential cultural reference. In the Antillean Black and Creole Atlantic, dishes such as *colombo* work as vehicles for creolization, a dynamic process that incorporates African, European, and Asian elements while creating a genuine Caribbean culture that surpasses the sum of its original parts.

To examine the representation of food in the postslavery era, however, requires going back to the centuries immediately following the very inception of the conquest of what has been known since as "America" or the "New World." I refer systematically to texts written from the European Renaissance to the nineteenth century when they explain certain racial or culinary theories or representations. Columbus's (blind) eyewitness account of his encounter with Amerindians is foundational of the very word and concept of cannibalism. Montaigne's "Of Cannibals," as I have just argued, offers the most modern visionary account of the representations and functions of symbolic cannibalism. Buffon's theories are also crucial to comprehend how Europeans began to classify race, and they offer an interesting interpretation of the variety within the human race as seen through a continuum. Gobineau's racist writings are also helpful in understanding how black hunger was constructed as monstrous and pathological. Seventeenth- and early eighteenth-century accounts by priests such as Père Dutertre, Père Labat, or the late eighteenth- and early nineteenth-century historical account of white Creole Martinican Moreau de Saint-Méry give us precious insights not only on ethnographic notes on eating practices but also about European fantasies about Amerindian and African eaters, and, ultimately, about their own pathological relation to food. As I show in chapter 2, Labat becomes the cruel cannibal he projects onto the African or Amerindian. As Cameroonian writer Achille Mbembe has so rightly claimed, colonial discourse is "an aberrant product of madness that threatens all domination" (*On the Postcolony,* 181). Thus this book is as much about European and Western pathology as it is about the response of the object of the colonizing gaze.

The Materiality of Hunger

While *The Tropics Bite Back* does not deal centrally with the politics of hunger,[20] the materiality of hunger serves as an intensifier in all the cases I discuss. Slavery, colonization, and neocolonialism have indeed plagued the Caribbean with hunger, from its European-African inception to the present: from the forced starvation of the slave plantation, to the impoverishment of the soil due to extensive land exploitation, to political blockades, to a bulldozer global economy armed with tourist resorts and sweatshops, Caribbean subjects have experienced hunger as a lived torment or threat. One of the interviewees of the 2009 documentary film *Poto-Mitan,*[21] which defines women as the pillars of a Haitian economy dominated by the global market, claims that hunger, in Haiti, has a name: Clorox. Hunger is thus an imported product, which, like the abrasive cleaning bleach, can destroy the body. It is therefore crucial to highlight the fact that this book not only deals with the figurative. Metaphors of hunger, juxtaposed with those of overeating, are steeped in a material experience of hunger.

The fear of going hungry is indeed grounded economically. In Martinique and Guadeloupe, where most of the food eaten is imported (more in chapters 1 and 2), local sustainability is limited to the private gardens of an educated financial elite. The majority of the land is still dominated by the monocultures of sugarcane and bananas, or else, the land that belongs to the white elite class of *békés* is now rented to French supermarket chains.[22] The current economy is thus still closely linked to plantation economy since supermarkets have replaced the plantation, implying the same relationship of dependence on foods that are not produced locally by the laboring body. Already in 1943, a local industrialist and planter in Martinique, J. M. Hayot, addressed a plea to the landowners of the town of Petit-Bourg:

> Gentlemen: if we want to eat, we must imperatively plant . . . not only yams, but also cabbages, peas, pistachios, manioc, etc. I plan to build a modern manioc factory on the farm, which could accommodate the manioc production of neighboring farmers as well, should they so desire. Cucumbers, eggplants, chayotes, papayas, as well as peppers, onions, etc. grow quickly and easily and guarantee a sure profit. We must plant everything. Everything can be eaten, everything can be sold. I guarantee you the easy sale of your entire production on the Fort-de-France market. I'm currently organizing a haulage system with wagons and drawn carriages that will provide you with easy and inexpensive transportation. Our duty and interest are but one. I'm sure you will understand. I count on you. The land does not lie.[23]

The urgent call for sustainable agriculture, already felt acutely in 1943, remains unaddressed to this day. The ingenious and visionary Hayot, providing solutions to all the problems of sustainability—from the suitability of the land to the modes of transportation, to profit, to distribution, to the possibility of a fully local agriculture—remains unheard.

The scream of the land, which "does not lie," remains unheard as well.[24] Planters are still not working for the land and for Martinique but instead for their own profit, which is more directly linked to a global economy. For lack of local sustainable agriculture, Antilleans are kept in the lurking fear of hunger if a relationship to France were to be severed. This might partly explain the result of the referendum quoted earlier, a point that Confiant fails to address.

Pathologized Hunger

African, Caribbean, or Tropical eaters have been systematically presented as less than human through their relationship to food in order to mask the responsibility of the colonial or imperial power for the hunger of the slavery or the postslavery subject, whether it is forced hunger or force-feeding by the dumping of goods onto consumers to maintain a desire for dependency. The two dominant images are that of an insatiable hunger and of a lack of a need to eat. These twin images, despite their apparent contradiction, work hand in hand. Sometimes they are even presented in the same paragraph by naturalists, historians, and philosophers. In Creole colonist Moreau de Saint-Méry's words:

> In health, the negro deserves the quality of "sober," even if he tends to be a gourmand, even a glutton, on occasions in which he is given the opportunity to eat profusely. Happy with little in his daily life, he may very well be, among all men, the one who consumes the least amount of food, especially in relation to his labor. . . . Since he often eats raw [food], he saves all the time in his disposal. The negro follows no rules when he eats, save that of his appetite. . . . He enjoys mixing several meals in the same dish, even in the same mouthful. . . . He has no other knife, spoon, and fork than his fingers and teeth. (*Description topographiqe,* 61)

Moreau's "negro," in spite of his gluttony, is, among mankind, the one who needs the least amount of food to thrive. These apparently contradictory statements actually point to two sides of the same coin, gluttony and asceticism, which will be prevalent in Césaire's *Cahier* and in Chamoiseau's *Creole Folktales* (see chapter 2). Thus the act of eating is never balanced; it is always oscillating between one extreme pole and the other. Moreover, the two attributions of gluttony and asceticism serve the same purpose of justifying and absolving the colonial enterprise. The fictionalized black people's gluttony and unruliness, their proximity to nature, their pretechnological state—their only tools are teeth and fingers—their lack of discrimination, their preference for the raw over the cooked, place them on the side of the natural, the bestial, and therefore justify their enslavement or domination. However, their natural frugality, demonstrated by an inherent sense of "economy," justifies their enslavement by a naturalist argument and absolves colonists and plantation owners from near-starving them. How can you starve someone who can survive without eating? As eighteenth-century French naturalist Buffon sums it up: "Ils supportent, dit-on, très aisément la faim" [They (Africans) take hunger lightly, I am told] (Buffon, 368).

This argument of frugality and endurance was often used historically, from Las Casas in a Spanish colonial context to Dutertre in the French case, to justify the enslavement of Africans as opposed to that of the Amerindians. This conclusion did not benefit the Amerindians since, while Africans were assimilated to slavery, Amerindians were annihilated. Dutertre provides us with a cold declaration on the contrasting needs and abilities of Amerindians and Africans: "As for enslaved savages . . . they are usually so melancholic that no work can be extracted from them, unless by flattery, and a local proverb says, to beat a negro is to feed him, but conversely, to scream at a savage is to beat him, and to beat him is to kill him" (480–81). Basing his construction on an observation of the naturality of Africans and "savages," Dutertre confirms the colonial assumption that Africans do not need to be fed, that a good beating is all the food they need, and that "savages" are unfit for work and thus unfit for life in the colony: "But if they lack food or water, they are soon reduced to despair, so much that . . . they take their life with their own hands" (477). Assimilation and annihilation are thus the only two alternatives for Africans and Amerindians in the colony. Interestingly, the fate of the Amerindian is fabricated as suicide, caused by a natural state of melancholy. The white man is thus doubly absolved, first by the deferral of responsibility onto the Amerindian, and second, by a natural legitimization of his state.

For Dutertre, the savagery of the Amerindian appetite equals that of the African. The Amerindians eat when they please with no respect for temporal order. They injest things inconceivable to the European palate, such as fish bones, nameless sauces, poisonous manioc, snakes, and a mixture that Dutertre calls "un beau tripotage" (an obscene mess) (430): "The uncouth nature of our savages is nowhere as evident as in their eating: for they are so unclean in all matters of drinking and eating that it sickens all who witness their concoctions. . . . While they eat, they burp, piss, and, . . . I will refrain from saying more for decency purposes. They find it completely natural to find hair, straw, leaves, caterpillars, and all sorts of junk mixed up with their food (429)." The Amerindian is placed in the state of an infant unable to discriminate between the bodily functions of eating or urinating. Dutertre's "savage," more than being on the side of the raw, which, according to Claude Lévi-Strauss, represents the pole of the natural in opposition to the cultural (*Le cru,* 341), is on the side of the inedible (hair, straw, leaves, caterpillars, and junk). Abject eating settles Amerindians in the position of the inassimilable, who need to perish figuratively and literally.

Disorderly eating is one abject trait of Amerindians and Africans, among many others; for Dutertre and Moreau, they also suffer from deviant sexuality, melancholic motherhood, lack of skills, and ill morality. Gobineau goes even further by reducing Africans to their stomachs or turning them into inverted cripples, as Nietzsche would call them.[25] Their unruly stomachs are the sites of a hypertrophic and indiscriminate appetite that come to define them entirely. This hypertrophy of the stomach explains, in part, for Gobineau an "inexistent or mediocre intellectual faculty" (1:214). According to racist Gobineau, the impulses of the "Melanian race" ("race mélanienne") are determined by their animal senses of smell and taste: "All types of food are good for him. Nothing disgusts him, nothing repels him. All he wants to do is eat, eat with excess, eat with a fury; no repugnant corpse is unfit for his engulfing stomach" (215). Because he feeds on the inedible, the abject, on corpses, like vultures or hyenas, he cannot be assimilated, needs to be expelled, vomited from Gobineau's definition of humanity. However, in his delirious language, complaisance for the abject, voyeuristic, and utter sadist, it is Gobineau's text itself that represents, for this reader, the indigestible and the abject. The two volumes of *L'Essai sur l'inégalité des races humaines* spoil my bookshelves, cause nausea and an urge to quickly get rid of the book. As a reader, I feel dirtied, and also perhaps in a position of voyeurism in reading these texts, which are abject because of their abject hatred. However, as a critic, I think it is essential to quote the filth of these texts, to read them closely, firsthand, in order to undermine their racism and to understand the origin of the circulating images, such as the ones I analyze in this chapter, that have determined the destiny of black subjects. As Frantz Fanon puts it, "At the start of my history that others have fabricated for me, the pedestal of cannibalism was given pride of place *so that I wouldn't forget.* They inscribed on my chromosomes certain genes of various thickness representing cannibalism" (100, emphasis mine). We could add to the inscription of the cannibal that of the savage-eater, of the happy-to-be-starved, and of the edible. Thus, *so that we wouldn't forget,* we should investigate not so much the state of the victim but the disease of the perpetrator. We should reveal the madness of texts, such as Gobineau's, that present an extreme, albeit rampant, case of white racist pathology.[26] Native American scholar Jack D. Forbes comes to a similar conclusion in his *Columbus and Other Cannibals.* Exploiters and colonizers, and we could add epistemological colonizers like Gobineau, carry a disease that Forbes calls *wétiko* after a Native American Cree term encompassing all forms of greed-prompted violence. The *wétiko* psychosis, which Forbes translates as "cannibalism," was imported by the very inventor of the term "cannibal": "I shall argue that Columbus was a *wétiko*, that he was mentally ill or insane, the carrier of a terribly contagious disease, the *wétiko* psychosis. The native people he described were, on the other hand, sane people with a healthy state of mind" (Forbes, 23).

Food Racism

Within this racist logic, or rather, racist madness, Amerindian, African, Black, or Tropical subjects are controlled by two figures that define them: the edible and the cannibal. The two stereotypes seem antithetical but actually serve the same function. Similar to the example of the frugal and uncontrollable hunger I just analyzed, one appears as the logical sanction of the other. If the "tropical other" as cannibal threatens to turn the European subject into food, then, the cannibal must be turned into food in order to be tamed and annihilated.[27] The potential eater is turned into the eaten following a simple preemptive logic. Additionally, both images relegate the Tropical to a subhuman state. As anthropologist Richard King has argued: "After 1492, cannibalism takes its place alongside incest, polygamy, infanticide, and more recently female genital modification as a privileged, even central marker of difference" (King, 109). The logical consequence of the cannibal, the edible, functions as another marker of absolute difference.

The figure of the cannibal and its twin lead to the assimilation or annihilation of the African or Carib, two gestures that, for Glissant, define what he calls the Western "pensée de l'un" or "thinking of the one" (*Poétique,* 59–63). The edible woman and man become digestible and assimilated in their metaphorical or metonymic association with ingestible products: bananas, sugar, rum, or chocolate. The metaphor of the cannibal, in contrast, annihilates the other by expelling her or him from humanity. Both gestures amount to the desire for racial purity and cultural uniformity responding to the desire for "the thinking of the one." The dysfunctional nature of Western thinking is therefore projected onto a fictionalized other.

In the collective Western psyche expressed in caricatures, in commercials, in Tintin comic books, in Tarzan movies, and in travelers' accounts, the twin image of this bipolar pathology abounds. The 1987 collection *Négripub* constitutes a rich archive of representations of black figures in French and other European commercials during the height of colonialism and its aftermath.[28] In this particular genre of advertisement, however, images of the edible prevail over representations of cannibals,[29] certainly because the image of the cannibal is not the most appetizing image to be served on the kitchen table to young children, and because the cannibal is, by definition, not assimilable but, rather, threatens to assimilate. The collection nonetheless includes several examples of grossly caricatured black bodies. I have chosen not to reproduce these degrading illustrations in my book since images can have an immediate effect on readers who would simply leaf through the book they picked up in a bookstore or library. I believe, however, that a discursive analysis of these commercials by way of textual analysis can efficiently undermine their mechanism. This choice responds to cultural critic Anne Donadey's call to privilege "the process of working through" colonial imagery while avoiding a "reactivation of colonial nostalgia" ("'Y'a Bon Banania,'" 10).

One such infamous example is a commercial for a fire extinguisher—not for a product to be ingested through the mouth (*Négripub,* 88). The animalized human subject has bones in its hair (remnants of a previous cannibal feast), rings in its ears and nose to mark its warrior-like strength, and an oblique excited gaze turned onto the pleasing features of whites simmering in pots. The caption reads: "Face au feu . . . extincteur et sang-froid" [Armed against fire: extinguisher and cold blood]. The white man put in the cannibal's pot with a smile on his face, cold-bloodedly extinguishes the fire under the pot, and thus, through his wits, and access to technology, wins over the savage cannibal and the fiery Tropics. Interestingly, the fire under the pot extends to the inner thigh of the cannibal, perhaps pointing to the torrid zone of its burning sexuality, and also, threatening to annihilate it. I use the pronoun "it" consciously to highlight the animalized features of the cannibal, and also because the subject, with its breasts and warrior-like musculature, looks androgynous. The infamous commercial was produced in 1965, a few years after the decolonization of most former African colonies, and during the civil rights movement in the United States. In spite of undeniable political progress, the image persists in stifling black subjects.

The most prevalent image from the *Négripub* collection is that of the edible. Women are metonymically associated with fruit by their adornment with bananas in the style that African American artist Josephine Baker made famous. On a metaphorical level, feminine and masculine figures alike are turned into rum or coffee, breasts become dates, mouths are watermelon slices, and eyes, cocoa beans. In these food metonymies and metaphors, bananas prevail. The banana waist belt, the only item of clothing on female and male black bodies alike, both conceals their genitals and replaces them. They simultaneously strip subjects of their sex and impose upon them the fictionalized image of an unruly sexuality in a double movement of castration and grotesque exaggeration. Bananas often point down, as in the case of Josephine Baker–style images. They can also point up or in disorderly directions when associated with masculine figures. Bananas are of course traces of the unruly and hypertrophic sexuality of these figures. A 1950 commercial for the banana-chocolate drink of the Maison Meunier "Nutri Banane" (*Négripub,* 74) depicts a black man holding bananas as a disorderly bouquet of flowers, an image juxtaposed to the background silhouette of a white woman sensually enjoying the chocolate drink. Her figure is surrounded by a halo of white, highlighting the purity of her features and a Christ-like holiness. In the foreground stands a black man holding more than a dozen unruly bananas escaping his grasp. The bananas no longer represent an erection but a loss of control. For Freud, a "multiplication of penis symbols signifies castration" ("Medusa's Head"). To reinforce this interpretation of castration, we note that the man's body is severed under the waistline, the letters advertising the product where his groin and thighs should have been. The man of the commercial is thus half a man: castrated, feminized, and tamed in the stroke of an image. The commercial produces structurally and visually what lynching practiced on the level of lived experience. A tender smile replaces the threatening grin, a look of admiration turned upward, perhaps toward the white woman that he now serves as a good eunuch should.

Such tamings and castrations of the savage, the hyperbolic, or the fierce are most famously presented in the French depictions of the Senegalese *Tirailleurs* in Banania commercials.[30] The Senegalese *Tirailleurs,* composed of recruits from West, Central, and East Africa, served France from 1857 on in the Franco-Prussian War, World War I, and World War II.[31] In these series of images, their military contribution to France is eclipsed. The domesticated soldiers are turned into edible products served on the breakfast table. The most striking of these photos is a 1915 advertisement (*Négripub,* 134), depicting a Senegalese soldier in his blue, white, and red war attire, taking a break from war by lifting a spoon of the chocolate drink to his grinning open mouth. As Donadey points out, images of "Black people consuming the product . . . and seeming to relax and enjoy themselves" are "colonial fantasies [that] serve to cover the fact that African people under colonization were rarely in the situation depicted. Rather than consuming these goods, many of them were exploited in producing them for exportation" (Donadey, 21–22). Thus the heroism and historical contribution of the Senegalese *Tirailleurs* disappear under the grinning image of an idle man seemingly indifferent to the ongoing war.

The man sits on a crate with the inscription "Aliment délicieux pour les estomacs délicats" [Delicious food for the delicate stomach]. The letters, bent like an arrow, point to the man sitting on the crate as much as the product his image advertises. Thus the soldier merges with the powdered chocolate drink. He is tamed enough to be digested even by the most delicate of stomachs. In the bottom-left corner, the handwritten inscription "Y'a bon" [Dat good!] is a fictionalized language called "petit nègre," literally translated, "little negro," pointing to a corrupt, degenerate form of French attributed to Africans and other black subjects. The note itself constitutes an act of cannibalization: the assimilation of a historical figure into the jumbled, infant, ridiculed speech of the fictional language. As Fanon explains, the French language swallows up the black man by speaking for him, thus depriving him of his own language and history: "Making [the black man] speak pidgin [petit-nègre] is tying him to an image, snaring him, imprisoning him as the eternal victim of his own essence" (*Black Skin,* 18). The black man is thus eaten up by language, and the white man or white discourse revealed as cannibalistic.

The image of the Senegalese soldier, infantilized, tamed, and speaking "Y'a Bon Banania," prompted the scream of negritude and Fanon's reaction in *Black Skin, White Masks.* About this infantilizing sentence and insulting image Senegalese poet of negritude Léopold Sédar Senghor wrote: "Mais je déchirerai les rires *banania* sur tous les murs de France" [But I will tear all Banania grins off the walls of France].[32] It is with this image that Fanon ends his litany of overdetermined images of the black man: "[D]eafened by cannibalism, backwardness, fetishism, racial stigmas, slave traders, and above all, yes, above all, the grinning Y'a bon Banania" (*Black Skin,* 92). The Banania image and the debasing language that swallows the black man stand *above all* other crimes inflicted upon him. In Fanon's analysis, then, the origin of the act of cannibalism is revealed as the colonial power itself. Cannibalism finds its source in visual and textual representations of black subjects as cannibals, in their assimilation in a fictional language, in the exploitation of their laboring bodies in the big industries of bananas, coffee, chocolate, and sugarcane, and in the historical use of the Senegalese *Tirailleurs* as cannon-fodder flesh.

Abolitionist Victor Schoelcher, in the 1800s, had already cleverly undermined the mechanism of cannibal discourse, bringing the logic of colonial oppression and dehumanization to its full conclusion. In other words, when white men turn black men into savages and cannibals, into animals, it is not the black men who are "savaged," to use a Césairian expression, but the colonial who is the cannibal, and thus the beast: "If Negroes belong to a species of brutes, we have a right to exploit them, to use them for our profit, like reindeer, cattle, and camels; it is even our right, it is a forced consequence, to eat them like chicken or deer. There is no middle ground here."[33] The logical consequence of the brutish colonial act and colonial discourse is thus cannibalism. However, colonizers, conquerors, and travelers have persisted in projecting it onto the fictionalized other.

The Caribbean Cannibal

The image of the cannibal is projected wherever difference starts—or needs—to emerge. For Pierre Chaunu, the cannibal "is the really other Other, that which is placed at the limit of alterity."[34] In early Renaissance European maps of the New World, the image of a cannibal appears at the liminal space between conquered and uncharted territories. Peter

Hulme explains that "the cannibal, like utopia, traditionally marks the limit of representation, and appears at the edge of the known world. Thus textual or visual representations of cannibals always contain the trace of the Columbian moment, signifying the European encounter with the Amerindian Other, and its ensuing battle between conflicting selves. . . . In texts, representations of cannibalism is a rhetorical strategy by which narratives signify voracity, hunger, and the dissolution of the Self into Other, or vice versa" (quoted in Sands, 7). The cannibal therefore acts as a marker of difference, and as a marker of the limits of humanity, inscribed in the spatial imagination. In his *Intellectual History of Cannibalism*, Cătălin Avramescu adds that cannibalism is geographically linked to insularity. The presence of the cannibal is explained by the natural state of the island. Because of their supposed insularity, remoteness, and unsustainability, islands lead to cannibalism as a necessary act of survival. Avramescu illustrates this argument by Diderot's "Supplement to the Voyage of Bougainville" (1772). According to this natural-history argument, "anthopophagy may have appeared at a very ancient date and would thus be insular in origin" (1). While the image of the anthropophagus has been prevalent since antiquity in the figure of the dog-headed ape or cynocephalus, the image of the cannibal appears as soon as Columbus and the Caribs meet. In short, cannibalism, we could argue, is a usurping Adamic gesture, whereby Columbus misnamed the Caribs by linking them to the image of the anthropophagus through a single name.[35] Thus, while cannibalism has been used to define images and practices in the whole world, its naming and original gesture are intimately linked to the Carib zone, including the Caribbean and the northern coast of Brazil. The mere definitions in the *Webster's New World Dictionary* illustrate the imagined proximity of the words "cannibal" and "Carribean," which define each other in an endless referral (Cannibal: see Caribbean; Carib, see cannibal).

This endless lexicological referral, a reciprocal hyperlink, so to speak, shows how the designation *Cariba*, the name of the Amerindian population, was swallowed and incorporated into the body of the Spanish language, to then be regurgitated with a brand-new meaning inspired by a loose phonetic resemblance: Cariba = caníbal. The word "caníbal" of course refers to the Latin image of the anthropophagus, the *canis*, the cynocephalus or dog-headed monkey. The preexisting name Cariba, referring to the Caribs and their possessions, was assimilated by, cannibalized by, the word "cannibal," and the "Cariba islands" naturally became the "Cannibal islands.[36] Benítez-Rojo describes this process as "the glorious cannibalism of men and words, carib, calib, cannibal, and Caliban" (13), which presents the Caribbean (Amerindian or later African) in a situation of ipseity with the savage cannibal and the Shakespearean Caliban. The entire American continent was named by such a misnaming, which swallowed existing names and imposed others. We could see this as an enormous act of linguistic ingestion. Once again, defining the other as cannibal reveals the name-giver, in this case the colonizing language, as cannibal. Such names were interpreted as bad or deformed Spanish, as illustrated by the example of the Columbus character, portrayed in Tzvetan Todorov's *Conquête de l'Amérique,* who plays the game of deciphering the "primitive gibberish" of "savages" unable to speak Spanish properly. Todorov—and the advantage of historical distance—teaches us that the creation of terms such as "cannibal" was not based on a mis-speaking, a state of speech infancy, or primitive "gibberish," but instead on a case of mis-hearing, or linguistic infancy by illegitimate name-givers such as Columbus.

As Roberto Fernández Retamar argues, and as we have seen above, the curse of the cannibal is not projected exclusively onto Caribbean subjects, and even less so onto Caribbean Caribs: "It is typical that we have applied the term 'cannibal' not to the extinct aborigine of our isles but, above all, to the African black who appeared in those shameful Tarzan movies. For, it is the colonizer that brings us together, who reveals the profound similarities existing above and beyond our secondary differences" (Retamar, 7). In short, the term "cannibal" extends from the Carib to the African slave, and to all images of "black" and Tropical "others" by a contamination transmitted from the land, and also through the common trait of savagery that Europeans projected onto these groups of humans.[37]

In spite of the extensive nature of the term "cannibal," first and foremost it is linked to the Caribbean, and to the circum-Caribbean zone of Brazil, a fact that gives a material grounding to the term in the texts of American authors reclaiming cannibalism, such as Brazilian modernist Andrade and Martinican Suzanne Césaire. In fact, when she writes "Martinican poetry will be cannibal or will not be," Césaire might very well mean "Martinican poetry will be Caribbean or will not be," as I argue in chapter 5.

Discursive Cannibalism

While cannibalism is one of the main controlling images forced onto the Caribbean and its inhabitants, Caribbean writers have also reclaimed it as a privileged mode of cultural resistance, or eating back. The gesture detours a curse in order to use it as a weapon. Reclaiming the cannibal also amounts to grounding oneself in Caribbeanness. The image acts as a potent metaphor to invoke a complex cultural creation, a discursive gesture, a blurring of borders between self and other, and a troubling of established hierarchies.

Cannibalism could be seen as opposite to the shapeless hunger that Gobineau attributed to the "Melanian race." As Montaigne had already observed during the height of the circulation of the image of the fierce cannibal in sixteenth-century Europe, cannibalism represents, countercurrent to received ideas of barbarity, a proof of civilization. By practicing cannibalism, for Montaigne, the Tupinambá Amerindians go beyond the basic need for food. Cannibalism is not about hunger but, rather, about the performance of a complex sacred war ritual: "This is not, as people think, for nourishment, as of old the Scythians used to do; it is to betoken an extreme revenge" (Montaigne, *Complete Essays,* 155). This extreme vengeance is organized around a discursive practice, in the Latin sense of *discursus,* or thinking in a sequence of logical steps. It also takes place amid war logic, in particular the need to defend one's territory (environmental or cultural) against an invader (whether the Spanish *Conquista* or passing priests, poets, or ethnographers). In war cannibalism, Montaigne specifies, the cannibal selects the head of the enemy. Hearts, livers, and other sites of power are chosen for ritual consumption; for example, the thigh of a good runner will be eaten. As Freud explains, "By incorporating parts of a person's body through the act of eating, one at the same time acquires the qualities possessed by him" (*Totem and Taboo,* 102). This is also why Andrade calls anthropophagy a "codification of vengeance" (41). Thus war cannibalism is discursive and strategic: selecting the best parts of the body in order to incorporate the other's strength. Chapter 5 elaborates on the discursive nature of cannibalism.

While this book does not evoke "real" cannibal practices but, rather, metaphorical ones, the characteristics of rituals and revenge will be key to the practice of a literary cannibalism. Cannibalism first intervenes in a context of war. This is what Andrade calls "Poesía y arte de guerra" in his *Escritos Antropófagos* (51).[38] The Caribbean subject, by asserting him- or herself as cannibal, reclaims the warrior-like strength of which the "Banania" figure evoked earlier had been amputated. As early as 1580, Montaigne performs the gesture of reversal of Oswald de Andrade, Suzanne Césaire, and Maryse Condé, among others, which places cannibalism on the side of civilization and so-called Western civilization on the side of barbarity:

> I am not sorry that we notice the barbarous horror of such acts, but I am heartily sorry that, judging their faults rightly, we should be so blind to our own. I think that there is more barbarity in eating a man alive than in eating him dead; and in tearing by tortures and the rack a body still full of feeling, in roasting a man bit by bit, in having him bitten and mangled by dogs and swine (as we have not only read but seen within fresh memory, not among ancient enemies, but among neighbors and fellow citizens, and what is worse, on the pretext of piety and religion), than in roasting and eating him after he is dead. *(Complete Essays,* 155)

While the description of the barbaric act of "eating a man alive" applies, in Montaigne's case, to the cruel attacks on Protestant reformists of the bloody religious wars of sixteenth-century France, it could easily describe the barbaric crimes of colonialism and slavery—such as legalized torture and tolerated lynching. In his raw analysis of lynching in the United States, Leon Litwack seems to describe exactly what Montaigne calls "an act of barbarity much worse than cannibalism" when he depicts the practice of burning alive a lynched woman or man as a "Negro Barbecue" (10). Litwack arrives at Montaigne's conclusion: the barbarity resides in the so-called call for civilization: "The inhumanity, depravity, bestiality, and savagery practiced by white participants in lynchings would be justified in the name of humanity, morality, justice, civilization, and Christianity" (22). Four centuries later, Montaigne's voice still resonates.

Montaigne's reverse association appears frequently in the texts I discuss in this book. The figure of the cannibal comes to be associated with colonial figures, structures, or discourses. In the Creole tales as well as in Aimé Césaire's *Cahier,* which I analyze in chapter 2, the cannibal is perceived in the plantation machinery. Richard King emphasizes this common perception of whiteness and the structures of oppression it carries as cannibalism: "Indigenous peoples and marginalized communities have elaborated nuanced interpretations of the West as cannibalistic. Although by no means universal, it appears to be quite common for non-Western peoples to understand Western individuals or institutions as cannibals."[39] Cannibalism has also been used as a trope for a milder form of cruelty and ingestion, but nonetheless violent, such as the enterprise of tourism. Dennis O'Rourke's 1988 documentary *Cannibal Tours* (the story of European and North American tourists in Papua New Guinea) seems to indicate that the tours are more about showing cannibals to the tourists. Instead, the tourists are revealed as the true cannibals in their compulsive habits of stealing photographic images and stuffing their bags with local crafts obtained for a few dollars. As the voice-over claims at the beginning of the movie: "There is nothing so strange in so strange a land as the stranger who comes to visit it." The strangeness of the cannibal resides above all in the act of the visitor to a foreign land, whether it is a tourist, traveler, missionary, colonist, or even cultural critic. Thus the enterprises of tourism, exploitation of the land, and urbanization, could and have been seen as a giant act of cannibalism or consumption.[40] To summarize, then, cannibalism is used as a tool for asserting a warrior position and as a mirror turning back the oppressor's own terrifying reflection into its face.

Another propensity of cannibalism is that of transmigration. From the Christian communion, to the sexual act, to Montaigne, to Freud, to Andrade, cannibalism acts as a privileged metaphor of mixing bodies and mixing texts.[41] In the Caribbean context, it thus becomes a powerful metaphor for *métissage* or creolization, depending on how cannibalism is conceived. Montaigne, again, illuminates us: "'These muscles,' he says, 'this flesh and these veins are your own, poor fools that you are. You do not recognize that the substance of your ancestors' limbs is still contained in them. Savor them well; you will find in them the taste of your own flesh. An idea that certainly does not smack of barbarity" (*Complete Essays,* 158). Cannibalism, thus, is not the annihilation of the enemy by the victor, nor of the father by the sons, according to the Freudian myth of origin, but rather, an act of destruction that necessarily entails an act of conservation. The limit of the revolutionary nature of cannibalism for our American authors as well as for the sons of the Freudian scene, then, resides in the fact that the violence used against a previously established power structure actually leads to its preservation or establishment. This order turned on its head could be patriarchy for Freud or cultural imperialism for the Brazilian modernists or the Antillean literary cannibals. Indeed, for Freud, the devouring of the father by the sons, which was intended to "make an end of the patriarchal horde," actually marked instead the very inception of paternalism, and all the systems that ensued—social organization, moral restrictions, and religion—(*Totem and Taboo,* 176), since the father, once consumed, became sacred in the form of a totem.

However, if cannibalism fails to eradicate the father—totemic or literary—it nonetheless troubles notions of origins and originality, since the eater and the eaten lose themselves, lose their discrete selves, in the very act of ingestion. Thus, literary sons and daughters such as Suzanne Césaire, by ingesting their literary father, also give birth to him by mothering or fathering him again in a new form. The image of the family is not to be taken only metaphorically. In fact, in Suzanne Césaire's essays, cannibalism is strongly linked to the process of *métissage,* or the mixing of racially different bodies through the act of reproduction. As I show in chapter 5, *métissage* is associated with the violent act of cannibalism. In both instances, the flesh of a body passes into that of another through an act that often implies violence. While in the act of cannibalism, violence originates in the mouth and teeth of the eater, the one who receives, in the act of *métissage* it resides in the violence of penetration. In this way, the respective violence of ingestion through the mouth and reception through the vagina are diametrically opposed. Both lead to a monstrosity of both the act and its product. In Suzanne Césaire's case, the passing white men are disturbed to see in *métis* children on the beach "the strange burgeoning of their blood" (*Le Grand camouflage,* 270). The product of *métissage* contains the same dose of horror for the white men as the act of cannibalism. Both represent excesses caused by the mixing of fleshes and bloods that should not mix, responding to the age-old taboo of cannibalism, and to the colonial taboo of *métissage.* While closely linked, the two forms of bodily mixing do not function the same way. While cannibalism leads to absorption and fusion, but also to excremental waste, *métissage* leads to fertilization and fusion, and to a human child. For Suzanne Césaire, the cannibalism practiced by Caribbean subjects acts as a sort of prophylactic or antidote to the violence of rape by white men, which causes *métissage.* In other words, cannibalism, the violent eating of the other, or eating at the other, allows for a freeing violence through which the *métis* (as an individual or as a people) can fight the father's violence. In other words, cannibalism allows the *métis* to function as a subject instead of as waste.[42]

Another slippery property of the cannibal metaphor is that it migrates easily from the mixing of bodies—through ingestion or sexuality—to the mixing of words and language. Caribbean writing of the 1940s, for instance, finds itself in a state of linguistic colonization, whereby the writer has to ingest the language of the colonizer, French, and throw it back in his colonizer's face as a curse, in Caliban style.[43] As I examine in chapter 5, and throughout the book, literary cannibalism is not simply a gratuitous term referring to any form of textual citation or plagiarism; it is an act of revenge, reclaiming, and cultural creation that is caused by the situation of linguistic colonization. In this, Caribbean literary cannibalism diverges from European self-declared cannibal texts such as Francis Picabia's "Manifeste cannibale dada," which acts on a theoretical level outside historical motivations.

As Carlos A. Jáuregui sums it up, cannibalism blurs all frontiers, temporal, subjective, and spatial: "In the cannibal scene, the devouring body and the devoured body, as the act of devouring itself, provide models of identity building and disintegration. . . . The cannibal does not respect the limits that establish difference; to the contrary, it flows on them in the act of eating" (13). For Jáuregui, it is the fluidity of the act of cannibalism that explains its propensity to move from the real to the metaphorical: "It is perhaps this evasive liminality . . . that engenders the thick polysemy and the nomadic meaning of cannibalism: its propensity to metaphorization" (ibid.).

Moreover, the fluidity of the cannibal leads to a critical trap.[44] The overuse of the metaphor of cannibalism is dangerous because it (1) reinforces the projection of cannibalism and savagery onto Caribbean people; (2) it can be culturally inappropriate because it is based on concept mistranslations; and (3) it loses stable meaning because of its overuse and conceptual slipperiness. In spite of the metaphor's imperfections, authors such as Oswald de Andrade, Suzanne Césaire, and Maryse Condé—as well as this book—see it as a necessary strategy to practice, analyze, and ultimately leave behind in order to build a culinary poetics independent from colonial confrontation.

Starving, Cooking, and Race

If cannibalism is a prevalent trope in this book, other material or metaphorical states or acts of starving, eating, and cooking are crucial sites for analyzing ethnic or cultural constructions within the Caribbean and the Black Atlantic, as well as intercultural exchange. Food is enmeshed in the question of race because it is used as a justification of enslavement or colonization. As explained above, Africans were represented as frugal eaters, an argument used to justify keeping the slave in a state of near-starvation or food paucity in which the slave would eat enough to be productive, but never enough to be satisfied.[45] Food, like sexuality, has been used to pathologize "black" women and men, as I suggest in chapter 4. Throughout this book, states or processes of racial or cultural mixing such as *métissage, Créolité,* creolization, and so-called racial purity are defined by food metaphors. The Creolists Bernabé, Confiant, and Chamoiseau indeed stated: "Our Creoleness is our primitive soup" (*Éloge,* 28). Lévi-Straussian categories of the raw and the cooked, which lead, respectively, to the inedible and to the palatable, are prevalent tropes in the texts. The raw, which Lévi-Strauss places on the side of animality, is also often associated with categories that resist assimilation into an economic and racial system. The nature of the inassimilable depends on which phantasmatic racial framework the authors put forward. In Moreau de Saint-Méry's model, and in other racial representations that follow Aristotelian categorical thinking, meaning that cannot be categorized is monstrous and thus incapable of being reproduced and linked to a genealogy. In such models, blackness is more digestible than varying forms of miscegenation. In visions privileging the mixed such as Buffon's, the different degrees of *métissage* represent the temperate or the tepid, which leads to easy assimilation. *Métissage* represents the cooked, the digestible, while so-called pure cultural and racial categories occupy the position of the raw or the inedible, to use Lévi-Straussian concepts.[46] Like *Banania,* it can be digested by even the most delicate of stomachs. In Bernabé, Confiant, and Chamoiseau's *Éloge de la Créolité,* the "East Indian," the "African," or the "European" (in short, categories that don't belong to a state of "Creoleness")[47] are on the side of the raw, while Creole or highly mixed linguistic, cultural, or racial categories are on the side of the concocted, the digestible.

The book moves away from stable Lévi-Straussian categories of the cooked or the raw to look instead at processes of cooking. The passage from state to process is also the one Glissant makes in his move from *métissage* to creolization. *Métissage*, for Glissant, is on the side of the fixed or the impoverished.[48] While *métissage* is not always used in the sense of an impoverished product, I will use Glissant's take on it throughout the book to keep the definition clear. In contrast with *métissage,* which is on the side of the cooked, creolization is a cooking process: never a fixed product, never a stabilized recipe, but not a lawless chaos either. The examples of gumbo, masala, or callaloo that I explore in chapter 1 represent on the culinary sphere what jazz is to music. These dishes are variations on a theme, based on rhythms, movements, continuity and interruptions, improvisation, and community. They are common dishes involving complex cultural creations. They also shift the focus from racial entrapments to cultural aesthetic processes. For writers like Pineau or Danticat, this movement of creolization through culinary production takes the Caribbean outside its geographical borders to create, with North African migrants in France, or Louisiana Creoles in the Bronx, a form of neocreolization that eventually leads to practices of globalization, pulling the Caribbean out of the position of deviance, exception, and monstrosity that colonial discourse assigned it to. In a nutshell, food, with all its constructive power and stifling potential, acts as a constant yet constantly shifting signifier of Caribbean cultural constructions within the Black Atlantic, and within the world.

Framework of the Book

Chapter 1, "From Gumbo to Masala," provides the theoretical framework from which this study emanates. It looks at the use of food metaphors in Glissant's theoretical texts as modes of practicing Relation or creolization. His privileged culinary example, the Martinican East Indian spice mix masala, with its adaptable and improvisational qualities, embodies the process of creolization as an open dynamic movement. The spice mix, a volatile example of cultural construction, provides an escape from the trap of essentialist difference in which Creoleness is at times caught. In choosing this culinary model, I also show that the construction of a Caribbean identity for Glissant, and for others with whom he engages, such as Cuban essayist Fernando Ortiz and African American critic Hortense Spillers, is primarily cultural rather than political. The choice of an East Indian spice mix to define West Indian identity also challenges the notion, embraced by Kamau Brathwaite or Lafcadio Hearn, that East Indianness is inassimilable to creolization and ultimately to Caribbean identity.

Chapter 2, "Not Just Hunger," relies mainly, but not exclusively, on Chamoiseau's collection of *Creole Folktales,* which he claims to have heard from his grandmother, who belonged to a lineage of plantation storytellers. It deals with hunger—literal, libidinal, aesthetic; individual and collective—and the influence of hunger on constructions of racialized, gendered, and cultural entities and communities. The main thrust of the chapter, however, is to use the Creole tales as a springboard to analyze the continuity of the Martinican obsession with hunger and overeating from the time of slavery in which these tales were produced, to postdepartmentalization contemporary Martinique. I put the tales into dialogue with slavery and postslavery texts, such as the travelogues by the Dominican priests Labat and Dutertre, Claude Lévi-Strauss's anthropological writings, and Aimé Césaire's *Cahier d'un retour au pays natal.* The reflections on hunger, eating, and cooking throughout these texts allows us to define how the borders between animality and humanity blur in a slavery and postslavery context. I focus specifically on the recurring trope of the talking bird, which troubles clear definitions between human and animal, abject and sacred. By moving from a state of dependence upon food and hunger to a practice of cooking (both literal and metaphorical), the characters in *Creole Folktales* emerge from the animality in which they were legally and discursively forced in order to master rationality and humanity, and to establish a Creole cultural specificity. Chamoiseau, Confiant, and Bernabé have famously trumpeted this *Créolité* or Creoleness in their 1989 manifesto: "Neither European, nor African, nor Asian, we proclaim ourselves Creoles" (*Éloge,* 75).

Chapter 3, "Kitchen Narrative," looks away from Creoleness to evaluate instead the process of culinary creolization beyond its geographically defined Caribbean borders. I look at texts by Gisèle Pineau (a writer with Guadeloupean roots living in Paris) and Edwidge Danticat (the famous Haitian American writer), which deal with young girls living in exile in European and North American capitals. Like Glissant, the young protagonists choose the kitchen as their privileged site to link the Caribbean and the Western metropolis, as well as to heal disrupted love and transmission between mother and child. When they write about food, Pineau and Danticat mostly write about writing, and more specifically about inscribing their identity on the written text of their novels—texts inhabited by the food culture inherited from their Caribbean grandmothers. By cooking up words and articulating ingredients in their texts, Danticat and Pineau perform a creolizing gesture through cooking, which preserves the quality of dynamism and the improvisatory nature of the Glissantian model, yet takes creolization a few steps further. First, by highlighting the power of women as transmitters of knowledge through culinary creations, they bring a material strength to the practice of creolization and shift the focus from the colonizer/colonized binary to the masculine/feminine split. Second, they practice a form of "neocreolization" by exporting the Caribbean movement into a host country and by combining it with the productions of other immigrant or minority groups. In short, they perform acts of "minor transnationalism," defined by Shu-mei Shih and Françoise Lionnet as the identification of "minority subjects" with other minority subjects instead of "identifying themselves in opposition to a dominant discourse" (*Minor Transnationalism,* 2). Danticat's and Pineau's kitchen narratives not only link a present of disruption and exile to an—often utopian—intact past of the Caribbean island and of childhood, but they also construct a common Caribbeanness that relates Guadeloupe and Haiti in spite of their historical and political disconnections. They perform creolization on a global level by combining their heritage with other minority groups. I read the novels in dialogue with women thinkers of food and writing in the Black Atlantic such as Ntozake Shange, Audre Lorde, Maryse Condé, and bell hooks. However, the chapter does not present food as an ideal mode of self-construction. I read food primarily as passion, in both the sense of an intense excitement leading to a positive construction and in its original meaning of enduring and suffering. Through the concept of "purging," I look at the intricate relationship of food and sexuality, whereby the refusal to eat or bulimic purging are bodily reminders of acts of sexual violence. Food, while it can heal, can also disrupt cultural and motherly channels of transmission.

Chapters 4 and 5 focus on acts of cannibalizing or "biting back" while, at the same time, highlighting the limitations of such gestures. The phrase "biting back"—*remordre* in French—entails a risk of settling Caribbean subjects in a state of temporal and psychological stasis. *Remords,* remorse, is a guilt-prompted feeling that incessantly bites back, that prevents both a temporal evolution and an emancipation from the father, as Freud has argued in his interpretation of the primal myth of sons who killed their oppressive patriarch, and who internalized his power through the very traumatic feeling of guilt they experienced through the killing.[49] We understand what the crime of the primal father means when translated allegorically into the colonizer/colonized situation: an increase of the colonizer's power through its very destruction. While this stage of devouring the father/colonizer is necessary, it also must be dissolved. The confrontational stage must give way to a poetic and aesthetic relation existing independently of Oedipal or colonial relationship. Thus chapters 4 and 5 lead to the conclusion that the oppositional practice of eating the other with a vengeance is a temporary state to be eventually overcome.

In chapter 4, "Sexual Traps," I analyze a particular type of text that I call "fake pornography." I examine specifically Haitian Canadian writer Dany Laferrière's novel *Comment faire l'amour avec un nègre sans se fatiguer* (1985) and Gisèle Pineau's novel *Chair Piment* (2002). Laferrière and Pineau, with their publishers' complicity, create novels that, through their title, front cover, and first paragraph, manifest all the exterior signs of a pornographic text. The two writers use stereotypes such as the fruity mixed-race woman, the fierce nymphomaniac, and the hypersexual black male to attract erotic-thirsty readers into the trap of their text in order to give them, instead of sexual satisfaction, a history lesson. The chapter also raises the question as to whether the Caribbean writers haven't themselves been entrapped by the same exoticizing and animalizing machine they attempted to pilot. The chapter also investigates the enmeshment of the pathologizing of eating and the pathologizing of sexuality in the two authors' representations. In Laferrière's novel, for instance, the hypersexual black man quickly merges with the memory of the castrated and "barbecued" lynched black man. Both Pineau's and Laferrière's endings point to a possible exit from the dual entrapment of reader and writer. For Pineau, the exit is the entrance of Caribbean women onto the stage of globalization; for Laferrière, it is the choice of the textual over the sexual, with the final image of the victorious black Remington having just given birth to a healthy and fierce novel.

It is this power of writing, or writing back, that I explore in chapter 5. After an introductory reflection on literary authority in the wake of colonialism, I analyze the texts of Martinican writer Suzanne Césaire and her Guadeloupean respondent, Maryse Condé, who have both declared "literary cannibalism" as a strategy for constructing Caribbean literature. While Césaire and Condé claim a similar gesture, their practices could not be more opposed. For Césaire, textual cannibalism is discreet, subtle, and lethal; for Condé, it is flagrant, hypertrophic, and ultimately, by its very exaggeration, self-defeating. My reading of Césaire's essays published in *Tropiques* (1941–45) focuses specifically on her cannibalization of André Breton, the passing surrealist poet who befriended the Césaires, and who developed an intoxicating infatuation with "Madame Césaire" in particular, and with mixed-race beauties in general. In both Césaire's and Breton's texts, the biblical story of Absalom, Tamar, and Amnôn, I argue, acts as a coded text for Breton and Césaire's camouflaged dialogue. While Breton saw Césaire as a "Tropical Nadja," as J. Michael Dash so cleverly put it, I propose to read her as a "Caribbean Tamar," the one who has been violated,[50] and the one who takes revenge by telling the world the story of her violation. Césaire's texts ingest the words of Breton, transforming them into speaking against the easy infatuation of passing travelers with tropical beauties, and to reveal the violence of *métissage.*

While Condé presents Césaire as her partner in crime, her practice of literary cannibalism, at least in *Histoire de la femme cannibale*, is a sort of farce. I mean the word "farce" both as exaggerated comedy and as "stuffing." The text, stuffed with innumerable citations from Shakespeare, Billy Joel, W. B. Yeats, Aimé Césaire, and *Sex and the City,* proclaims the end of cannibalism by generalizing it. Yet for Condé and Césaire, for Columbus and Montaigne, for Andrade, Retamar, and Fanon, and for this very text, the figure of the cannibal—and its cousin figures of the *banania*-man, the sugary *doudou,* or the untamed eater—need to reach center stage before becoming obsolete.

Thus, all chapters are concerned with cultural construction of a Caribbean self—individual or collective—through cooking or ingesting; with mixing identities, through Creoleness, *métissage,* creolization, or neocreolization. Creolization and cannibalism both deal with mixing substances—linguistic or corporeal—and incorporate discrete elements to turn them into objects that go beyond the sum of their original parts. Both creolization and cannibalization lead to the blurring of frontiers, and eventually to a practice of globalization that goes beyond Caribbean particularity while staying grounded in the Antilles. Yet creolization and cannibalization are based upon different original metaphors. While the first is grounded in the mixing of languages, the second evolves from a mixing of bodies. Sexuality, a prevalent question in chapters 3, 4, and 5, gives us an entryway into articulating the relationship between the consumption of food and the consumption of human bodies. Indeed, the sexual act is often represented in terms of metaphors of eating; the children of "mixed-race" sexual encounters or *métis* are often metaphorically turned into consumable exotic fruit or spices. The book will reflect on the proximity of the two acts of consumption—

culinary and sexual—while emphasizing the risk of confusing the two. This confusion, in essence, reduces the human object of desire to a consumable good.

I use the term "culinary coups" in order to encompass these multifarious gestures. The culinary, as Brillat-Savarin and Lévi-Strauss have famously shown, elevates the consumption of food from a basic animal need to a cultural assertion of the human.[51] Cooking or culinary art, as opposed to just eating or even making food, involves rules, a grammar, a poetics, a politics, and an aesthetics. On a literal level, a *coup* is a blow. A "culinary coup" can thus be interpreted as a strike, physical or emotional, inflicted upon the Caribbean subject using the culinary as its mode of expression. This would be equivalent to the phase of "biting back." A coup also refers to a political act of resistance, dissidence, or revolution, usually using military force as in coup d'état. Fittingly, Suzanne Césaire, Patrick Chamoiseau, Édouard Glissant, Gisèle Pineau, Dany Laferrière, and Maryse Condé all use the culinary as a political tool of resistance. Finally, a "culinary coup," as in *coup de maître,* in the language of culinary magazines, television cooking channels, and blogs, refers to the aesthetic accomplishment or victory of a gifted chef. This aesthetic side is crucial to highlight the culinary as a mode of artistic expression that could be detached from a bellicose relation.

The chapter order is neither chronological nor teleological. The strategies of culinary reconstruction and creolization featured in each chapter could be read in their logical simultaneity, and not as dialectical consecutive phases. Suzanne Césaire's literary cannibalism performed in the 1940s could, for instance, coexist logically with Glissant's theory of creolization developed in the 1990s. In fact, each practice reciprocally illuminates the other. The afterword calls for a mode of thinking, a creative hunger, in which texts, Caribbean or otherwise, speak to one another ethically, politically, poetically.

1 FROM GUMBO TO MASALA

Édouard Glissant's Creolization in the Circum-Caribbean

Eating is rhizome.
—Édouard Glissant, *Tout-Monde*

ARGUABLY THE MOST INFLUENTIAL and conceptual theorist to have emerged from the Caribbean, Édouard Glissant paradoxically accords a privileged modality to the materiality of food, hunger, eating, and cooking. The paradox, however, is only an outward appearance. This chapter shows precisely that the materiality and corporeality of food, hunger, and eating must be articulated in tandem with the conceptual dimensions of these spheres, in order that they might make sense as cultural traits, signs of humanity. Cooking is the ultimate articulation of the corporeal and the cerebral. It is also the human, cultural, and theoretical response to the basic bodily need of feeding oneself and the other. In his philosophical portrait of the Martinican author, *Édouard Glissant: One World in Relation,*[1] Malian filmmaker and cultural critic Manthia Diawara titles one of the film's sections "Broccoli and Opacity." While the subtitle attempts to make Glissant's philosophical concept accessible to a wider audience,[2] the juxtaposition is not as inane as it seems. Opacity, one of the fundamental elements of Glissantian ethical thinking and practice, cannot be thought of in a vacuum severed from the daily materiality of exchanges with the other, among which the culinary is the most elementary. In other words, the culinary cannot be reduced to a material practice, and even far less to an insignificant daily distraction or need.

This chapter, the main critical engine of the book, reflects on culinary creolization in Édouard Glissant's theoretical texts. It juxtaposes the particular example of Martinique to the broader scope of Circum-Caribbean food discourse,[3] and ultimately to what Glissant calls the *tout-monde,* an alternative way of thinking about the world outside the model of "globalization." In crucial moments of complex definitions of Martinican identity, Glissant turns to culinary metaphors. Perhaps because of the perceived trivial nature of the culinary, Glissant's critics have overlooked his fertile reflections on food.[4] This chapter explores the concretization of highly theoretical concepts, such as Relation, Creolization, and Caribbeanness, through food metaphors. My corpus here is limited to Glissant's theoretical texts precisely because the highly theoretical and the very ordinary are closer than they seem,[5] fusing into what Parama Roy has called a "grammar of gastropoetics."[6] We can identify two poles of Glissant's theoretical writings: on one end of the spectrum, his pathbreaking *Discours antillais* (1981) and *Poétique de la Relation* (1990); on the other, *Tout-Monde* (1993) and *Traité du Tout-monde* (1997). Between the earlier and the later texts, a shift appears on the level of the function of food, and running parallel, of the position of Martinique within the Caribbean and within the world.

In Glissant's early texts, Martinique faces a series of culinary impasses: it cannot recognize itself in the French dominant culinary model that forcibly appends Martinicans to the colonial power; nor can it fully associate with an African cuisine that exists through undeniable and numerous traces but not as integral presence;[7] nor can it exclusively embrace a local production in a gesture that would isolate Martinique in narrow provincialism. In contrast, *Tout-Monde* and *Traité du Tout-monde* offer a constructive culinary model that frees Martinique from these impasses by linking the island space to the "tout-monde." Glissant's *tout-monde* or "whole-world" is a nontotalitarian totality, in which the particular place is in constant interaction and transaction with the world. In this model, Martinique, no longer a mere extension of the French colonizing nation or the lost African homeland, becomes an agent in the construction of a relational world model. While the process and theory of Relation runs through all of Glissant's writings, it adopts a concrete form in *Tout-Monde* in the avatar of masala.

Intriguingly, Glissant selects an East Indian spice mix, masala, as a privileged example of this striving, newly forged Martinican identity. I will reflect on the implications of his choice of masala in representing Caribbeanness and will contrast it with other culinary metaphors used to define race, ethnicity, language, or nation in the Black Atlantic. For instance, how do gumbo, *ajiaco,* callaloo, or *awara* signify mixed ethnicities of Louisiana, Cuba, Trinidad, or French Guyana in a different way from the volatile culinary spice mix? Moreover, why choose the East Indian spice, as people of Tamil origin constitute a relatively small percentage of the Martinican population? Why not choose instead Creole dishes such as *calalou* or *soupe-zhabitan,*[8] which share with masala qualities of improvisation, adaptability, dynamism, instability, and complexity that could exemplify Glissant's concepts of Creolization and Relation? Ultimately, I elucidate how Glissant exemplifies his "whole-world" through masala because this model allows him to position Martinique outside national entrapments to avoid the assimilating and annihilating forces of globalization. This chapter precisely situates the culinary as a crucial site of political expression and interaction.[9]

A "Taste" of France

Glissant suggests that "Martinican consumers 'belong' to what they possess. . . . All imported goods seem beautiful and all domestic goods seem inferior" (*Discours,* 459). Martinique gets a "taste" of France on many levels. By "taste," I mean the literal act of tasting France in Martinique, where a vast majority of objects consumed are imported and where the largest local production is trash.[10] Glissant calls this unbalanced economic model "an overstimulated consumption and an annihilated production" (461).

By "taste" of France, I also allude to the fragmentary nature of the act of tasting, as opposed to receiving a generous helping, or nourishment. Indeed Glissant refers to what France bestows upon Martinique as leftovers, "colonial crumbs" (403). Historically and economically, France has forced Martinique into the status of perennial dependent, within what Françoise Vergès has called an economy of debt. This clearly differs from an economy based on a reciprocal exchange of goods. In an economy of debt, the colonial power entraps the colonized recipient, such as France ensnared Martinique, in a perpetual position of need:[11] "Dependence and debt were the operative elements of the [French] colonial family's dynamics. Its rhetoric displaced social relations determined by the symbolic and economic organization of exchange between the colony and the metropole, and replaced them with the theme of continuous debt of the colony to its metropole" (Vergès, 6). This nonreciprocity and overwhelming dependence, which turn the colonized into perennial children, translate economically into the disequilibrium between the high quality of Martinique's exported food and the inferiority of the produce France dumps on its colony. As Glissant writes: "The issue of banana conditioning (the legitimate demand of French importers on the quality of the fruit leaving Martinique) prompts us to evoke the overripe pears and the half-rotten grapes that Martinican consumers choose to buy . . . on the Fort-de-France supermarket shelves" (*Discours,* 119).[12] The sustained illusion of a debt to France masks the economic gift that Martinique provides its colonizer, and turns what should be a reaction of disgust into a grateful disposition in the Martinican consumer, who is happier to eat insipid French apples than fragrant mangoes left to rot on the sidewalks of Fort-de-France.[13] The instilled false impression of being indebted, hence appreciative, deprives Martinicans of the right to make demands and, ultimately, of the right to legitimacy.

Martinique's overwhelming economic dependence makes it particularly vulnerable in times of crises and wars, during which the island, forced into the position of a minor, faces death by starvation. In Martinique, *an tan Wobè,* or "the time of the admiral Robert," governor of Martinique during the economic blockade of World War II, remains inscribed in Martinican memory as a period of hunger.[14] The joint culinary history between France and Martinique is thus one of nonreciprocity, inequality, dependence, and fear. As Richard Burton claims, the memory of colonialism is clearly inscribed in the body that remembers starvation, and the memory of colonialism coincides with that of hunger: "In the Martinican collective memory, colonialism is above all hunger" (*La Famille coloniale,* 254).

The experience of satiety, which has replaced hunger in contemporary Martinique, leads to a similarly overwhelming dependence. On an island where French subsidies have eradicated hunger, where a third of the population is unemployed and receives state funding,[15] satiety, like hunger, creates a form of ideological dependence, which discourages desires and actions toward political independence. As Eric Prieto has argued, in a neocolonial situation where the "former oppressors have become the benefactors . . . the region can't achieve political and economic independence without making huge, perhaps unbearable sacrifices" ("The Uses of Landscape," 244). Martinicans' experience with food, oscillating between hunger and satiety, is at the heart of a complex economic, political, and ideological relationship of dependence upon the Métropole.

Tasting French food also necessarily implies tasting French language and ideology. A "taste" of France, colloquially, has come to mean a violent lesson, a bad medicine to swallow, such as in "have a taste of me" or "feel my fist upon you." A taste of France is indeed a violent lesson of imposition. As Burton has shown, "The civilizing mission starts at the dinner table" (245). The Guyanese poet Léon-Gontran Damas demonstrates this very well in his poem "Hoquet," in which a mother forces her child to chew on a bone the "proper" way, the "civilized" way, read, the "French" way ("You must eat your bone with restraint and discretion," *Pigments,* 36). In Damas's poem, the civilizing of the organs of digestion, the stomach and the tongue ("a belly must behave," 36), go hand in hand with the civilizing of speech, whereby eating French equals speaking French. The mother in the poem admonishes the speaker both for his unruly eating and verbal conduct: "Be quiet / Did I command you to speak French or did I not" (37). The tongue is thus the target of a double colonization, a double civilization: that of eating and that of speech. A taste of France is thus inextricably linked with a silencing taste of French.

For Glissant, this double colonization of the tongue also afflicts Martinicans. French language or *palé-fwance* (in parallel with French food or *manjé-fwance*) exiles Martinican subjects from their potential Martinican community. Food and language, instead of constituting the common heritage necessary to the constitution of a collective experience, disrupt the community because they exile subjects from their most immediate environment. As it were, Martinicans' language and food are already spoken and consumed by others:[16] "The characteristic feature of the French Antilles is that the official language is a language of consumption. As a result, the speaker is deported between and by these two impossible realities: the 'suspended' nature of a (Creole) language that fails to produce or create anything, and the 'disenfranchised' nature of a (French) language whose sole function is consumption" (*Discours,* 357).

Glissant accentuates the parallelism of functionality between food and language by metaphorically equating language with an act of consumption devoid of the power of creating meaning: "In Martinique, it's a pleasant spectacle to see our personalities spinning French language on television. This one rounds it up in warm curls. . . . That one sizzles it with the tip of the lips, to get a better taste of the delicate dish. His puckered lips *[la bouche en cul de poule]* elevate his entire being" (*Discours,* 85). Glissant refers to the ridiculous spectacle of the Martinican elite emulating the restrained lip movements of Parisian French, puckering their lips for perceived social elevation—"cul-de-poule" literally means "chicken's ass" in French. For Glissant, the upper class fails to represent its people: "Here, the elite does not exploit others for its own sake—in spite of its monstrous privileges—and remains servant as much as master" (403). The Martinican elite is subject to a false ontology that equates speaking and eating French with a superior state of being. There is a world of difference between this superficial, constrained, and subservient act of tasting and Suzanne Césaire's then-forty-year-old prophetic advocacy of cannibalizing French language and culture in an act of radical appropriation and transformation through the Martinican body: "Martinican poetry will be cannibal or will not be" (50).

Yet the Martinican subject of *Discours antillais* and *Poétique de la Relation* seems oblivious of the violent taste of this medicine and deaf to Suzanne Césaire's call, and so continues to adulate French food, or "manjé-fwance." In the Creole term, *manjé-fwance,* or "French food," one can also hear "eating France," once again linking the act of eating with epistemic colonization. In "Les écart déterminants," a chapter of *Poétique de la Relation* in which Glissant reflects on the economic intrusion paired with the emotional violence brought about by the importation of food and culture, Glissant exposes the chiasmic model according to which local foods are mentally deported, while imported products become emotionally domestic: "With a ferocious 'tsk!' from the lips, these [Martinican] children dismiss breadfruit thinking *[la pensée du fruit à pain],* relishing instead in salami thinking *[celle du saucisson sec].* In countries where importations rule, childhood is the first thing to be deported" (*Poétique,* 163). Glissant reads the Martinican act of food consumption as a complex model of incoming and exiting movements, imperial rule and exile. Children who favor imported goods not only leave behind their own childhood but also the communal past of persistence, resistance, and revolutionary acts. Food and flesh become thought and word in a model where words and thoughts are severed from any agency that could forge an emancipated community.

In *Traité du Tout-monde,* Glissant elaborates further on the disconnection between Martinican identity and eating French: "Many of us had never seen nor considered anything French, even if we gulped down france-flour *[farine-france],* france-onion, and white butter" (*Traité,* 44). By ingesting *farine-france,* the subject activates the global machine of production while also developing the illusion of becoming subject by ingesting the other's food. It is no longer a matter of substituting being with having, as Fanon once put it,[17] but being with ingesting. Pay close attention to the words used to describe these global products: "farine-france," "onion-france." These denominations do not necessarily refer to products imported by France, but to products distributed by the globalized forces of what Michael Hardt and Antonio Negri call "Empire."[18]

A century before the shift identified by Hardt and Negri, Lafcadio Hearn remarks that in Martinique all imported products, whatever their provenance, are perceived as French: "Although certain flours are regularly advertised as American in the local papers, they are still *farine-Fouance* for the population who call every thing foreign French. American beer is *bié-Fouance;* canned peas, *ti-pois-Fouance,* any white foreigner who can talk French is *yon béké-Fouance*" (*Two Years,* 275). As early as 1890, Hearn remarks that the Martinican population *still* confuses the process of what we can anachronistically call "globalization" with French imperialism. In Glissant's *Tout-Monde,* wheat flour is *still* called "farine-france." In *Les Meilleures recettes de la cuisine antillaise,* published in 2000, imported onions are *still* called "oignons-france." This enduring perception of global market forces and anything foreign as French extends from the nineteenth to the twenty-first century—which leads us to an important observation. France, mostly thanks to its massive food exportation to Martinique, has instilled the illusion that eating French equals being French, hence successful; more important, it has managed to camouflage international forces of capitalism as French, thus maintaining a fictional image of the old French Empire as the sole indispensable provider, as it had been before the independences of the early 1960s.

Breadfruit Thinking

"With a ferocious 'tsk' from the lips, [Martinican] children dismiss Breadfruit Thinking" (*Poétique*, 163), claims Glissant. Curiously enough, Glissant's *Discours antillais* and *Poétique de la Relation* do not propose breadfruit or root vegetables such as "igname" (yam) or "dachine" (dasheen or taro root),[19] which are associated with resistance to the plantation system, marooning, survival, local production, and which bear a memorial trace of Africa,[20] as possible alternatives to French products. As Glissant clearly states: "It won't be easy (here) to replace products of intense emotional power, such as Coca-Cola, wheat bread, and butter, with yam, breadfruit, or with a revived production of 'madou,' 'mabi,' or any other local product" (*Discours,* 162). Glissant explains this failure only by acknowledgment of capitalism and market rules. However, it seems to be more complex than the mere consequence of market economy. Indeed, the real and the metaphoric, the practical and the theoretical, are never fully separated in Glissantian thought. Significantly, this seemingly concrete reflection on the colonial and capitalist economy, and more specifically on the failure of tuberous roots, appears only four pages after Glissant dismisses root-identity ("l'identité-racine") as a violent form of reterritorialization: "Thus, root-identity stiffly grounded the thinking of oneself and that of the territory" (*Poétique,* 158). Beyond the fact that root vegetables permit an easy metaphor for a linear past, they are also linked historically and linguistically to Africa. The fruits and vegetables, as well as their names, have followed the enslaved Africans in their Middle Passage. Cristine MacKie claims that the breadfruit was "first introduced to the West Indies from West Africa in 1792 by Captain Bligh" (*Caribbean,* 17).[21] Sidney Mintz gives a slightly conflicting interpretation as he claims that the same Captain Bligh, commissioned by the Jamaican assembly, brought the "breadfruit *(Artocarpus altilis)* from Oceania" (39). Mintz also "suspect[s] that the yam came from Africa, possibly carried by the slaves themselves" (39). The word "yam," derived from the Fulani word *nyami*, "to eat," which passed into English through the Portuguese *inhame (Webster's)*, could provide a historical and direct bridge to Africa, and has often been exploited as a symbol of cross-diasporic connectedness and community.[22] While Glissant does not make explicit the link between yams and Africa, these products bear a memory trace of the African past through their routes—real and imaginary, and through their roots—etymological and metaphorical. However, the search for authentic and identifiable African traces is a minor concern in Glissant's texts. Far more important is the resistance to idealizing the local, which would isolate Martinique in a detrimental parochialism.

Throughout his theoretical texts, Glissant has dismissed "root-identity," favoring instead "rhizome-identity." "Root-identity" carries along the fiction of an original past and place, legitimately connected by lineage to the origin of a chosen people. This rootlike foundational myth legitimizes the presence of a people on a given land, as well as the national drives emerging from this imagined fiction. Glissant claims that the root is monolingual (*Poétique,* 27), privileges the One, and allows only one form of relationship to the other: either assimilating or annihilating. In Martinique, tubers are simply called *racines,* or "roots." They thus bear a strong resemblance to Glissant's ideological model. In contrast, the *identité-rhizome* allows for relation, creolization, and respectful opacity.[23]

By dismissing root vegetables as privileged metaphors for Martinican identity, Glissant refuses to elect any given origin as an exclusive path to the past. Indeed, these root vegetables become productive cultural references when they stop functioning as roots: "The practice of *métissage* . . . establishes a Relation, in an egalitarian mode . . . between histories that today, in the Caribbean, are known to converge. The civilization of manioc, of sweet potatoes, of peppers and tobacco, faces toward the future of this Relation. Hence, it strives to conquer the memory of these crossed-out histories" (*Discours,* 462). Instead of electing one past, these Caribbean civilizations build a functional *métissage,* situated in the present ("today") and branching out to an open-ended future.

If Glissant's relational model denies a putative single past, it also resists desires of territorialization and exclusive grounding on the Martinican land, which would lead to new forms of atavisms and sectarianisms, and which would lock Martinique into a sterile particularity, Glissant's "folklorism." In *Poétique de la Relation,* Glissant reflects on the relationship of the Caribbean subject to the land and proposes that even a choosing of an Arawak or Carib origin—the closest scenario to a creational story—is bound to failure. Such a nostalgic return to a single ground and to roots would bar access to a total expression of the collective. Glissant substitutes an "aesthetics of upsettings and intrusions," highlighting the importance of differences between cultures in failed "ontological thinking" (*Poétique,* 165). Hardt and Negri join Glissant in their criticism of a foundational root-identity by describing the defense of the local as "a kind of primordialism that fixes social relations and identities" (*Empire,* 45).

The consumption of food harvested locally does not reestablish an exclusive culinary relationship between the eater and the land. For

Glissant, the local crawfish ("écrevisses-habitants") have more claim to Martinique than its human tenants: "These large river-crawfish make you think that they have lived on this land well before the Caribs Blacks Buckras [*békés*] Mulattoes . . . that they have been here since the timeless times" (*Tout-Monde,* 479). This statement is a clear antiterritorialization. Unlike certain localists who, as Hardt and Negri claim, justify local political action by the "terminology of ecology" or "the defense of nature and biodiversity" (45), Glissant resists the easy temptation of turning ecology into an ideological, if not mystical, claim to the territory, an ecology that, "going above and beyond its concerns with what we call the environment, seems to us to represent mankind's drive to extend to the planet Earth the former sacred thought of Territory" (*Poétique,* 146).[24] Nature leads us not to an authenticating stance, but to the humbling human relationship to a soil to which only crawfish and stones seem naturally linked. Avoiding autochthonous genealogy evades the formation of clear boundaries between communities, which would, by their ideological grounding to the land, exclude others. Thus the inclusive and nonhierarchical list of communities uninterrupted by commas: "Caribs Blacks Buckras Mulattoes."

"Manjé-Fwance" and "Breadfruit Thinking" are both bound to fail since they present Martinique with an impasse: "Martinique will experience a forced passage between African beliefs increasingly devoid of content, and French ambitions, which are, by definition, empty of meaning" (*Discours,* 402). By opting for Africa or for France, the Martinican subject would oscillate between a vanishing past and an empty future. Politically reclaiming the Caribbean land would also fail since it would lead to a reductive territorialization. Masala, a productive culinary model that Glissant introduces in *Tout-Monde,* rescues Martinique from these impasses by placing it instead within the "whole-world." Before moving to Glissant's privileged example of masala, we will take a detour through other culinary models that ground different zones of the African diaspora into a common creolization.

Our Common Creole Stew

It seems to be a universal fact. Human communities define themselves by one or several dishes that they prepare and consume as a group: *choucroute* for Alsatians, couscous or *tajine* for North Africans, fondue for the Swiss, pizza for Southern Italians, paella for Spaniards, apple pie for North Americans, *magluba* for Palestinians, *yerba mate* for Argentines, *fufu* for West Africans, *pho* for Vietnamese, *bok choy* for Koreans. Regional, ethnic, or national communities invest pride in these dishes, which come to symbolize them as their flags, heroes, or national monuments. Food functions as a powerful national or communal symbol because, unlike a flag, a dish can be taken in, assimilated, in other words, internalized by the human body. Ethnic or national groups, thus, are consolidated by the consumption of a meal in a secular form of communion. The use of food as a metaphor to define a particular human community associated with pride or valorization, however, is rare. A Swiss citizen wouldn't call herself fondue; nor would a Palestinian call himself *magluba* without a note of derision. However, defining an ethnic or national group in an insulting way is common practice. The French call the British "Roast-Beef," the British respond to the insult by the well-known "French Frogs"; immigrant communities are invariably reduced to the metaphor of the simplistic perception of what they eat: "Macaronis" for Italians in mid-twentieth-century France; "Krauts" for German immigrants in the United States. The community, instead of actively consuming its dish as a point of pride, is assimilated to it, swallowed up by its name, its national or ethnic pride and identity erased under the all-consuming food metaphor.[25]

So far, I have left the Caribbean and the Black Atlantic aside, since multiple examples drawn from the African diaspora in the New World offer a striking contrast with the negative food metaphors evoked above. Self-claimed positive culinary metaphors define cultural, ethnic, or national identities. Callaloo, gumbo, and *awara,* for instance, are used metaphorically to define proudly mixed identities in, respectively, but not exclusively, Trinidad, Louisiana, and French Guyana. In those cases, the culinary metaphor does not reduce the other to the debased state of a done-for dish, but rather is claimed by the self as an active and dynamic model of identity. Neither the dish nor the group is assimilated to the other, but both merge in a comfortable and interactive ipseity. The community houses the dish and the dish houses it in a reciprocal embracement.

While not presenting the following list as inclusive,[26] I reflect on *ajiaco*, pepper-pot, callaloo, gumbo, *feijoada,* and *awara.*[27] Like jazz standards, these dishes are based on unlimited variations on a basic theme. Hence, my descriptions do not aim at a stable and definitive definition, and I am sure my readers will have in mind very different manifestations and contexts of the dishes. *Ajiaco* is a meat stew, cooked with corn, potatoes, and, occasionally, tomatoes. The dish can be found in Cuba as well as in Colombia. Its color is usually dark yellow, or else red, if tomatoes are added to the mix. Pepper-pot is a dish typically consumed on Sundays in Barbados, where it is also a traditional Christmas dish. A variety of cuts of meat (beef, pork, duck, fowl, oxtail) are thrown into an earthenware pot *(canaree)* with hot peppers and brown sugar. The dish is also consumed in the rest of the Anglophone West Indies.[28] The national dish of Brazil, *feijoada,* is a slowly cooked stew prepared with black beans, sausage, salt-pork trimmings (tongue, ears, tail, feet), and collard greens. Once perceived as a slave survival dish made of bits and scraps, it is now also served in the finest restaurants on Saturdays. *Callaloo* is a name with many manifestations.[29] Consumed in most of the Caribbean and the African diasporic American South, *calalloo* is cooked down to a thick, smooth soup or sauce of mashed leaves of dasheen or taro, callaloo, okra, or spinach for a pale imitation. Added to the mix are salt pork or crabs, according to the season or the location. Callaloo is often consumed on special occasions such as the Sunday meal or, in Guadeloupe, for Easter. Louisiana Gumbo is also a stew with okra or roux for a base.[30] While chicken, smoked pork, or sausage often form the base of the gumbo, various seafood (crawfish, shrimp, oysters, crab) and vegetables (green leaves, peppers, celery, onions, and tomatoes) can be added according to the season and the availability of products. *Filé* or *gumbo filé* (pulverized sassafras leaves) can be added to the mix for taste and slipperiness. *Awara*, a rich broth from French Guyana, and the object of a film with the same name,[31] is consumed by the diverse community of South American French Guyana, composed of descendants of Amerindians, Africans, French, Portuguese, and contemporary Chinese, Hmong, Brazilian, and Surinamese communities. The stew's preparation is an affair lasting a few days. It is usually consumed on Easter Monday and is composed of cooked-down meats and crabs and vegetables such as spinach, eggplant, cabbage, cucumbers, and the indispensible Amazonian *awara* fruit. Awara soup has a greenish pale brown color.

Continuing to think about food through the analogy of jazz, what appears striking is the infinite number of variations on one single theme. The multiple symbolic dishes are all unique in the variety of ingredients and spices they require. The particular tastes they create unmistakably link us to a cultural, ethnic, or national specificity. However, what appears strikingly standard in all these varieties is the commonality of the stew's structures, preparations, consumption, and social and symbolic functions. In other words, the ensemble awara–ajiaco–callaloo–gumbo–pepper-pot–feijoada, to which we could assign the common-denominator name "Creole Stew,"[32] could be seen as one single manifestation of an extended Caribbeanness,[33] as a repetition with endless variations. In that, cuisine provides a helpful way to think concretely about notions of a submarine unity, as articulated by Kamau Brathwaite, or by Benítez Rojo's notion of a repeating island.[34] The Creole Stew offers a concrete illustration of repeating patterns, rhythms, and material units, which unify the Caribbean despite its political, linguistic, and cultural disconnections. The functions and attributes of cooking and sharing practices associated with these meals exemplify Glissant's notion of creolization as an encounter where violently different sources do not blend but congregate, resulting in a richer product than the original; a creolization that also builds on the lacks, interruptions, and violence of the immense exile of bodies, techniques, and ingredients of the diaspora; and a creolization that brings "word," language, signifying, out of the void of the diaspora or out of the scream of the enslaved. This word of food places in a continuum the parameters of the cultural, national, or social fragments of this extended Creole identity.

The parameters of the Creole Stew as common denominator consist of the following. The stew is based on plurality in oneness by mixing in one single pot a rich variety of ingredients. While it is sometimes served with side dishes—callaloo can be served in Guadeloupe with "cod chiquetaille,"[35] gumbo with corn bread, *feijoada* with deep-fried cassava or pork rinds—the Creole Stew is a complete dish in itself, rich in fat and proteins, and can sustain a family or a community for several days. In contrast with the common daily plate in the Caribbean and the Black Atlantic, usually a juxtaposition of meat or fish with rice and root vegetables, the ingredients are cooked together, forming a new entity. The unity of the pot provides an easy metaphor for the space of the Plantation, which is one enclosed space in which people of different origins were thrown together precipitously.[36] The pot, called *canari* or *canaree* in the Antilles, is usually earthenware, and therefore establishes a link to the earth and, by extension, the land. The pot, like the Plantation walls, contains ingredients that are as varied as the multiple origins of the cooks and consumers. The dish is equally inspired by world-dimension techniques: aboriginal (corn, potatoes, sassafras, *awara*),

African (okra, dasheen, earthenware), French or Spanish (smoked sausage, roux, beans, salt cod), or Asian (curry, callaloo). The origins of these ingredients and techniques are often debated and thus reproduce the uncertainty of origins in the context of communities displaced by the Middle Passage and other massive movements of migration.[37]

The nature of the stew also diverges from blended soups, since, through the action of cooking, each ingredient affects the others' nature without turning them into unrecognizable, melted, passive relays. In that, the cultural construction symbolized by the stew differs from the American idea of the melting pot, representing a community evolving toward sameness, blending, conformism, and uniformity, that is, a national construct in which one is either assimilated or annihilated.[38] In other words, the Creole Stew performs neither a blending (melting pot) nor a juxtaposition (Creole plate of meat, roots, and rice), but an agglutination. The linguistic meaning of agglutination describes precisely the cooking process of the Creole Stew. In linguistic terms, agglutination is "the systematic combining of independent words into compounds without marked change of form or loss of meaning." According to the medical definition, agglutination is "the clumping together of micro-organisms . . . suspended in fluids" *(Webster's)*. Thus, the Creole Stew is the aggregate of culinary elements that form a whole without losing their specificities, which is exactly, for the *créolistes* and for Glissant, the definition of "Créolité." The authors oppose *créolité* to *métissage*, a blend in which the specificities of the original product are lost in the synthesis.[39] I should also add that the aggregated pieces are linked without being glued together by the viscous, performed by the addition of the sticky okra to gumbos and callaloo stews and of *awara* fruit to the Guyana mix. The quality of viscosity, fluidity, and stickiness contributes to the unclassifiable nature of the dish within the categories of solid or liquid.[40] The concept of viscosity thus defies Lévi-Strauss's classification, which did not allow for intermediate stages, in a culinary grammar based on opposites.[41] The viscous, the slippery, the dynamic also correspond to Glissant's notion of a creolization always in movement. In his *Anthologie de la poésie du Tout-Monde,* Glissant includes African American writer Jayne Cortez's poem "Okra," which praises the often-despised fruit as the "inventor of secret paths" and as "the main connector between visible / and invisible forces" (Cortez, quoted in Glissant, *Anthologie,* 219). In its slipperiness, okra becomes a vector of creolization that alters the hard edges of the ingredients therein gathered without dissolving the elements it agglutinates. In short, the okra stew resists both blending and categorizing all the while unifying.

This resistance to categorization, however, does not indicate a lack of order, rules, and discipline. There is, to use a linguistic term, a grammar of the Creole Stew. To use the example of gumbo, it should be prepared with the indispensable okra, and according to the majority, prepared with the Cajun or Creole "holy trinity" of celery, onions, and bell peppers. The fact that not everyone agrees on the grammar—the cooking wars between roux gumbo and okra gumbo proponents can be fierce—is very proof of the existence of a grammar or an order. As a Guyanese woman interviewed in *Bouillon d'awara* sums it up for us: "In the *awara* soup, you can put many things but not any old thing." In the preparation of *awara,* cooks are trained with scientific precision because it is believed that only expert cooks can assure that the dish will do no harm. In Paes's documentary, there are countless examples of people whom ill-prepared *awara* made sick. As one of the interviewed cooks states: "Awara soup can make you sick if it is not well prepared" (in Paes). The *awara,* thus, goes beyond its function of feeding or pleasing the palate and appears close to the art of pharmacology, where the lack of precision of the concoction, or the *pharmakon,* can turn a healing brew into poison. The necessity of rules and grammaticality, or of the presence of a standard, is a fact essential to note since, through its grammar or standards, the Creole Stew establishes itself as cuisine, as gastronomy (rational, cultural), and not simply as food (survival, natural).[42]

Once the standard is mastered, improvisation—often forced by hardship or unavailability of food due to seasonal, economic, or geographic reasons—adds its genius signature to the cuisine. Lafcadio Hearn sums it up: "Any one who has ever paid a flying visit to New Orleans probably knows something about those various culinary preparations whose generic name is 'Gombo'—compounded of many odds and ends, with the okra-plant . . . but also comprising occasionally 'losé, zépinard, laitie'" (*Gombo*, 3). In Hearn's description of gumbo, we can clearly identify the standard or genre ("generic") and several possible variations or improvisations on a theme.[43] When a culinary grammar is established, it can be transmitted, communicated, and, like a common language,[44] begin to unify communities.[45] As many critics have shown, the sharing of a common food inheritance functions as a common language in situations in which common linguistic forms of expressions have been taken away, voluntarily left behind, or forgotten in situations of diaspora, migration, and exile.[46] Our Creole Stew acts as the common language at the level of the familial, the local, the religious, the national, and the transnational. The Creole Stew is based on duration. This food concoction simmers slowly and at times, like *awara* or *ajiaco,* requires several days of preparation. It is not instantaneous but inserts itself and the consuming community into a shared duration.[47] Moreover, the stew is not a daily staple but rather is consumed on specific days of the week or religious or national holidays: Sunday for Bajan pepper-pot; Easter for callaloo and *awara*. While dishes such as callaloo are eaten at a Christian feast, their consumption is also reminiscent of African religious and communal feasts. Mme. Prudence Marcelin, one of the *doyennes* of the "syndicat des cuisinières" in Guadeloupe, describes callaloo as a sacred dish, referring explicitly to the rebirth of Christ, and also less explicitly to the African sacredness of the earth and the roots: "You have to fetch the crabs under the earth. Callaloo is a sacred dish, and that's why you can't find it in restaurants. Callaloo is sacred."[48] Callaloo thus is a double-signifying sign, which helps to reformulate notions of sacredness and religiosity outside the Western Christian norms. Independently from the origin of the sacredness associated with the stews, their consumption on specific days or holidays consolidates communities as they inscribe memorialization on specific dates, which become significant to the community through the simple gesture of tasting the common dish.

The single-pot nature of the dish also brings us back to the term "religion" as *re-ligere* or relation. Several hands and mouths will eat from the same pot, thereby disseminating a unity, and a single performance of the dish, to the consumers. Implying that the dishes are consumed in the traditional way, reminiscent of the West African sharing of the *fufu,* a paste made from cassavas, yams, maize, or plantains, eaten without utensils and rolled into a small ball with the right hand, the encounter of the hands in the single dish literally links the bodies through the tangible relay of the common pot. Caribbean proverbs and testimonies attest to this eating practice. For instance, a proverb from Haiti collected by Hearn indicates that "Nîon doight pas jamin manjé calalou [You can't eat callalou with one finger'] (*Gombo Zhèbes,* 27). Danticat refers to the same proverb: "We [in Haiti] also have another expression, 'It takes more than one finger to eat kalalou' because of the slippery nature of it. It's a statement of unity. The fingers have to work together to pick up the kalalou" ("Dyasporic Appetites," 37). The singular hand and plural fingers come to symbolize the community's union in their diversity.

The example of *awara* speaks particularly to this notion of community building. The documentary *Bouillon d'awara* focuses on the community of Mana, a town of fifteen hundred inhabitants speaking thirteen different languages, including Guyanese Creole, French, Surinamese, Hmong, Galibi, and several South Asian languages. In this New World babel, *awara* acts as the common denominator, a common tool of communication and communion that links the members of the disparate linguistic communities. According to one of the interviewees, the legend goes that, long ago, a white man fell into a pit. After the Amerindians saved his life, a young woman fell in love with him and cooked a stew for him, mixing in it whatever ingredients she could find. The storyteller adds that the soup looked like "ce que vous savez" [you know what], implying that it had the color and texture of excrement. Instead of causing him disgust, the soup attracted the outsider, who returned to the cook. The commentator concludes that the stranger who tastes *awara* always comes back to Guyana.

This account evokes rich interpretations. First of all, a new community is formed out of the sharing of the meal. In this sense, food mirrors sexuality and reproduction, the traditional ways of consolidating a family. The soup also links the stranger to the excremental and forces him to eat it in order to become a member of the group. Community building is therefore a mix of sacred and profane, inclusion and debasement. The perception of the meal as culinary or excremental depends on the position of the eater in relation to the community. Outsiders perceive it as excremental and therefore cannot become part of that community. Outsiders who perceive it as food are taken in by members of the community and become insiders. An interviewed Surinamese man living in Mana, who considers himself an outsider, recounts that after eating *awara,* 'il a fait caca toute la nuit" [he went to the bathroom all night], concluding that one has to be Guyanese to eat it. The *awara* soup thus stands on a fine line between food, in the context of feast and community, and dejection, which chases out those who cannot assimilate it and who therefore cannot be assimilated. *Awara*, in this case, acts as a strict community consolidator, at the price of excluding those who cannot assimilate it. An elementary-school director who complains about the afflux of migrants in Guyana and who declares that her country wants to remain Creole ("On veut rester créoles") claims: "In the past twenty years, we've had to digest tons of communities. It's hard!" The double-edged sword of *awara*, which seems to decide who is included and excluded from a community, represents here a form of closed *creoleness* that does not have infinite properties of agglutination, a creole model strongly linked to the territorialization of the land. One Guyanese speaking against the exportation of *awara* paste claims: "Awara cannot be exported and must remain in Guyana." This conception of the Creole Stew as closed Creoleness contrasts with Glissant's notion of open creolization through his theorization of masala, which I explore below.

Creole Stew as a metaphor for community is further explained by the rich range of possible colors of the stew. A Trinidadian friend of mine once claimed that he was "callaloo," that is, a perfect blend of the African, European, and Indian ethnic groups present in Trinidad and Tobago. Marlon Riggs, in his 1995 documentary film on defining who is black, *Black Is, Black Ain't,* intersperses interviews of people evoking their multifarious definitions of blackness with images of his mother's gumbo slowly simmering on the stove. "Everything that you can imagine can be put into gumbo," the narrator explains. The rhythmical repetition of the gumbo's images implies that blackness in America follows the same rules. Its slowly evolving color from green to brown in the movie indicates that the changing colors of gumbo offer a fitting illustration of the varied spectrum of colors associated with blackness in the United States. And indeed, the tints of Creole Stew vary from dark yellow (*ajiaco*), to greenish-brown (callaloo, *gumbo zhèbes*), to light yellowish-brown (*awara*), to mahogany (roux gumbo), to dark brown or black (pepper-pot), to dark-purplish-brown (*feijoada*). The Creole Stew therefore represents the varied color scale of the inhabitants of the Caribbean and plantation zone. Creole Stew becomes skin; skin becomes food. The continuum and variability of the colors of Creole Stew encourage us to think of race as fluid in nature, escaping the trap of fixed categorization.

The repetition of the Creole Stew, with its multiple avatars in the Antilles, Brazil, Guyana, and the United States, also creates a transnation through the repetition of this food standard, which is not the only one pertinent to the Black or Creole Atlantic, but which is nonetheless one of its major themes. In her hybrid book made of recipes, memoirs, and historical narratives, *If I Can Cook, You Know God Can,* Ntozake Shange does extraordinary work demonstrating that the diasporic peoples of South Carolina, Haiti, and Brazil are linked by common culinary practices and poetics. In her equally complex *Vibration Cooking*, Vertamae Smart-Grosvenor, does similar work thinking about transnational diasporic cuisine as sharing what she terms a "poetics of vibration."[49] I will not repeat Shange's and Grosvenor's extensive transnational studies; I will simply state that dishes such as callaloo create or consolidate a community of people separated by national borders and seas, but united by culture, inheritance, and creolization.

As Shange and Smart-Grosvenor demonstrate, a common culinary grammar, syntax, and cooking and eating rhythms allow communication between segments of time and space separated by generations or by seas. A grandmother will speak with her émigré granddaughter through food.[50] A Grenadian will speak to a Haitian via callaloo or *kalalou*. This seems like a universal fact of the daily experience of immigration and exile accompanied by the loss of linguistic tools of communication. Communication thus happens through culinary channels when common linguistic tools are lacking.

However, the substitution of language with food has its pitfalls. Assimilating a particular language to a dish can deny the given parlance its status of language and reduce it to an act of consumption instead of an act of creation. While reflecting on late nineteenth-century New Orleans, Hearn described the attitudes of non-Creolophone speakers toward the mixed language: "Such English-speaking residents of New Orleans seldom speak of it as 'Creole'": they call it "'gombo', for some mysterious reason I have never been able to explain satisfactorily" (*Gombo Zhèbes*, 3). The reason does not appear to be so mysterious. The refusal of the word "Creole" denies its existence as a language linked to a particular ethno-cultural reality and replaces it with a dish, gumbo, which could be perceived, by the antagonist eye, as an exotic, whimsical, and garbled mix. "Speaking gumbo" is thus not speaking but instead being reduced to the primary act of eating. The debasing utterance of the English-speaking mouth above is internalized by the black children of the same Creole speakers: "In like manner a young Creole negro or negress of New Orleans might tell an aged member of his race: 'Ça qui to parlé ça pas Créole: ça c'est gombo!' I have sometimes heard the pure and primitive Creole also called 'Congo' by colored folks of the new generation" (ibid.). The passage from Gombo to Congo, cousins in rhyme but separated by much history, language, and geography, further associates Creole language, "gumbo language," with a form of perceived primitiveness of the African continent and its derivations.

In his *Pays sans chapeau,* a narrative recounting the return of a Haitian exile to his native country, Dany Laferrière pushes the degrading association of Creole language with food to an extreme. In the northwestern Haitian town of Bombardopolis, an international commission, including emissaries from the U.S. Food and Drug Administration and the National Aeronautics and Space Administration, and a Belgian linguist study a strange case of inhabitants who are believed to be able to survive without eating. In his cynical allegory of Western media representations of hunger in Haiti, Laferrière invents a scientist whose conclusions consist of the following. The inhabitants of Bombardopolis do not have to eat in order to survive because of a curious property of a particularly pure form of Creole language: "C'est le créole qui permet ça" ("It's all thanks to Creole," *Pays sans chapeau,* 194). What could be perceived as an absurd proposal—that the purity of Creole language is enough to feed its speakers—makes a lot of sense if we read it allegorically. The observation presents Creole language as food, in a manner similar to Hearn's "gombo." The strange case of Bombardopolis is presented as a solution to world hunger. According to the fictional Belgian linguist, "In less than two hundred years, Creole could become the universal language, which would put an end to world hunger" (196). If the miracle can be universalized, it would absolve Westerners of the guilt, duty, and responsibility of feeding those who have fed the world for centuries. More crucially, the allegory presents Creole speakers, in this case black Haitians, as beyond the basic need to eat. This last proposition is very close to the common colonial myth that descendants of Africans in the colony do not need to be fed as much as others. As Moreau de Saint-Méry asserts, "In health, the negro could be called sober . . . he is perhaps, amongst all humans, the one who consumes the least amount of food especially in relation to his work" (61). In Laferrière's model, Creole speakers are shriveled up into an exceptional section of humanity, beyond the basic need of hunger, a fact that consequently absolves the West of its past and present responsibilities. Creole language is reduced to the alimentary, the basic, the animal. This book struggles with this very debasement of food and language, suggesting instead that food is an articulate, functional, and complex language.

In order to avoid the traps just described, it is necessary to keep two things in mind: first, the presence of a common culinary language is to be taken metaphorically. Language doesn't feed its man. Second, if we want to use food as a powerful metaphor for language, it is crucial to insist on Creole food's complexity and grammaticality and not to reduce it (or the language it represents) to a shapeless stew. Many literary and academic publications have done just that. The leading journal in the literatures of the African diasporas, *Callaloo,* made this complexity clear in the publication of two special issues devoted to thinking about callaloo. The title of the special issue presented the dish as a readable text.[51] In the same spirit, Hearn titled his 1885 collection of proverbs from Mauritius, Louisiana, Trinidad, Guyana, Martinique, and Haiti *Gombo Zhèbes,* granting gumbo all its complexity. Practicing Creole transatlantic studies *avant la lettre,* Hearn lists proverbs in various Creole languages with their French and English translations: "The literature of 'gombo' has perhaps more varieties than there are preparations of the esculents above referred to;—the patois has certainly its gombo févi, its gombo filé, its 'gombo zhèbes,'—both written and unwritten" (3). Creole here is presented in its rich diversity and replaced in a context of literature and literacy (both oral and written). The number of literary and scholarly texts that use the Creole culinary metaphor in their title is high: *Un Plat de porc aux bananes vertes; L'Espérance-macadam; Gumbo Ya-Ya: Folktales of Louisiana; A Pepper-Pot of Cultures: Aspects of Creolization in the Caribbean;* or *Breadfood or Chesnut: Gender Construction in the French Caribbean Novel.* In these examples, cultural complexity is not assimilated to a shapeless dish, but instead, the culinary complexity is what comes closer to "creolization, a form of *métissage* with a result that goes beyond its original elements" (Glissant, "Métissage," 50) or to Bernabé, Confiant, and Chamoiseau's definition of Créolité as an "interactional and transactional aggregate of Caribbean, European, African, Asian and Leventine elements" (*Éloge,* 87).

With the example of the masala, Glissant takes the model of creolization a step further. He links the culinary to the more abstract and theoretical place of Relation and projects Martinique into the *tout-monde* or "whole-world."

Martinique-Masala

In his *Tout-Monde* and auxiliary *Traité du Tout-monde,* Glissant concretizes his model of Relation developed in earlier theoretical work. *Tout-monde,* or "whole-world," unlike Hardt and Negri's Empire, is a totality, which does not lead to totalitarianism, and does not dominate the world by multiple, capitalized sites of power. Instead, "whole-world" offers a constant interaction, an oscillating model of self-creation, between the particular place and the global world, on the one hand, and among the fragments of whole-world, on the other. The hybrid novel-treatise *Tout-Monde* relinquishes the usual setting of Glissant's earlier novels, the Martinican plantation and land, to explore various fixed and mobile world sites such as airports and airplanes, Colombia, Senegal, Montenegro, Savoy, Martinique, Lagos, Berlin, and Liguria. J. Michael Dash has called this new relationship between the particular island space of Martinique and the world a "relational insularity," which involves a constant interaction between the island space, the archipelago, and the world (Dash, "Martinique/Mississippi," 94). For Dash, Glissant "seems to suggest that only in this way can the island space be freed from the preoccupation with creating a grounding center and opened out to new possibilities of representation" (95). This model does not lead to the disappearance of Martinique but chooses the Martinican place as one among the many other possible pieces of whole-world.

Two apparently incompatible refrains punctuate Glissant's *Tout-Monde*: "le lieu est incontournable" [the place is unavoidable] (*Tout-Monde,* 29) and "il n'y avait plus ni Ici, ni Là-bas" [Here and There are long gone] (477). Whereas the first statement seems to praise place, the second quickly negates the exclusivity of a particular place. In a passage of *Tout-Monde,* between two repetitions of "il n'y avait plus ni Ici, ni Là-bas" emerges the inevitable reference to masala, which extends for three pages. Let's draw out its most significant ingredients, which will allow us to grasp the paradoxical relationship between the local and whole-world, and to understand how this "place-world" is a valid response both to grounding and globalization:

> Look at Indian cuisine for instance. . . . It was like a bondless chain, a meshed net drifting away. From where did it drift? From masala, or masalè. The base, the primary element as you might say, the cuisine's earth-water-air-fire. . . . In order to make masala, mix together curcuma rhizome or powder, onion or green-onion, parsley, garlic, chili pepper, grilled or fried rice, cloves, and fried cumin. We'll keep the proportions secret to let you experiment a little. . . . See the meshed net, the continuum with neither here nor there, with neither periphery nor center, massala [*sic*] is essential, yet it disappears in the mix, it's the basis for everything, with so many different results. . . . You will understand the invariant, that eating is rhizome, and once you

> grasp the primary element, you'll never let it go. . . . Mix the masala with vegetables or meat and you will get a Colombo; with cumin-flavored meat, garlic, and oil, you will obtain a talchou. . . . If you add left-over split peas to masala, green peas, and cubed potatoes, you will obtain samosas . . . Lason is made with the same lentils, but after having been processed . . . and mixed once more with masala. . . . In short, masala is the invariant element of the culinary Chaos that Antillean Hindus taught us to adopt in our maelstrom. . . . Believe me, Here and There are long gone. (477–79)

Movement defines masala as it does Glissant's Relation. The orthographic instability (*masala*, *massala* or *masalé*, used indifferently) produces even more versions of mixtures: *colombo*, *talchou*, *samosa*, *dol*, and *lason*. The primary element ("l'élément premier") is defined by its indeterminacy ("Let's keep the proportions secret"). The very definition of the "primary element" refutes the possibility of primary elements since water, earth, air, and fire are hyphenated as a unit ("earth-water-air-fire"). The engine of this culinary machine, the masala, becomes a product that can be reactivated by itself in an endless recycling: *lason* is *dol*, already mixed with masala, "mixed once more with masala" (478).[52] Its major property is paradoxically that it escapes a stabilizing definition as movement characterizes it: "It was like a meshed net drifting away" (477). This instability, however, in which no particular ingredient is elected as dominant, in which no product can be stabilized either in orthography or in a culinary recipe, links concrete elements. These vital, fluid parts create a nongrounded particularity and allow us to imagine—and to remember.[53]

It is also significant that Glissant selects masala—a spice mix, a volatile object, a virtual meal—instead of a finished product such as *colombo,* the Martinican Indian curry. The spice appeals to the nose before the palate and incites one to imagine and remember, rather than to taste and consume. Timothy Morton's definition of "spice," as "a linguistic and ideological operator rather than an essentialised object" (*Poetics of Spice,* 18) and its qualities as a "complex and contradictory marker . . . sacred and profane, medicine and poison, Orient and Occident; *and the traffic between these terms*" (9, emphasis in original) closely resembles Glissant's Relation, which is defined not by any of the individual terms but by the relation, or movement, between these terms. In short, the volatility, virtuality, versatility of masala lets the reader imagine one concrete application of Glissant's Relation: "Relation is open-ended . . . totality is virtual. . . . Relation is movement . . . its results alter each time the elements that make it, and, as a result, the relation that emerges from them and that modifies them once again" (*Poétique,* 185–86). Recall, as an example of Relation, the masala, which becomes lason, blended up and mixed once again to become masala.

Despite the fact that masala appears as a clear concretization of Glissant's concept of Relation, we must look further and not be satisfied with this purely theoretical answer. It is also politically significant that Glissant would take the Indian spice mix as his privileged example for the constitution of Martinican—and whole-worldly—identity. He could, for instance, have chosen one of our common Creole Stews such as the *calalou*, a more specifically Creole dish of Dahomean origin, which functions according to the same versatile, adaptable, and changeable nature. *Calalou,* which can take many shapes in Martinican cuisine, mixed with ham and salt meat, pig tails, or alternatively crab, which could take the form of a soup or a sauce, could easily exemplify the constantly creolizing and recreolizing Martinican identity (*Meilleures recettes,* 28–29). *Calalou* has indeed been documented since the nineteenth century as one of the staples of Caribbean and, more specifically, Martinican cuisine. Hearn in his 1890 *Martinique Sketches* defines it as one of the two most typical soups of Martinican "*manjé créole*," "the food of the people proper, the colored population" (*Two Years,* 274). In this *manjé créole*, "there are only two popular soups which are peculiar to authentic Creole cuisine—calalou, a gumbo soup, almost precisely similar to that of Louisiana; and the soupe-d'habitant, a country soup" (275). Lelia Taylor in the first issue of the journal *Callaloo* explains that "the West Indian soup called Callaloo is much like the Louisiana gumbos, and recipes can be found in Trinidad, Jamaica, Grenada, Haiti, Martinique, and Guadeloupe" ("Callaloo Anyone?" 248). For MacKie, "callaloo remains one of the cornerstones of Caribbean cooking and is remembered nostalgically by all who have eaten it" (*Life and Food,* 81). Ary Ebroïn makes it a paradigm of diasporic crossings and contacts: "Among African dishes often consumed in Martinique . . . the calalou, which came from Dahomey and crossed the South-Atlantic before reaching Louisiana, deserves a special mention" ("Les origines," 81). Significantly, Glissant does not mention *calalou* in his theoretical works, despite the fact that the dish would make an ideal candidate to allegorize the transatlantic relations between Martinique and the American South dear to the Martinican theorist.[54] Instead, he chooses the East Indian masala as the privileged metaphor of his "whole-world."

Electing masala, a marginal yet essential component of Martinican creolization, is significant in that it frees Martinique from the atavistic relationship to the French Métropole and from desires of territorialization and provincialism. By being at once unquestionably Martinican, Indian, and cosmopolitan, masala troubles the pattern of opposition between the global and the local and thus settles Martinique as a privileged transactional place between the two.

Additionally, Glissant's choice of a marginalized yet indispensable constituent of the Antillean cultural landscape appears as a significant political gesture. Indeed, in her pioneering *Diasporic (Dis)locations,* Brinda Mehta calls for the need to examine the East Indian component of the Caribbean, too often overlooked in "contemporary anthologies and critical studies" (1).[55] Massive Indian migration to the Caribbean started with the official abolition of slavery in 1838, when "a second wave of 'voluntary immigration' was mobilized from India in the form of the indentured labor trade" (2). While in Guadeloupe and Martinique the proportion of people with East Indian descent, mostly Tamil, is much less significant in numbers than in Trinidad or Guyana,[56] their cultural, literary, political, religious, and of course culinary presence is indispensable to understand contemporary Martinican identity. For random examples of this representation, we can think of Ernest Moutoussamy, a Guadeloupean politician and writer, Gerty Dambury, a Guadeloupean playwright, Vincent Placoly, a Martinican writer of Tamil ancestry; of figurines of Ganesh present in many altars and temples; and of the *colombos,* curries, dhal, coconut milk, masalas, and *dosai,* now integral parts of Antillean cooking. For Mehta, "colombo or curry [is] considered the national dish of Guadeloupe and Martinique. As an affirmation of the East Indian presence in the Antilles, colombo charts the history of Indian indenture through the migration of spices and curry flavours attesting both to the distinctiveness of Indian cuisine and its creolized adaptations in the Caribbean" (*Notions of Identity,* 39). Mehta infers that the strength of the culinary palliates the marginalized religious, ethnic, and political East Indian contribution to the Antillean cultural landscape.

In spite of their many contributions, culinary or otherwise, the discourse on Indians and Indianness remains marginal in Martinican and Guadeloupean literary and cultural studies.[57] The representation of East Indians in Martinican or Guadeloupean novels, who are often referred to by the derogatory "couli" or "couli-malaba," reflects and arguably perpetuates a strong xenophobic sentiment. East Indian characters are often portrayed with an irreducible difference that hinders the process of creolization. For instance, the Ramsaran family in Maryse Condé's *Traversée de la Mangrove* remains ostracized in spite of their social and economic success: "Many people . . . sang meanly: 'Kouli malaba / Isi dan / Pa peyiw' [Malabar Coolie / This here / Is not your land]" (20). At the end of his *Ravines du devant-jour*, Raphaël Confiant inserts a glossary repeating rampant violent stereotypes: "Coolie: Dog-eater, urine-smelling, gutter-cleaner, street-beggar, negro-heckler" (211).

It appears that Glissant's centralizing of the masala metaphor does justice to the Indian contribution in the establishment of a Martinican identity. In many other places of his theoretical texts, Glissant refers to the Indian diaspora, or to Indian philosophy, as a counterexample of the destructive, conquering force of Western philosophies and politics. In *Poétique,* Glissant praises the nonlinear Indian philosophy: "Everywhere, in India, for instance, where time is not conceived as linear, where philosophies do not meditate on the One but on the Whole, myths of foundation did not generate the process of filiation" (59). However, in spite of his taste for things Indian, Glissant is far from "praising Indianness" as an archetypal model of Caribbeanness. His gesture has nothing to do with, for instance, the Mauritian poet Khal Torabully's "coolitude" (coolieness), an ode to East Indians in Creole cultures.[58]

The privileging of the Indian culinary example is rather the desire to recenter the marginal, whatever its cultural or national adherence. This is precisely masala's function: to destabilize dominant categories. This poetics of leaps, upsetting, and intrusion invites Caribbean subjects to imagine alternative routes to the old colonial and "authentic" paths of reconstruction, whether French, African, or aboriginal. As Mehta argues, Indian cuisine, because of its marginal position in the Caribbean, allows one to "simultaneously reveal and resist the colonizing imprint of otherness in the form of reconfigured culinary routes" ("Gisèle Pineau," 26). The choice of the spice mix transmitted by the South Asian Martinican minority, often ignored or expelled from the construction of a Caribbean identity, clearly indicates Glissant's antinationalist drive. Kamau Brathwaite's model for a Caribbean nation, in contrast, excludes the East Indian component.[59] Masala represents the nontotalitarian totality in which a minority culture (Indian) becomes a necessary (but nonassimilating) engine to create a constantly shifting creolizing model of political identification.

Importantly, Glissant's masala is not exclusively linked to a Martinican model of identity but represents an attempt to resist the force of Empire and globalization by offering an alternative way to think about whole-world. In the new battleground that has become the world, the Martinican subject has to act on this new terrain: "We have to fill-up with the idea of globalization *[mondialisation]* . . . lest we become obsolete in relation to those who will use the possibilities of globalization in a harmful and wicked way" (*Introduction à une poétique,* 102–3). Since, as Hardt and Negri demonstrate, "empire establishes no territorial center" (*Empire,* xii), it cannot be resisted by a singular locus or body. As Glissant puts it, "You could fight physically with the King of France who was the head of French capitalism. Fight with the colonist. With the boss. But you cannot fight physically, I mean physically, with multinationals" (*Introduction à une poétique,* 102–3). Hardt and Negri, in a movement apparently similar to Glissant's, present a positive global response to the crushing globalization of Empire through the achievement of a "global citizenship" by "the mobile multitude" (*Empire,* 361) through the "ethical practices" of "Nomadism" and "miscegenation" (362). This "common human species" becomes for Hardt and Negri "the multicolored Orpheus of infinite power," a universal singular unit in which "bodies are mixed and the nomads speak a common tongue" (362). This is where the danger of universalism lies, however, namely, in the creation of a utopian-blended entity, devoid of any particularity, crushing localities ideologically. This echoes the capitalist strategies by which the Empire economically suppresses local peoples. As Glissant bluntly states:

> The place is unavoidable. Globalization *[mondialisation]* doesn't come from a series of evaporations in the air. . . . The more I will become aware of the relationship between Martinique and the Caribbean and between the Caribbean and the world, like in a system or rather an anti-system of differences, the more I will be Martinican. . . . The more I will say: Martinique is Martinique, the less I will be Martinican. . . . The true relation is not between the particular and the universal but between the place and the world-totality, which is not totalitarian, but its opposite in diversity. (*Introduction à une poétique,* 105)

Through the example of masala, Glissant inextricably links the particular place to the world-totality. Doing so, he destabilizes the oppositional model between the Empire and the local that Hardt and Negri develop. This mobile spice mix, undeniably and simultaneously local and global,

Martinican, East Indian, Circum-Caribbean, and transnational, can fight globalization on its own ground. It responds to a difference-crushing globalization with a product linking Martinique, India, the Circum-Caribbean, and the world in reciprocal and boundless chains of influence. Glissant presents this particular-becoming-totality as the only valid defense against Empire. This system (or rather, antisystem) exemplified and performed by masala clearly prevents reterritorialization and nationalism. Masala, in spite of its unmistakable bold taste and smell, which marks every store and kitchen housing it, reverts in the end to the single engine of Glissant's theory of whole-world and Relation: "In a nutshell, masala is the invariant of this culinary chaos" (*Tout-Monde,* 478).[60]

While Glissant undoubtedly gives cooking a long-awaited central place in his texts, the references to spices and recipes seem to slip through our fingers because of their volatile theoretical character. Indeed, where does the food come from? From itself, it seems. Recall the description of the masala as "a bondless chain, a meshed net drifting away. From where did it drift? From masala, or masalè" (*Tout-Monde,* 477). The culinary chain is linked to its ipseity and the theoretical model to its own referentiality. Where is the materiality of food? Where are the references to starved bodies and an overfed plantation? To creative modes of survival in situations of near-starvation produced by slavery, war, or exile? To bodies laboring to plant and harvest products of secret Creole gardens? Where are the references to the overheated kitchen? To cooks' sweating foreheads and hands that grind up spices and burn their fingers on the stove? Where are the bodies receiving pleasure and pain from the presence of familiar dishes and in their absence? The authors I will discuss in the next two chapters, like Glissant, present food as a major site of creolization and cultural construction. Moreover, Patrick Chamoiseau's *Creole Folktales,* Aimé Césaire's *Notebook of a Return to the Native Land* (chapter 2), Edwidge Danticat's *Breath, Eyes, Memory,* and Gisèle Pineau's *Exil selon Julia* (chapter 3) provide us with this warranted acknowledgment of the materiality of the culinary crucially grounding Glissant's theoretical drive.

2 NOT JUST HUNGER

Patrick Chamoiseau and Aimé Césaire

> Ils supportent, dit-on, très aisément la faim. [They take hunger lightly, I am told.]
>
> —Buffon, *Variétés dans l'Espèce humaine*

IN 2009, PATRICK CHAMOISEAU, Édouard Glissant, and other writers from the French Overseas Departments and Regions of Martinique, Guadeloupe, Guyana, and Réunion cosigned a pamphlet entitled "Manifeste pour les 'produits' de haute nécessité."[1] Published in the wake of the general strike in Guadeloupe and Martinique,[2] the manifesto argues that the "prosaic" needs of daily survival, cost of living, and agricultural sustainability go hand in hand with a claim to a "poetics":

> Behind the prosaic homemaker's basket lurks the essential part of what we lack and of what brings meaning to our lives, i.e., the poetic. Every human life . . . gets articulated between, on the one hand the immediate need of drinking-surviving-eating (the prosaic); and on the other, the desire towards a self-realization, for which food is made of dignity, of honor, of music, of songs, of sports, of dances, of readings, of spirituality, of love, of free time obtained by the accomplishment of the great intimate desire (the poetic). ("Manifeste pour les 'produits de haute nécessité,'" 3)

In other words, hunger is not just hunger. The basic need for survival is necessarily inhabited by a means for self-assertion—artistic, creative, or philosophical—that lurks behind the homemaker's shopping basket. The manifesto constitutes a significant political gesture to make the metropolitan French public and government understand that the general strikes in Martinique and Guadeloupe were not simply about consumerism and the high cost of living ("les grèves contre la vie chère")[3] as the media qualified them, but also about a generalized desire for more cultural and political autonomy.[4]

This chapter focuses on food as the very site or metaphor where cultural, linguistic, and political identities, in short, high-necessity products, get cooked. I will primarily focus on Patrick Chamoiseau's 1988 renditions of Creole folktales told on the Martinican slavery and post-slavery plantation. In choosing these tales dominated by themes of hunger and survival, I aim to show that the prosaic partakes in the creation of a complex poetics. I intend "poetics" in its Greek etymological sense of "making," the building of a human creation through artistic forms, which Aristotle exemplifies with drama as well as lyric or epic poetry. Glissant's definition of the poetics, which he evokes in the manifesto as well as in his 1990 *Poétique de la Relation,* clearly entails the idea of building and construction through aesthetics forms of expressions. In his essay "La Barque ouverte," after having listed the unfathomable manifestations of the abyss linked to the experience of the Middle Passage and enslavement, Glissant proposes poetry as the only form able to speak the unspeakable of slavery and to advance constructively toward the future: "Nous crions le cri de poésie. Nos barques sont ouvertes, pour tous, nous les naviguons" [We cry our cry of poetry. Our boats are open, and we sail them for everyone] (*Poétique,* 20). The palimpsest of the French verb "crier," "to scream," hides and reveals the Creole verb "crier," "criar," "criare," "créer," at the origin of the word Creole, which means to be born, to be raised, to create, to build, or to name. In this last meaning of the word, "crier le cri" thus means to name the scream of poetry, to identify the moment in which Martinicans can name their own poetry. Poetry is thus, for Glissant, a constructive scream and an act of naming closely tied with the process of creolization. Food constitutes one of the privileged sites of creolization where bread and poetry, to use Aimé Césaire's analogy, or the prosaic and the poetic meet.[5] While food in the tales that I will analyze reflects an experienced situation—rampant and acute hunger naturally leads to an obsessive representation of gluttony in the tales—it also assumes a poetic function. Food "makes" humanity through a process of aesthetization. Food acts as a site of poetic creation and reclaiming of cultural identity, when it starts to function, as Lévi-Strauss would have it, as a form of active cooking, as a language with its own grammar: in short, as an agent of cultural complexity and grammaticality.[6]

In other words, the control, cooking, and poeticizing of food maintains humanity—by consolidating familial and communal links and by expressing cultural specificity—in a context in which legal, economic, political, and discursive structures stripped the enslaved and the exploited from their basic human rights. The tales are set in a context in which the borders between animality and humanity are troubled, in which, as we see below, a Dominican priest grants more compassion to a parrot than to an enslaved African. It is paradoxically through a characteristic that humans share with all other animals, the basic necessity of eating, that they first preserve their humanity and, second, create cultural particularity, in this specific case, Creole culture.[7]

Tales of Survival

In "Lieu clos, parole ouverte" (*Poétique,* 77–89), Glissant provides a useful contextualization to situate Chamoiseau's *Creole Folktales.* He lists three phases of Martinican literature: survival, lure, and memory. The first, "literature of survival," practiced under extreme conditions during slavery, operates through what Glissant calls a "practice of the detour," whereby the storyteller uses symbols in order to voice political and social concerns that could not be expressed openly without reprimand. Food and eating, gluttons and starved characters, express a situation of enslavement in a cryptic way.

The phase of the "lure" defines an elitist literary practice by writers who overemphasize the beauty of the island while "possessed by the throbbing need to justify the [Plantation] system" (*Poétique,* 84). In this second phase, food simply contributes to the construction of an exotic, palatable, and ultimately misleading paradise (84). Phase three, or "the work of memory," describes writers from the zone of the Americas dominated by the Plantation system—Frankétienne, Toni Morrison, William Faulkner, Gabriel García Márquez, Derek Walcott, Kamau Brathwaite, Alejo Carpentier, and Glissant himself—who practice "a creative marooning, whose multiple expressions begin to forge a continuity" (*Poétique,* 85) beyond historical gaps and fragmentation.

The folktales I will consider in this chapter, significantly, belong both to phase one and phase three, insofar as Chamoiseau, by his contemporary intervention, gives these tales of survival a critical distance and a contemporary bend, granting them a continuity that makes them relevant to understanding the present experience of hunger in Martinique as well.[8] The figure of the starved slave foreshadows the contemporary departmentalized recipient of French sustenance.[9]

The twelve stories included in Chamoiseau's *Creole Folktales* are saturated with allusions to food: states and acts of starvation, vomiting, gluttony, cannibalism, scatophagy, talking dishes, copious lists of prepared meals. The following synopsis of the five tales will provide context for the issues I examine in this chapter.

First, in order of appearance in the collection, "La Madame Kéléman" recounts the trials of a young girl—her mother's fourteenth daughter—lost in the woods. She encounters an ogress who promises to resume feeding her when she finds out the ogress's name. The crabs teach the girl the name of Madame Kéléman. The ogress then stuffs the girl but vengefully decapitates the crabs. In "Une Graine de giraumon" [A Pumpkin Seed], a starved woman comes upon a wounded bird. She nurses it back to good health. The healed bird returns with a magic pumpkin seed, which provides a daily fully cooked meal for her new owner. In "Glan-Glan, l'oiseau craché" [Glan-Glan, the Spat-Out Bird], a kind and gentle man is forced by his voracious wife to go hunting on Good Friday. He captures a talking bird and brings it back home alive. His wife kills it and eats it. The bird, speaking from the woman's guts, urges her to vomit. The bird thus reappears, and husband and wife dismantle their house to find one last missing feather needed to reassemble the bird. "Yé, Maître de la famine" [Yé, Master of Famine] is, so to speak, the main course of the collection, and also a classic of Martinican folklore. It is also a centerpiece in Hearn's transcriptions and has received the most critical—if dated—attention.[10] Yé refuses to work on the slave plantation. His mouth perpetually agape, he roams the woods and gobbles up a termites' feast and a devil's dinner. The devil jumps on Yé's shoulders and orders him to bring him to Yé's home. The "thing" forces Yé and his family to eat excrement. Yé's son Ti-Fonté ultimately frees the family from this devil of gluttony. Finally, "Nanie-Rosette et sa bouche douce" [Sweet Mouthed Nanie-Rosette] is about a ravenous little girl who remains skinny as a stick in spite of her gluttony. As she walks deep into the woods where she can eat undisturbed, she sits on the stone of the "devil of gluttony." She gets stuck on the mineral. The villagers build a protective cage around her. Her mother orders her to open up the gate only when she hears her sing. The devil asks a blacksmith to hammer his tongue thin so that his voice could sound as aerial as the girl's mother's. When all this fails, he opens up his belly to let out food scents and Nanie-Rosette opens up the door.

Because of their multifarious temporal implications, I put folktales into dialogue with interlocutors from different periods of Martinican history in whose texts these tales resonate: French Dominican priests Jean-Baptiste Du Tertre and Jean-Baptiste Labat, who were missionaries in the French Antilles in 1640–58 and 1696–1706, respectively; traveler and anthropologist Claude Lévi-Strauss, who visited Martinique during World War II, Martinican poet Aimé Césaire, whose *Cahier* exposes hunger and the fragmentation of a Martinican communal consciousness in the immediate pre–World War II period; and Édouard Glissant himself, Martinican thinker of creolization in the period of departmentalization.

Creole Folktales was originally published in French under the title *Au temps de l'antan: Contes du pays de Martinique.*[11] Chamoiseau explicitly situates them in a slavery and postslavery plantation context in his introduction, titled "Tales of Survival": "The Seventeenth and Eighteenth Centuries. In Martinique. First of all, imagine it is nighttime on one of those great sugar cane estates called plantations" (*Creole,* xi). The back cover of the American edition claims that "Chamoiseau recreates in truly magical language the stories he heard as a child in Martinique." It should also be noted that several of the tales are sometimes inspired by tales told in Creole collected and translated by Irish traveler Lafcadio Hearn in the late 1880s. Hearn's versions of the tales, which he transcribes directly from oral Creole performance, are closer to the literature of survival that Glissant describes than Chamoiseau's. I will sometimes refer to this first transcription when alluding to important passages absent from Chamoiseau's versions.

While Chamoiseau's own introduction gives the storyteller a privileged place in his collection,[12] he also inscribes himself as the writer of the tales: "Read these stories only at night. Remember, I wrote them with the moon as my sole companion" (*Creole,* xiv). The tales therefore result from an alliance between plantation and postplantation time, between the orality of the storyteller and the contemporary Martinican writer's text. Thus they allow us to focus on the continuity, instead of the epistemic break, between slavery and postslavery Martinique. The structures of oppression have changed names, but food still acts as a tool of oppression and cooking as an act of emancipation. The tales written in the 1980s, with their remnants of oral literature from the seventeenth to nineteenth centuries, allow us to discern both the stifling nature of food and the liberating and creative properties of cooking in the time of slavery, in postabolition times, in the 1940s *an tan Wobè,* a time of starvation, and in the contemporary situation of departmentalization where forceful consumption has replaced starvation. Across this literary and cultural span, the fear of hunger pervades as a way to maintain the drive for political dependence.

We mustn't minimize the enormous physical and symbolic violence of imposed hunger; the same is true of hunger's correlate, namely, food dependency or gluttony, accomplished through strategically encouraged overconsumption in slavery and postslavery Martinique. Chamoiseau explains the obsession with food by the state of constant starvation in which slaves were kept: "Our Storyteller speaks for a people enchained: starving, terrorized, living in the cramped postures of survival" (xii). In their "Introduction au folklore martiniquais," written in the 1940s, Césaire and René Ménil had similarly emphasized the obsession for food in Martinique.[13] By way of explanation, the authors remind us that multiple laws periodically reinforced the nature, quantity, and frequency of the food masters should feed their slaves: "Recall that no less than a law (18 July 1845), an ordinance (5 June 1846), a ministerial memo (13 June 1846), a governor's appeal (October 1846) were needed to request that the master feed his slave six pounds of manioc flour and one and a half kilo of codfish per week; a sign that ordinary rations of food remained everywhere below these modest proportions" ("Introduction au folklore," 8–9). Two years before the definitive abolition of slavery, and almost two centuries after the 1685 *Code noir,* the French law has ordered, in the repetitious and poor monotony of the prison world of the Plantation, that the masters feed their slaves the same survival food: barely sufficient portions of manioc flour, cassava, salt meat, or fish.[14] In spite of the shocking scarcity and monotony of the food portions mandated by the French state, Césaire and Ménil point out the painfully precise way that the French laws were ironically benevolent next to the inhuman treatment of slaves by masters, namely, by assuring their bare survival.

The monotony of food also barred slaves from the access to food variety. This limitation not only had dire consequences on health but also performed an act of *acculturation*, adding poetic paucity to experienced poverty. Reading the term with the privative "a-", I mean not to define a state of being without culture, but rather the active stripping away of culture from the slave or the plantation worker. After psychologist Paul Rauzin, Michael Pollan argues that food diversity in humans, as opposed to the limited choices of highly specialized animal eaters, requires in humans mental operations such as memory, selectivity, and culturally constructed habits that might have increased their level of rationality: "Many anthropologists believe that the reason we evolved such big and intricate brains was precisely to help us deal with the omnivore's dilemma" (4). Stripping the enslaved of food choices thus also attempts to stifle their rational thinking.

The 1685 and 1724 versions of the *Code noir* punished with uttermost cruelty the theft of food that would have allowed the slaves to add variety, or simply essential nutrients, to their food intake: "Thefts of sheep, goats, swine, poultry, sugar cane, peas, manioc or other vegetable by slaves will be punished . . . by judges who will . . . condemn them to be whipped . . . and to be branded with a *fleur de lys*" (*Code noir,* art. 36, 30). Slaves were not only deprived of food but also were pushed a step closer to animality, treated like the food cattle, branded and burned. In the postslavery 1880s, when Hearn heard the tales he transcribed, and in Chamoiseau's informants' early twentieth century, hunger was still experienced as a constant, widespread torment. Between 1940 and 1943, Martinique experienced acute hunger because of the blockade imposed on the island by the Vichy regime. This period, referred to as "*an tan Wobè,*"[15] is still very much alive in the Martinican psyche.[16] In light of this long and sustained crisis of food in pre- and postslavery Martinique, we acknowledge hunger as the primary explanation of the omnipresence of food in the tales: "Take this as you wish. This people is a hungry people. Not one tale without a recurrent obsession with empty bellies, without visions of gorging and drunkenness" (Césaire and Ménil, 7).

Food is not just about hunger, however. Reducing Martinicans' relationship with food to enslavement or dependency would repeat, on the discursive level, a gesture of political and economic impoverishment performed by slavery and colonization. While acknowledging that hunger provides an indispensible and compelling explanation of the tales' saturation with food references, restricting our analysis to hunger would neglect the "high necessity" function of food, to go back to the 2009 manifesto. As Lévi-Strauss explains, "Empirical categories—such as the categories of the raw and the cooked, the fresh and the decayed, the moistened and the burned . . . can nonetheless be used as conceptual tools with which to elaborate abstract ideas" (*The Raw,* 1). Clearly, Chamoiseau's folktales perform much more than he himself gives them credit for. Food establishes the vocabulary, syntax, and style for the emergence of a Creole poetics. Roland Barthes compellingly argues that while "food is, anthropologically speaking . . . the first need . . . ever since the first man has ceased living off wild berries, this need has been highly structured. Substances, techniques of preparations, habits, all become part of a system of differences in signification; and as soon as it happens, we have communication by the way of food" ("Toward a Psychosociology," 22–23). For Barthes, assigning significance or nonsignificance to food items and practices amounts to a "veritable grammar of foods."

In line with Barthes's argument, humans perform their humanity through the cooking, control, and grammaticalization of food. For instance, in the tale "Yé, Master of Famine," a family moves from the immediate consumption of rotten and unripe "junk" to a successful relationship to food mediated by work, intelligence, restraint, and, eventually, cuisine. The passage from animality to humanity constitutes the first step toward independence in the tale of "Yé." The step that most concerns us, however, is the move from acculturation to a culturally marked identity. In short, food is not only an act of survival but also is an "art of survival," a term that locates the cultural stratagem in culture itself.[17]

Shackled Bodies

Most of the characters in the tales are imprisoned in their bodies, which are themselves shackled to literal or metaphorical, internal or external, controlling factors. Hunger, which impedes the characters' acts of liberation, is the most obvious controlling force, which can play on all of the aforementioned levels.[18] Food and eating are in situations of excess, polarized around the two apparent opposite extremes of starving and feasting. Characters can be divided into two apparently opposite types: the starved and the gluttonous. Characters such as Yé and Nanie-Rosette oscillate between the two extremes, however, never reaching equilibrium. The relationship to food is thus incessantly extreme and pathological. In his *Cahier*, describing Martinique in the 1930s, a few years before the great starvation of *an tan Wobè,* Césaire presents the same extremely polarized relationship to eating. Excessive feasting—

"and it's cozy in here ["et l'on est bien à l'intérieur"] and there's good eating, and hearty drinking, and there are blood sausages, one kind only two fingers wide twined in coils, the other broad and stocky . . . the hot one spiced to an incandescence, and steaming coffee, and sugared anise and milk punch" (15–16, translation modified)—is juxtaposed with acute starvation: "at the peak of its ascent, joy [la voix] bursts like a cloud" (16, translation modified). Feasting is limited to the short time of Christmas, which brings sensual indulgence in food, songs, and bodies.

In Césaire's description, the satisfied bodies enter in a fluid continuity with the world. Content stomachs, sexes, and voices flow among each other in a sensual feeling of intoxication. The references to the *boudins,* or Creole sausages, remind us, in their variety, of a Rabelaisian feast where the guts of humans and animals are not clearly delineated. The Martinican Creole meaning of *boudin,* referring to the belly, reinforces the proximity between the human body and the culinary product. Death feeds life in a flowing way. The references to the *boudins* and their attributes, evoking a variety of masculine sexes, juxtaposes a virile energy to the sweetness of anise and milk punch.[19] This sensual feast in which eating and sexuality bring a feeling of corporeal wellness is soon interrupted by the daily fear, misery, and hunger brought about with yet another depressive and wretched dawn, illustrated by the endless pedaling of the poet persona's mother, who works on her old Singer day and night for her children's bottomless hunger: ". . . and my mother whose legs pedal, pedal, night and day, for our tireless hunger" (10). The children's hunger is directly linked to the mother's labor, incessantly pedaling on the sewing machine, to which her body is perpetually linked. This inescapable circle of oppression, emphasized in Césaire's poem by the hammering repetition of the verb "to pedal," links the children's mouths to their mother's legs, which merge with the machine's pedal. Hers is a subsistence labor that does not allow for saving. The mother is reduced to a Sisyphean act of labor that cannot feed the children who face a perpetual state of hunger and need. Interestingly, it is not the mother who feeds—or rather fails to feed—her own children, but the contraption to which she is shackled. The same relationship characterizes Martinique, an overexploited land shackled to the economic machine of exportation that cannot sustain its inhabitants.

In contemporary Martinique, as in the eighteenth- and nineteenth-century plantation and urban pre–World War II periods, a specific form of enslavement to eating persists. Even though literal hunger touches only a minority of Martinicans, who have a living standard superior to their Caribbean neighbors,[20] the juxtaposition of excess consumption is the mark of the contemporary economy of the French Antilles, which have, for instance, both a high number of cars per capita and one of the highest levels of state assistance.[21] Hunger and overconsumption need to be considered as logically related, yet unbalanced, attitudes toward food, rather than opposites. As Martinican anthropologist William Rolle lucidly explains: "It is as if the habits of great-grand-parents who ate to maintain a 'stout' body—i.e., a body able to endure extreme physical labor—when transmitted to younger generations, led to a comportment of devouring hunger ill-adapted to a different economic situation. Such a comportment is indicative of a cultural tradition inherited from the conditions of slavery" (Rolle, 94). Hunger, transmitted between generations by its inscription in the body, becomes an atavistic trait. The "devouring hunger" Rolle alludes to must also be understood to extend to exaggerated product consumption logically linked to the memory or fear of past, present, and future famine and poverty.

In a context in which an overwhelming majority of the food is imported,[22] Martinique is vulnerable and could easily fall into famine in the event of an embargo or breakdown in the transportation system. Cultural production is also defined by a ravenous relationship: gluttony in the face of the bounty of exported, or dumped, French cultural products stemming from implicit hunger for locally produced and controlled cultural productions.[23]

Whether the literal experience of hunger of the plantation characters of *Creole Folktales* or the metaphorical cultural hunger of contemporary Martinicans, starvation and gluttony are pathological results of a single dysfunctional relationship to food or culture, a function of the availability of food or culture at a specific moment and in specific circumstances. In the case of *Creole Folktales,* characters experience a fragmented animal temporality where meals cannot be planned, and starved humans cannot control their food intake once food is present. Starvation and gluttony drive the same stifling, paralyzing consequences. The characters of Chamoiseau's tales are neither purely starved nor purely gluttonous, but are both at once. They are starved gluttons. Like plantation subjects and contemporary Martinicans who are culturally force-fed with indigestible—imported—elements, kept in a situation of perpetual dependence, the characters of *Creole Folktales* literally consume food that their bodies cannot absorb. The starved gluttons' bodies in the tales become prosthetic extensions of the plantation factory. They are bodies out of bonds, and out of bounds, overflowing clearly delineated selves, disappearing, liquefying, mineralizing, decomposing, or merging with the plantation structure that oppresses them.

The relationship to the land, tied to the memory of slavery, is not a romanced one. The soil fails as the site of projection of an origin or as a site of cultural grounding.[24] Nor does it exist in a balanced relation where worked land and working bodies would nurture each other in a reciprocal gesture. The land represents violence and disconnection in a situation where most of the crop is exported (sugarcane, bananas, coffee), unsustainable, and of miserable profit to the slaves or workers. In fact, in both fictional texts and anthropological accounts, the land and industry feed the working bodies only waste. A telling example is the situation in which, on working sugarcane plantations, children only had access to, and gorged themselves with, the "sirop de batterie" (battery syrup). The term alternately refers to a dense concentrate of sugar used to make rum, or the waste product dripping from the fifth and last boiler of a sugarcane refinery.[25] The overconsumption of sugar in Martinique has historically caused severe disease in otherwise undernourished children and adults. A high dependency on sugar continues to plague Martinique with a disproportionate number of people afflicted with type 2 diabetes.[26]

Illustrating the situation of a land where crops grow in abundance but offer no sustenance, *Creole Folktales* includes numerous characters who constantly ingest food but don't grow an inch. The ogress Madame Kéléman is as dry as drought land: "The old lady sucked down, down, down, as though her throat were South of a burning desert" (*Creole,* 20). Nanie-Rosette has "an abyss for a stomach, a riverbed for a throat, and a kind of grinding mill where mouth and teeth should have been" (104). Nanie-Rosette's attributes—the grinding mill or the eroded land—evoke the plantation machinery: "This food seemed to go entirely to waste: instead of being a plump dumpling, Nanie-Rosette was a scrawny little thing for her age" (154). Nanie-Rosette's body loses flesh and shrivels to skin and bones.

In the process, Nanie-Rosette loses her previous sensual appeal, an appeal based on the fact that she herself is seen as ready to be eaten ("a plump dumpling"). The French title of Chamoiseau's tale, "Nanie-Rosette et sa bouche douce," invokes a metaphor of taste. The title can be alternately interpreted, in view of the tale's content, as Nanie-Rosette's sweet tooth. In this light, she is cast an indiscriminate consumer of food. Reading her as a glutton, we would place her predicament or sin on her. However, the title is more complex since the word *dou* in Martinican Creole also means "sugar." In this sense, Nanie-Rosette's "bouche douce" would be a sugar mouth, candy tempting a taste, ingestion by the reader. Thus a continuity is established between Nanie-Rosette's body and the object of her uncontrollable compulsion. Nanie-Rosette eats sugar and *is* sugar. In this way, she is also part of the machinistic extension of the sugar industry, a piece in its clockwork, which does not gain anything from it.[27]

The word *dou* also evokes the sweetness and sensual appeal of women. Martinican writer Raphaël Confiant gives a telling example in the following definition of the word in his online Martinican Creole Dictionary: "A! Siwo, fanm Sen-Piè dou" [Oh Lord! How sweet are the women from Saint-Pierre!] (*Dictionnaire du créole Martiniquais*). Whether an extension of the sugarcane factory or a plump treat, Nanie-Rosette is destined to be eaten up either by work or by men. The most important question to ask is not exactly to whom we should attribute this reductive representation of women. Chamoiseau's writing intervenes in a long archeology of presenting Caribbean women as consumable sweets.[28] In this example, as in several other tales, the woman is presented as the cause of evil, responding to the stereotypical description of the "breeder," the woman who cannot control her fertility, and who carries responsibility for social dysfunctions, which in turn absolves the structures of oppression that led her to that state in the first place.[29] Nanie-Rosette's "sweet mouth" is yet another projection of responsibility and blame on the victim. While controlling images projected onto women in Chamoiseau's tales are not the primary focus of this chapter, it is nonetheless essential to note that female characters are attached to an epistemic apparatus that augments that of the plantation. One could argue that the representation of women as reproductive machines is already part of the plantation machinery, which reduced women's bodies to the production of children as profit.[30]

Like Nanie-Rosette, other starved gluttons are described in bodily terms as machinistic extensions of the plantation. Gluttons and the machinery of the plantation share the same epithets: "devils of gluttony" are accompanied by "small explosions" (*Creole Folktales*, 79) and "the barking of chained dogs" (108). Dogs in the plantation context were traditional tools and weapons of the master. The devil of gluttony in Yé's tale is "a shapeless being, made of hide, tender flesh, and lustrous mahogany" (70). The devil of gluttony, thus, appears as a composite object made of animated and inanimate plantation objects: leather (whip), tender flesh (the whipped body), and lustrous mahogany (the fine wood used in plantation houses for furniture and floors and also to make boats). The "thing" incorporates instruments of torture and tortured flesh in the same unit, thereby eliminating the boundaries between the torturers and the tortured, who equally become extensions of the same machinery.

Césaire's *Notebook* and *Creole Folktales* present very similar examples of confusion between human bodies and plantation machinery. In Césaire's *Notebook*, the humanized landscape bears marks of disease and torture ("the hungry Antilles, the Antilles pitted with smallpox, the Antilles dynamited by alcohol," *Notebook,* 1), while the human face looks like a landscape disfigured by industrialization: "His nose which looked like a drifting peninsula. . . . One could easily see how that industrious and malevolent thumb had kneaded bumps into his brow, bored two bizarre parallel tunnels in his nose (29). Oppressed human bodies and landscape share their marks of torture and become part of the same imbricated machine: "Sweet-mouthed negroes saw themselves led by their maw to the most hellish among the plantations" (*Creole Folktales,* 92). The mouth of the starved leads them straight to the cannibalistic mouth of the plantation that swallows them like the mouth of inferno. Césaire's factory shares the cannibalistic features of the Plantation of *Creole Folktales*: "The hill [translation modified] crouching before bulimia on the outlook for tuns and mills, slowly vomiting out its human fatigue" (4). The metaphors of engulfing and vomiting arrive at the same result: each destroys the plantation workers' humanity and reduces them to abjection.[31] Once again, the worker is not treated as the origin of production, and therefore as the origin of wealth for the planters, but rather as a body that should be discarded, like waste, once used up and useless for economic production.

Yé, the perpetually agape and wretched slave, constitutes the most striking and complex example of enslavement to hunger. In contrast with slaves or plantation workers swallowed by the mouth of the factory, Yé refuses to work on the Plantation. As Suvélor, Césaire, Ménil, and Hearn have pointed out, Yé is the maroon who lives outside the plantation structure. Yé's predicament thus demonstrates that there is no outside of the plantation, that the act of marooning is not an act of resistance, but rather an act of submission. No redemptive maroon pride here.[32] Yet, Yé's situation as a maroon is not explained as an act of resistance, but rather results from the laziness of the character: "Lazy, he fled from the work in the planters' [*békés*] fields" (Hearn, quoted in Césaire and Ménil, 68).[33] The maroon is presented not as a revolutionary hero but simply as a lazy outcast. Living outside the system means a fight for bare animalistic survival.

Lafcadio Hearn, who first transcribed the tale of Yé, gives a slightly different version of the "Yé" type in his own observations of Martinican people. Instead of attributing Yé's predicament to his own vices, Hearn gives more weight to the oppressive economic structure that enslaves Yé: "Poor old Yé, you keep on living for me intensely, outside of these stories about eating and drinking that reveal the cruel and long hunger of your race of slaves. For I did see you . . . climb up from plantation to plantation, cutlass in hand . . . across snake-infested fields . . . to pick up a saw palmetto, always starving, always needy" (Hearn quoted in Césaire and Ménil, 7). Like Césaire and Ménil, Hearn reads in Yé the epitome of the oppressed condemned to continual precariousness. The tale of Yé does occupy the mimetic function of integrating into oral literature the suffering of the enslaved, constructing the potent archive that Césaire and Ménil urged the critics to analyze: "Once all the archives have been pillaged . . . all the abolitionists' papers searched, these tales will be the ones to reveal, to those who want to comprehend it, the great, eloquent, and pathetic misery of our enslaved fathers" (*Tropiques,* IV, 8). The tale also provides us with a theoretical tool that allows us to read beyond a simple dichotomy of plantation power. The story of Yé, in particular, blurs the borders between humanity, animality, gods, and devils. It also reveals that a categorization of characters into victims and torturers is not too simple. Yé and his relationship to the devil of gluttony serve as a synecdoche of the large dynamics of hunger maintained on the Plantation, in which the victim internalizes the power of the oppressor. The devil of gluttony, hence, bites from within.

For example, the tale of Yé presents a striking inversion of roles of animals and humans. The wretched character Yé encounters en route a group of termites holding a banquet and devours all their food. In contrast with the "poux-de-bois" or termites holding an organized and communal feast with singing and order (the termites walk in line), Yé eats and acts like an animal.[34] While Chamoiseau does not list the food

Yé indiscriminately consumes along the road (he simply calls his booty "des cochonneries," junk), Hearn's transcription of the Creole tales offers more details: "Then he ate green plums, coco plums, carata—all the tart junk he could find!—his teeth were icy when he returned home; he could barely order his wife to start cooking" (Hearn quoted by Césaire and Ménil, 46).[35] Yé's food consumption is reduced to the inedible, unripe fruit that is unfit even for animal consumption. He is practicing uneducated gathering, defined by what comes to him, without any sense of discrimination or organization. In other words, food appears to him as an undifferentiated mush, in a pregrammatical state, to use Barthian language, that Yé cannot process intelligibly but can only swallow. Yé's eating is below language since it is not organized, cannot be transmitted or reproduced in time, and ignores difference or discrimination. He is stuck in Lévi-Strauss's phase of the raw, or the natural, away from the cultural. We could argue that he is even a step below this, since the food he consumes is not only raw but also unripe, inedible, and even harmful. As the tale indicates, Yé's glacial and paralyzed mouth cannot utter the words that would command his wife to cook.

Yé, reduced to the position of something less than an animal predator or gatherer, steals the food and songs from the community of termites: "He ate up all their food while singing all of their songs" (*Creole Folktales,* 69). The termites put a curse on Yé by way of lifting their behind in his direction. Already, they frame him in a scatological state, linking his body to the excremental, the nonedible. The termites' malediction results in Yé's encounter with a "thing," "the devil of gluttony," several years later, from which Yé again tries to steal. The blind devil jumps on Yé's shoulders and asks Yé to bring him home.[36] Once again, we could read this episode as synechdotic comment on plantation oppression: the coerced man, reduced to the most basic survival relationship to food, is condemned to be ridden not by a benevolent spirit but by a stifling devil, the evil of the plantation economy.

Suvélor interprets the devil's blindness as an attribute of the white man or the planter. Chamoiseau's devil has "no eyelids or even any eyebulbs" (*Creole Folktales,* 79); Hearn's beast has "les yeux crevés" [was violently blinded] (Hearn in Césaire and Ménil, 43). Suvélor argues that "his blindness . . . in the colonial society, is the symbolic attribute of the master. For the master does not see the other. His gaze goes through him without seeing him, because seeing him consciously in his real state of servitude and misery would bring a threatening element in the system's equilibrium" ("Yé," 55). Yet the distance between master and slave, oppressor and oppressed, collapses even further than Suvélor allows. The devil is the master (of famine), the oppressor, but he is also the oppressed victim, Yé himself. As Suvélor indicates, if the devil is a parasite of Yé, he is also his own projection (55). Recall that the title presents Yé as the master of famine. He is the one who keeps his family starving by failing to deliver them from the devil, and by failing to share his food with them: "He hated the starvation that dogged his idle heels, and he skulked all-over with wide-open mouth, a bottomless pit looking to take a taste or a bite wherever he could" (*Creole Folktales,* 77). After devouring the feast of snails of the devil of gluttony himself, Yé becomes enslaved by the devil, and by his own gluttony, dragging down his family with him into misery: "The paternal responsibility becomes plain as day. Nothing indicates that he shares his robbed meals and rummaged fruit with his familial cell" (Suvélor, 58). The malfunctioning transmission of hunger undermines the role of the father as provider and therefore deeply disrupts the family. The devil of gluttony brings the family a step below starvation by forcing them to eat the devil's excrement. Hearn puts it plainly: "Then, the devil would jump on the table, eat the meals, and relieve himself on their plates. . . . He would tell them: "Eat that!" and the family, starving to death, had to gobble up the devil's excrements" (Hearn quoted in Césaire and Ménil, 45).[37]

The story of Yé thus presents us with a break in the circulation of food, where exchange, outside the original feast of termites, does not take place, where there is neither growth nor profit. This situation where food has stopped circulating and gets reduced to an abject waste evokes the plantation situation, where laboring bodies received nothing in return for the land they cultivated but were forced instead to consume its waste. Eating excrement also amounts to the collapse of humanity below even a state of animality. While critics have abundantly denounced the dehumanization of slaves, Africans, or Natives through their rampant assimilation to cannibals,[38] the association with cannibals can grant—as Montaigne famously showed—a certain warrior pride, if not a mark of civilization.[39] However, we would be hard-pressed to find any remnant of humanity in the figure of excrement-eaters. Forced scatophagy places humans into the category of the abject in an extreme act of dehumanization. In her fascinating book on cannibalism as a metaphor for national construction in the New World, Zita Nunes insists on the importance of the remainder in the cannibalistic model.

The remainder or the excremental, that which cannot be processed by the body, is also, for Nunes, that which cannot be assimilated in the national construction: "The indigestible residue," she claims, "prevents a sense of completion and haunts the discourse on/of national unity" (*Cannibal Democracy,* 13). In the example of Yé, it is not only that the enslaved are excluded from the plantation system as its "indigestible residue," but also that they are reduced to the consumption of the waste of what is already waste, an extreme act of humiliation and annihilation.

Busy Tongues

"Mais qui tourne ma voix? Qui écorche ma voix? Me fourrant dans la gorge mille crocs de bamboo" [But who misleads my voice? Who grates my voice? With a thousand bamboo fangs stuffing my throat?] (Aimé Césaire, *Cahier,* 31; *Notebook,* 21), asks the Martinican poet. Aimé Césaire's *Cahier* points to an essential stifling of the slave or the oppressed human in a slavery or postslavery context. If bodies were shackled, undistinguishable from the machinery of the plantation, one of the most violent forms of dehumanization was the severe injury inflicted on the tongue—the tongue as the organ of speech, and also the tongue as speech itself. Césaire's evocation expresses this double violence metaphorically, defining actual instruments or acts of torture ("écorcher," "tourner," "fourrer des crocs") as hurting simultaneously the voice and the throat and tongue, the site of speech, its production, and so language itself.

While tongue as organ and tongue as speech are expressed by the same word in a multitude of languages (Creole, *lang;* English, *tongue;* French, *langue;* Spanish, *lengua;* Arabic, *lissan*, for example), and while the linguistic passage from the organ to the voice is widespread if not universal, the specificity of the slavery context is expressed by the actual ablation of the tongue to prevent speech, or the use of the tongue as a lethal tool. The literal act of cutting the tongue prevents speech, swallowing one's tongue is literally an act of self-inflicted death. While the *Code noir* of 1685 legitimizes many forms of branding, torture, and amputations (amputated ears for first-time fugitives, amputation of a leg for recidivists),[40] the cutting of the tongue is not mentioned in the *Code*. However, the practice was common: rabble-rousers among the slaves or the emancipated often had their tongues severed, as Haitian writer Marie Chauvet's novel *Danse sur le volcan* exemplifies.[41] Swallowing one's tongue was also the only way shackled slaves could commit suicide, as Césaire's powerful image evokes: "le suicidé s'est etouffé avec complicité de son hypoglosse en retournant sa langue pour l'avaler" [the suicide chocked with a little help from his hypoglossal jamming his tongue backwards to swallow it] (*Cahier,* 11; 4).[42] The tongue is thus a historically overdetermined organ and idiom in the slavery and post-slavery Martinican context. Understood as native language, the tongue was taken away when slave traders separated people sharing the same language upon their arrival in the Antilles. Creole language, as we know, is still stifled in Martinique in a state that Glissant calls "artificial Frenchification."[43]

Yet the dominant image in *Creole Folktales* is not that of the severed or swallowed tongue, but rather that of the "thick" or busy tongue. Characters like Nanie-Rosette or Yé are too busy eating or wanting food to speak to attain their freedom, or that of their family or community. The devil of gluttony, in retaliation for Nanie-Rosette's selfish *gourmandise,* affixed her to a stone in the woods. Her family and friends built a shelter around the stone to protect her from the devil. She cannot resist opening the door to the devil when she succumbs to the aromas emanating from the depths of his belly. Her stomach made her forget her mother's command to open the door only when she heard her mother's song. Nanie-Rosette thereby compromises her family, her mother, and, ultimately, her mother's song—that is, her articulated and aestheticized voice for her uncontrollable desire for food: "possessed by her vice (without even thinking that her mommy would not find a trace of her and that the night creatures and werewolves would experience a mighty nocturnal feast), she opened up the lock and opened the door wide" (*Au temps,* 102). The glutton Nanie-Rosette in essence offers her body as a feast for the devils. The loss of food control turns the eater into the eaten.

Similarly, Yé fails to gain his freedom and that of his family through the inability to control his eating compulsion. Yé consults with "Bondié" (Goodlord), who sends him back home with a magic formula that will annihilate the devil, on the condition that Yé stop eating. Stuffing his mouth with junk all the way back home, Yé forgets the formula and reenslaves himself to the devil. As a result, the food he absorbs chases the words away: "And all the way back, our man gummed up his teeth—and his memory—with whatever junk he could find" (*Creole Folktales,* 82).

The busy tongue seems to be a lesser evil than the severed tongue. It gives the illusion of keeping the Martinican body intact. An occupied tongue—eating, talking—avoids manifest traces of torture. However, the tongue that is too busy eating directly undermines freedom. The constant obsession for consumption could refer not only to the state of famine in which slaves were kept but also to the status of assistance of Martinicans by the French state since departmentalization. The breast of France, so to speak, stuck in the mouths of the Martinicans, smothering their scream for autonomy.[44] Therefore, in the contemporary context in which the tales were written, characters such as Yé could be read not only as the wretched maroon but also as the Martinican RMIste,[45] reduced to receive the scraps that France deigns to send, maintained in a state of idleness. This subjugation is of course not as extreme as slavery's, but nonetheless it stifles the desire for "high-necessity products" by reinforcing the need for "low-necessity products," usually accompanied by an eagerness for imported goods.

In the tale, Ti-Fonté, or "little rascal," Yé's youngest son, offers a counterexample to his father's failure. By refraining from eating, he brings agricultural and economic sustainability to himself, his immediate family, and his community of villagers. Ti-Fonté hides in his father's pocket during his last trip to Good-Lord, hears the magic formula, eats nothing along the road, and rids his family of the devil of gluttony. The son reestablishes the family order and well-being: "Ti-Fonté heard everything, and clearly, too. He wrapped those words up in his entire brain, and sealed them fast with a good dollop of memory. He moistened his tongue so that the words would ring out nicely" (*Creole Folktales,* 83). Words are absorbed, processed, enveloped, and sealed just as precious dumplings or *accras* would be. The tongue uses its digestive property, by moistening words, rendering them digestible. In this way only can the tongue be linked to the reasoning and history-making functions of mind. The natural thereby develops into the cultural, the "prosaic" and the "poetic." Words are turned into food, into something that has to be swallowed, processed both by the mind and by digestive fluids, turned into an aesthetic object in the form of an articulated song that "would ring out nicely." Again, to contradict the manifesto's split between food for tongue and food for thought, this tale suggests that both culture and nature should be linked in the same gesture to achieve artistic production, and thereby true bodily satisfaction.

It is therefore through moderation and resistance, control of food intake, and articulate and poetic association of eating and speaking that Ti-Fonté liberates not only his family but also the whole community: "The entire region became a blessed garden called Gros Morne" (*Creole Folktales,* 84). In Chamoiseau's tale, the "blessed," Creole garden,[46] clearly refers to a stage of relative independence and sustainability in which, as opposed to the work on the plantation, individuals' cultivation will provide food gained from their direct labor. The *morne* or "hill" also evokes the "sad" space of marooning away from the Plantation. The land, instead of the place inhabited by demons, becomes blessed, invested with religion, and agriculturally successful. The meal that closes the tale provides an example of moderation and self-sufficiency: "three blue crabs and a breadfruit which was rich fare indeed" (84). The simplicity of these dishes jumps out at us; they are in a readily available state in nature and ask for little process; they are also composed of hunted and gathered food, local and sustainable staples on which the Amerindians or the maroons lived.[47] It is via a detour to the past—both native and diasporic—that Ti-Fonté succeeds in going beyond the fragmented time of his father, beyond himself and into the future.

Talking Birds

While human tongues in *Creole Folktales* (with the exception of those of a few heroic figures like Ti-Fonté) are often too thick with food to speak, wise animal tongues often accomplish more than the tongue of the enslaved, hence further blurring the distinction between humanity and inhumanity. The animal endowed with speech therefore functions in diametric opposition to the muted glutton. The tales offer frequent examples of a reversal whereby speech-impaired humans regress into animality and animals with organized speech become more valuable than humans.[48] Anthropomorphized animals are universally woven into folktales. However, in the particular context of Martinican slavery or postslavery, the humanization of animals in folktales and travelers' accounts offers an ironically sharp contrast to the widespread animalization of humans, whether enslaved or native.[49]

The prime example of the savvy animal is that of the talking bird, which abounds in Chamoiseau's tales.[50] In a provocative interpretation of Chamoiseau's "Glan-Glan, the Spat-Out Bird," Seifert reads the bird as a manifestation of the author himself—Chamoiseau, whose last name contains the word "oiseau," or bird.[51] Indeed, Chamoiseau often refers himself as "Oiseau de Cham."[52] Seifert's interpretation is certainly grounded, and the bird convincingly appears as a self-inscription of the author into his own text, adding a useful layer to the reading of the bird in his texts. However, the talking bird is too omnipresent in Caribbean, Amerindian, and African folklore and literature well beyond Chamoiseau to allow us to stop at this single explanation.[53]

Sometimes birds remain unnamed or unnamable because of their sacred or taboo nature. ("It was a small bird that had never been named by the Creole tongue, and, as for [French language] it has no idea that it even exists" [31]; "A Pumpkin Seed"; "A bird that no hunter had yet named," *Creole Folktales,* 70.) Often, however, they are explicitly linked to the native species of the parrot, either by their name ("When the devil was just a little boy, there was a parrot that had stopped talking" [11]) or by their multicolored bright plumage. The talking birds in Chamoiseau's tales share this dimension of sacred or divine character.[54]

The importance of the talking bird in the tales could simply be explained by the presence of such birds in the Antilles.[55] Du Tertre (1610–1687), in 1654, gives them a prominent place in his description of the Martinican and Guadeloupean fauna: "The taste of the parrot's flesh is excellent, but variable, according to what it feeds on . . . but the taste of the parakeet is much more delicate. They learn to sing, to talk, to whistle, and to imitate all sorts of animals very easily" (*Histoire générale des isles,* 198–99). Strikingly, in Du Tertre's description, the culinary qualities of the parrot come before its dashing looks and talent for imitating speech, both animal and human.[56] I will come back to the association of palatability with speech below, as it is one of the parrot's main characteristics in *Creole Folktales* and other ethnographic accounts. The coincidence between the gift of speech and comestibility further blurs the lines between animality and humanity, introducing a cannibalistic edge to the treatment of the speaking birds by humans. Eating a parrot is a case of quasi-cannibalism, whereby humans eat part of their human characteristics: speech or its uncanny imitation.

The volubility of the parrots troubles the frontiers between humanity and animality and threatens the definition of the human. In his *Histoire naturelle des animaux,* French naturalist Buffon (1707–1788) presents the monkey and the parrot as two most troubling creatures, which appear to men as "particular beings, intermediates between the human and the brute." His explanation continues: "the monkey for its external resemblance with man, the parrot for its ability to imitate speech" (*Œuvres,* 1150). Buffon immediately praises the goodness of nature, which refrained from attributing the parrot's talent for speech and the monkey's talent of imitating human gestures to the same creature: "It is therefore a desirable thing for our intelligence that nature has separated and placed in two very different species the imitation of speech and that of our gestures; and that having endowed . . . [a few animal species] with shapes and organs similar to those of man, reserved to him the faculty of perfectibility; a unique and glorious trait that . . . establishes the empire of man on all other beings" (*Œuvres,* 1151). While the economic, palatable, and culinary empire of humans over other animals was saved by this separation—if some animals have human traits, they, as if by design, are limited to a fragment of humanity short of perfection—the parrot nevertheless continues in literature to violate defined boundaries of humanity. Such category shifting occurs even more acutely in a context in which conquest, colonialism, and slavery are based on the fictional assumption that Amerindians, Africans, savages, and other nonwhites or enslaved are fitted to their fate as less than humans. Buffon himself notes the fascination of "savages" for talking animals: "Savages, insensitive to the great spectacle of Nature . . . are only astonished by parrots and monkeys; they are the only animals who can catch their dull attention" (1150). While Buffon attributes the "savages"' fascination for parrots to their stupidity, the reader cannot but notice Buffon's own fascination for the talking bird. The fascination imputed by Buffon to "savages," attracted to parrots because the savages' own humanity is in peril, affects no less the conquerors, colonizers, European travelers, or encyclopedists. In short, their own fascination is also a mark of the threat to their own humanity. In this moment of encounter between the Westerner and its threatening "Other," the borders of humanity are threatened on all sides.

The chronicles of Dominican priest Jean-Baptiste Labat, who was a missionary in the Antilles between 1693 and 1705 (more specifically in Martinique and Guadeloupe), offer further examples of not only the confusion but also of the reversal of humanity and animality. In short, Labat attributes to certain animals more humanity than the "savages" and "negroes" he frequented. Without going into detail into Labat's particularly brutal treatment of his slaves,[57] the following description encapsulates Labat's perception of black subjects: "We were five persons in the canoe and five negroes" [Nous étions cinq personnes dans le canot avec cinq nègres] (*Voyage aux îles françaises,* 65). In this evocation, black humans are clearly excluded from personhood and from humanity, illustrating compellingly Fanon's description of the black man as being defined by his ontological lack.[58] Any short-lived Christian guilt that Labat may have felt vanishes soon after his arrival in the Tropics: "Many negroes came on board . . . with the scars of previous whippings on their back. This excited the compassion of those of us who were not accustomed to this, but we soon get used to it" (38). While Labat's cruelty and perception could be seen as a sign of its time, his cruelty and sadism appear much sharper than that of his contemporary and brother in the faith, Du Tertre, who at least presented as unfathomable mystery the theological foundation of the "curse" put on one section of the humanity: "I must adore with full humbleness the deep and inconceivable secrets of God, for I do not know what this unfortunate nation did, to which God attached, like a particular and hereditary curse, the blackness and ugliness of body, together with slavery and servitude" (Du Tertre, *Histoire générale des isles*? 480). While Du Tertre does not challenge the servitude of the black race, which he associates with its physical misfortune, simplistically associating physiognomy to divine curse, he at least acknowledges the theological mystery of this curse, and thus recognizes an impenetrable contradiction within the Christian faith. We find no such soul-baring doubts in Labat, who never questions the theological foundations and contradictions of the predicament he witnessed. He simply, and quickly, gets used to the enslavement and torture of the bodies that slavery—and himself—exclude from humanity: "We soon get used to it."

By comparison to his reaction to the abuse of slaves, Labat's experience with a parrot comes much closer to instilling Christian repentance, albeit, once again, very temporarily:

> Of the three parrots I bought, one came from Guadeloupe, the two others from Dominique. The one from Guadeloupe was so big that I thought that it was old and that it would never learn. It would shriek all day, and since it had a very strong voice, it would have broken my ears; which led me to kill it, an action I regretted almost immediately. Some of parishioners came to see me while my negro was plucking it. They assured me that it was very young, and that its screeches were called "chitter-chatter" [*cancaner*] in the Islands, and that it would have learned how to talk in very little time and would have surpassed the others. Since the ill had no remedy, I had him

> cooked in a stew [en daube] since its meat was fine, delicate, and succulent." (*Voyage aux îles françaises,* 153–54)

The slaughtering of the bird provokes a religious sentiment of regret never felt by Labat in relation to the manifest mistreatment of native and enslaved human beings. His short-lived regret has to do with the parrot's ability to speak, to be trained, and thus with its anthropomorphic qualities of speech and perfectibility. Believed to be old, the parrot is also deemed useless, since it cannot be tamed, trained, civilized, and marginally humanized. The bird is soon put to another use, namely, meat for a dainty stew. Labat thus presents the parrot as a highly specialized animal, his properties, so to speak, whether talking entertainment or gratification for the palate and belly. The one who cannot speak is thus destined to be swallowed up. The bird therefore belongs to a utilitarian economy that makes interchangeable the speech-endowed being with the consumable, the human and the animal. The use of the verb "cancaner," which refers both to the quacking of certain birds and to the human act of gossiping, further complicates the human or animal nature of sound utterance. Furthermore, talking about the other two parrots, Labat attributes to them the verb "to speak": "I boarded the two others . . . at the home of one of my female parishioners, which is the best I could do to teach them how to speak. It is a well-known fact that women are gifted talkers, and that they love to use their gift" (*Voyage aux îles françaises,* 154). While we can only be amused at the feminization of speech, and by its derogatory description, the recognition of potential for speech in the birds stands in stark contrast to Labat's systematic animalization of speech of blacks in the colony. To cite only a few examples, "newly-arrived negroes who spoke a corrupt language" (45), "The ordinary gibberish [baragouin] of negroes" (52). Labat clearly projects more humanity on the speech of the parrot than on the corrupt speech of the African humans.

Labat's satisfaction and indifference to the fate of the anthropomorphic bird shocks the community: the parishioners denounce the priest's bad judgment. What appeared to be an old and useless bird was indeed a young and trainable parrot, which would have been able to eclipse the two other parrots. Eating the young bird is metonymically equivalent to eating the young speech it was about to utter. The chitter-chatter of the bird from Guadeloupe could also be read, like Creole itself, as the young language about to emerge in the late 1600s. Swallowing the bird therefore reads as a swallowing of Creole language, turning it into a well-cooked and very French stew: *la daube*.

The delectation in describing the meal as "delicate and succulent flesh," as well as the cruel sarcasm in the justification of the irremediable crime by consumption of the bird, evokes an even greater horror in the reader who reads into Labat's act, through the eyes of the parishioners, a sacrilegious act of eating a sacred bird, a reversal of Christ's act of divinizing what he ingested. The horror of the act increases when we see it as the action of a "Father," old man and priest, who eats a young, or his own.

The culinary appreciation of the parrot is not an exception in the text. The omnivorous and mostly carnivorous Labat takes great pleasure in eating all sorts of unusual animals, displaying a violent exotic curiosity for anything unknown to the European palate.[59] From the turtle (61, 188), to the *ver palmiste* (a worm found in the head of cabbage palms) (101), to frogs and lizards (102), nothing escapes Labat's insatiably curious stomach. Anticipating criticism from fellow Christians, Labat offers counter-arguments for all the theological attacks that might come his way. To justify eating birds during Lent, he argues that certain types of birds, the "diables" or "devils," a type of small bird, are not technically meat, and he justifies the necessity of their consumption with a convoluted health argument.[60] He also confesses that his accounts contain "too many cooking documents for an apostolic missionary" and justifies his obsession for pleasurable eating by the necessity to learn: "all the while, we have to get instructed by many things" (188). Learning the Tropics, for Labat, necessarily entails eating the Tropics. The cognitive gesture is also an act of violent, guilty ingestion and incorporation. Labat repeats, on an individual basis, the immense act of cannibalism of "civilization."

Labat's formidable appetite became legendary in Martinique. Indeed, other than giving his name to a type of rum and a technique for processing sugar, Labat's ghost still haunts Martinican hills and Martinican children. "The Creole imagination incorporated him," claims Aurélia Montel in her creative biography of the Dominican priest. "He became a sort of sorcerer, a zombie who sometimes makes his presence felt. . . . In Martinique, grandmothers . . . threaten the grandchildren who will not go to sleep . . . by telling them '*Le Père Labat* will come and get you'" (Montel, 178–79). As John Edgar Wideman cleverly demonstrates, the consumer of the Antilles, the omnivorous and cannibal figure, has been devoured in turn by the Martinican folklore and imaginary: "Ironically, in a delicious creolized twist, Père Labat . . . became embedded in the island's folk history as a bogeyman and hobgoblin" (Wideman, xxvii).

Approximately two hundred years after both Buffon's account of parrots and savages and Labat's sacrilegious act, Lévi-Strauss picks up the coupling between borderline animality and humanity by observing, again, the privileged place of the parrot in Amerindian mythologies. The anthropologist evokes a third troubling property of the parrot, namely, the introduction of the sacred into the profane world of earthly humans and animals. Parrots' speech—their Word—turns them into consistent sacred objects in the lore of the Amerindian region of Brazil, particularly in the Matako and Bororo myths (*Le Cru et le cuit,* 43–45). Bororos cover themselves with parrots' plumage during highly sacred rites of passages (55). Lévi-Strauss's extensive analysis of Bororo and other Amerindian stories of creation documents the privileged place of talking birds in mythology.

One of the types of myths he identifies is "Myths which have a bird-nester as their hero" (*Le Cru et le cuit,* 99). To give only one example, Lévi-Strauss summarizes the following story of origin found in Alfred Métraux's text:

> A man went fishing with his wife. He climbed a tree to catch parrots, which he threw down to his wife. But the wife devoured them. "Why are you eating the parrots?" he asked. . . . As soon as he came down from the tree, she killed him by breaking his neck with her teeth. . . . She showed [her children] their father's head, saying it was the head of an armadillo. During the night, she ate her children and ran away to the bush. She changed herself into a jaguar. Jaguars are women." (Métraux, *Myths and Tales of the Matako Indians,* 60–61, quoted in Lévi-Strauss, *Le Cru et le cuit,* 99)

In this myth of origin, namely, of jaguars, the transgressive gesture of eating the talking bird is associated with cannibalism. The devouring of the wife's own children appears as a logical and similarly transgressive act in the wake of her eating the parrots, a crime denounced by the husband. The wife, after devouring parrots and progeny, joins the animal reign by turning into a jaguar. The association of the cannibal-predator with women ("Jaguars are women") appears widespread in travelers' accounts of eating practices in the Americas. Du Tertre also noted the voracity of women in an episode of ritual war cannibalism: "Above all, it is an astonishing and marvelous thing to witness the habit, or rather the rage, of women who eat the flesh of their enemies: they chew it and chew it again; they grind it in their teeth; they are so afraid to lose any bit of it that they lick the sticks on which fell a few drops of fat" (*Histoire générale des isles,* 451). While Amerindian men's eating of their enemy's flesh is limited to the highly coded war ritual of cannibalism, the women's gesture is marked by rage and obsession, and therefore escapes the limits of ritualized cannibalism to join with the animalistic savagery of eating human flesh. The eating of human flesh fails to function as the act of incorporation that implies conservation (of the warrior's strength) and destruction (of what needs to disappear in the inimical). Women's cannibalism appears as an act of selfish autarky instead of exchange and transmigration. The women chew and chew again, attempting to clench the flesh in their teeth, and therefore fail to take part in any transformative exchange.[61]

The scenes of eating talking birds in Chamoiseau's tales offer a striking resemblance to both Lévi-Strauss's Matako myth and Du Tertre's evocation of women's rage. In all these instances, men are presented as ascetic vegetarians, while women are sacrilegious and merciless devourers of meat. In "Glan-Glan, the Spat-Out Bird," it is also the cruel and carnivorous wife who coerces her husband into killing a talking bird. While the evocation of cannibalism is not as explicit in the Matako myth, the eating of the bird, whose human voice survives after being swallowed and who urges her eater to spit him out ("Spit me out, my lil' daughter," *Creole Folktales,* 72) clearly evokes cannibalism. While the husband limits himself to eating vegetarian fritters, "his wife feasted royally. She ate everything, sucking on the bones, eating up the gravy" (72), reminding us of Du Tertre's description of the cannibal women, closer to the jaguar than to the human.

The voracious wife of "Glan-Glan" also violates a ritualized moment. Indeed, the tale takes place on Good Friday, a day when meat, in remembrance of the body of Christ, should not be consumed. Like in the Matako myth, it is also the cruel and transgressive wife who coerces her husband into killing a talking bird. The eating of the bird, whose human voice survives after having been swallowed, also evokes anthropophagy, or eating of one's own kind. This time, however, the wife does not eat her children, but rather her father. Father bird exhorts her to spit him out using the following words: "Spit me out, my lil' daughter" (*Creole Folktales,* 72). "Father" could be here understood as the paterfamilias, but also as God, or its human manifestation through body, the body of Christ turned into a speaking bird. The following description evokes the Christian scene of transfiguration: "L'oiseau bientôt prit chair, puis on vit sa silhouette, enfin, le corps trembla entre leurs doigts damnés" [The bird soon became flesh, his shape soon became visible, and his body shivered in their cursed fingers] (*Au temps,* 66). Essentially the bird that becomes flesh takes the place of the "Word" in the Christian expression. The bird, then, can be seen as word, as speech, or as God himself. Swallowing the bird or the word thus amounts to a religious sacrilege, but also to an act of swallowing up every chance of a future autonomous expression.

It would be pointless, in this context of intertextuality and juncture of many intercultural myths (Amerindian, African, European, Judeo-Christian), and in light of Chamoiseau's own fictitious creations, to attempt to impute this characteristic to any specific source. Rather, we should see it as part of a discourse as old as humanity in which Eve talks Adam into eating the fruit, or in which the Matako woman eats the speaking sacred bird. However, in this context of othering, or "savaging," the savage can always be projected onto the other, whether via race or gender. While for Buffon the less-than-human was the savage as a generic, nongendered group, for the Boboros, the Matakos, and Chamoiseau, this dehumanizing is projected onto the female "gendered" category of oppressed humanity. The less-than-human can always be projected elsewhere like an endlessly rebounding ball.

The origin of the sacred fascination for the talking bird cannot itself be situated. One could reasonably read the bird in *Creole Folktales* as the direct descendant of the native myth, conserved in Martinican folklore by a miraculous transmission in the time when Caribs and African slaves coexisted in Martinique. One could also read the centrality of the bird as a remnant of African mythology, since birds such as Sankofa clearly have survived in tales of the African diaspora. However, it is not my goal to trace the origins of the animals in Chamoiseau's folktales. Nor am I trying to re-create a filiation that would offer only an ill-fitted way of reading the fragmented bits and pieces composing Caribbean creolization. The bird Glan-Glan is described as a "puzzle beyond measure," not as a family tree. The fragmentation of the pieces, like San Lucian poet Derek Walcott's fragmented vase of history,[62] does not deny its integrity, its autonomy, as a site of creolization, but makes its scars and fissures part and parcel of the object.

The bits and pieces of the regurgitated bird urge the woman and her husband to put him back together again: "Stick me back together my lil' daughter" (*Creole Folktales,* 73). Subsequently, husband and wife search all the cracks of their home, tear the house to pieces to reconstruct the bird through duration and pain, until they find the last missing feather. As a result, the wife is liberated from her fate and becomes a vegetarian. In his evocation of the same tale in his poem, "beau sang giclé" (*Ferrements*), Aimé Césaire refers to the slaughtered bird in the following terms: "L'oiseau aux plumes jadis plus belles que le passé / exige le compte de ses plumes dispersées" [The bird with wings once prettier than past / demands the accounting of its dispersed feathers]. In Chamoiseau's tales, as in Césaire's poem, it is a question of dispersion, diaspora, subsequent reconstruction, and historical reparation. Thus we could read the talking bird, the parrot, as the act of active creolization that would perform an act of reparation. We should understand "reparation" both in the sense of sticking back together and as juridical, political, and ethical duty. As in the South African post-Apartheid context, both Césaire's poem and Chamoiseau's bird demand an "accounting" of their dispersed feathers: "l'oiseau refit ses comptes" [the bird cooked his books again] (*Au temps,* 66). "Glan-Glan" could therefore be read as a highly political tale with contemporary demands for reparation of the diasporic fragmentation of people, land, and language performed by colonizers and slaveholders.

What is surprising in Chamoiseau's tale is that the ones who pay for the crimes of the past are a poor couple, husband and wife, who do not seem to represent the perpetrators of colonization and slavery. The price they pay amounts to physical exhaustion, consumption of soul ("their souls in ashes from exhaustion"), and dismantling of their house: "They explored between the planks, ripping them apart one by one. Then they took out the roof, and demolished the hut, reducing it to rubble" (*Creole Folktales,* 74). The act of reparation here involves not only the perpetrators of violence, but their victims as well, who have to destroy their house, look under its foundation—in other words, the foundation of their own history—in order to free themselves from the guilt caused by the bird: "glaring at them with a cold and angry eye" (ibid.). Historical reparation is thus a work of memory, which involves a piece-by-piece destruction of the house, or frame of history, in order to reconstruct something significant and living in the margins of essential definition, the boundaries of the human condition.

The conclusion to the tale is surprising. Instead of restoring the couple's happiness, their common work leads to their separation: "The shrewish wife became a loving and kind woman, and even a vegetarian, so that the poor husband grew tired of this happiness and married someone else" (74). The wife's expiation and her drastic change—she becomes "douce" [sweet, soft] and vegetarian—leads to a cynical ending whereby the man is presented as needing the evilness of a different woman. Beyond cynicism, the ending of the tale works against a positivist and idealistic message of redemption through reconstruction, or against an idealistic message of harmonious and complete creolization. The tale remains open on a false note.

My reading of the tales through the model of creolization is only one path among many. This plurality of interpretation might be precisely one of the interests, and dangers, of studying Creole cultures: the tension between the re-creation of—often severed or troubled—historical filiation and the examination of juxtaposed bits and ends that make sense through their very loud juxtaposition. The French word for "loud," *criard,* which refers simultaneously to shrill sounds and bright colors, describes the situation well. "Criard" is precisely the characteristic of the parrot, loud in sound and sight, surprising and unheard of in the contrast of its colors, just like Creole itself. Through a false etymology, the words "Creole" and "cri" are indeed linked. The word Creole comes from the Spanish "criar" (from the Latin "creare"), meaning to create, to grow, or to raise. "Criar" is thus phonetically just a hair away from the French *crier* or "to scream." Let us then call for the *criard* parrot to stand for Creole and for the scream of creation.

Creole Food Poetics

Chamoiseau's stories are, as he himself writes in his preface, "tales of survival." Hunger and food paucity, which stifle the enslaved or their contemporary Martinican descendants, often reduce individuals to a state of impotence or dependence upon the machine of slavery—in other words, the political economy of colonialism. However, what emerges from even the most pessimistic tales, such as "Yé" or "Glan-Glan," is a movement toward construction. Before a cuisine can be shared, the community that it will eventually define has to be reconstructed.[63] Ti-Fonté, Yé's youngest son, we will recall, not only saves his family but also his community from hunger. In "A Pumpkin Seed," sharing food is the key to a well-functioning community. Food disrupts the passive state of what is "already cooked from the sky"—dumped from a benevolent welfare state. The selfless and kind-hearted old woman of the tale finds a wounded nameless bird. In spite of having survived for years exclusively on watercress, the old woman refuses to listen to her stomach and chooses to nurse the bird back to health instead of eating it. Her own culinary exodus, or crossing of the desert, surviving on bitter herbs, comes to an end when the healed bird drops a seed that produces a fruit containing "a fully-cooked meal: a ragout of good meat and rice, garnished with a sprig of parsley" (*Creole Folktales,* 33). The old woman, after satisfying her hunger within measure carries the leftovers to her closest neighbor in order not to waste them. This ethical practice of sharing food illustrates a primary characteristic of Creole cuisine, according to Guadeloupean writer Simone Schwarz-Bart, who declares: "Creole cuisine is above all about sharing" (80).

Ti-Fonté's and the old woman's gestures go beyond the state of survival or providential state to place the control of food back into the hands of the family and the community. For food anthropologist Sidney Mintz, the control of one's own crops by each member of the enslaved community reinstated family links that had been disrupted by slavery: "Organizing production and processing of food meant that the slave family gained autonomy despite the plantation structure and was an arena of socialization in which childhood and parenthood took on what are, for us, familiar meanings" (*Creole Folktales,* 43). Eating alone, in contrast, disrupts further the community and the family and ultimately reenslaves the selfish eater. Such is the case of the old lady's neighbor, who, not satisfied with the abundant leftovers bequeathed to her, searches for her own magic pumpkin. She finds the nameless bird in good health, wounds it, puts it on an old damp rag, and feeds it only filthy water. Later, the bird comes back with a pumpkin seed. But, surprise, "Out sprang a hellish mob of snakes, spiders, and fat brown mabouyas all under the unfortunate impression that she was their mother. Their cold maws gaping, they lunged for her breasts" (34). For her selfishness, the woman is not only deprived of food but is also expelled from the community, never to reappear, inscribed in a devilish motherhood.

In one of Hearn's tales that is not included in Chamoiseau's collection, the exchange of food within a market economy is key to family and community cohesion. In "Zhistouè piment," or "Pimiento Story," a poor woman with many children at her charge begs at her neighbor's door for some food. The thoughtful neighbor, instead of providing her with a fully cooked meal, gives her "yon gran trai piment" [a big tray of pimientos] (Hearn, *American Writings*, 473). The friend advises her to sell them at the market and buy other ingredients with her profit. Instead, the hopeless mother, in a panic to feed her family, hastily cooks a "calalou piment" [a spicy callaloo] (474). Her children drown in the river, where they had expected to find solace from the burning pain in their throats. The pimiento tale is once more about rupture in the functioning of the community. Without food circulating outside the family unit, the family literally dies. The burning feeling of the pimiento is also that of hunger itself. Without mediation and exchange, there is no solution to hunger, no functional community. The circulation of food highlighted in the Creole tales, however, is not that of a capitalist circuit based on the exchange of goods for profit. In "Zhistouè piment" as well as in "A Pumpkin Seed," the food circulation relies upon human relationships of mutual respect. Rolle describes this Martinican practice as *bokantage*: "*Bokantage* cannot simply be defined as an economic practice outside of the economic circuits regulated by the exchange of money; it depends on a cordial and direct human relationship. It is the hand we give our neighbors when we give them a little respect [quand on ne les mésestime pas trop]" (Rolle, 83).[64]

The first step toward the creation of a proper Martinican cuisine is thus to restore a relationship with the community, with the land, and with a temporality based on continuity that would break with the compulsion or necessity for immediate consumption. *Bokantage* implies local food harvesting, production, and exchange to restore the disrupted links between family and community members and between humans and their land. Shared and sustainable food not only satisfies primary bodily needs, but it also serves as the vessel of a shared cultural production and consciousness: it teaches this "crowd which doesn't know how to be a crowd" to become a community through a shared cultural product and provides Martinicans with a consciousness of a Martinican Creole production.[65]

Significantly, the birds that are instrumental in sparking the process of the creation of a cuisine are often unnamed in the tales I have analyzed. The bird of "A Pumpkin Seed" is "A little bird that Creole language had not yet named. As for French language, it didn't even suspect its existence" (*Creole Folktales,* 37). The bird is categorically presented outside the realm of French language. However, it is only "as yet" unnamed, with the eventual possibility of being named, within the particular context of Creole language. The bird represents freedom as an open potentiality—a freedom of choice, a freedom of construction, of a neo-Adamic naming grounded in Martinique and Creole language. The bird represents the power of naming and thus of creating what is in the people's hands. In her Nobel Prize speech, Toni Morrison presents us with an allegory: two young people come to a blind old woman with a bird in their hands. They ask her whether what they hold in their hands is alive or dead. The old woman answers only that the bird is in their hands. The potentiality of life and death lies in their hands. They are free to determine its potentialities. Morrison, putting herself in the young people's shoes, chooses to "read the bird as language" (*Nobel Lecture,* 14). Chamoiseau too invites us to name the unnamed bird. The cuisine that emerges from the good care of the bird, its motherly nurturing, is also, in Chamoiseau's tales, about naming and language. Moreover, the cuisine circulating in the text further grounded in a local context is clearly marked as Creole. Countless are the lists of Creole specialties—fritters, "papaya au gratin and zabitan soup" (*Creole Folktales,* 90), "Angola peas, breadfruit, codfish fritters, peppery octopus, crawfish cooked in a court-bouillon" (104)—just to give an appetizing sampling.

The following description—"categories of things au gratin, series of fricassees, theories of fishes cooked in court-bouillon" (*Au temps,* 32)—explicitly presents culinary items not only as a contribution to a new vocabulary but also as a new syntax. The words "categories," "series," and "theories," closely associated with culinary terms, present cuisine as an organized discourse, a grammatical ensemble. Food leaves the pragmatic realm to perform the needful poetic act. The abundance and variety of dishes listed in Chamoiseau's text counterbalance the common-lot impoverished monotony of foods distributed to slaves in times of oppression. The combination of dishes is also significant, as it incorporates maroon food, slave fare, and Big House preparations: breadfruit, yams, and blue crabs were products on which maroon slaves survived when away from the plantations; codfish fritters or accras were brought by Africans;[66] complex preparations such as *au court-bouillon* or *fricassée* were prepared by the plantation cooks to be served at the master's table.[67] The cuisine operates through a grammar of creolization, which connects fragments while preserving their particularity.

Creole food is also defined by the diversity of cooking techniques that were imported by African, European, and East Indian migrants. As we can decipher in the list, the ingredients involved in Caribbean cooking are also of various origins. In the section "The Origin of Foods" (*Tasting Food,* 38–40), Mintz attempts to draw a history of various Caribbean foods. Breadfruit came from Oceania; yam is suspected to have come from Africa, "possibly carried by the slaves themselves" (39). The adjective *zabitan*, "inhabitant" or "native," is used here to describe a local variety of crawfish. It is the very assemblage of foodstuffs with eclectic origins sprinkled with a few local products that make for its Creole "specificity." "Creoleness is the interactional or transactional aggregate of Caribbean, European, African, Asian, and levantine cultural elements, united on the same soil by the yoke of history" (*Éloge,* 87), claim Bernabé, Confiant, and Chamoiseau in their Creole manifesto. A Creole food can therefore only be in the amalgamation of these various sources. In this encounter, the various elements are in a relation of "interaction," a reciprocal action in which none dominates the other, and "transaction," in which each renounces a part of their characteristics: a stew. In this juxtaposition, the elements do not blend but are distinctively recognizable. Chamoiseau's folktales have proved that food is the site of *créolité* or creoleness, a positivist cultural construction rooted in the local while tending toward the universal. The next chapter examines how the experiences of immigration and exile simultaneously detach the culinary from its immediate Creole environment and enhance the process of creolization.

3 KITCHEN NARRATIVE

Food and Exile in Edwidge Danticat and Gisèle Pineau

Vant pété, manjé pas gaté! [Bursting belly: no waste of food!]
—Gisèle Pineau, *Un Papillon dans la cité*

I took yet another cookie, and another, until the whole box was empty. . . . "I cannot read American," I said. . . . "It is not American," she said. "They are French cookies. That says *Le Petit Ecolier*." I stuffed my mouth in shame.
—Edwidge Danticat, *Krik? Krak!*

IN *Brother, I'm Dying,* EDWIDGE DANTICAT RECALLS her father, extremely weakened by a pulmonary disease, ordering a bowl of rice. This food request signals to her the certainty of his imminent death. Danticat comments at length on this episode in her interview with Nancy Mirabal: "He just wanted plain white rice and I hated the whole idea. . . . What I learned through this experience, is that one of the things that happens when you're dying is that you completely lose your taste. . . . You completely lose your desire to eat or drink. Food is that core connection to life" ("Dyasporic Appetites," 38). Eating a bowl of rice, evidently the plainest act of survival, signals the end and the last breath. However, eating represents more than individual life sustainability. The migrant father's dying words, ordering the plainest of food, also epitomizes the cultural death of migrants leaving their culinary complexity behind as they assimilate into the new culture. Hence Danticat's "hating" the idea of "just plain rice," since it reduces food to a basic staple of survival. In Danticat's case, Haitians migrating to the United States constitute the privileged example of culinary survival in exile. Danticat juxtaposes the memory of her father's last request to one of his favorite practices as a healthy man. He would cook newly arrived Haitian migrants to Brooklyn a Haitian meal, hoping "they would feel, as he did, that one could easily return home, simply by raising a fork to one's lips" (*Brother,* 259). More than plain survival, thus, cooking and eating mend disjointed communities and restore the link to their original land. More than life support, these gestures sustain culture and humanity.

As the two epigraphs at the beginning of this chapter exemplify, food constitutes the core of Pineau's and Danticat's narratives of childhood and exile. Food is the original pleasure, food is missed; food is painful, food is shame; food is language, fluid and interrupted, untranslatable yet essential. By making food the archive of women's history within texts written by women, Danticat and Pineau braid the uneven threads of Caribbean homes and sites of exile, of the urban and the agrarian, erase borders between mind and body, and intermingle writing and cooking, reading and eating. They invalidate the distinction between the private and the political, overcoming Western dualisms, through the pain of remembrance.

Pineau's and Danticat's resemblances are striking both in their similar biographical journeys and in their fictional representations. Both writers are marked by a personal experience of exile that ultimately structures their works. Their young protagonists share the experience of displacement from the Antilles to a Western metropolis such as Paris or New York, a strong link to their grandmother, alienation from their mother, and a passion for eating, cooking, and sharing food. I insist on the word "passion," which should be understood as both enthusiasm and suffering. Indeed, for the young protagonists, food represents both a tool of survival and thriving in the world, as well as a constant torment.

Gisèle Pineau was born in France to Guadeloupean parents and only encountered Martinique and Guadeloupe during two childhood family trips.[1] Most of her novels involve displacement, exile, or touristic travel. This chapter focuses mainly on *Un Papillon dans la cité,* a book for young readers published in 1992, and *L'Exil selon Julia,* a novel published in 1996. Both texts provide a first-person account of a Guadeloupean girl exiled in a Parisian *banlieue* with her mother.[2] In both texts, the grandmother, visiting from Guadeloupe, establishes the missing link between the land of origin and the land of arrival.

Edwidge Danticat moved from Haiti to the United States at the age of twelve, where she reunited with her mother and father. Her first novel, *Breath, Eyes, Memory,* published in 1994 in the United States, recounts the journey of twelve-year-old Sophie Caco, who left her grandmother and her native Haiti to meet her estranged mother in Brooklyn. Danticat's and Pineau's narratives share the striking similarities of recounting the exile of a young girl, of telling the story of a cross-cultural coming of age, and of recounting the passage from a Caribbean island to a Western metropolis. Moreover, Danticat's Sophie and Pineau's Félicie create a creolized self through the actions of eating and cooking. I use creolization in the Glissantian sense: the process of combining elements from two or more original cultures, which leads not only to an impoverishing synthesis but also to an enriched processual movement, amounting to more than the sum of its originals.[3] For instance, Pineau's character Félicie reinvents the Caribbean Sea by concocting in Paris a *court-bouillon* fish with improvised spices in the absence of the Guadeloupean pimiento. More crucially perhaps, Danticat, Pineau, and their characters combine the acts of cooking and writing in a single gesture that I call a "kitchen narrative." The word "narrative" conveys the act of recounting a story and links disparate fragments separated by time, space, and traumatic experiences. I am thinking particularly of Paul Ricoeur's reflection on narrative, which, he explains, humanizes the experience of the past, by measuring, rendering visible, and organizing fragments in a story.[4] For Pineau and Danticat, cooking and writing both participate in this narrative reconstruction.

In their kitchen narrative, cooking and writing become interconnected forms of resistance. This association, which Danticat calls a "braiding" of cooking and writing (*Krik? Krak!* 220), transforms the daily gestures of women into political acts and home and kitchen into sites of political resistance. Women's previously written bodies graduate to writing bodies. They become the agencies for culinary constructions instead of predetermined works inscribed by their domestic labor. Paule Marshall's concept of kitchen poets, to which Danticat pays tribute in *Krik,* serves as the major theoretical tool for interpreting the links Danticat makes between cooking and writing, and between the home and the political sphere. In *Reena and Other Stories,* Marshall demonstrates that kitchen literacy is a prerequisite, not an obstacle, to scholarly education.

As Andrew Warnes has shown in *Hunger Overcome,* culinary practices have not only been overlooked in the study of literary construction, but they have also been highly trivialized. If food is considered at all in the study of literary construction, it is viewed as a form of subwriting at best, and, at worst, as an obstacle to literacy.[5] Danticat and Pineau, like the African American writers Warnes examines, "draw a profound connection between writing and cooking, insisting on the capacity of both to replenish two disabling voids—hunger and illiteracy—that external forces have invested with special prominence throughout American history" (Warnes, 2). Danticat's and Pineau's characters and narrators move toward that very goal. Sophie Caco and Félicie Benjamin learn to master a kitchen narrative through which they voice their self, family, and communal history. As the epigraph above drawn from *Krik? Krak!* indicates, learning how to read and learning how to eat are irremediably linked.

Danticat's and Pineau's kitchen narratives not only link the disjointed present of the northern metropolis to the intact past of the Caribbean island, but they also construct a common Caribbeanness, an "Antillanité,"[6] that links Guadeloupe and Haiti, separated by historical and political breaks.[7] In spite of their historical differences, Pineau's and Danticat's focus on food allows their readers to see that Guadeloupe has much more in common in its culinary practices with Haiti than with the French Metropole. Culture thus, more than historical and political status, becomes a powerful lens through which to explore trans-Caribbean links. The transcultural Caribbean that the two writers build is not limited by the geographic bounds of the Caribbean archipelago, but also extends to the zones of the diaspora, which have become new centers of Caribbean culture, such as Brooklyn, Miami, Atlanta, Montreal, London, or Paris. Therefore, the diaspora does not correspond to its etymological definition of dispersion, but rather to a newly formed Caribbeanness, gaining strength through its transcultural links, building upon its fragmentations, and reinserting its marginal nodes into the center of cultural, economic, and political centers of power.

Moreover, Danticat's and Pineau's texts extend beyond Caribbeanness since their use of food transcends the local, that is, Haiti, Guadeloupe, France, and the United States, to join a transnational or "transcolonial" network of women,[8] such as Ntozake Shange, Paule Marshall, and Audre Lorde, who stitch their ripped memories by turning food into a historical text and mode of communication. "Mainstream" American philosophers of the body and the environment, such as Susan Bordo and Wendell Berry, even though they do not deal explicitly with immigration and exile, also provide a crucial interpretive sounding board for the novels. Bordo's and Berry's descriptions of a contemporary America plagued with disconnections of the body and its environment resonate with the two Caribbean writers' narratives. Conversely, the Caribbean writers provide a framework for understanding contemporary issues in mainstream American culture. Pineau's and Danticat's reflections on environmental respect contribute a crucial reflection on the timely discourses of sustainability. Such connections ultimately show that Danticat's and Pineau's texts are not only significant as exotic vernacular texts, but first and foremost as agents toward the construction of U.S., French, and, ultimately, world modernities.

Because Danticat and Pineau speak the same cultural language, my reading of their texts is based on a methodology of braiding. In a practical way, I do not compartmentalize Danticat's and Pineau's texts into discrete segments. Rather, I braid their stories throughout this chapter in order to emphasize their topical resemblance. This interweaving establishes synergistic connections, which are essential to a proper appreciation of Danticat and Pineau and the transnational writers they epitomize.

The characters and tropes of the grandmother, the mother, and the daughter punctuate the chapter. More than individual family functions, each of the three positions allegorizes, respectively, the native land, the adoptive nation, and a state of exile. The figure of the grandmother is strongly linked to the land-of-before, whether rural Guadeloupe or Haiti.[9] She is also the integral cook, the food literate, and the provider of abundant nourishing, in a symbiotic, if often utopian, relation with the land. The protagonists' mothers, exiled, respectively, on Flatbush Avenue in Brooklyn and in the *banlieue* of the French capital, exemplify the position of first-generation migrants who assimilate into their host culture, force-feeding themselves with its food while rejecting the island's culinary products and practices. Exilic mothers interrupt the relation between themselves, their daughters, and their land of origin and fail to nourish their daughter, both physically (literally feeding them food) and emotionally (providing the nourishment of well-being). The daughters, or second-generation migrants, practice creolization. They link to their culture by combining food products, and, more important, by "using their ten fingers," to use Danticat's expression, in order to braid food and writing. As a result, their creolization is not only a mixture of diverse cultural elements but also a feminist gesture. They combine activities traditionally relegated to women, to the rural, and to natives—cooking, oral storytelling, hair-braiding—with the reclaimed masculine, Western, and urban-coded acts of writing with a pen or computer. As a result, creolization is not just a matter of cultural mixing but also of reinserting gender into the equation, a gender component absent, for instance, from Glissant's masala theory examined in chapter 1.

"Le Mal de Mère": Mother's Ache

In Danticat's and Pineau's novels, the grandmother is the embodiment of relation and the substitute for an absent or defective mother's love.[10] It is a common cliché to say that grandparents and children develop a privileged relationship because of a shared enemy: the parents occupying the middle position. Moreover, Danticat's and Pineau's narratives indicate that the failed relationship to the mother is not limited by a link to a single person, but that the figure of the mother is overdetermined by the past and present experiences of slavery, exile, and political and masculine violence against women. In other words, the mother stands for more than her function in her family unit: she is also a figure that has been stifled by centuries of oppression and negative representations. First, obviously, comes to mind the experience of slavery in which the mother-child relationship was invaded by economic definition.[11] Moreau de Saint-Méry, a white Creole born in Martinique, observed quite perspicaciously in his 1789 *Description* that enslaved mothers were victims of "le mal de mère" (61)[12]—a phrase that could translate both as "mother's ache" or "mother's evil."[13] This double meaning does justice to Moreau's puzzlement over the tension between the intensity of the slave mother's love and her act of aborting or killing her children.[14] The "mal de mère" indicates the complexity of motherhood during slavery. It refers simultaneously to the sufferance of the mother, in that case, "mother's ache," and also to the bad mother, or "mother's evil." In a nutshell, the term reflects the complex history of motherhood during slavery and its aftermath, in which the mother oscillated between the excruciating pain caused by the love for her child juxtaposed with the necessity of saving the child from slavery by inflicting death. Toni Morrison and many critics have brought this contradiction into the open in their fiction and histories.[15] Danticat's and Pineau's heroines, who come of age in the 1960s and 1970s, seem far from slavery. However, the violence of the plantation structure is still felt by their mothers and by themselves through inheritance. Sophie's mother, Martine, is raped in a cane field, a space intimately associated with slavery. Félicie's grandmother, Julia, is beaten and abused by her husband, who repeats the violence inflicted upon slaves.

Bad or failed motherhood is also made more complex by the experiences of political or private violence, by exile, and by the neocolonial forces and cultural imperialism of, respectively, France and the United States, which disrupt the nourishing function of the mother. As I discuss below, the mothers in Pineau's and Danticat's texts are strongly associated with the "host" country through their culinary practices. In *Monsters and Revolutionaries,* Françoise Vergès discusses the belittlement of the enslaved or colonized mother—and father—by the all-powerful symbolic figure of France, the Mère-Patrie, mother and father at once. The colonized parents become perennial children (Vergès, 3–5). In this position, the real mother becomes invested with characteristics of the symbolic mother, France, and represents its values even in the absence of the colonial power. Félicie's mother feeds her daughter French food, French manners, and French language and thus acts as the henchman of the colonial.

In *Breath, Eyes, Memory,* the relationship of the mother Martine to the United States is best approached through a different angle than that of the symbolic Mother-Nation since, in spite of its long neocolonial presence in Haiti, the United States, unlike France, never presented itself as the *Mère-Patrie.* If a symbolic figure should be used, it should be that of the militaristic, paternalistic father, saving Haitians from their own misery, while at the same time erasing the responsibility of France and the United States in Haiti's economic exploitation. Martine, rather, seems to embody the typical position of first-generation immigrants, who tend to swallow the new and reject the old in order to be fully assimilated—ingested and erased—by their host culture. This assimilation entails a consumption of American values and a rejection of Haitian practices in a movement of self-erasure. More precisely, Martine ingests tasteless, unhealthy, and accultural globalized fast food.[16] Danticat's model would then present a classic case of immigrant attitudes. The first generation, or parents, get assimilated by ingesting the food of the host country, while the second generation, or children, become agents of creolization. The children both digest products of their host country and combine them again with elements of the original country, and with the other immigrant cultural elements that surround them to create an improved product, which amounts to more than the addition of its original elements. The grandparents represent the intact country of origin, nostalgic and irretrievable.

Grandmother's Love

In this state of affairs, the grandmothers embody the past of Guadeloupe and Haiti through their acts of cooking and oral storytelling. They are simultaneously cooks, soothsayers, and storytellers. They come to stand for the lost and irretrievable land of childhood, representing wholeness, authenticity, and soothing. As Brinda Mehta cogently argues for Guadeloupean migrants in France:

> The inability to claim a political motherland in the absence of nationhood further complicates the interrogation of maternal roots in the context of colonization and the consequent severing of ontological origins. The ambivalence represented by the symbolic mother is . . . confronted by the grandmother as the figure of a pre-symbolic or "arche" sensibility. . . . The grandmother. . . becomes the marker and preserver of a dynamic prehistory of cultural productivity. (*Notions of Identity,* 95)

The term "prehistory" is crucial because it not only situates the grandmothers in the past of their exiled granddaughters but also propels them into a plane outside history, irretrievably lost. Both Danticat and Pineau portray this certain yet irretrievable past through the figures of grandmothers Man Ya and Grandmè Ifé.

In Pineau's *L'Exil selon Julia* and *Un Papillon dans la cité*, Man Ya is the site of interconnecting relations, an open body facilitating symbiotic relations between land and women, and between women themselves. The little girl and her grandmother are first and foremost linked through the grandmother's organs, her breath, her smell, and her belly: "I would find myself stuck with my nose in her pungent armpit. We were Siamese twins. Her breath resounded in me as did each of the movements of her big belly agitated by resonant gas" (*Papillon,* 12). The description of the grandmother as twin is significant on several levels. First of all, temporal separations are collapsed and the forebear becomes sister, creating the illusion of a stagnant time protected from ineluctable progression. Moreover, the image recalls the "marassa" or twinning,[17] a trope drawn from *Vodun* spirituality. Thus, twinning performs a rooting in local traditions and in sacredness: a sacredness embedded in the digestive and respiratory functions of the body.

The grandmother's sacred function is also expressed in her storytelling. Like Trinh's storyteller, Man Ya is the site of "[h]umidity, receptivity, fecundity . . . her speech is seen, heard, smelled, tasted, and touched. Great mother is the goddess of all waters, the protectress of women and childbearing, the unwary sentient healer" (Trinh, 126–27). In Pineau's memory of a childhood without angles and separations, the grandmother brings to all her senses memories of the past. Her groaning, digesting, sweating body—an image that would disturb contemporary Western codes of politeness—constitutes the site of relation between the little girl and the land. By taking in the products of soil, the human body exits its shell to enter into a Rabelaisian relation with the world. This flowing interaction between humans and land defines a world preceding the introduction of divisions and hierarchies between human bodies and products of the earth.

A frequent practice in the Antilles consists of "twinning" a newborn with a tree by planting the placenta or the umbilical cord in the roots of a tree. Man Ya herself becomes tree: "She would even adopt a plant-like posture, would remain still until numbness, thought herself to be a mamma-tree, dark-barked, earth-marbled-toes, sky-saluting-arms" (*Exil,* 190). More than a gratuitous metaphor, the image of the tree situates Man Ya in a privileged position of remembering the land. Not only does she reminisce about the land, but she also *re-members* it by becoming one of its members or growing limbs. Her memory of the land is in the flesh, and she is the flesh of the land, occupying a posture that evokes the relational aesthetics of Cuban painter Wilfredo Lam's tree-human figures in which human breasts, sprouting shoots, penises, heads, and trunks are linked in an uninterrupted flow.

Similarly, like Trinh's writing of the body, Man Ya's memory does not isolate itself from the rememberer's body or its environment. "We do not have bodies, we are our bodies. And we are ourselves by being the world. . . . We write—think and feel—(with) our entire bodies rather than only with our minds and hearts," Trinh explains (36). It is precisely this absence of separation between specialized parts of the body that counters the Western overspecialization of body parts. Man Ya illustrates precisely the absence of separation between body and mind and between body and environment. She also challenges the definition of inscribing memory through the act of writing with a pen on paper.

Her illiteracy does not impede her power to tell a story. On the contrary, it is the rooting of the plants in the earth and the rooting of human bodies with plants that allows memory to flow. A land without trees, such as Man Ya's space of exile in the urban *métropole,* is a land "deprived of the essential wisdom" inscribed in "the leaves of the breadfruit and soursop" (*Exil*, 179). In contrast with the mnemonic properties of plants, pen writing, which her children try to teach her in vain, appears like a dangerous stain linked to the colonial power: "Ink soils. The things called letters come from France, as they say" (131). As a logical response to this perception, as well as a way to save and recycle valuable supplies, Man Ya launders the writing on school notebooks: "she lets cold water run on the pages and watches the undone marks of writing run into the sink, quietly . . . she watches words as she would watch the large uprooted trees . . . after a hurricane at the bottom of the ravine" (166–67). The removal of the dirt of the ink makes room for the processed paper to take root again through the recalled image of uprooted trees. Only the natural support, linked again to the trees, remains. Instead of using the prosthetic pen and distancing her story from the earth, and instead of projecting her thoughts on paper, Man Ya coincides with the original source of this paper, the trees. Her static, receptive, and arboreal posture reminds us of Suzanne Césaire's "human-plant." For Césaire, the "Ethiopian" and, by extension, the Martinican and the "Antillean," are human-plants. Instead of the Western attributes of passivity and inactivity usually associated with being a plant, Césaire claims that Martinicans have appropriated a meditative "Ethiopian" sense of being-in-the-world, which consists not in acting upon the world, but in being acted upon by the world.[18] Césaire's visionary essays, which send humanity back to its humble place, provide a powerful criticism of the destruction of nature by civilization: "Conversely, mankind is the instrument of civilization, a simple mode of expression of an organic power infinitely larger than it" (*Le Grand camouflage,* 28). Based on Leo Frobenius's observations on "Ethiopic civilization" in the dawn of the twentieth century, Césaire's analysis emphasizes the creative and fertile nature of this being in life. Like the Ethiopian, Man Ya represents the seamless past, and hopeful future, a state in which civilization has not introduced splits between humans and nature, body and mind, orality and writing, cooking and storytelling, natural and cultural memory. She is a live memory.

The flowing profusion of the island is linked to a fertile body out of bounds. A character explains to children at a community dinner: "Vant pété, manjé pas gaté!" (*Papillon,* 120). Food should not be wasted, the body should expand, and if necessary burst, letting itself be filled by the abundance of food during the feast. This perception of the body bursting as a desirable state is violently contradicted in the experience of exile, both for Félicie and for Sophie. Even before Félicie leaves Guadeloupe, in her trip between her rural Haute-Terre to the capital of Pointe-à-Pitre, the bursting of food appears as indecent, as her mother's friend voices:

> —Félicie, Your suitcase is way too heavy. What did your grandmother put in there?
> —My clothing, ma'am and my notebooks. And yams, sweet potatoes, and a small breadfruit I think.
> —Your grandmother is a crazy old woman. You'll have to leave it all behind. (*Papillon,* 20)

Food abundance, a sign of health in the Haute-Terre community, is dismissed as insanity in the urban Pointe-à-Pitre, and the grandmother is labeled a "crazy old woman." In clearly split associations, the mother represents restraint, rationality, and the *métropole,* while the grandmother is associated with outburst, insanity, and Guadeloupe. However, the narrative dismisses the urban friend's Western discourse by charging food with meaning. The breadfruit, as I explored in chapter 1, is strongly associated with maroon resistance on the hills, away both from plantation and globalized economy. The yams and sweet potatoes are root vegetables and symbolize an attachment to the earth. As Métraux indicates in his observation of the sacred festival of "manger yam" ("Yam eating") in Haiti, yams are sacred roots that can only be consumed after a ceremony in which the tubercules are laid down under the eyes of the Gods (*Le Vaudou,* 200). This ceremony, Métraux reminds us, is a repetition of the vegetable offerings of the Fons in Togo and Dahomey (200). The word "yam" itself provides an etymological root to the basic act of eating, and to Africa. Moreover, yams are rhizomes,[19] whose roots develop transversally, thus establishing a metaphorical connection not only with the native land and with Africa but also with the diasporic African community in the Americas.[20] Therefore, the food items carried in the suitcase are heavy not because of their actual size and density but because of the weight of the history they hold.

The connection between grandmother and original land, overflowing food, health, community, sanity, and storytelling in *Breath, Eyes, Memory* are so close to Pineau's narratives that they could be the continuation of the same voice. The setting of the first part of the novel, the village of Croix-des-Rosets, is best summed up as the place of connection between Sophie Caco and her land, her community, and her grandmother and maternal aunt. Tante Atie's and Grandmé Ifé's homes act as shelters protecting Sophie from incessant violence and disruption. Haiti as a whole is far from being represented as a utopian land of relation.[21] Away from home, people die of heatstroke in the cane fields, women are abused and raped, and *Tonton Macoutes* terrify the villagers and torture and kill young protestors.[22] However, Danticat's allusions to political violence in *Breath, Eyes, Memory* remain "the most gently glancing of references," as Ethan Casey puts it (525).[23] These glancing references could be explained by the fact that before her departure for Brooklyn, in Haiti Sophie is most focused on the connection and love flowing between her and Tante Atie and Grandmé Ifé. After they witness the murder of a young student protestor by the army on their way to the airport, Atie asks Sophie, "Do you see what you are leaving?" Sophie responds, "I know I am leaving you" (*Breath,* 34). At this point, in the narrator's mind, the country is equated with Tante Atie, and family love obliterates political violence. As the narrator analyzes her initial perception of Haiti, she admits her incomplete vision of her lost homeland: "I did not press to find out more. Part of me did not understand. Most of me did not want to" (61). This initial construction of Haiti is thus dominated by nostalgia, a self-deceptive experience that contrasts with the remembering Sophie achieves at the end of the novel. It is a longing to go home rather than a return to an ambivalent land.

The elements of this initial self-sufficient wholeness are organized around eating and cooking. Food acts as a vital link, unifying the members of the community in a living macro-organism, and provides a necessary amniotic liquid between humans and the land. "Eating alone" in the Caribbean, Guadeloupean writer Simone Schwarz-Bart reminds us, "is not eating" ("manger seul n'est pas manger," "Du fond des casseroles," 80), but rather it is the action of receiving nature and of maintaining links to the community. Schwarz-Bart recalls the example of her grandfather, who lived at a time when "the Antillean way of life was still intact" (75). The forebear, when he picked fruit from the trees or vegetable from his garden, "would leave part of it on the side of the road. . . . This gesture had a double meaning: to give back to nature a part of its due, and to share ahead of time the products of his crop" (78). This cultural definition of eating, inscribed in an "intact" time, based on the double relation of humans within their community and that of humans and their land, also defines Sophie's childhood in Croix-des-Rosets. Childhood time is marked by a unity that precedes Western industrialized practices based on exaggerated individualization. One of its highlights is a village potluck: "Tante Atie said that the way these potlucks started was really a long time ago in the hills . . . the women would cook large amounts of food while the men worked. Then at sunset, when the work was done, every one would gather together and enjoy a feast of eating, dancing and laughter" (*Breath,* 11). Food traditions act as the link of the community to its history, particularly to a historical tradition of resistance[24]—the people of the hills were the ones who escaped slavery and thus kept their West African heritage intact. The communal feast also consolidates the members of the *konbit*, who share the labor associated with food gathering and preparation.[25] The reward for community and cooperation is feasting, dancing, and laughing together. In Pineau's Guadeloupe, the communal feast evokes the same lost relation:

> All year long, Robert would fatten a pig for Christmas. . . . In Guadeloupe, the traditional way to serve a roast pig is with . . . tender yams. The entire day was bubbly with the preparation of the meal. Yet, Christmas really began when the drummers [tambouyé] came, their *ka* drum on their back, haloed with the authentic glory of being the heirs of the *nèg-mawon* . . . "Christmas Eve is about singing the coming of Christ" . . . but it is also about filling up bellies, drinking, laughing, and forgetting hard times. (*Papillon,* 49–50)

The scene, reminiscent—for its exuberance, its rhythmic beat, its celebration of the body—of the Christmas feast in Aimé Césaire's *Cahier,* performs relation on several levels.[26] The feast grows out of communal physical work in which all members are associated through a defined role. The physical work is inscribed in duration: the feast is the result of a year of waiting; the meal, of a full day's work. The preparation and consumption is thus linked in a temporal memory that inscribes it onto a collective. The ingredients, the direct product of the consumers, are anchored in a specific tradition of resistance and independence. Yams and other root vegetables constitute a link to Africa and to independent local production. The presence of musical instruments during the feast, such as the *ka*, consolidates the eating ritual. The *Ka,* or *Gwoka,* an African drum, represents a form of resistance in Guadeloupe, as well as a sacred object.[27] The presence of *nèg-mawon* or maroons, reinforces both the Africanity and Caribbeanness of the event. Food is thus linked to a temporality, a community, a history, and a religion. The celebration of Christ is swallowed up and appropriated through its investment in local food, music, and sacredness. Christianity is assimilated instead of assimilating.[28]

Just as food consolidates links to the members of its community, it establishes a vital relationship between the inhabitants and their immediate environment. The goods consumed come directly from the land. In the absence of refrigeration, food is obtained daily, from the local market or the garden. Therefore, production, preparation, and consumption of food frame time and community in a sustainable manner. By repeating the gestures of planting, gathering, and preparing, associated with cyclically repeated seasons, the working women embody a memory that transcends the instant that would be an isolated point in a linear progression. In the body is inscribed a memory of time that transcends the limits of individual bodies. Since the body is seen as the extension of the land, as a tool shaping it, through work, and shaped by it, through cooking and eating, its memory is extended to the land. Memory transcends, in space, the limits of the individual body. To the dimension of time and space, the feast adds the dimension of community to the extension of memory. Therefore, in the Haitian context presented in the first part of *Breath, Eyes, Memory,* there cannot be a disruption of memory since there is no individualization.

Food's healing properties are inseparable from its nutritional functions. It serves to cure a body or a mind struck by illness. Body and mind, a Western distinction, fits badly the concept of Sophie's grandmother's conception: "To my grandmother, chagrin was a genuine physical disease. Like a hurt leg or a broken arm. To treat chagrin, you drank teas from leaves that only my grandmother and other old wise women could recognize" (*Breath,* 24). Vegetal essences and body fluids, such as blood, permeate and nourish each other; they flow to become only one life: "We washed down our meal with watermelon juice. Tante Atie always said that eating beets and watermelon would put more red in my blood and give me more strength for hard times" (56). This description, where the food consumed flows into and becomes the body, echoes in Shange's *If I Can Cook,* where the blood of African ancestors flows in the breadfruit tree, symbol of runaway slaves: “You’ve peeled and seeded the breadfruit already. Don’t be afraid when it changes to a blood-red color, that’s the mourning of our ancestors, hungry for us to live now” (*If I Can Cook,* 31). Nurturing, rather than flowing in one direction, merges into a continuous cycle where food passes through the body and where the body relives in food. Eating what your ancestors ate is a way to remember them in the strong sense of the word, that is, to incorporate into your living body their dispersed members.

Elisa Sobo’s concept of “body-in-relation,” which she draws from her analysis of a rural Jamaican community, supplies a theoretical context in which to interpret the properties of food highlighted in this chapter. For Sobo, “The concept of a body-in-relation may seem foreign to U.S. or Western European readers who tend to view the body like they view the self—as autonomous, individual, and independent” (257). Food links bodies to the earth, and to other individuals who share the same meal. It is therefore important, according to these criteria, that the body be constantly well fed, since starving it would, in effect, disrupt the community and efface the daily cultural memory of the community. As Sobo describes, “Weight loss signals social neglect” (258). “A thin, dry body reveals a person’s non-nurturing nature and his or her lack of social commitment” (262). These initial remarks on body-and-food-in-relation provide a stark contrast with Sophie’s and Félicie’s consecutive dislocation and amnesia in a Western, urban, compartmentalized, individualistic world where all familiar and environmental relations fail.

Eating and the City: Mother’s Box

“Random concoctions: frozen dinners, samples from global cookbooks, food that was easy to put together and brought me no pain” (*Breath,* 151), “Fried chicken, glazed potatoes, and broiled vegetables. Everything came frozen out of a box” (198), “bacon and eggs and extremely sweet café au lait” (188), “spaghetti. I would boil it and eat it quickly before I completely lost my appetite” (183), “multicolor cans and cellophane-wrapped products” (*Papillon,* 83), “a silvery platter with lined-up little sausages [boudins]” (50), “oysters and a big turkey for Christmas Eve” (46), “a white tablecloth, china plates, finely decorated glasses with delicate tiny flowers” (51).

The list above provides a sampling of what Sophie, Félicie, and their respective mothers eat or refuse to eat, in Brooklyn or the French *banlieue*. These foods are "global" and anonymous (samples, spaghetti), or strongly linked to a French tradition (raw oysters and Christmas turkey). They disrupt the rituals of preparation that mark time—the dishes are "frozen," prepared "quickly," and eaten hastily; they are incomplete (concoctions), disordered (random), and unhealthy (fried, extremely sweet). In the French context, the food products are invaded by a sense of forced order (alignés), and by the luxury and whiteness of the table accessories (white tablecloth, china, delicate tiny flowers), which forbid the overflowing evoked in the Guadeloupean Christmas. The meals alienate mother and daughter from the native land because they bear no memory of it. They cut, fragment, organize, compartmentalize, and sicken instead of making whole, wholesome, and healthy. The image of the box, associated with the food consumed and with the mothers' respective spaces (tall buildings, square apartments, and coffin for Martine), dominates the period Sophie and Félicie spent in their mother's homes. The mothers's images are also "boxed up." Félicie's mother "grins on a photograph that [her] grandmother locks up in a white iron cookie jar" (*Papillon,* 5). Similarly, Sophie "only knew [her] mother from the picture on the night table . . . her grin never went away" (*Breath,* 8).

From the get-go, Sophie's mother's French universe is dominated by the omnipresence of the box and the grid restricting life, sounds, smells, and tastes. The ceremonial space of Félicie's mother's apartment is "mute like an empty church" (*Papillon,* 34). The building looks like "un kalòj à poules" or henhouse (32). The slippers that the mother asks her daughter to wear in order not to soil the "gridded floor" (34) inexorably separate outdoors and indoors, and, importantly, remove any trace of earth from the kitchen space. The slippers, which the mother's friend wears as she dances, silence the rhythmic *Ka* beat, essential to the Christmas feast in Guadeloupe.

This is in sharp contrast to the common practice of the outdoor kitchen in the Caribbean or with the communal, outdoor space of *lakou* or courtyard. Culinary practices respond to the same conformist imperative. On Christmas Eve, Félicie's mother buys "oysters and a big turkey," explaining to her daughter that "it is the tradition here and one has to adapt to the French way of life" (*Papillon,* 46–47). The mother swallows, not only literally but also metaphorically, what Rosello named "la culture du Blanc" (*Littérature,* 126). She assimilates to laws of market and capitalist consumption and the predetermined categories they presuppose by ingesting them.

The French and Guadeloupean Easter celebrations clearly distinguish between anonymous and serially produced food and personalized and meaningful consumption. The French Easter eggs offer the illusion of variety in the "carefully disguised painted eggs" (*Papillon,* 119). Under the mask of variety, everybody consumes the same boiled eggs. The Guadeloupean Easter feast is based on an opposite gesture. From a unique product, crabs, are created truly varied dishes: "There were only crabs. Crabs Everywhere. People served them in callaloo, in *matété* [rice dish], or in curries [*colombo*]" (ibid.). Creativity counteracts mass consumption. The meals prepared in Guadeloupe are linked to a temporality of the earth, of what the earth offers in the now, instead of the uprooted serialized products of consumption. The interchangeable cans that Félicie's mother collects "like in a museum," objects of a past disconnected from their context (83), fail to connect to any "live memory" or *hypomnesis.* As French philosopher Michel Picard explains, the so-called ephemerization of products of consumption in capitalist societies leads to a collective amnesia: "The first world economy market multiplies disposable objects such as pens, razors, tablecloths, miscellaneous containers. . . . A continuous consumption of the ephemeral goes hand-in-hand with the loss of control over memorization" (Picard, 37).

The elaborate art of preparing *kalalou* and *colombo* allows, by contrast, the double connection to a duration and a community. The preparation time is linked to the anticipation and pleasure of consumption, and the community—present and past—is fully involved in the preparation. Instead of a collective amnesia caused by the consumption of ephemeral products, we witness a collective temporal remembering. Both Danticat and Pineau insist on the link between past, community, preparation, and consumption of *kalalou* and *colombo* in their respective interviews: "It takes more than one finger to eat kalalou because of the slippery nature of it. It's a statement of unity; the fingers have to work together to pick up the *kalalou*" (Danticat, "Dyasporic Appetites," 37). Pineau says in an interview with me, "Colombo dish includes all the spices that have crossed the ocean to reach Caribbean shores. It also represents for me the victory of humanity over pain, adversity, and exile" (Loichot, "'Devoured by Writing,'" 337).

Danticat's protagonist experiences a similar radical disruption of the link between present and past as she moves to her mother's Flatbush apartment. Sophie and her mother, Martine, forcefully swallow urban contemporary American values and forget their Haitian past. Their experience of migration is not only a transnational passage but also a transition between agrarian and urban living areas. In that, they are also American and go beyond their immigrant status as they share the plight of rural Americans losing their bearings as they move to cities. In his *Unsettling of America,* Wendell Berry describes a similar moral and physical crisis in the life of contemporary Americans. He presents this malaise as a direct consequence of the agricultural paradigmatic shift between the production and consumption of local products to globalized and deterritorialized market practices. The body, severed from the land, and the mind, disconnected from immediate corporeal needs, function without bearings: "And the modern household's direct destructiveness of the world bears a profound relation—as cause or effect or both—to the fundamental moral disconnections for which it also stands. It divorces us from the sources of our bodily life; as a people, we no longer know the earth from where we come, have no respect for it, keep no responsibilities for it" (Berry, 52). Berry's description of a flight from agrarian America to urban industrial life, even though it deals solely with an internal national rural exodus, can easily be applied to Sophie's situation. Sophie moves from a rural land to a metropolis, from a place where food is daily taken from the land to a kitchen oblivious of the environment. She finds herself in a culture that, as Berry puts it, is destroying the world by ignoring it. Putting Danticat and Berry into dialogue—two texts that apparently belong to different contexts—allows us to read Danticat's novel as a central contributor to an American cultural discourse. Danticat in turn complicates and enriches Berry's definition of an "unsettled America" through the diasporic element she adds to his definition. For example, the mother's Haitian boyfriend's advocating of food as a luxurious product directly contradicts the bounty of food available in the United States: "'Food is a luxury,' he said, 'but we can not allow ourselves to become gluttons or get fat. Do you hear that Sophie?' I shook my head yes, as though I was very interested. I ate like I had been on a hunger strike, filling myself with the coconut milk they served us in real green coconuts" (*Breath,* 56). In Sophie's mind, if food is a luxury, then it shouldn't be wasted; rather, it should be consumed immediately. Or, as Pineau's character echoes: "Vant pété, manjé pas gaté!" The American abundance of food and the urgency for consumption experienced in Haiti cause a contradiction in the act of eating, a revaluation that emerges from the clash of two economic situations and societal behaviors. Sophie's mother was herself victim to this dilemma before her daughter: "In the beginning, food was a struggle. To have so much to eat and not to eat it all. It took me a while to get used to the idea that the food was going to be there to stay" (179).

The meals prepared by the mother and later by the daughter are not cooked but are simply heated or boiled quickly, a direct consequence of the collision between their hand-to-mouth conception of eating and capitalism, which reduces maximally time spent on nonmarketable labor. Communication, cooperation, effort, love, and time are no longer part of the actions of cooking and eating. The latter have become mere acts of survival and commercial process, having lost their socializing properties. bell hooks similarly observes that industrialized practice alters the organism of a community: "Industrial capitalism was not simply changing the nature of black work life, it altered the communal practices that were so central to survival in the agrarian South. And it fundamentally altered black people's relationship to the body" (*Sisters,* 179).

As Sophie becomes disconnected from the food of her land, she loses control of her own body. It is significant that the only Haitian meals Sophie eats in the United States are consumed in restaurants, in public spaces, the opposite of home, in particularly faraway places: "He started taking her to restaurants, always Haitian restaurants, sometimes ones as far as Philadelphia. They even went to Canada once to eat at a Haitian restaurant in Montreal" (*Breath,* 60). Haitian food becomes an exception, a commercialized event rather than a daily habit, an occasion for dislocation. It also capitulates to the ideology of capitalist and colonialist consumer economy whereby the only Haitian cultural elements tolerated are culinary dishes severed from the practice of communal relation and offered as commodified and entertaining diversions for the American urban palate.

The loss of food control deprives the mother of her capacity to hold the community together. When Sophie's grandmother asks her if Martine still cooks Haitian, she replies: "I don't know if she remembers cooking Haitian" (*Breath,* 106). Food, in the mother's practice, becomes a tool to disrupt rather than feed the community. This amnesia of cooking Haitian is central to the split in *Breath*'s Haitian immigrant community: "You will have to choose between the really old-fashioned

Haitians and the new-generation Haitians. The old-fashioned-ones are not exactly prize fruits. They make you cook plantain, rice and beans and never let you feed them lasagna" (80). The irreducible clash between traditional and Americanized Haitians resides in food differences. Lasagna and plantain rice are presented as incompatible traditions. The link is not there anymore, or it has not yet been reestablished.

The disconnection of Danticat's and Pineau's characters from their land, community, and mother—with food as the absent link—provokes a discomfort shared by displaced women of diaspora. Toni Cade Bambara in *The Salt Eaters,* her novel on healing, reflects on the disruption of communities of African American women, on their loss of a history grounded not in books but in the product of the earth: "What is happening to the daughters of the Yam? Seem like they just don't know how to draw up the powers from the deep like before" (quoted in hooks, *Black Looks,* 13). It is the loss of this sense of connection that Berry regrets. The isolation of the individual entails, according to him, an ill-fitting idea of health and modern Western medicine. It is not the body alone that needs to be cured but the body-in-relation: "The concept of health is rooted in the concept of wholeness. To be healthy is to be whole. . . . The body cannot be whole alone. Persons cannot be whole alone" (Berry, 103).

Another disconnection Berry identifies is the incompatibility of a healthy body with the model constructed and imposed on American society: "For the appropriate standard for the body—that is health—has been replaced, not even by another standard, but by very exclusive physical models. The concept of 'model' here conforms very closely to the model of scientists and planners: it is an exclusive, narrowly defined ideal that affects destructively whatever it does not include" (112). Similar to the domestication, construction, and eventual mechanization of the land, the body, disconnected from nature, becomes the prey of an artificial and forceful construction.

Purging the Body

Once severed from its nourishing environment and its memory of the past and of community, the isolated body turned into prey develops tools of resistance. Controlling food intake appears to be the only, albeit illusionary and risky, way to master the body. Thus it seems almost unavoidable that Sophie should develop bulimia. The relationship she experiences in the United States with her environment and her kin is one of disconnection, illustrated by an abundance of random food samples leading to amnesia. Sophie's body, like the serialized food products she consumes, becomes detached from any coherent system of reference. The body-turned-thing does not fit the predetermined Western mold. As a consequence, Sophie rejects the food her body ingests and develops bulimia. Moreover, this disease, which her Haitian grandmother does not understand, makes her body untranslatable to the Haitian language and system of communication. Sophie's body becomes a floating sign, which can belong neither to her native nor to her acquired language. Her illness seems to be prompted by yet another cut: the body-and-mind split.

Susan Bordo analyzes this schism helpfully in her *Unbearable Weight* (2). This dualistic conception influenced by Western theology and philosophy necessarily brings about a hierarchy, the body often cast as the inferior element: "The body as animal, as appetite, as deceiver, as prison of the soul and confounder of its projects: these are common images within Western philosophy" (3). A dichotomy between body and mind turns the body into a mere thing, reserving the mind for all thinking and ruling functions. The body-made-object therefore becomes a separate entity, demanding control, open to violence. As Berry explains: "By dividing body and soul, we divide both from all else. We thus condemn ourselves to a loneliness for which the only compensation is violence—against other creatures, against the earth, against ourselves" (106). This separation is what allows Sophie to develop and name her eating disorder—a name that holds meaning only in its American context: "After I got married, I found out that I had something called bulimia. . . . I have never heard of a Haitian woman getting anything like that. Food, it was so rare when we were growing up. We could not waste it" (*Breath*, 179). Her body has become a separate object. It has been externalized and projected into a net of images of alien, constructed bodies. This U.S. construction follows a previous constraint of female bodies in Haiti, where, as Chancy demonstrates, "women are subject to the same outdated Victorian codes of sexual behavior as their female counterparts in the United States and Europe" (*Framing Silence,* 107). Sophie, once more constructed, once more separated from community, cuisine, and corporeal soul, perceives her body as something that does not fit the model, something that intrinsically, interminably, has to change.

This isolation of the body puts it in the vulnerable position of incorporating negative stereotypes. As hooks argues: "Estrangement from nature and engagement in mind/body splits made it all the more possible for black people to internalize white supremacist assumptions about black identity" (*Black Looks,* 179). Sophie's body enters the network of negative connotations associated with black women's bodies in the United States. As Bordo adds, racist white supremacist discourse has constructed the black body as "'primitive,' 'savage,' 'sexually animalistic'" (*Unbearable Weight,* 9), as a "property, to be 'taken' and used at will. Such a body is denied even the dignity accorded a wild animal; its status approaches that of mere matter, thing-hood" (11). Sophie not only struggles to escape the stereotyping of being black in a white-dominated society but also of being a Haitian immigrant in the United States. When Sophie goes to school, her body is perceived as unhealthy and takes on the negative connotations associated with an objectified Haitian body: "[Haitian children] were accused of having HBO—Haitian Body Odor. Many of the American kids even accused Haitians of having AIDS because they had heard on television that only the four 'Hs' got AIDS—Heroin addicts, Hemophiliacs, Homosexuals, and Haitians" (*Breath,* 51). The negative stereotypes of corpulence as ugliness depend intrinsically on Western and capitalist assumptions, as is clear from the value ascribed to corpulence within many African and African American societies.[29] As Marvalene Hughes describes: "The interrelatedness of the concepts 'big' and 'beautiful' is African. Bigness represents health and prosperity, but in America, thinness is beautiful. Having learned these American values, could it be that the black woman (and black man) enjoy making White America fat and 'ugly' by its standards?" ("Soul, Black Women, and Food," 273). We could add that the cultural and aesthetic particularity of the intersection between "big" and "beautiful" is also strongly linked to the association between fatness and wealth. As Danticat herself explains in her interview with Mirabal, "Food was also an expression of wealth and I think that corresponds to people's body size and the belief that fat things were good. If you were skinny things weren't so good" ("Dyasporic Appetites," 39). The association between a well-fed body and beauty seems to be prevalent not only in African and Caribbean contexts but also in European cases in which class demarcations become visible through the quantity and type of food people are able to consume.[30]

The solution, however, is not simply to import or readopt the values of bigness advocated by Hughes or by Sophie's Haitian grandmother. It would mean reimposing foreign black models on their already serially Americanized bodies. The illusion of the easy adoption of African values within the context of American society leads black American women to experience a deep loneliness and invisibility in their struggle with food. bell hooks comments on the invisibility of eating disorders such as bulimia in African American women: "Concurrently, in black life 'fat' does not have many of the negative connotations that it has in the dominant society. Though black women are the most obese group in this society, being overweight does not carry the stigmata of unattractiveness, or sexual undesirability, that is the norm in white society. This means, however, that it is very easy for black women to hide the food addiction" (*Black Looks,* 71). The struggle of these invisible women cannot be named and understood within their community. As Bordo argues: "[She is] left alone to deal with an eating-disorder that she wasn't 'supposed' to have" (63). The insurmountable distance between the impulse to gorge oneself in situations of hunger and the need to limit one's food intake in a situation of food overabundance, as illustrated by the two epigraphs to this chapter, also means that Sophie cannot go back to her original state.

Sophie, alienated from her female forebears—and also distanced from the daily experience of hunger—cannot understand her fear of fatness and is isolated from an American serialized body into which she will never fit. Her body becomes the currency of exchange between two incompatible cultural values and economic contexts. In the situation of immigrants, these two systems clash in a head-on collision. To become American, Sophie rejects her Haitian body.[31] When she returns to Haiti, her grandmother remarks on her bony and hollow figure. She swallows the cultural sign of skinniness and purges the food she would have eaten as a Haitian. Sophie's body is therefore alienated from the American ideal but is also isolated from the Haitian conception of the body, since her struggle does not make sense in a culture favoring a well-fed body.[32] The state of bulimia, consisting in painfully swallowing a plethora of incompatible nutrients and vomiting them forcefully, is the embodiment of Sophie's forced amnesia. This amnesia is the direct consequence of the indigestible combination of Haitian ideals of fullness and relation and urban capitalist individualistic consumerism. Isolation is multiplied to the extent that Sophie attempts to take nourishment in and from the new land: the more she swallows of the American model, the more sick she appears within the American context, and the more she is unable to reintegrate into the once-healthy bosom of the Haitian community. The novel ends with the partial patching of these ill-fitting elements; healing, and a culturally complicated understanding of eating disorders, requires the re-creation of a transcultural space, through a memory concocted from Haitian and American ingredients.

This impossible integration into any community, which has its roots in an original disruption of food integrity, has further implications and causes of a sexual and sensual nature. In Danticat's texts, food and sexuality are often presented as two correlated plagues for women. In Sophie's case, the inadequacy of pleasurable sexual relations is not only motivated by the "American" rejection of the body. It also acts as a continuation of family behaviors, traditions marked by violence: Sophie's mother was raped in a cane field and became pregnant. Building on this traumatic experience, she repeats the family tradition of "testing"—checking her daughter's vagina with her fingers to verify her virginity. Sophie, in order to put an end to this "rape" by her mother, rips her flesh apart with a pestle, repeating the act of violence endured by her mother, continuing the vicious circle of victim/torturer. This cycle of violence continues her Haitian past, whereby women, such as Martine, have internalized the socially constructed "codification of women's bodies as vessels for male gratification in marriage" (Chancy, *Framing Silence,* 121). The extreme pain inflicted on the body is a violent act of memorization, the embodiment of the pain of women before her. As Chancy asserts, "sexuality . . . serves as a pivotal symbol of Haitian women's attempt to formulate empowering identities" (107). It also serves as protection against the repetition of violence. One remembers in order to prevent. The deflowering-ravishing pestle renders impossible any future violence from the mother since there is nothing left to "test." It protects Sophie's daughter, Brigitte, born at the end of the novel, from potential violence. The cathartic pestle, tool of memory, breaks the cycle of violence by repeating it.

Significantly, the tool used for the self-rape is the cooking utensil used uniquely for the preparation of Haitian dishes. It consolidates the link between rape and the Haitian family tradition, and it also mingles cooking tradition and sexuality in the same coercive structure. The mother's mortar and pestle finds antithetical echoes in Audre Lorde's

Zami (71–80). For Lorde, the two objects standing proudly in the kitchen cabinet are the necessary tools to authenticate West Indian dishes and thus to conserve their memories by making the dishes "unforgettable" (72). In Lorde's experience, the use of the mortar is accompanied by ritual sentences inscribed in "the script written by some ancient and secret hand" (73). As in *Breath, Eyes, Memory,* the past of West Indian foremothers is etched in these monumental kitchen objects. Another similarity between the two texts is the transference of cooking gestures to sexuality. In Lorde's text, the last time the narrator uses her mother's mortar coincides with her first period. The pestle's action in the mortar is explicitly described as sensual sexual intercourse, with the repetition of the refrain "Back and forth, round up and down, back, forth round, round up and down" (74). The pestle's movements transfer themselves into the girl's body: "the tidal basin suspended between my hips shuddered at each repetition of the strokes" (79). As in Danticat's novel, Lorde's mortar and pestle bears the inscription of female West Indian history and is strongly linked with sexuality. Lorde, however, describes these cooking gestures as a healing and pleasurable experience where both the mortar and pestle interact with the mashed, moist garlic balm between them. Contrast this with Danticat's language of violence, disconnection, and rupture where the pestle alone acts against a silenced mortar-vagina.

In Danticat's "Women Like Us," a young Haitian girl relates her mother's two rules: "Always use your ten fingers, which in her parlance meant that you should be the best little cook [and] never have sex before marriage, and even after you marry, you shouldn't say you enjoy it or your husband won't respect you" (*Krik? Krak!* 219). In the mother's rule, cooking and sexuality are presented as the two major subjections of a woman. In Sophie's case, the forbidden pleasure of sexuality is displaced to the guilty pleasure of eating, as becomes clear in the following episode, where she gorges herself after sexual intercourse with her husband: "I waited for him to fall asleep, then went to the kitchen. I ate every scrap of the leftovers, then went to the bathroom, locked the door, and purged all the food out of my body" (*Breath,* 200). Sophie's remembering body is, however, not a cured body. Sexuality (and food with its associated activities and utensils) is still perceived as violence; men, even the loved, loving, and careful ones, still loom as potential rapists. The purged food is again the symptom of an unacceptable sexuality, in both senses the lasting memory of the mother's rape.

Purging the body, not only expressed through the act of vomiting, also manifests itself in the various failed or successful abortions of Sophie's mother. Her original rape is repeated through the use of cooking utensils, which deviate from their original purpose of feeding and healing and transmitting mother's love. In Martine's case, her subsequent pregnancy with Sophie is seen as a mere continuation of the original violence, and the unborn child is imagined as the faceless rapist who has invaded Martine's body. In the attempted act of abortion, Martine also deviates food and cooking utensils from their primary functions of feeding and healing to turn them into lethal weapons. She confesses to her daughter that she once used food in an attempt to abort her: "When I was pregnant with you, my mother made me drink all kinds of herbs, vervain, quinine, and verbena, baby poisons. I tried beating my stomach with wooden spoons. I tried to destroy you but you wouldn't go away" (*Breath,* 190). In Martine's experience, the child and the rapist figure become one single being. Since the rapist was faceless and masked, the actual face of Sophie, and the imagined faces of Martine's subsequent aborted children, are the only incarnations of the missing face of the rapist: "I never saw his face. He had it covered when he did this to me. But now, when I look at your face I think it is true what they say. A child out of wedlock always looks like its father" (61). Purging the body, then, also links mother and daughter in a bond of violence, through the acts of ridding the body of its food, and of its child. When Sophie throws up food, she also vomits herself, purging her own body of the product of her mother's rape and purging herself of the mother who tried to kill her. However, by the same token, she also saves herself, vomiting her mother's lethal dreams and poisoned body.[33]

While the themes of abortion and bulimia are absent from *Un Papillon dans la cité* and *L'Exil selon Julia,* they are central to Pineau's 2008 novel *Morne Câpresse.* As in Danticat's novel, body purging and illusionary food control respond to the lived or inherited experience of sexual violence. In *Morne Câpresse,* Line, a young, urban, upper-class, professional, single, and independent Pointe-à-Pitre woman, searches for her sister, who disappeared after sinking into a life of drugs and violence. Line's quest begins—and ends—in an asylum for raped, battered, or drug-dependent women, sheltered away from men on the hilltop of Câpresse. Two half-sisters, "Mère Pacôme" and "Sœur Lucia," abandoned at birth by the same father, head the community that distrustful villagers called "Plantation." The two matrons built the isolated community to protect women from men's violence, inspired by a creolized mix of Christian faith, Buddhist philosophy, vegetarianism, and Aimé Césaire's poetry. As the novel progresses, the devilish side of the two sisters is slowly revealed.

In the world of Morne Câpresse, as in Danticat's *Breath, Eyes, Memory,* the act of purging the body links the control of food intake to abortion and infanticide. The women and girls confined to the shelter are subjected to a forced diet that forbids the consumption of meat, sugar, and synthetic and imported products. This diet could be read as a mindful gesture motivated by environmental and historical concerns. When Line asks for sugar to sweeten her tea, she is told that "sugar is the origin of Caribbean slavery . . . with sugar, humanity made a deal with the devil" (*Morne Câpresse,* 118).[34] However, instead of an efficient response to the exploitation of past and present generations because of sugar production, the limitation of food intake is instead perceived by Line as a way to starve the women's bodies (117). Therefore, the unfortunate recipients of this so-called political action are the women stuck in the shelter, not the production system at which it apparently aims. Instead of an act of emancipation, the coercive act of withholding food repeats the violence of the system it was fighting in the first place.

Vegetarianism is not justified by an ethical respect for animal life but rather used as a violent tool of war against masculine violence confused with meat-eating. It is the type of practice Derrida describes as "a reactionary and compulsive vegetarianism always inscribed, in the name of denegation, of inversion, or refoulement, in the history of cannibalism" ("Il faut bien manger," 295). Mother Pacôme practices this compulsive vegetarianism by purging her body of "animal corpses" by ingesting raw vegetables, gallons of water and bitter teas: "She sustained herself with vegetables. Carrots, tomatoes, cucumbers, radishes . . . She engulfed gallons of water and bitter teas to purge her body, purify her guts, rid her organs of the toxic waste left by the corpses of animals she had swallowed . . . Dead flesh, seasoned with devilish spices only there to mask the scent of death" (*Morne Câpresse,* 96–97). Flesh is clearly associated with the devil, a devil tied to men's sexuality. The phrases "purify my guts" and "swallowing animal corpses" evoke both a purging of food and rape. The evocation of spices masking the smell of rotting flesh also recalls Pineau's *Chair Piment,*[35] where the pimiento flesh forms a nexus in which food ingestion, violent sexuality, the destructive power of fire, and the woman's body meet. While the practice of vegetarianism in itself is an ethical act, the confusion of eating flesh alongside female flesh consumed by violent sexuality leads here to disastrous consequences. Line and the readers soon learn that the purging of the sexual and maternal body is pushed to a literal extreme. After wondering why all children born on Morne Câpresse are female, Line discovers that all male newborns were murdered at birth by Lucia, her sister's head executioner: "When her criminal hands chocked the male infants . . . she was just doing her job with the same professionalism as an executioner from the State of Kansas. . . . The twenty-three tiny creatures she had sacrificed did not give her any guilty feelings" (190).[36]

The mass murder of male children is accompanied by euphemistic references to abortion. Sister Lucia tells Neel, one of the women grounded in Morne Câpresse, that she will "have to swallow up teas to unhook it" (157). The term "unhook" presents the fetus as a parasite to the mother's flesh, like a worm. The event reminds Line of her own past abortion, prompted by her unsupportive married lover: "Line bit her tongue in order not to speak. To tell Regina that she had swallowed up a pill to kill her baby. A pill that twisted her guts before expelling the little one from her womb" (135). The euphemism of the action of "taking a pill" is contrasted with the physical severity of the uterus spasms caused by the apparently anodyne swallowing. The words "kill the little one" also link the contemporary scene to the hidden and banal abortion of children during slavery. "Drinking tea," "swallowing a pill," clearly evokes the motto "manjé tè pa fè Yiche pou lesclavage" (eat dirt don't make children for slavery) used by enslaved women to get rid of their fetus.[37] Swallowing as purging is thus strongly associated with the passing of the unborn child, a response to masculine and colonial violence.

Through her exposition of Line's predicament, Pineau is not linking her voice to antiabortion movements motivated by Christian beliefs. Instead, she exposes the graveness of the act of abortion, a painful experience too often trivialized or closeted. In Pineau's narrative, slavery and postslavery women are thus linked not by identical, but by a familiar, denial of their right to a loving motherhood, whether by the institution of slavery or by men's cowardice in contemporary Guadeloupe. Line, the urban, educated, upper-class protagonist, aborts because her married lover denies her the right to become a mother mothering:

"To comfort her, Terence swore that they would make another one. As if a baby was a disposable and interchangeable object" (*Morne Câpresse,* 134). The disposable and interchangeable qualities of the unborn child remind us of the mathematical unit of production that defined children during slavery.

However, once the link between contemporary Guadeloupean women and their enslaved forebears is acknowledged, Pineau sharply criticizes the neo-plantation, coercive, murderous world of Morne Câpresse, which, under the guise of a response to that violence, only perpetuates it. The novel ends with the congregation burning, leading both to destruction and the possibility of revival. This revival consists in dissociating eating from sexual violence in order to link acts of ingesting and cooking to the creative power of writing.

Writer's Pot, Daughter's Plot

In what could be called "Autobiography of My Grandmother," *Victoire, les saveurs et les mots,* Maryse Condé imagines her grandmother's forgotten life and culinary art by inscribing them into a written narrative.[38] Victoire was a house cook whose story had been buried into oblivion, especially by her daughter—Condé's own mother. Once more, the mother disrupts the transmission of a story from grandmother to granddaughter. Through Condé's pen, writing and cooking become aesthetic, structural, and functional equivalents, which reestablish a continuity between the writer and her silenced grandmother: "What I want is to reclaim the legacy of this woman who apparently had left none. Build a bridge between her creative powers and mine. Easily move from the tastes, colors, and scents of flesh and vegetable to those of words. Victoire could not name her dishes and did not seem to give it a second thought. She was locked up for the brightest of her days in the temple of her kitchen . . . absorbed in front of her stove *[potajé]* like a writer in front of her computer screen" (Condé, *Victoire,* 85). Cooking and writing relay each other in one fluid technological network. The traditional Guadeloupean *potajé* works hand in hand with the high-tech computer.[39] By placing these two forms of expression in a continuous line, Condé also dismantles the opposition between "high" and "low" cultural forms of expression and technologies, and between tradition and modernity. In her presentation of food as a site of technological creativity, Condé redefines her grandmother's craft as art, not as subservience. The narrator's mother, when prompted by her daughter's question about her grandmother's job, responds that Victoire "hired herself" for a living (14). Condé's book masterfully demonstrates that cooking, while also undeniably a subservient act—Victoire works as a domestic—is a place of memorialization as valuable as writing.[40] Or, rather, more plainly, cooking is writing.

In Danticat's texts, heroines similarly connect with their female forebears through the gesture of cooking. Sophie painfully overcomes the burden of food by engaging with it through cooking. In *Breath, Eyes, Memory,* cooking intervenes in a literal manner. Through a meal she prepares, Sophie links the four generations of women of her family. Danticat complicates the action of cooking further in her story "Women Like Us," where she links cooking and writing in a reciprocal metaphorical relation. Women's cooking gestures are poetic acts, just as writing becomes a "survival soup" (*Krik? Krak!* 220). These interchangeable activities establish a link between the formerly divided: past and present, local and global, mother and daughter, male and female, literary and digestive categories.[41]

The reconnection with the original land is Sophie's first step toward healing. Against her therapist's recommendation, who thinks it is too early for a "confrontation," Sophie takes her infant daughter to Haiti to meet the aunt and grandmother who raised her. What Sophie seeks is not a confrontation but, rather, a mutual "nourishment" between herself, her mothers, and her original land. Almost magically, considering her previous estrangement to food, Sophie offers to cook for her elders a dish of "Rice, black beans, and herring sauce" (*Breath,* 149). Even if Sophie's biological mother is physically absent, she is included in the sharing, since the dish, as the grandmother remarks, is her "mother's favorite meal" (149). Food defines this community of women and links the four generations in a collective, physical ceremony of tradition and memory: "My grandmother chewed slowly as she gave my daughter her bottle" (151). The theme is a familiar one. Shange ritually feeds her ancestors by preparing for them a New Year's Eve meal that she eats on her own: "Though I ate alone that New Year's Eve, I knew a calm I must attribute to the satisfaction of my ancestors. I tried to feed us" (*If I Can Cook,* 9). With equal ritual and sense of tradition, the young narrator of Danticat's work reinserts herself into the organism of the women of her community. By cooking a Haitian meal in Haiti, she regrounds herself in the space and time of her childhood, buying the best plantain on the market, taking time to cook, away from the pace of capitalist societies: "My grandmother and I spent the day watching the beans boil" (*Breath,* 121). The act and ritual of cooking, intrinsically a communal act, reconnects Sophie to orders and rhythms of time connected to community and environment.

Re-creating oneself as whole also heals the wounds between the self and others. Sophie, during one of her doublings, meets her mother, whom she calls her *marassa*:[42] "Finally, as an adult, I had a chance to console my mother again. I was lying in bed with my mother. . . . I kept thinking of my mother, who now wanted to be my friend" (*Breath,* 200). According to bell hooks, forgiving those who have hurt us is essential for recovery, which is that of the self-in-relation to the community *(Sisters)*. Through cooking, Sophie is now better equipped to erase the personal boundaries between herself and her mother, and to embrace her past.

The necessary forgiving that leads to healing can happen only if the cause of her suffering is acknowledged, only if the mother's individual gesture is replaced in the chain of violence to which it belongs, only when the individual and the political can be articulated, jointed, joined. Sophie calls it "piec[ing] together my mother's entire story" (*Breath,* 61). Her mother's story is in fact put together again when the body of Haiti has regained all its parts. Opposed to the nostalgic land of relation constructed in Sophie's initial stage in her remembrance process, the country represented at the end of Sophie's journey regains its limbs of violence. The experience of a violent political event, the murder of a villager, directly leads to Sophie's remembering of her mother's life of violence: "Somehow, Dessalines's death brought to mind all those frightening memories" (140).

The full-fledged narrative of the mother's rape, her insanity, and her life as a *restavec*[43] comes back to Sophie's mind directly after political awareness is heightened in Haiti. Sophie perceives her epiphany as vain: "It took me twelve years to piece together my mother's entire story. By then, it was already too late" (*Breath,* 161). Too late because Sophie's knowledge will not allow her to cure her mother, or to prevent her from aborting violently and from killing herself by stabbing. While too late to join with her mother, it is not too late to join her land and her past. After her return, Sophie's husband remarks that Sophie, for the first time, called Haiti home, whereas before "Home ha[d] always been [her] mother's house, that [she] could never go back to" (195). Again, we see that Sophie's mother in North America stands as an individual fragment, separated from her history, her past, and her community. Such a disconnected house allows no return, no joining home.

The joining of land and the past is reached when the collective and the individual meet, when the land of origin becomes more than an imagined haven. When the individual stories of violence and oppression of women are connected with their political sources, they are not isolated anymore but enter a space where stories become histories. Only after acknowledging this violence can Sophie reconstruct for herself a syncretic space, new values, and a solid self. Only then can she build her transcultural self by braiding values of the Haitian and U.S. histories that she bears.

The building of this transcultural space needs a specific medium. A syncretic vessel emerges from the reconciliation of writing and cooking that Danticat develops with another Haitian American character in her epilogue of *Krik? Krak!* ("Women Like Us"). In Haiti, as frequently stated in Danticat's stories, writing is an activity forbidden to women: "And writing? Writing was as forbidden as dark rouge on the cheeks or a first date before eighteen. It was an act of indolence, something to be done in the corner when you should have been learning to cook" (*Krik? Krak!* 219). The activity of writing is seen both as an act of sexual transgression ("dark rouge") as well as a threat to both the domestic work imposed upon women and the agrarian activity that her family practiced: "We are a family with dirt under our fingers, do you know what that means? . . . That means we've worked the land. We're not *educated*" (*Breath,* 20). The narrator's mother perceives her daughter's writing as a betrayal, believing that she is denying the activities of her ancestors: *"There are nine hundred and ninety-nine women who went before you and worked their fingers to coconut rind so you can stand here before me holding that torn old notebook that you cradle against your breast like your prettiest Sunday braids. I would rather you had spit in my face"* (*Krik? Krak!* 222; emphasis in original).

From the perspective of a young Haitian living in the United States, writing for others is not a betrayal as the mother sees it, but, rather, it is an innovative expression of solidarity toward her mothers and her sisters. "A thousand women urging you to speak, even if they speak in a tongue that is hard to understand. Even if it's patois, dialect, Creole" (222). Even if these women will not be able to read the words and understand the English language used, it is *their* voice that Danticat remembers in writing. Through writing (and writing about food and culinary traditions), Danticat heals not only herself but also the anonymous Haitian women calling to her. Cooking and writing appear braided together, far from the two irreconcilable activities the mother describes. In fact, the notebook is the braid that the young girl "cradles against her breast" to her mother's despair. To describe the equivalence between writing and cooking, Danticat borrows the concept of kitchen poets coined by Marshall in *Reena*: "Are there women who both cook and write? Kitchen poets. . . . They slip phrases into their stew and wrap meaning around their pork before frying it. They make narrative dumplings and stuff their daughters' mouths so they say nothing more" (*Krik? Krak!* 219–20). Danticat's putative sisters' cooking is presented as a form of expression similar to an art, like writing: "They carve onion sculptures and potato statues" (221).

For women like Pineau's Man Ya or Condé's Victoire, who do not have access to pen and paper, cooking acts as a tool for communication and a method for transmitting a lived history. Together, cooked product and cooking body become the site and text of the historiography of generations of silenced women. The kitchen is not any longer a marginalized place outside history where women are "locked up," but a center of collective women's memory. Paule Marshall's perception of the kitchen also evolves in this direction. In her text, initially, the kitchen evokes women's alienation: "There again was that awful image of women locked away from the world in the kitchen with only each other to talk to, and their daughters locked in with them" (*Reena,* 3). Later in her essay, it becomes the place of "ordinary speech," which makes for the best narratives. The kitchen is presented as a prerequisite, not an antithesis to writing: "I graduated from the corner of the kitchen to the neighborhood library" (9).

Another split no longer of value in the context of Caribbean American women is that between the private and the political. The communal memory that is passed on from mothers to daughters is not only that of good cookin' but also that of political activism: "In this man world you got to take yuh mouth and make a gun!" (*Reena,* 7). This discourse of empowerment, as Marshall describes, takes place in the kitchen. Danticat's and Pineau's heroines, like Marshall's, participate in this politicizing of the private kitchen.[44] Writing, perceived as a humiliating "spit in [the] face" or as a sign of transgressive sexuality—a degrading "dark rouge"—by mothers, becomes a war mask that daughters put on the palimpsest of their mothers' indelible text: their cooking history.

Unifying the themes of gender and physical and cultural healing, Danticat's writing is described alternatively as cooking or as a female activity. It is a writing that, like Marshall's, originated in the mother's kitchen: "Your mother, she introduced you to the first echoes of the tongue that you now speak when at the end of the day she would braid your hair while you sat between her legs, scrubbing the kitchen pots" (*Krik? Krak!* 224). It conjures the memory of the past just as cooking does. It braids women together just as food reunites them in an action of solidarity:

> When you write, it's like braiding your hair. . . . Some of the braids are long, others are short. Some are thick, others are thin. Some are heavy. Others are light. Like the diverse women in your family. Those fables and metaphors, whose similes, and soliloquies, whose diction and *je ne sais quoi* daily slip into your survival soup, by way of their fingers. (*Krik? Krak!* 220)

The action of cooking becomes the writing of a collectivity, the difficult braiding of women's histories. Writing is a "survival soup" made by these women's hands. Chancy shows that Caribbean women escape what she calls "culture-lacune" "through the written text, through the actualization of identity in language, the world of words shaping a new reality within the inviolable space of the imagination" (*Framing Silence,* 115). The action of cooking projected within Danticat's novel doubles and reinforces this liberating function of writing. It also, and perhaps more important, expands the definition of the written text beyond its culturally ratified definition (ink, pen, and paper in hand) and endows women cooks with authority, and through authorship. The inclusion of cooking in this wider definition of writing corresponds to what Angelia Poon describes as "a re-writing of the male 'text' or a redrawing of its textual borders to include perspectives and areas of experience hitherto excluded or marginalized" (Poon, paragraph 2).

The protagonists of Pineau's books, like Danticat's heroines and Marshall's kitchen poets, devour books and concoct letters, write history by cooking meals from their native lands. Through their kitchen narratives, the characters move from the status of consumers to that of producers of discourse. Writing exhumes the land of before. But the actions of eating and cooking, both digested by the text and transforming it, allow for the experience of a living memory of the past, according to the narrator of *L'Exil selon Julia:*

> The void of the land can happen anywhere at anytime . . . to feed that void is to buy fresh water fish in France, bathe it in a mock marinade—no lime nor bonda-man-jak here—leave the fish alone, cook it, eat it . . . and then, dream about the Land. Search for mouth scents and pleasures within memory. Reinvent a Caribbean Sea . . . suck on a snapper's head, mash a breadfruit chunk in the court-bouillon and sweat with the fire of a hot pepper. Re-live all the tastes. Breathe in [inspirer] and burp. (*Exil,* 169)

The reinvented dish is not the simple reproduction of the original but a new creation using substitute products available on the land of exile, a form of creolization that keeps creativity in motion. This cooking practice corresponds to the act of "writing" that Homi Bhabha calls "mimesis." The mimetic process introduces a difference that surpasses the original gesture: "What emerges between *mimesis* and mimicry is a writing, a mode of representation, that marginalizes the monumentality of history, quite simply mocks its power to be a model, that power which supposedly makes it imitable" (Bhabha, *Location,* 88). Pineau's reinvented Creole *court-bouillon* is described as an "imitation," an "offense," but, more important, a reinvention. Cooking and eating therefore act as vessels of creolization in a situation of exile. The situation of exile, paradoxically, facilitates modes of turning private gestures into political acts that gain resonance outside the walls of the kitchen and the walls of the island of origin. In her reflection on Caribbean women writers in exile, Chancy contends that "Caribbean women can ironically politicize their discourse and be heard in more than one culture simultaneously, making their consciousness and those they reach 'contrapuntal' at once" (*Searching,* 5). The writer-eater in exile, then, transforms the host country by inserting into it her own literary and culinary techniques, and also by practicing an epistemological model in which basic corporeal functions of digestions and soul inspiration, burping and creative breath, are united in the gestures of memory and transnational communication.

The narrator not only heals the exiled subject, the intimate, the familial, but also reinvents the collective history of the Caribbean people and diaspora, the private and the political: "All these long vacation days, she taught us how to . . . use a pestle to grind spices on the masalè rock: mandja, rice, coriander, clove . . . to make the colombo paste that the local Indians—those who came from faraway India, Calcutta—had brought with them to Guadeloupe, along with their Gods Maldevilin, Maliemin and Kali" (*Exil,* 305).[45] Home cooking then, an activity traditionally reserved for women relegated to the kitchen, tells the narrative of a people on the same level as a historical archive. In the example above, the history of various Antillean diasporas and exiles can be seen through the juxtaposition of the East Indian spices with native Caribbean and African elements.[46] Bhabha evokes the encounter of private and public spheres in the texts of minority women writers, in particular Toni Morrison: "Private and public, past and present, the psyche and the social develop an interstitial intimacy. It is an intimacy that questions binary divisions through which such spheres of social experience are often spatially opposed" (Bhabha, 13). The young narrator of *L'Exil selon Julia,* in a gesture that resembles Pineau's writer's mission, puts on the same cutting board, on the same writing case, the tools helping her to rebuild the past: "I spent entire days collecting leftovers, old bones, rancid food, aching writings, yellowish photos. . . . I wanted to collect each saying, stuff it, turn it inside out, and bite into it. A hunger you can't fathom" (*Exil,* 25). In this recollection or *hypomnesis,* the independent units of writing and cooking weave into each other to form a tapestry of the past.

"Thanks to the cuisine, they call themselves Creole," Pineau declares in our interview (Loichot, "Devoured by Writing," 328). It is precisely by inserting their language and cuisine into Metropolitan centers that *négropolitains* regain proud Creole identities.[47] To use Barbadian critic George Lamming's concept, frontiers of the Caribbean are extended by the movements of migrations of Caribbean subjects such as Pineau or Danticat: "There is a Caribbean world that exists . . . in many Metropolitan centers, whether in North-America or in Europe. . . . These centers comprise what I call the external frontier . . . [which] has a very decisive role to play in the future cultural and political development of the Caribbean" (9). Caribbean migrants thus reverse the movement of colonization since they re-create Kingston, Port-au-Prince, and Pointe-à-Pitre in London, New York, and Paris.

Pineau and Danticat add to this expansion of frontiers a movement of neocreolization, where new elements enrich the already Creole culinary products of the Caribbean diaspora.[48] The result is more than the sum of the parts of France and Guadeloupe or Haiti and Brooklyn. Marc, Sophie's husband-to-be, recognizes himself in Sophie's Creoleness: "'We have something in common. Mwin aussi. I speak a form of Creole too. I am from Louisiana. My parents considered themselves what we call Creoles. Is it a small world or what?'" (*Breath,* 215). The agrarian South and the rural space of Haiti reconnect in the urban space of Brooklyn to aggregate into a form of neocreolization, adding to the previous sediment of cultural creolization.

Félicie adds yet another element to the processual movement of neocreolization. Hers consists of braiding Antillean cultural elements with her North African neighbors. This transversal, rhizomatic cultural formation creates a cultural unity excluding both the French Metropolitan center and the Caribbean Plantation as places of rootedness and origin. Paul Gilroy describes these new connections between peoples drawn from disparate diasporic movements: "This change of perspective [of the African diaspora] is aimed at transforming the more familial unidirectional notion of diaspora as a form of dispersal which enjoys an identifiable and reversible originary movement, into a much more complex 'chaotic' model in which unstable 'strange attractors' are also visible" (Gilroy, 21–22). Félicie's multidiasporic friends are "all perched up . . . in the tall buildings of the projects [la Cité]. They are French, North-African, Caribbean, African" (*Papillon,* 38). In spite of their ethnic and national differences, the friends are linked by a common positionality in French society and in the urban space. They live in the margins of the city, "perched"—the word recalling images of birdhouses—in tall buildings. This societal commonality, this common marginalization, is therefore what allows for a new phase of creolization. We are not far from the reality of the closed space of the Plantation, having given birth to innovative forms of expression such as Creole language, jazz, or Caribbean cooking, otherwise understood as creolization.[49]

Once again, this neocreolization is dominated by a kinship emerging from culinary resemblances. Félicie changes her name from Félicie Benjamin to Félicie Ben Jamine, to establish a familial link with her friend Mo (*Papillon,* 105). Their kinship also appears through the phonetic proximity of the name of two sweets, "doukoun" and "loukoum," prepared, respectively, by their Guadeloupean and Algerian grandmother (56). It is also through food that Mo and Féli reclaim global cultural elements imposed on them by television. They ingest and incorporate the characters of the series *Dallas* in their own cultural system by ingesting and transforming their words and by making them ingest their own dishes: "I cooked this couscous especially for you, Bobby." "Thanks sweetheart, you are an excellent cook" (69). Thus the children swallow up the words of the American television characters in a process that Françoise Lionnet would describe as "a radical and subversive appropriation of the cultural codes by a subject who constructs herself through her discourse" (Lionnet, *Postcolonial Representations,* 175). The apparently trivial transformation of the American popular series elevates a child's game to the level of political gesture.

The Caribbean geography of the land is also apparently reinvented through a playful game associating the phonetic cousins of "lentilles" and "Antilles": "When I eat lentils I think of the Antilles. Lentils, Antilles [lentilles, Antilles]. Is it true to think that Guadeloupe is an Antille among so many others? Each seed is an island on my plate (*Exil,* 202–3). The reconstruction of an Antillean geography with lentils exemplifies once more the contribution of the private and the culinary to the political. This gesture looks like an avenging against the French imagination of the Antilles as insignificant rocks in the sea. We will recall Charles de Gaulle's infamous metaphor evoking the Antilles as a "dust of islands," as well as the violence inflicted on the world by the tracing of European maps described by Benedict Anderson: "European style maps worked on the basis of a totalizing classification. . . . [T]he entire planet's curved surface had been subjected to a geometrical grid which squared off empty seas and unexplored regions in measured boxes. The task of, as it were, 'filling in' the boxes was to be accomplished by explorers, surveyors, and military forces" (*Imagined Communities,* 173). The reference to the imagination of the Antillean by European cartographers appears even more striking when we juxtapose Pineau's scene with Cuban writer Antonio Benítez Rojo's *El mar de las lentejas (Sea of Lentils)*, a demystifying of the conquest of the Antilles by Spanish conquerors. The last chapter of the novel reflects on a map by cosmographer Guillaume le Testu, called "La Mer de Lentille" (Sea of Lentils). Rojo's characters invest the restrictive naming by assigning a new meaning to the word.[50] Whether the association between Antilles and lentils in Pineau and Benítez Rojo is due to coincidence or intertextuality, both gestures similarly expand a reductive label. By reading the world in her plate, Pineau's narrator, like Danticat's kitchen poets, confronts the flat, static, totalizing map of European geographers and colonizers with an open, dynamic, and domestic map, performing an intimate, culinary, and feminized version of Glissant's creolization.

The next chapter also reflects on the juncture between writing, food, and sexuality, albeit on a different level. While the heroines of *Breath,*

Eyes, Memory, Papillon, and *L'Exil selon Julia* strive to dissociate writing from sexual transgression and eating from sexual violence in order to mend individual, familial, and cultural fragmentation, Pineau's *Chair Piment* and Laferrière's *Comment faire l'amour avec un nègre* empower their writing precisely by using sexual and culinary coups as tools of the reader's seduction.

4 SEXUAL TRAPS

Dany Laferrière and Gisèle Pineau

> As for humming-bird-women, tropical-flower women, four-raced women and dozen-blooded women, they are long gone. . . . Yet they're here.
>
> —Suzanne Césaire, "Le grand camouflage"

COLONIAL DISCOURSE, EXOTIC LITERATURE, and sex tourism corner Caribbean subjects in a double sexual trap. On a discursive level, travelogues and exotic poetry assimilate mixed-raced bodies to palatable fruit or to astonishing exotic flowers such as the ones evoked by Suzanne Césaire in the epigraph above. On a material level, sex tourism, old and new, allied with the economic superiority of European and North American travelers, increases the vulnerability of women and men, as well as that of boys and girls. The sexual depravation and uncontrollable lust attributed to figures such as the mulatto boy or the *métis* woman in colonial discourse absolve the sexual acts of violence committed by travelers or writers by placing the responsibility onto the victims. This chapter demonstrates how contemporary Caribbean writers Gisèle Pineau and Dany Laferrière highjack the sexual trap by turning it against readers seeking exotic eroticism. In short, they regurgitate at the forefront of their text sexual stereotypes associated with exploited female and male Caribbean bodies in order to disarm the mechanism of such cultural presumption. This digestive process of literary ingestion, regurgitation, and, ultimately, excretion of stereotypes should clear the ground for an "empowering eroticism," to use Audre Lorde's expression, freed from the stifling pornography affixed to Caribbean bodies.[1] Suzanne Césaire, in her 1945 essay, deploys the same strategy. The beautiful humming-bird women are no longer available for Western readers and travelers ("they're long gone"). However, their presence is strong ("Yet they're here"). Césaire crosses out the image of palatable exotic Caribbean women in order to ensure their comeback as poets. She draws in exotic-thirsty readers with a familiar trope, only to let the trap of the image close upon them.

The touristic reader, out to consume sugary and colorful exotic male and female flowers, becomes, I argue, the meal of the coveted carnivorous plant. Haitian-Canadian writer Dany Laferrière's *Comment faire l'amour avec un nègre sans se fatiguer* (1985) and French-Guadeloupean novelist Gisèle Pineau's *Chair Piment* (2002) serve as two privileged examples of what could be called "fake pornography." In this subgenre of Caribbean, African, or diasporic writing that I am putting forward, I include texts that regurgitate in the face of—mostly white—readers' images of stereotypical blackness such as the nymphomaniac, the hypersexual male, or the cannibal. This is done with a sense of humor and an ironic distance, delivering a politicized analysis instead of the expected erotic product.[2]

Metaphors of ingestion, digestion, and regurgitation are not innocuous when referring to sexuality. Eating and sexuality are linked by the organ of the mouth, simultaneously the site of erotic pleasure and the site of eating. Gisèle Harrus-Révidi, in her book on psychoanalysis and culinary pleasure, sums it up for us: "The oral stage is genetically the first stage of the child's libidinal evolution, essential for . . . the pleasure of filling up linked to that of suction. The relation to the mother is a relation of the mouth . . . eat me if you love me, I eat you because I love you" (*Psychanalyse,* 22–23). This original matrix of the mouth as the double site of sexuality and food is at the crux of Freudian-based psychoanalysis.[3] In the oral stage of early infancy, the mouth sucking the mother's breast and taking in the mother's milk has not yet separated erotic pleasure from feeding. In the oral phase, which he also calls "cannibalistic pregenital sexual organization," Freud argues, "sexuality has not yet been separated from the ingestion of food. . . . [T]he object of both activities is the same; the sexual aim consists in the incorporation of the object" ("Three Essays," 64). The continuation of this stage of infancy is seen as pathological in habits such as thumb sucking. The enmeshment of sex and cannibalism frequent in Pineau's and Laferrière's novels can thus be seen as the pathologizing of black sexuality as constructed by the white gaze.

If we move from an ontogenic to a phylogenic model, in other words, if we transport the premise of confusion of eating and sexuality from the early stage of individual human development into the development of a group, we observe that Caribbean communities have been pathologized jointly at the level of eating and of sexuality. No need to return to the pathologies of eating forced upon Caribbean subjects highlighted in the preceding chapters: the theft of the enslaved children's mother's milk; the severing between laboring bodies and the product of the land they cultivate; the association of Caribbean subjects with figures of dysfunctional or monstrous eaters such as the glutton, the starved, the hunger-less, or the original and originating figure of the cannibal. The section below questions the possibility of Caribbean eroticism in the context of this violent control of black female and male sexuality.[4]

Facing the Satyr and Jezebel

Black women and men face, as they enter the "white world," as Frantz Fanon puts it,[5] an image of blackness that precedes them, circulates in spite of them, and flattens their cultural, ethnic, historical, cultural, literary, sexual, and individual specificities with steam-roller strength. The stereotype creates a fiction for each of the sections of their humanity—their physical appearance, their rationality, their clothing, their family relations, their food habits, and their sexuality.[6] As Laferrière lucidly puts it: "En tant que Noir, je n'ai pas assez de recul par rapport au Nègre" [As a Black man, I don't have enough distance from the Negro] (*Comment faire,* 49). Negotiating the relationship between the subject ["je"] and the image ["le nègre"] is crucial to reclaiming self-definition. The particular segment of the stereotype, of Fanon's "overdetermination from the outside," or yet of Patricia Hill Collins's "controlling image," at stake here is the encoding of the sexuality of male and female black bodies.[7] To schematize, two extreme and apparently opposite images have dominated this realm of representation: a threatening hypersexualization and a stripping of sexuality.

Racialist discourse has defined men by the figure of the perverse black satyr or by equivalent representations of a threatening figure with a grotesquely oversized phallus.[8] "For the Negro has a hallucinating sexual power" (Fanon, *Black Skin,* 136). This mark of monstrosity, along with the projection of cannibalism, justified the "taming" or annihilation of the black man in acts of enslavement, murder, or lynching. Women have also been presented with an overflowing sexuality and an insatiable appetite for men, particularly for white men.[9] Such representations based on rumors or fantasies became beliefs, official history, which first justified the act of colonization, in that it provided a reason for taming the black subjects' wild animality, and, second, absolved white men from the rape of black women. Black and mulatto women were in essence unrapable since they were represented as initiators of the sexual act.

On the other end of the spectrum stands the figure of the desexualized black woman, and that of the tamed black man, often rendered impotent by castration, figurative or literal. Black and colonized males, as a result of their hypertrophic virility, become castrated, and therefore incapable of rape.[10] From Lafcadio Hearn, to André Gide, to contemporary sexual tourists, colonized boys and men are the passive partners or feminized objects of desire.[11] If not literally raped or castrated, such as in acts of lynching or sexual exploitation through sexual tourism, black men become passive, feminized, or sexless beings who can enter the white home without constituting a threat. Thus the asexual, tamed, benevolent, and boxed-up domesticated slaves Uncle Tom and Uncle Ben can find a place on the kitchen table and become "part of the family."[12] In the French colonial and contemporary context, the Banania figure stands out.[13] In the infamous commercials, the Senegalese soldier loses all warrior masculinity, disappearing behind a eunuch-like smile. Thus little French children can safely ingest the Banania-man.

Women are stripped of both sexuality and maternity as they dissolve under the image of the "mammy" or the "Da" in the Antillean context.[14] Not unlike the case of the Banania figure, the desexualization of the mammy, Da, or wet nurse allowed her to penetrate safely the big house or upper-class home intimacy without constituting a threat to the white family. The blindness of the white family to the Da's own children eclipsed the sacrifice of a mother forced to give her own milk, intimacy, bodily warmth, and caresses to the child of her masters or employers, while her own children received some ill-adapted ersatz. Thus, by stripping the mammy or Da of her own family, the white family turned the mother into a childless orphan, stuck in a perennially ageless and sexless body.

The two extremes of hypersexualization or desexualization of black women and men go hand in hand. One is the natural sanction of the other: desexualization responds to uncontrollable drives; castration is the preemptive sanction of the fear of rape. The image of black sexuality is thus organized around these two transgressive, and pathological, poles. Sexuality can never reach a balance, a middle ground, and is bound to be deviant and monstrous. In white representations, black women and men are lecherous and impotent at once, in a manner reminiscent of the pathologizing of hunger in the figure of Chamoiseau's "starved gluttons."[15] Black people's eating and sexual habits, their appetite for food and their appetite for sex, are thus constructed according to the same schema: black eating and black sexuality are pathological appetites that need to be cured, tamed, or suppressed.

On the level of human experience, particularly in the context of slavery and its aftermath, the sexuality of the enslaved was, in an enormous generalizing movement, dissociated from pleasure, love, and desire and linked instead to economic profit. Copulation equaled economic reproduction in a world where men were stallions and women were mares. Sexuality was thus separated not only from sensual desire and pleasure,[16] but also violently severed from motherly and fatherly love, whereby the products of the sexual act, children, were treated as dehumanized capital.[17]

Black sexuality was thus the object of a double theft, first in the realm of experience, and second on the level of representation. The association of black sexuality with grotesque, immoral, and pathological features, the actual dehumanization of the sexual act relegated to an animalistic reproducing machine during slavery, and sexual violence (rapes and forced breeding) to which women and men were subjected during slavery led to distorted self-representations of erotic relations. African, African American, and Black Caribbean novelists and poets of Africa write the erotic under the constraint of, and in tension with, the awareness of the hypertrophic and pathological representation of black sexuality in white texts. "Caribbean sexuality is very complicated," Carole Boyce Davies argues, by the tension between the "prescriptions to reject" an exotic and stereotypical sexuality with the expression of "open sexuality in the larger community" ("Secrets," 292). In her introduction to the 2010 anthology *Caribbean Erotic,* "Creating a Safe Space," Donna Aza Weir-Soley contends that "Caribbean women, in particular, have been reluctant to write about sex. . . . Historically, Western discourses have grossly misrepresented and impugned the Caribbean woman's sexuality—so much that she has felt it necessary to deny or repress her sexuality in order to gain 'respectability'" (16). In a special issue on eroticism in the literatures of Africa and its diaspora, J. L. Joubert defines sexuality in black texts—Antillean and African—as veiled by a "timeless decency" or "shame" *[pudeur immémoriale].*[18]

While the expression of—overwhelmingly heterosexual—eroticism is common in Caribbean literature, it is often interrupted by the intrusion of slavery, colonization, racial politics, or else used as a political tool.[19] In her important dissertation, "Sexual Edge," Jacqueline Couti has unearthed an impressive "archeology of sexuality" in Martinican literature. She goes beyond the hasty dismissal of representations of the female body in Confiant's and Chamoiseau's texts as derogatory and chauvinistic to highlight instead the political nature of these hyper-heterosexual scenes of master *coqueurs* ("fuckers") and genitalized females. For her, terms such as *coquer* ("to fuck") and *coucoune* ("pussy") are misread by non-Creolophone French readers, who see in them only their sexual meaning.[20] Couti convincingly argues that these terms also refer to the political gesture performed by the sexual acts. So, if eroticism is present, it doubles up with a political function.[21]

In his erotic novels and celebratory essay "Vive l'érotisme solaire!" [Long live solar eroticism], Haitian writer René Depestre develops a praxis and a theory of blissful eroticism.[22] He identifies a Caribbean erotic exception, divergent from both African and European relationships to Eros. This Caribbean exception, for Depestre, can be attributed to a certain Magic Realist aesthetic, which celebrates nature as the farmer who "passionately digs and plows the adorable depths" ("Vive l'érotisme," 125) of the "garden-woman." Depestre problematically presents emancipating eroticism as a welcome result of the conditions of enslavement proper to the Caribbean plantation: "In times of colonial order on the plantation, sexual games represented perhaps the only freedom left to my enslaved ancestors. They were free to dance their solitude, and to forget their unhappiness for a short while, in a carnal gift of themselves" (126). While we can't deny the fact that slaves did experience sexual pleasure and love, Depestre's obliteration of plantation sexual violence is problematic. Caribbean sexuality for Depestre is a pain-free, guilt-free experience far from the Western obsession of the "morbid erotic consciousness" of a Georges Bataille, for instance.[23] However, in a portrayal reminiscent of the most naive exotic representations of Caribbean eroticism as spice, Depestre casts a Western eye on the Caribbean erotic scene.[24] Caribbean sex is a palatable exotic dish. "In our horizontal bed business," Depestre claims, there is "a sexual whimsical surrealism sparkled with Creole spice" (ibid.). The self-exoticism of the Caribbean sexual act is felt even more acutely when Depestre juxtaposes it with the proposal that lovemaking is a remedy to thirst and hunger: "In the Caribbean . . . men and women . . . surrender themselves to death by thirst or starvation when they are outside whereas they make love as sovereign beings" (127). This portrayal of lovemaking as a solution to hunger repeats the age-old colonial belief that blacks didn't need to be fed in order to be happy or even to survive.[25] Who makes love, dines, Depestre implies. His solar and sovereign eroticism appears more like an idiosyncratic fantasy than a valid comment on Caribbean sexuality.[26]

On the polar opposite of Depestre's solar eroticism stands the testimony of Marie Vieux-Chauvet's character Claire, who defines sexuality in Haiti as lurking in the shadows. Haitian writer Vieux-Chauvet's novel *Amour,* first published in 1968 by Gallimard, offers the most explicit example of this closeted sexuality while courageously bringing it to light in the novel. Claire, first-person narrator and eyewitness, is an unmarried woman in her late thirties, who occupies a situation that expels her from all groups of Haitian society. She is excluded from her bourgeois family because of her dark skin. She cannot integrate the community of dark-skinned workers of the land because of her privileged class status. Thus she is excluded from circulation through the marriage market and, as a consequence, from sexual relationships either because of class or because of race.

As opposed to Pineau's and Laferrière's novels, which present themselves as the exteriorization of black Caribbean male and female sexuality, as sexual marketplaces or *trompe-l'oeil* metaphorical brothels, Chauvet's book is a doubly locked closet. Its subtle title, *Amour*, clashes with the explicit sexuality exposed in Pineau's and Laferrière's titles. However, the discreet external appearance of the book, like the discrete contours of Claire, "effacée comme une ombre" (*Amour,* 9), contains a sexuality screaming to be heard. While Pineau and Laferrière exteriorize in their literary trap an eroticism that reveals itself not to be a true eroticism, Vieux-Chauvet's novel hides in its walls a true screaming erotic desire.

Claire's predicament, primarily defined by race and class, is also owed to her sexual status, which she presents as the common lot of women in rural Haiti: "I am thirty-nine years old and still a virgin. The unenviable fate of most women in small Haitian towns" (*Amour,* 5). What starts as an observation of the status of women in Haitian society soon moves to a more intimate, if not genital, description: "I am old. I must smell rancid down there, clutching this starving, virgin sex between my legs" (39). In the atmosphere of "age-old shame" or in the silenced expression of female sexuality in Haiti, Vieux-Chauvet's intervention seems earth-shattering.[27] Through her character, she gives voice to an individual Haitian woman (who herself speaks for a wide section of Haitian women: "most women in small Haitian towns") in a direct language that avoids metaphorical or metonymical detours. More important, Claire's speech exposes to the light of day a sexual expression independent from male fantasy: the sexuality of a middle-aged woman, who describes her sexual organ as rancid, and therefore miles away from the sugary, fruity object of desire of male Western and local fantasy.

In contrast with Depestre, who declared lovemaking the antidote to hunger, Vieux-Chauvet presents sexual desire as a devouring act:

> My door is double-locked and I keep a key in my pocket. I do not let anyone in. . . . Still, just in case, I have hidden under my bed the romance novels I devour and the pornographic postcards sold to me one night. . . . There is no such thing as purity, and the needs of the flesh are normal. Can anyone live without eating or drinking? I twist on my bed, prey to desires that nothing slakes. . . . When [Felicia and Jean Luze] leave the bedroom, I go and touch, I smell the sheets on which they made love, starving for this smell of seaweed mixed with male sweat, which must be the smell of sperm and which blends with Felicia's bland perfume. (*Amour,* 10–11)

The vagina is metaphorically presented as a starving mouth ("this starving sex"). The ravenous pleasure-seeking woman devours pornographic postcards. Vieux-Chauvet's association between sexual hunger and hunger for food goes beyond the Freudian anatomical coincidence of oral and sexual pleasure located in the mouth and, more generally, beyond the metaphorical.[28] Sex is as essential as food to life sustainability. By associating the question: "Can anyone live without eating or drinking?" with the need for sexual relations, Vieux-Chauvet makes a compelling political claim that to deny Haitian women the right to sexuality and eroticism is to challenge their basic survival. Sex is not a luxury, it is a staple, it is hunger. Vieux-Chauvet also powerfully responds to the images of deviant sexuality discussed above by insisting on the normality of sexual need (not desire).

However, while Vieux-Chauvet's intervention is revolutionary in its audacity and courage, we can only wonder about its impact. Claire's words are shared with her readers. However, we can't help but notice the references to locks and enclosures inscribed in the scene. The door is locked twice and the key is safely kept close to Claire's body. And indeed, when is Claire—and Vieux-Chauvet—heard and by whom? As Chancy indicates, Vieux-Chauvet was ill received by contemporary Haitian intellectuals, who criticized her for making "little or no use of Haitian creole" and for having a French mind-set (Chancy, *Searching,* 169). Her portrayal of Haitian society was dismissed as "utopian" (169). Because of Vieux-Chauvet's criticism of the American occupation, and of various dictatorships, including the Duvalier régime (1957–87), her family, who had remained in Haiti, bought back "all remaining copies of *Amour* from the French publishers" (169) in fear of retaliation. For several decades, Vieux-Chauvet's trilogy was circulating undercover in the form of rare saved copies of the book and illicit photocopies until the editors Maisonneuve et Larose/Emina Soleil republished the trilogy, *Amour, Colère, Folie,* in 2005.[29] An English translation was soon to follow the publication of this monumental work in 2009.[30] *Amour* was therefore locked up, like Claire, like her sexuality, for many years before seeing the sun. Despite this silencing, Claire's scream cleared a space for the expression of female and male sexuality on the literary front, which Pineau and Laferrière turn inside out.

Roughly two decades after the original publication of *Amour*, Laferrière and Pineau express Caribbean sexuality loud and clear. Dany Laferrière, born in Port-au-Prince in 1953, left Haiti for Miami in 1976 and later moved to Montreal. Gisèle Pineau was born in a suburb of Paris in 1956 to Guadeloupean parents and spent several years in Guadeloupe and Martinique during her childhood and adult years. Thus both Pineau and Laferrière write from North American or European metropolises, away from their country of origin. However, both travel back and forth between their various homes, and both write texts that deal with France, Quebec, Guadeloupe, Haiti, and spaces in between. Laferrière calls this transnational space "l'Amérique"; Pineau calls it "the World." Both writers stand out for their use of sexual provocation or evocation, even if Laferrière's has a more pronounced tendency for the scandalous. Laferrière and Pineau use sexuality to disarm specific imposed sexual images such as those of the "satyr" and "Jezebel."

While Pineau and Laferrière broach sexuality in a variety of ways in their other novels, I have isolated two texts that represent a particularly interesting case of reclaiming the sexual space: the fake pornographic novel. Pornography is the depiction of explicit sexual subject matter for the purposes of sexual excitement. Pineau and Laferrière, while they depict explicit sexual acts involving graphic descriptions of male and female genitals reminiscent of hard-core pornography, do not fulfill the pornographic purpose of sexual excitement. Or else, they mix sexual excitement with a discourse on the history and politics of the black body. In other words, they entrap the readers through sex, swallow them up in sex to give them a taste of the oppression of black bodies instead of the anticipated pleasure. When the reader expects sexual satisfaction, he—or she—gets a moral history lesson instead. Like the mucilage, bright colors, inviting cupules of the carnivorous flower, the exterior signs of the book immediately perceptible to the buyer's eye—the title, the back cover, the cover art, the first paragraphs—are used to eat up the one who was about to eat them.

We could say that the exhibition of the book with the exaggeration of its most external features repeats the colonial act of exhibiting black women's bodies by externalizing, hypertrophying, and exhibiting its sexual features.[31] Sander Gilman discusses the case of Sarah Baartman,[32] whose cut genitalia were exhibited at the Musée de l'Homme in Paris, as the most famous—and infamous—example of this exteriorization of the intimate: "According to Cuvier, the black female looks different. Her physiognomy, her skin color, the form of her genitalia label her as inherently different. In the nineteenth century, the black female was widely perceived as possessing not only a 'primitive' sexual appetite but also the external signs of this temperament—'primitive' genitalia" (Gilman, 213). Laferrière's and Pineau's gestures of externalizing the genitals and selling them in the cultural marketplace reiterate the methods of the exploitative and degrading colonial gesture. If their books are genitalized objects on display in the marketplace of French, Canadian, or American major publishers like Gallimard, their function is not to satisfy the public's voyeurism, but instead to disarm it. Their mechanism, as opposed to Baartman's severed organs left without context and interiority, lead the reader to see their own interiority, and to face their political responsibility. Laferrière tells its captive audience: "If it's porn you were looking for," you came to the wrong place (*Comment faire,* 46).

We could find an equivalent to this movement of entrapment in the sexual "teeth" of the title and the paratext in the world of criticism, for instance, in bell hooks's chapter on the commodification of black women's sexual organs and sexuality in the United States entitled "Selling Hot Pussy: Representations of Black Female Sexuality in the

Cultural Marketplace" (*Black Looks,* 61–77). Like Pineau and Laferrière, hooks externalizes in the title the most immediately visible and epidermal part of the book, the most stereotypical representations of black sexuality, more precisely, its genitalia. This gesture, like Laferrière's and Pineau's, is a double-edged sword. On the one hand, Pineau, Laferrière, and hooks clearly reclaim the most dehumanizing and racist stereotypes to appropriate them in their texts and therefore to disarm them, in a use similar to the reclaiming and revalorization of other racist or chauvinistic slurs. On the other hand, by playing with fire, they put themselves at risk of perpetuating these stereotypes, making them circulate in the "Cultural Marketplace" once more, and of falling into their own trap. The carnivorous plant at the origin of the game of entrapment ultimately dies from opening up too many times. The success or failures of these traps depend on which eyes and hands the books fall into.

Vulnerable Super-Males

Laferrière's *Comment faire* was published in 1985. Its protagonist, a black man nicknamed or named Vieux,[33] spends most of his time writing a novel in his seedy Montreal apartment with his black roommate Bouba, who mostly sleeps and reads Freud, Nietzsche, and an incomplete dictionary on his filthy sofa. The main plot revolves around a cataloguing of the protagonist's young, white, Anglophone, McGill-educated conquests, all sarcastically nicknamed after a salient feature (Miz Literature, Miz Sophisticated Lady, Miz Cat, etc.). Another plot revolves around eating and cannibalism, and yet another on reading and writing. Vieux himself writes a novel entitled "Paradis du Dragueur Nègre" [Nigger Cruiser's Heaven], which is obviously reminiscent of Harlem Renaissance patron Carl Van Vechten's controversial 1926 *Nigger Heaven.*[34]

As Jana Evans Braziel has shown in her book *Artists, Performers, and Black Masculinities in the Haitian Diaspora,* Laferrière's novel enters into a richly woven dialogue with writers from the Harlem Renaissance, and more generally with African American intellectuals and musicians who have reflected on black masculinity. Another striking connection is the quasi-simultaneity of the publication of Laferrière's first novel with Spike Lee's first full-length feature movie, *She's Gotta Have It* (1986). Like Lee, Laferrière attempts to pull black sexuality out of the closet, albeit in a different style and with a different focus.

Lee's film focuses on the sexual life of Nola Darling, an African American woman who entertains a sustained and simultaneous sexual/love/friendship relationship with three African American men. Although Nola would be thought promiscuous, her African American female psychiatrist considers her a "very healthy human being." Like Laferrière, Lee puts in the foreground an externally constructed image, that of the black polygamous nymphomaniac, and reinserts her in a discourse of normality.[35] However, in contrast with Laferrière, white sexual partners are excluded from the equation,[36] and the focus is put on the African American female, a player entirely absent from Laferrière's novel.[37] Laferrière, as opposed to Lee, seems stuck in the Fanonian white/black dialectics of sexuality.

Before scrutinizing the "insides" of *Comment faire,* it is helpful to follow the external path that would lead a reader to read the book, since Laferrière targets the reader precisely through these most external signs of marketing and book design. As Braziel has shown, Laferrière's novel caused scandals in Montreal, Paris, and New York, misunderstood as a first-degree treatise buying into the stereotype of the black man as a hypersexual being.[38] While some of the novel's passages are clearly ironic, it is also complicit in repeating pornographic mechanisms to please the erotic-thirsty reader. The line, therefore, between using sex to sell and increasing the reader's consciousness about sexual exploitation is a fine one.

A search on Amazon.fr placed *Comment faire l'amour avec un nègre sans se fatiguer* among the following titles: *Comment faire son pain, Comment faire l'amour toute la nuit, Comment faire l'amour à un homme, Comment faire l'amour à une femme.* The book thus gains visibility among "how to . . ." self-help guides, from the innocent "making one's own bread" to the less innocuous guides that define the sexual act as performance ("making love all night"), or the partner in the act in a perfect symmetry: a man or a woman (the guides are geared toward a heterosexual public). Laferrière's title, however, troubles from the outset the predictable self-help category of the Amazon list. In *Comment faire l'amour avec un Nègre,* the title's racial slur destabilizes the quiet heterodox self-help category. While the word "nègre" was translated as "negro" in the American English version,[39] the French word also refers to the more violent racial slur.[40] The American title lost its second part in the 1987 translation. This severing could be read as an interesting act of literary castration, so to speak. "Sans se fatiguer," "without getting tired," or "effortlessly," first adds an aspect of derision to the first part of the title, then absolves the targeted buyer from doing any work in the sexual act: a passive spectator in a comfortable movie theater seat.

Amazon readers' reviews are revealing about how the sexual trap functions. The following comments are representative of two diametrically opposed ways readers have received the text. An anonymous dissatisfied client gives it two stars out of five. She titles her review "C'est dommage," "It's too bad!": "Yep! It's too bad [c'est dommage]! When I read the book, I couldn't see what the content had to do with the title. *How to make love to a Negro Without Getting Tired* was a promising title. It's well written, full of successful images, in a style proper to our Afro-Caribbean authors. Yet, a little something was missing. A little something that could have made a big difference. What's more, the ending disappointed me, too abrupt. It's too bad!"[41] First of all, it is helpful to situate the anonymous reader. She seems to be a woman since she added the feminine "e" in the past participle "demandée." Her ethnic or racial identity is harder to pinpoint. She does use the term "Afro-Caribbean writers" "nos auteurs afro-caribéens," which shows a certain, if somewhat dated, "diaspora literacy." The most troubling detail, though, is the use of the appropriating possessive adjective "nos." If the reader is herself a member of the African diaspora, it is understandable that she would use the pronoun as a sign of common identification. However, if she is white and French, her possessive incorporation would appear as a neocolonial gesture submitting the "Afro-Caribbean" text to a submissive position in the white readership's hands. The reader's disappointment is great. She repeats the word "dommage" (too bad!) no less than three times. Her frustration lies in the discrepancy between the title and its content. The book is thus declared a teaser. Here the removed object of consumption is clearly sexual pleasure and, more specifically, the male sexual organ. The statement "a little something was missing . . . that could have made a big difference" is almost too stereotypical to believe.

At the other end of the spectrum, another customer, this time satisfied (four out of five stars), and this time named Eric Marmet alias "Bluesbeauty," sees beyond the sexual trap and reads Laferrière's novel as a serious political artifact: "*How to Make love to a Black Person of Color Without Getting Tired* targets racial clichés and prejudice with an exquisite ferocity and leaves a powerful after-taste of the US Civil

Rights uprisings of the 60's and 70's. Dany Laferrière, armed with his Remington 22, shot first. Target reached." First, note the respectful purging of Laferrière's title by the substitution of "nègre" by "black person of color." Marmet's reading continues this purging by stripping the text of its sexualized content and by reading it as a literary weapon: "Dany Laferrière shot first."

The interest of Laferrière's novel lies precisely in that it oscillates between these two readings, and that the targeted reader is never clearly the woman in search of sexual thrills, or the politically conscious activist reducing the text to its political function, since, for Laferrière, one is clearly enmeshed with the other: "fucking" equals "historical reparation" (*Comment faire,* 19).

The potential reader is explicitly addressed both by the author of *Comment faire* and by its protagonist. The author responds to the reader in quest of erotic satisfaction in the explicit following manner: "All the readers who expected to learn something about Miz Literature's sexual habits can go home. There's plenty of porn books out there" (*Comment faire,* 46) thus denies the classification of his novel as pornography. The answer is not as clear-cut as Laferrière claims it to be since some passages do offer the reader the contemplation and enjoyment of pornographic scenes. However, Laferrière is right in claiming that his book is not a "porn book" per se. It both fails to satisfy the eroticism-seeking reader and offers more than sexual arousal by entangling the politics of black sexuality with historical racial violence.

Laferrière's character responds to anticipated readerly criticism of his own novel by explicitly addressing the complicity of the author with the circulation of sexual stereotypes of black men in the cultural marketplace. While daydreaming of literary success, Vieux imagines a conversation between himself and a journalist in a Q. & A. session:

> "How have Blacks reacted to your book?"
>
> "They want to lynch me."
>
> "Why is that?"
>
> "Because . . . they say I've sold out, that I'm playing the white man's game . . . that my book is worthless and that it was published for the sole reason that whites need a Negro to make faces and to give them a clear conscience." (*Comment faire,* 163)

The author within the text is therefore seen as the black man willing to play the white "game" of reducing the "negro" to a palatable and comic jester who amuses the gallery ("to make faces"). By representing himself as a degraded, yet happy, human being, he absolves and justifies his oppressors' crimes. The affirmation that other "blacks" want to "lynch" him is surprising. The historically specific white form of violence becomes attributed to black men who become the torturers of their own "brother." The daydreamer entraps himself and black people in an inescapable circuit of violence in which the game has only changed the color of its pawns.

And indeed, in the epigraph directly following the title, Laferrière situates his novel outside the "fun" game of sexual entrapment, and deep into the juridical violence in which the enslaved were entrapped, by citing an article from the 1685 Code noir: "'Le nègre est un meuble.' Code Noir, art. 1, 1685" (9).[42] Three hundred years after the Black Code, Laferrière claims that the "nègre" is still a "bien meuble," a "movable asset," a commodity, a disposable object who is owned and does not own himself.

As Braziel has convincingly shown, Laferrière's text enters a rich dialogic relationship with Frantz Fanon's *Black Skin, White Masks,*[43] particularly as it refers to the entrapment of the black man in an overdetermining image of white-created masculinity. Laferrière's novel presents the complex relationship not so much between black men and white women, I would argue, but, more important, between the black man, or simply the man, and the negro. Laferrière claims, we will recall, "As a Black man, I don't have enough distance from the Negro." *Comment faire* is first of all about the dissolution of masculinity, and of humanity, under the overpowering image of the "nègre."

The situation Laferrière describes, that of a black man copulating with and occasionally making love to white women, repeats the angst of the black man who can only become legitimized as a respectable object of love if his "blackness" is denied. In his chapter "L'homme de couleur et la Blanche" (*Black Skin,* 51–66), Fanon focuses on the French Guyanese writer René Maran's character Jean Veneuse, a black man in reciprocal love with a white woman. Veneuse seeks the white woman's brother's legitimization of their union. The white brother responds that his race is not a problem because, "You have nothing in common with a real Negro. You are not black; you are 'very, very dark' [excessivement brun]" (50). Thus the black man has to sacrifice his blackness in order to enter into a loving relationship sanctified by marriage and to exit the act of fornication. The same hunger for love and tenderness is sometimes found, always limited to brief moments, in Laferrière's novel: "I take a nap right there. I'm her kid. . . . Her negro kid. She touches my forehead with gentle strokes. Happy, sweet, fragile moments. I am not just a Negro. She is not just a white woman" (*Comment faire,* 46). The sexual relationship becomes imbued with tenderness only if the frock of race is left behind.

In the scene above, the term "kid" introduces tenderness in the previously strictly sexual relationship. In addition, and in a more problematic gesture, it presents the moment as a scene of adoption in which the black man finds himself mothered again,[44] here by a young white woman.[45] Miz Literature, the adoptive mother, is a white woman, a situation that excludes the adult black woman from the family relation. The maternal endearments repeat on the private sphere global and national representations of France as the surrogate mother to an absent black mother.[46] Additionally, he is mothered by a very young woman, and thus infantilized.

Miz Literature is herself turned into a baby because of her powdery smell: "Whites tend to forget that they too smell. Most of the McGill girls smell like Johnson's baby powder. . . . As for me, I can't help to tickle-tickle her" (27). This description appears as a potent retort to the age-old association of smell to the "negro" and, more significant, to the classification, exposed by Fanon, of the "Negro" as occupying the "negative" pole of the positive-neutral-negative model of humanity, the white man occupying both the neutral and positive. Here whiteness becomes marked as other than neutral. The scheme is disarmed. There is no more neutrality, only marked white and black bodies. Through this humoristic description, in sharp contrast with the crude descriptions of the sexual intercourse of the two protagonists, the narrator infantilizes the white Anglo-Saxon Judeo-Christian woman.[47] Her sexual appeal, and the protagonist's own sexual edge, vanishes under the infantile tickling game. Yet it is this cute pink baby who mothers, albeit briefly, the protagonist. The erasure of racial difference ultimately fails since the man doesn't simply become her child but her "negro kid." This moment of desexualized—albeit problematic—tender love is short-lived. Miz Literature's motherly tenderness is quickly followed by a re-erotization of the moment: "Miz Literature glances surreptitiously at my penis." The adverb "surreptitiously"—etymologically a theft from below—reintroduces the illicit, the perverse, and the fraudulent in the gaze. The man, the tender child, disappears under the blinding metonymy of his racialized sexual organ.

The protagonist's sexual relations are inextricable from the politicization of the sexual act Fanon described in 1952. Quoting Veneuse's words, Fanon portrays black-and-white love as playing on the terrain of political revenge: "And so I wonder whether . . . I won't look as though I'm stating that not only do I despise women of my own race, but drawn by the desire for white flesh that has been off limits to us blacks since the white man rules the world, I am unconsciously endeavoring to take my revenge on the European female for everything her ancestors have inflicted on my people throughout the centuries" (*Black Skin*, 51). Veneuse's statement compellingly enmeshes the individual and the collective, and the sexual and the historical. The interracial amorous relationship is always bellicose, Veneuse implies. Such an invasion of the private, the tender, and the amorous by political violence abounds in Laferrière's novel: "I want to fuck her subconscious . . . fuck her identity. Force the racial debate into the guts" (*Comment faire,* 81), "What's an innocent pick-up line in relation to the slave trade?'" (57).

Moreover, in Fanon, via Veneuse, via Maran, the black man's sexual desire for the white woman is always constructed as transgressive, and, more particularly, enmeshed with the taboo of anthropophagy as demonstrated by the expression "the desire of white flesh," which conflates sexual drive with cannibalistic desire.

Disarming Cannibals

Sex, the main plot of *Comment faire,* shares the stage with the no less significant plot of food. Laferrière's readers are forced into a position of voyeurism, forced to watch the grotesque constructions of the hypermasculine and allegedly cannibal black man, while also witnessing the absurdity, demise, and racism of these representations.[48] Eating and sexuality become tangled in the novel's portrayal of politics and pornography. The chapter titles, providing a sort of menu to the book, mix references to eating with pornographic evocations: "The Negro Belongs to the Vegetable Kingdom" (25), "Humane Cannibalism" (29), "And Now Miz Literature gives me some Blow Job" (45), "Like a Flower at the tip of my Negro Cock" (77), "The First Vegetarian Negro" (147), "The Black Penis and the Demoralization of the West" (131), "My old Remington Reaches Bliss While Whistling *ya bon banania*" (153), or "Negroes are Thirsty" (165). The humane (vegetarianism) is mixed with the bestial (cannibalism), the vulgar (pornography), the bucolic (botany), the sophomoric (sexuality), and the political (intellectual history).

In a dialogue he establishes with Fanon's "The Lived Experience of the Black Man," Laferrière intermingles the two degrading stereotypes of the rapist and the cannibal. In Fanon's famous "primal" scene, we will recall, the black man who enters the "world"—read the "white world"—is confronted by the gaze of a child who expresses terror toward him. While clinging to his mother's arm, he cries out: "*Maman,* look, a Negro; I'm scared!" (*Black Skin,* 91). A page later, Fanon interweaves the white boy's inner thoughts with those of the black man: "Look, a Negro; the Negro is trembling, the Negro is trembling because he's cold, the cold that chills the bones, the lovely little boy is trembling because he thinks the Negro is trembling with rage, the little white boy runs to his mother's arms: '*Maman*, the Negro's going to eat me" (93). This emotionally charged passage introduces a violent plurivocality in which two conflicting voices nevertheless intermingle into one voice without any distinctive mark of the origin of each perception. The assault of these schizophrenic voices turns the black man, the object of the gaze, and turns his own subjectivity, into passive recipients of voices that speak to him from the outside. The bodily manifestation of trembling is interpreted in two radically incompatible ways. The rational interpretation, which would read the shivering as a physiological reaction to cold, is immediately dismissed by the emotional interpretation of trembling as anger, an anger that immediately leads to the fear of cannibalism. The trembling, however, is shared by both watched and watcher, linking the child and the image he fears in one violent continuum.

In a passage clearly citing the Fanonian moment, Laferrière shifts the focus from the dominant stereotype of the cannibal to that of the rapist: "Go back to the bush, li'l negro. And harakiri yourself you know where. Look mommy, says the young White girl. Look at the cut Negro. A good Negro, her father replies, is a Negro without balls" (17). Laferrière shifts from the fear of cannibalism to that of the sexually threatening male, who is sent "back" to his imagined origin, the place of savagery of the "bush," to go castrate himself. The words of Fanon's white boy—"the Negro's going to eat me"—become, in the mouth of Laferrière's white girl: "Look at the cut Negro." The two images, while seemingly different, arrive at the same result. A man viewed as cannibal is a castrated man, amputated of his humanity, an object, to use Fanon's terms, circulating among other objects. It is no surprise that the cannibal in "The Lived Experience" appears directly after the evocation of the commercial of the popular French chocolate drink consumed by white children such as the terrorized white boy. The Banania figure, we will recall, is the tamed cannibal. Not the one who eats, but the one who is repeatedly eaten, with eyes, mouth, nose, and skin turned into edible substances such as bananas and chocolate. The Banania figure is to the cannibal the analogical equivalent of what the castrated man is to the rapist. The rapist becomes castrated, and ultimately raped; the eater becomes eaten. Therefore, Laferrière's scene is a direct continuation of Fanon's. Interestingly, though, Laferrière substitutes Fanon's white boy who finds solace in his mother's arms with a white girl still at her mother's arm, but with the addition of the father's maximlike verdict: "A good Negro . . . is a Negro without balls." Castration and *bananiazation* are both direct consequences of the same white fear. In white racist fantasies, both the act of cannibalism and rape lead to the fear of annihilation of the white man: the first by swallowing him up, the second by "contaminating" his progeny through the rape of white girls and women. Cannibalism and miscegenation thus lead to the same fear of disappearing whiteness.

Beyond the analogical relationship between the dyads rapist/castrated and cannibal/Banania, sexual intercourse and ingestion are metaphorically related. Jacqueline Couti argues that the two acts are confused in Caribbean contexts where the same word is used to describe both: "Mwen ké mangéw" [I'm going to eat you] can also mean "mwen ké koupéw" [I'm going to fuck you] (Couti, 222). Couti explains that the verb "couper," "to cut" in Creole, also means "to fuck." If we follow that lexical association, then, for Laferrière, "un nègre coupé" is also a "fucked" black man: not the sexual aggressor he so emphatically appears to be throughout the novel but a sexual prey.

In Laferrière's novel, food and sexuality are similarly linked as they originate and reside in the same organ, as Freud and Melanie Klein have taught us. Laferrière is clearly aware of Freudian theories. He himself points us in the Freudian direction, if ironically so. Freud occupies a significant place in Laferrière's novel, since the protagonist's roommate Bouba crowds the tiny apartment with his twenty-four-volume complete works. Freudian psychoanalysis is thus an imposing presence at least in the physical space (if not in the psyche) of the novel. In short, Freud takes up space.

However, in contrast with the fusion of mother-child mixing pleasure of food and sexual pleasure, the sexual acts in Laferrière's novel lead, for the most part, to interruption and violence. The mouth and genitals are not sites of bonding but tools of harm. The protagonist precisely reconciles with an image of a sane eater after undermining the image of the cannibal. It is through a practice of a "cannibalisme à visage humain," as one of the chapter titles ironically indicates, that the protagonist regains his virility and, ultimately, his humanity.

Fanon's black man sitting in a French café censures and controls each of his gestures, gestures as simple as the lighting of a cigarette, protecting himself against the "definitive structuring of my self and the world" (*Black Skin,* 91), that is, against the overdetermination of each of his gestures by the white gaze. No action is perhaps more under scrutiny than that of a black man eating. The image of the cannibal and that of its consequential tamed counterpart, the Banania man, are the two main culinary poles that structure the "epidermal racial schema" (92) of the black man. The menacing cannibal and the ridiculed Senegalese soldier of "Y'a Bon Banania" bookmark Fanon's reflection on his "overdetermination from the outside" as well as Laferrière's.

The image of the cannibal is omnipresent in the roommates' conversations. What could have been a peaceful domestic scene—Miz Literature having just finished cleaning up around the apartment and putting away the dishes—turns into the gruesome fantasy of cannibalism. The narrator's daily life is invaded, predetermined, and structured by the "legends, stories, history . . . historicity" (*Black Skin,* 92) always lurking around his image. The narrator imagines the following scene, through the eyes of the Montreal daily *La Presse:*

> What if we ate her right here, one bite, yum-yum, with salt-and-pepper. I can already see the headlines in *La Presse.*
>
> IT IS THE TALK OF THE TOWN
>
> "Did you see that! A McGill student eaten up by two Negroes."
>
> "How do we know this?"
>
> "The police found an arm in the refrigerator."
>
> "Oh God! This is what immigration policy is all about now! Importing cannibals."
>
> "Did they rape her as well . . . ?"
>
> "We can't tell ma'am, they ate her up." (*Comment faire,* 44)[49]

I should first underline the comedic undertones of the scene, replete with gross exaggerations and onomatopoeia ("yum-yum"), which spice up the barbaric act with a civilizing culinary touch (salt and pepper). Laferrière's humor and sarcasm undermine the lurking cannibal image while at the same time crumbling under its weight. However, the evocation succeeds in demonstrating the lack of logic in drawing hasty conclusions about cannibalism. The remaining limb, evidently, does not forensically prove the act of consumption. The body could have simply been cut into pieces. This contemporary scene evokes centuries of accusations of unobserved cannibalism. As Peter Hulme explains, while not denying the existence of cannibalism, so-called cannibal scenes observed by Western travelers and anthropologists are often "bereft of actual cannibals: the primal scene of 'cannibalism' as 'witnessed' by Westerners is of its aftermath rather than its performance. At the center of the scene is the large cooking pot, essential utensil for cannibal illustrations; and surrounding it is the 'evidence' of cannibalism: the discarded human bones" (Hulme, 2). Therefore, the accusation of cannibalism is a crime proven not by evidence or witnesses, but by a fallacious association between cannibalism and race or ethnicity. We could call this a form of situational cannibalism in which blackness would serve as sufficient proof of the barbaric act.

Race becomes itself a cannibalizing signifier under which all other particularities are swallowed up. The socioeconomic, cultural, and political status of the roommates vanishes under this omnivorous signifier. The immigration status of the men, which should be the focus of the newspaper reporting on daily events, becomes invaded by centuries of legends that become an all-consuming reality. In brief, the politics of immigration consists of importing cannibals.

It is one matter when the popular press, guided by sensationalism, leads itself to such absurd associations. It is another when the highly educated McGill women buy into such fears. It is yet another matter when public rumor invades the intimate sphere of the bedroom. Miz Literature, probably the protagonist's most kindred of spirits, in spite of her literary culture and her kindness, voices one of the most hurtful comments retold here by the narrator: "It moves her to see me eat. Miz Literature is quite a thing. She was trained to believe everything she hears. It's part of her culture. . . . She is moved. If I tell her that I eat human flesh, that my desire to eat white flesh is programmed in my genes somewhere, that her hips haunt my dreams, her breasts, her thighs . . . I can tell her all that and she'll believe me" (*Comment faire,* 31).

The black man is once more overdetermined from the outside, under the surveillance, however well meaning, of the white woman's gaze. The striking fact is precisely the "moving" character of watching the intimate Other eat, which would be the equivalent of the emotion of seeing a wild animal, a faun, a lion, tamed enough to eat out of a little girl's hand. Through this soft-heartedness, the protagonist is turned into a tamed animal, which leads him automatically to see himself as the beast he is in the eyes of his sexual partner: the cannibal. In this inescapable dialectic, the white woman becomes the prey of the beast, her body parts turned into the prey's edible meal, sexual desire turned into the need to devour the other, the metaphorical forced back into the realm of the literal. Both are equally entrapped in this lion's den, the man because of his "race," the woman because of her "culture."

The use of the grotesque, which consists of pushing the image of the cannibal to its absurd extremity, provides an efficient strategy of escape. When the protagonist visits another of his conquests' upper-crust apartment, he recirculates the image of the cannibal to which he was subjected in the first place. After Miz Cat, named after her love for the eponymous pet, comes back from her shower, perhaps a ritualistic cleansing act before offering her body to the cannibalistic god, the man provokes her with the following: "You know, back home, we eat cats. . . . Not me of course. Too late, that was it" (139). The narrator's revelation is a definite turnoff for the erotic atmosphere.

For the purpose of undermining his revelation, we could question the phrase "chez moi" [back home]. Where is "chez moi"? What is this rootless immigrant's country? Home? Mother? Although the word "novel" is written under the title, *Comment faire* has often been read as an autobiography.[50] And although it contains certain autobiographical components (the exile of a black writer in Montreal), Braziel's term "alterbiography" is preferable. Indeed, we know nothing about the country of origin, ethnicity, family, or mother of the protagonist. In no place does he refer to himself as Haitian. When a homeless man asks him to point to his home on a map of Africa he happened to be carrying in his pocket, the protagonist points to the first country he spots out: "Ivory Coast. Look, it's right there" (128). The protagonist is thus detached from ethnic or national origin, interchangeable, assignable to any "Black" part of the world precisely because he is not an individual being situated in a specific geography and history but instead, he is a stereotypical image: "un nègre." Thus the claim "back home, we eat cats" is a ludicrous statement. Miz Cat, who believes him, is horrified at the idea of this near cannibalism. Eating pets in a culture where pets are members of the family is, after all, a form of cannibalism or "eating one's own kind." Significantly, though, the thought of the protagonist eating cats disturbs her more than the thought of him eating humans: "If I had told her that I thought human flesh was quite refined . . . she would have thought me acceptable. . . . But cats, it's another matter altogether" (140). Eating human flesh is thus more acceptable, in Miz Chat's imagination—itself imagined by the black man—because it is included in his "epidermal racial schema" (Fanon, 92). Eating pets is not planned in the serialized model of the black man.

We could also note that the act of "eating pets" introduces another popular urban myth: that of Asians consuming cats and dogs. The "racial schemes" of the McGill-educated woman and her categorization of (sub)humanity are disturbed by the cat-eating references. It is not what she ordered.[51] By its implicit association with Asian men via the street legend of cat-eating, the former predator also loses his hyper-virility. Indeed, Asian men, as Jeffrey Lesser has shown, occupy a position of undervirility on the sexual scale of racial stereotyping.[52] On the same line of thinking, the vegetarian "Negro" also upsets established racial categories. In the middle of the night, Miz Sophisticated Lady wakes up horrified by the sight of her lover's roommate Bouba devouring "a head of . . . . . . lettuce" (ellipsis in original, 85). Cannibals are no longer what they used to be. Black men turned vegetarians or even herbivores lose all virile power, undermine their power as super-males, and trouble deeply set white epistemological categories.

A similar critique of the category of the cannibal as it relates to blackness, whiteness, and power is eloquently expressed in Haitian American filmmaker Michelange Quay's *Mange, Ceci est mon corps [Eat, for This Is My Body].* In Quay's 2007 allegorical film about race, hunger, and cannibalism, an elderly white woman lying in the bed of a colonial house regurgitates a disturbing monologue. The viewer, intimately connected through the extreme cinematic close-up to the speaker's face, becomes engulfed in the speech as well as in the metaphor of consumption:

> My beloved and reluctant children, they take, they take . . . they cut my bones to turn them into coal . . . they spit on me . . . they turned my body into a desert. Forgive them, for they know not what they do. Forgive them for they are hungry, so hungry. . . Who am I? Who am I? . . . I am this island and I am its people. I am food . . . I am the food eater . . . Come with me and

> eat me . . . Eat, for this is my body . . . eat, cannibals, savages, prognathous, pygmies, eat 'til your swollen bellies burst. (00:17–00:21, my translation)

In this vignette, and in the film overall, Quay, like Laferrière, takes in the spectators with the promise of a meaning they do not get, to offer them instead something other than their initial expectation. The sacredness of the eucharistic script leads to utter profanity with the racial slurs associated with blackness and cannibalism. The woman who lies dying quickly moves from the position of the colonial mother victim of the ungrateful children she fed to that of the Haitian land itself, destroyed by the ravages of colonialism and exploitation. What makes the scene so disturbing is that the woman's body is both things at once: allegory of the colonial or neocolonial power *and* exploited land; food eater and food, cannibal and cannibalized. At the very moment the white woman accuses her putative enemy children of cannibalism, she is herself revealed as cannibal by the very position she occupies: a woman living in a colonial house on a devastated, eaten-up island with its very starved people.

In the novel, the "decannibalization" of the black man is also logically accompanied by the "cannibalization" of the White Anglo-Saxon Judeo-Christian woman, which happens in a double movement of slippage. The attribute of the cannibal thus experiences a double displacement. First, it migrates from the black man to the white woman, who becomes the cannibal. Second, the site of cannibalism moves from the mouth to the devouring or castrating vagina. The black man therefore exits both the image of the rapist and that of the cannibal, to become the vulnerable prey of the castrating white woman. The initially subservient Miz Literature, washing dishes, bringing carrots and cheese and literary conversations to the roommates, in short, the good domestic white girl, claims the position of the predator in the sexual act: "and she dives in, mouth wide open, onto my penis like a piranha . . . she rides me. We're miles away from the innocent, naïve, vegetarian fucks to which she's used. It's a carnivorous fuck" (50). The pink-white mouth and the pink-white vagina become the bestialized and teethed sites of ingestion and of carnivorous, cannibalistic sex.[53] For Miz Sophisticated as well, the vagina, instead of being the site of rape and violence ("you've got to penetrate her violently, almost to the blood," 80), becomes the active, carnivorous mouth that turns the black man into a vulnerable, trembling being: "I wouldn't have expected the small voracious insatiable beast nested in the depth of her vagina. I feel my legs trembling, my neck stiffening" (80). The vagina here becomes insatiable, and the former cannibal the trembling, suffering prey. The use of "Miz" to introduce all of the protagonists' white lovers certainly plays into the slave rhetoric in which slaves and servants call their mistress or their master's wives by the same prefix. The sex scene set in late twentieth-century Montreal thereby carries the weight of plantation sexuality.

This role reversal, however, does not constitute an exit to the violent eating/copulating relationship between the white woman and the black man. The two players are still entrapped in a sexual scene enmeshed within a history of raced violence and suffering. What I call Laferrière's rhetoric of deferral seems like a more helpful strategy to avoid these stereotypical and historical entrapments. I began this chapter with the idea that Laferrière and Pineau use the genre of fake pornography to trick their readers into seeing a history of the oppression of black bodies. In the case of Laferrière's text, the adjective "fake" could be questioned because some passages of the novel offer a textbook illustration of the pornographic genre—the depiction of explicit sexual subject matter for the purposes of sexual excitement. While Pineau's text dissociates the depiction of the sexual act with its function—the sexual voyeurism of the reader is never satisfied—Laferrière's novel clearly accomplishes that function. The following passage, for instance, feeds the erotic-thirsty reader what she or he wants: "You've got to fuck her viciously. She gladly gets on all four, I take her gently. At my own pace . . . I take her from behind and she roars . . . I take her to the bed . . . holding her, so to speak, at the tip of my cock. Like a flower at the tip of my negro cock" (*Comment faire,* 80). The passage represents a sexual act in the most banal of heterosexually coded norms: the agency and power of the male ("at my own pace"), the submission and animalization of the woman "on all four," and the crude macho vocabulary. However, the last sentence is troubling. It introduces an aestheticized object, the flower, into an animalistic pornographic scene. It also introduces the racialization of the sexual organ ("my negro cock"). The erect penis replaces the body, becomes the body, in a cannibalistic metonymy that eclipses the black man behind his raced sexual organ. In a parallel gesture, the woman's body vanishes under the metaphor of the flower. The scene has slipped from a literal crude description of the sexual act to a poetic image involving an interplay between metonymy and metaphor, as well as an ironic juxtaposition of bucolic imagery with racial and sexual violence.

The purpose of the description goes beyond sexual arousal and satisfaction with the insertion of both the political and the aesthetic at its center. Such is the case for all the erotic scenes in the text, which are subjected to this constant interruption destabilizing the reader seeking sexual arousal. Once again, it is not exactly what she or he had ordered. The promised pornography has been replaced by lessons in culture, literature, and history. Just to give a few examples from a selection that would be too long to list, sexual acts are interrupted by passages from the Quran (47), by allusions to Immanuel Kant as a pornographer ("Kant is a porn writer," 47),[54] by Billie Holiday's "Strange Fruit" playing in the background, or by diegetic interruptions when Bouba emerges from a comatose sleep on his sofa or comes home unexpectedly. One could argue that interruption is a common mechanism of pornography, such as in the classics of the genre by Marquis de Sade, whereby the reader's or viewer's desire is held spellbound by the intrusion of political musings. However, the following passage indicates a sequence of events more complicated than just the mere sexual titillation increased by interruption:

> Miz Literature gives me some blow job. . . . I don't know why—it has nothing to do with anything that's happening here—I remember a song I've heard. . . . It was about a lynching. About the Saint-Louis lynching of a young black man. They hung him and then castrated him. Why castrating him? Good God! I would love to know, I would love to be absolutely certain that the myth of the animalistic, primitive, barbaric Negro who only has sex on his mind, to be absolutely certain whether it is true or false. (49)

The pleasure received by the black man from the white woman's mouth automatically evokes lynching. Sexual pleasure leads to the fear of castration. The white woman's mouth stands metaphorically for the castrating teeth of racial violence. The private moment becomes invaded by a collective history of oppression, and particularly by the castration of black men often amputated and lynched for having only glanced at a white woman. Recall Emmett Till, among many others, lynched after allegedly whistling at a white woman. The black man's sexual pleasure is self-perceived as a transgressive act leading to the fear of lynching, in an automatic thought process in which the man loses control at a heightened moment of power in the sexual act ("it has nothing to do with anything that's happening here"). In this invasion of sexuality by history, pleasure and horror get mixed in the most confusing of ways. Not only does history invade the sexual scene, but more interestingly, the horrific history of racial violence becomes the site of sexual voyeurism. As the narrator claims, "history becomes our aphrodisiac." In the context of lynching, this provocative claim becomes painfully concrete as the staging of lynching appealed to voyeuristic titillation mirrored in pornography: the sadistic pleasure of watching dismembered bodies mixed with sexual desire.[55] In her discussion of the common act of castration in the act of lynching, Robyn Wiegman argues that "in the disciplinary fusion of castration with lynching, the [white] mob severs the black male from the masculine, interrupting the privilege of the phallus, and thereby reclaiming, through the perversity of dismemberment, his (masculine) potentiality for citizenship" (446) and, here, his potentiality for a violence-free sexuality.

In this confused conflation between the lynched dismembered black man's body and the sexual act, Laferrière's text, moving beyond the pornographic genre, becomes a historical document of suffering. Sexuality appears as the site of uttermost confusion where the borders between the "I" and the "nègre" become painfully blurred.

While Laferrière repeats strategies of the pornographic genre and pretends to give the reader what the title promised, he also feeds the reader the end of jouissance, the end of sexuality, through the haunting evocation of the lynching and castration of the black man. The erotic-seeking reader is at worst entrapped, at best disappointed. Let's recall the "It's too bad!" of the dissatisfied French Amazon commentator. However, this gesture is far from being victorious, since the protagonist, the black man, is himself entrapped in the image, demanding the truth from God: "Good God! . . . I would love to be absolutely certain." The sexual scene remains a trap both for the reader and for the protagonist as long as race invades it.

The victorious one is Vieux's finished book manuscript, evoked in the last page of the book: "Dawn has come. . . . The novel stares at me, there, on the table, next to the old Remington, in a big red folder. He is plump as a mastiff, my novel. My only chance. Come on" (*Comment faire,* 169). The only productive and hopeful relation is not sexual but textual. One escapes the trap not by conquering the white female body, but by conquering the white page. We should say, however, that the textual relation is itself highly sexual. Throughout the text, the protagonist copulates with his black Remington (which once belonged to Chester

Himes). Together, they give birth to an object, a white page marked with black letters, which appears to be the only child, and the only black-and-white child at that, in the novel. With its agency, its gaze ("he's looking at me"), its vitality (the adjective "dodu," "plump," is commonly used to describe a healthy baby), and with the bite of a mastiff, the text is ready to start life anew. The exit is thus literary, and only literary.

From Wounded Flesh to Open Eyes

Like Laferrière's novel, Pineau's *Chair Piment* (2000) is deceptive. Its opening pages, which graphically depict an avid woman's body penetrated by male sexual organs, evoke pornography. However, I argue that Pineau uses this initial titillation to entrap her readers, like her character Mina entraps men, in a story of a different kind. The first part of the novel narrates Mina's uprooted life in France as the twentieth century draws to a close, where she lives an unbridled sexual life. Mina, not unlike Vieux, is a Caribbean person of color displaced in a Western metropolis—in this case, a young woman from a fictional small town in Guadeloupe (Piment) living in the suburbs of Paris. Soon, the story of Rosalia, Mina's dead older sister, who lacked oxygen at birth and remained in the mental state of a three-year-old, punctuates Mina's Parisian story. Her sister's ghost interrupts the sexual narrative and brings into the private space of the bedroom her violent stories of raped, cursed, beaten, and orphaned female bodies. The second part of the novel recounts Mina's return to her native Guadeloupe, a quest that will provide her not with a reconnection to her familial and collective ancestry, but with another solution to heal and reconnect: Mina creates a form of transversal genealogy based on friendship and transcultural relationships, where Caribbean women become the spectators of cultural globalization instead of the objects of an exotic eroticizing discourse. Eventually, the initial sex story vanishes to make room for a narrative of platonic friendship between a white man and a black woman.

Like Laferrière's novel, the surface materiality of Pineau's book points to the erotic. The book cover of the Mercure de France edition features a photograph revealing a black woman's nape and oblique profile in a background of enflamed orange. Alternatively, the paperback edition by Folio Gallimard uses a photo of a nude black woman on a bed with a furtive gaze, legs closed yet slightly ajar. This last image invites the male reader to open the book-object as the photographed woman seems to send a sexual invitation. The book is explicitly (and falsely) marketed as an erotic text. The Folio Gallimard website advertised it as a Valentine's Day special among thirty other "aphrodisiac" titles.[56] An article on *Réseau France-outremer,* a French-Caribbean media network, warned readers that even though Pineau has previously published children's literature, "her new novel . . . is not a bedtime story!"[57] The French publisher, Mercure de France, the Folio Gallimard edition, and "Zananas,"[58] a Martinican tourist site, all quote the same exact passage to advertise it: "She would open herself up. Arch her back. . . . Ask for more. She wanted to feel them hard inside her. . . . She had to be taken, possessed. Screwed without words, by male organs. . . . She consumed sex, the hard sex of men."[59] Mina's image seems to offer a textbook example of the male fantasy of the nymphomaniac and of the white male fantasy of the black woman as insatiable temptress. The object of her desire is not her own satisfaction but instead embraces that of the male rapist: she needs to be "taken," "possessed," "pierced," without words. In the end of this composite paragraph (a compilation by Gallimard exteriorized on the back cover), the objectified, violated, silenced, raped Mina appears as mistress of the situation: "She consumed sex, the hard sex of men." In an interesting marketing twist, the consumed and discarded woman's body is portrayed as the predator: the insatiable mouth that entraps male sexual organs, that reduces men to the metonymy of their genitals, and makes them interchangeable. Their sexual organs, as well as their respective individuality, become reduced to the partitive "du sexe," like one would say "du pain," "some sex, some bread." An easy interpretation would read this passage as a woman's empowerment through sexuality. Indeed, the control of pornography reclaimed by feminist critics has been seen as a form of assertion of feminine sexual subjectivity and empowerment.[60] For instance, bell hooks has interpreted Tina Turner's hypersexual body as a transformation of the oppressed body as weapon. In other words, the formerly aggressed body becomes the aggressor and the agent: "Turner's video 'What's Love Got to Do With It?' also highlights the convergence between sexuality and power. Here, the black woman's body is represented as potential weapon . . . rather than being a pleasure-based eroticism, it is ruthless, violent; it is about women using sexual power to do violence to the male other" (*Black Looks,* 68–69).

Couti similarly reflects on female sexuality as power in Martinican literature. She elaborates on the trope of the "coucoune dentée," or "toothed vagina." In the Martinican context, the Creole expression *koupé*, "to cut," becomes synonymous with the act of copulation. The "koupeur" refers to male initiators of the sexual act. The man, then, semantically, cuts as he penetrates a woman. The female sexual organ, however, responds to the violent act by returning the threat of "cutting." Couti argues that the emphasis put on the constricting muscles of the vagina in texts such as Chamoiseau's *Texaco*, for instance, "depicts the vagina [coucoune] as a mouth that threatens the male lover with assimilation and castration" (Couti, 226). Mina's sexual scene seems to respond to this definition. The men's sexual organs become the consumed bodies and Mina the consumer. Like in Laferrière's scene of the consuming vagina, the men seem to be swallowed and threatened by castration or devouring, albeit briefly, in the sexual encounter.

In these instances, we are far from the "pleasure-based eroticism," a force based on spirituality and "depth of feeling" (Lorde, "Sister," 54) that Audre Lorde severs from pornography. Pineau, hooks, and Couti assert that some power can be gained through the confrontational side of sexuality, which Lorde would dismiss as yet another imprisonment within a "European-American" (59) and male-dominated discourse. Indeed, like the cannibalistic stance adopted by Suzanne Césaire, analyzed in the next chapter, this oppositional reaction is limiting. It turns women's bodies into weapons to be used against the enemy instead of "the sharing of joy" forming "a bridge between the sharers which can be the basis for understanding much of what is not shared between them, and lessens the threat of that difference" (Lorde, 56). However, we can ask, like we will ask of the cannibalistic moment in the following chapter, whether this piloting of the sexualized body does not provide a necessary space-clearing gesture to assert not only a spiritual eroticism but also a bodily sexual pleasure.

Basing her analysis on contemporary Haitian and Martinican women poets such as Kettly Mars, Nicole Cage-Florentiny, and Suzanne Dracius, literary critic Hanétha Vété-Congolo develops the concept of "douboutism," based on the Creole term *fanm doubout*, "the strong woman who stands up for herself" (Vété-Congolo, 303). She analyzes, among other texts, a poem written in Martinican Creole by Suzanne Dracius, "Fantasm Famm," which Vété-Congolo translates as "Women's Wicked Desires." The poem plainly and directly claims the right to assert women's sexual pleasure: "Pou fanm tou sé bèl plézi / Di monté adada osi" ("Women too revel in riding / Thighs apart," Dracius, 94, 92). This inscription of women's sexual pleasure within a realm dominated by men, "women too," seems to be a needed complement to the spiritual side of the erotic.

Dracius's poem, in contrast with Pineau's *Chair Piment,* takes place away from the confrontational moment. It is conductive, like Lorde's empowering energy, to a sharing of joy. In Pineau's novel, the positioning of the black woman as eater, as castrator, even if it gives a brief illusion of victory, still contributes to absolving the true perpetrator of sexual violence. Mina is still stuck in the image of the unrapable Jezebel, since she initiates the sexual contact. Mina, the victim, is simply represented as the winner, the man-eater, in order to mask her status as raped and consumed body. Such stereotypes are constructed to absolve the rapist or sexual violator and to displace the responsibility of sexual violence and sexual subversion onto the black woman as temptress.

More important perhaps than Mina's representation by Pineau, it is helpful to reflect on the marketing strategy performed by Gallimard, which explicitly participated in reinforcing the "controlling image" of the black woman as sexual temptress, Jezebel, or animalized nymphomaniac in Pineau's novel.[61] Indeed, the passage quoted on the back cover is a marketing construction in which all the complexity and interruptions referring to a historical and social context have been carved out. It forges a fake pornographic text from an original narrative that problematizes pornography by its interruptions. It plays the same role as the inviting erotic cover art.

However, the case of *Chair Piment* seems more complicated than an "overdetermination from the outside," to use Frantz Fanon's expression. It would be simplistic to consider Pineau's novel as an innocent victim of the editorialist or marketing apparatus. Indeed, Pineau herself is complicit in this construction: it is, after all, her words that publishers and marketing professionals quote. The title of her book, literally, "hot pepper flesh" seems to be drawn straight out of an erotizing reduction of Caribbean women's bodies to hot, exotic objects of consumption, potentially dangerous for the European consumer. hooks gives special attention to the use of spice as a form of commodification specific to "exotic" or "raced" women: "The commodification of Otherness has been so successful because it is offered as a new delight, more intense, more satisfying than normal ways of doing and feeling. Within commodity culture, ethnicity becomes spice, seasoning that can liven up the dull dish that is mainstream white culture (*Black Looks,* 21). The specific choice of the word *piment* inflects the general characteristics associated with spice with a further racialized meaning. *Piment* shares the Latin etymon, *pigmentum,* with the word *pigment.* Skin color thus becomes charged, through the common word origin, with the exotic and erotic characteristics of a torrid sexuality. In Pineau's title, "Chair" and "Piment" are juxtaposed like a first and last name, erasing the main protagonist's face and name from the outset. Black female flesh and spice are united in a duo that seems to announce a spicy dish. However complicit (and risky) it might be, Pineau uses this simultaneously culinary and sexual invitation in order to attract unlikely readers to her novel, to make them see what lies behind the construction of this stereotype, namely, the sexual oppression of women's bodies in the context of postslavery Guadeloupe.[62]

Indeed, "piment" is not a particularly friendly spice for the tourist's palate. The traveler to Martinique or Guadeloupe needs to be instructed, for instance, on the use of *piment bonda-man-jak*—literally "Mamma-Jack's-ass-pimiento," known in North America as *habanero*—to avoid rendering the meal inedible, and setting the uneducated eater's mouth on fire. The tip of the knife has to gently brush the hot pepper before lightly touching the sauce accompanying the dish. The pimiento is also associated in Antillean folklore with particularly destructive and selfish women.[63] From this viewpoint, we are far from the initial vision of the palatable, available, and digestible exotic woman of Pineau's novel.

More important, the pimiento is deeply embedded in the history of oppression of enslaved women and men in the Caribbean. The use of the "pimentade" was a particularly sadistic way to increase the pain of the whipped slaves. It was one of Dominican priest Père Labat's favorite methods of torture.[64] Not only did the mixture cause horrible pain, but it also turned the slaves literally into "flesh," their bodies seasoned like a dish. The juxtaposition of "Chair" and "Piment" also clearly evokes the turning of human bodies into raw flesh during slavery. For Hortense Spillers, the flesh, normally protected under the skin, is "turned inside out, in acts of branding, lacerations, and wounding" and becomes the "primary signifier" of the black enslaved bodies' histories, which comes to signify beyond the racializing of skin: "This body whose flesh carries the female and the male to the frontiers of survival bears in person the marks of a cultural text whose inside has been turned outside"

(Spillers, 207). As I discuss below, it is also this history of oppression that the "pimiento flesh" turns inside out.

Indeed, as soon as we turn the first page of the novel, *Chair Piment* is not what it appears to be. We soon realize that "piment," instead of a seasoning that can "liven up the dull dish" (hooks) and increase sexual arousal, can also harm its consumer and put an end to the sexual act. Similarly, the external signs of eroticism, the title, the various book covers, the opening pages, are all misleading. The reader discovers that "Piment" is not a spice but the name of Mina's native small town. The apparent emphasis on the commodified woman's sexual body is thus quickly displaced onto the geographical place, which is much less titillating, and which also shifts the focus from the woman's body to the body of the land, raped and violated by colonialism. In the colonial situation, the political is coupled with the erotic. As Cameroonian thinker Achille Mbembe has it: "There is no violence in a colony without a sense of contiguity, without bodies . . . engaged in particular forms of fondling and concubinage—a commerce, a coupling" (175). We could argue that symmetrically, there is no sexual relation in the colony without the complication of the political, both united by what Mbembe calls "a spirit of violence." *Chair/Piment* links the flesh and the place, the intimate and the political, in an inextricable relationship.

From the third sentence of the novel, violence interrupts the erotic text. Significantly, the Web advertisements and the back covers of the Gallimard and Mercure de France editions systematically excise these violent passages. The violence acts on several levels. First, Mina comments on the pain inflicted upon her body. She thus denies her classification as a pleasure-seeking nymphomaniac since she loathes and suffers from the sexual act. The men's "words hit her flesh, attempt to pierce her" (*Chair Piment,* 11), and as soon as men penetrate her she wants them out (13). Odile Cazenave points out that the narrative is dominated by "a difficult and unhappy sexuality" in which "love scenes, at times precise and graphic, at times erotic, highlight a total split between love and sex" (Cazenave, 60).

This "difficult sexuality" owes its unhappiness not only to Mina's individual situation but also to a buried history of sexual exploitation that has marked Mina's family and her extended community of diasporic and enslaved ancestors. The violence inflicted upon Mina's individual body automatically recalls the traumatic violence of Mina's collective and familial past. The sexual intercourse evokes memories of insect corpses lying on the ground of Mina's childhood home ("the ground was filled with corpses . . . of shriveled roaches and red spiders"; *Chair Piment,* 11). The vision of insects' corpses brings Mina back to memories of human bodies lying on the abyss of the ocean. Personal memories are intertwined with the collective traumatic past of the Middle Passage: "She was sucked into the purple depths of the ocean . . . where dead stars, wooden skeletons of pirate ships, fish cemeteries, and cannonballs lie. . . . [S]he thought she could hear strange chants, women's laughter poisoned by curses rising from the abyss" (12). Through her sexual penetration, Mina's body communicates with the silenced voices and laughter of the collective body of the sunken Africans. Her physical posture of fully opening up her body to men during sexual intercourse (17) resembles the sacrifice of the unnamed slave woman in Glissant's *La Case du commandeur,* the "open recumbent," who opens up her body to all the slaves of the plantation to cleanse herself from the original rape on the slaveship, and to communicate with the tortured of the plantation through a shared passion of pain.[65] Like Sophie, the main character of Danticat's *Breath, Eyes, Memory,* who experiences "twinning" or *marasa* during sexual intercourse,[66] Mina's body and mind split in a gesture of survival. The objectified body lies on the bed like an empty chrysalis, a vessel where men's desires, and bodies, circulate freely, while her mind becomes the recipient of another story, another history: "Two in one, because of her body tense with sexual pleasure and of her head assaulted by words of madness" (*Chair Piment,* 13). In this initial posture, neither the body nor the spirit functions as a site of agency. Both are occupied: the body assaulted by men, the mind invaded or squatted by ghostly voices of the past. The sexual scene thus deviates from its apparent intent: the reader's sexual arousal and satisfaction is diverted to make room for the recovery of a tormented past.

In the third page of the novel, sexual intercourse brings yet another memory of violence closer to Mina, that of her older sister Rosalia, burned alive in a fire: "Rosalia would always appear after Mina's sexual satisfaction. . . . Rosalia rose from darkness on September 11, 1998, the twenty-year anniversary of the fire in which she had burned alive. Braided fire-crowns circled her head. Astonished burned face. Grilled skin. Nylon night gown melted with flesh. Mute screams. Rosalia, a star shooting from the ignited cabin. Grilled skin" (*Chair Piment,* 13). This initial interruption of the sexual narrative by personal, familial, and collective histories of violence will dominate the novel. From that moment on, the novel will deliver to the captive reader a history of sexual and political oppression inflicted upon contemporary women's bodies and their deported ancestors. Like in Laferrière's novel, the vessel of sex is highjacked to tell a story of historical, political, and sexual oppression.

The reader finds out late in the novel that Mina's uncontrollable sexual drive, which compels her to offer her body to indiscriminate men of all ethnicities—"Men picked up on the parking lot . . . young and old . . . Blacks, Whites, and Arabs" (17)—results from a curse put on her by Suson Mignard, a female relative, herself victim of abuse, incest, and abandonment. Suson's spell doomed Mina to the state of nymphomaniac without ever being able to love, a state reminiscent of the controlling figure of the proverbial Jezebel of racist and exotic representations. We also recognize in this curse the transmission of the hereditary situation of slavery, in which love and sexuality were often disjointed. The oppressive historical repetition of violence is reinforced by the names of the cursor and the cursed, Mignard and Mina, victim-victimizer of plantation and postplantation sexual violence. In addition, the curse of incest, a repeating motif in Plantation literature, provides an additional reference to the legacy of slavery.[67] Since illegitimacy and secrecy marked sexual relations between masters and enslaved, and between slaves themselves, family relations were often kept in the dark, and, in consequence, unbeknownst incest was common.[68] Incest contaminates Mina's contemporary space and time even though she is a century away from slavery and an ocean apart. Mina is therefore the victim of a double entrapment: the sexual commodification of her own body under the sexual power of men, and the crushing paralysis caused by a heavy heredity of violence.

Yet *Chair Piment* succeeds in escaping this last subjugation. The narrative soon breaks away from sexual violence and from sexuality altogether. The readers are deprived of another sort of voyeurism based on the contemplation of sufferance, what Mbembe terms the "cult of victimization" (5). Mina escapes her violent sexual and genealogical bondage by returning to Guadeloupe to evaluate her familial and communal past of violence not as victim but as spectator. Elizabeth Wilson argues that in Francophone Caribbean writing, "The journey, except in rare instances . . . takes the form of journey as alienation. Self-knowledge often leads to destruction of self" (45). *Chair Piment* provides one of these "rare instances" in which the journey leads to productive results. In *Chair Piment,* destruction, incest, and curse do not lead to madness or self-annihilation, as in many novels by Caribbean women writers,[69] but to an alternative solution of reconstruction based on contemplation and spectatorship. In "Eating the Other," bell hooks recalls her childhood realization that spectatorship was not a universal right: "Amazed the first time I read in history classes that white slave-owners . . . punished enslaved black people for looking, I wondered how this traumatic relationship to the gaze had informed black parenting and black spectatorship" (*Black Looks,* 115). Pineau's novel precisely responds to this injustice by moving the black woman from the position of "spectacle" to that of spectator. She ironically relegates the evils of history—curses, incest, infanticide, family revenge—historically attributed to black subjects to the most globalized cultural site: television. After Mina's grandmother unveils family secrets shaped by incest, poisoning, cursing, and infanticide (a Daniel Moynihan–style collection of stereotypical popular and scholarly representations of the African-Caribbean family), another relative casually remarks that these deviant practices cannot compete with the U.S. television screen: "Mad about the soap operas that she watched daily on television, Fifine didn't find anything fascinating in Nana's story, nor her characters very interesting. But with the intrigues and reversals of fortune of *The Bold and the Beautiful,* now we're talking" (*Chair Piment,* 357). The comment dismisses with one stroke the deviant characteristics projected onto the Caribbean and black postslavery family by commenting on their trivial nature in a white, North American soap opera.

The contemporary female characters of *Chair Piment* establish links of kinship based on the globalized world created by television and popular culture. Médée, Mina and Rosalia's mother, "relearns to love herself" by establishing a link, through her blood-red lipstick, with "Ava Gardner and Marilyn Monroe" (33). The community of Piment despised Médée because of her dark skin. Médée re-creates links of kinship and solidarity beyond the community and beyond racist classifications. Instead of skin color, she opts for lipstick color to re-create a kinship with Hollywood vamps. Beyond that link with Hollywood, Médée re-creates a globalized family by identifying with television icons and moments: "Farah Diba's fairytale, Doña Fabiola's marriage to the King of Belgians, John Fitzgerald Kennedy's murder, de Gaulle in Martinique. . . . 'Had I been born in America, I could have been like Marilyn'" (34). In *Chair Piment,* the fire's date, September 11, establishes another link with the globalized world and settles Guadeloupe at the heart of televised history and beyond Caribbean deviance.[70]

Comment faire and *Chair Piment* both succeed, to some extent, in undermining the figure of the black male rapist and cannibal and the black female nymphomaniac by turning sexual stereotypes on their head. However, sexuality still entraps both protagonists: for Vieux, who finds liberation in the act of writing, and for Mina, who finds it in the act of reclaiming the position of the spectator. This oppositional moment clears a space for another form of resistance that I explore in the next chapter: that of literary cannibalism, which displaces the relationship with the other from the sexual battleground to the textual terrain. However, we are left to wonder whether Laferrière and Pineau, by posing this sexual trap for their readers, do not entrap themselves in the complicit gesture of reproducing racialized stereotypes, even if they do so for a pedagogical reason. More crucially, the disarming of sexual stereotypes does not lead to an empowering Lordian use of eroticism and to the reconciliation of sex and love. *Comment faire* and *Chair Piment* end, respectively, with the images of a writer copulating with his old Remington and with a traveler contemplating the clouds with her non-erotic white male friend. Unlike hooks, who calls for "space where our sexuality can be naked and represented, where we are sexual subjects—no longer bound and trapped" (*Black Looks,* 76–77), Laferrière's and Pineau's novels are still traps that remain situated in the second phase of an oppositional dialectics.

5 LITERARY CANNIBALS

Suzanne Césaire and Maryse Condé

For the colonized, there is nothing authentic, nothing traditional. Let's face it: we are just Tupis playing the lute.

—Maryse Condé, *Le Monde,* July 5, 2002

LITERARY CANNIBALISM UPSETS CATEGORIES of the devourer and the devoured, the robber and the robbed, the original and the secondary, the colonizer and the colonized. This chapter deals with the theory and practice of literary cannibalism as a response to literary colonialism in the Antilles and the Americas. By literary colonialism, I refer to the practice of European or colonial writers who write the Tropics with the effect, intended or not, of subjugating landscape, flora, fauna, humans, and texts to an imperial gaze and desire. By literary cannibalism, I mean the conscious effort of Caribbean writers to devour fragments of texts written mostly, but not only, by European or colonial writers. This act of ingestion, not to be confused with assimilation or plagiarism, is driven by a violence that responds to revenge or of justice. Literary cannibalism entails the transformation of both the eater and the eaten in a paradoxically simultaneous movement of destruction and conservation. It is not a lawless chaos but a discursive practice with its own rules and grammaticality. Finally, literary cannibalism acts on the level of the metaphorical: it is not a devouring of human flesh but a feasting on words.[1]

The essays of Martinican writer Suzanne Roussi Césaire serve as our privileged examples of literary cannibalism in the Americas.[2] Her dialogue with French surrealist André Breton provides a rich, textured, and ambivalent terrain to broach the relationship between the colonial act and its undermining by the violated "cannibal" Caribbean writer.

I also put Césaire into dialogue with predecessors and heirs such as Brazilian modernist Oswald de Andrade and Guadeloupean writer Maryse Condé. Like Césaire, Condé presents literary cannibalism as a major modus operandi of the writer of the Americas. Thus Suzanne Césaire's essays constitute our *plat de résistance,* preceded by a theoretical appetizer, and followed by a dessert reflection on postcannibalism in Condé's *Story of the Cannibal Woman.*

Originality and Colonial Pillage

Oswald de Andrade's "Tupi or not Tupi, that is the question" ("Cannibalist Manifesto," 38) is a speech act that performs its own call for action. In short, the cry for cannibalism is already cannibalistic. While Andrade's declaration associates Brazilian writers with the local figure of the "cannibal" Tupi,[3] it also ties them to European literary tradition. Andrade's sentence evidently feasted on Shakespeare's famous soliloquy in *Hamlet.* It conserved it and modified it, preserving from it the echo of a universal human condition ("To be or not to be"), while adding to it cultural particularity ("Tupi or not Tupi"). However, the relationship between Andrade's and Shakespeare's sentences is more than a simple line between devoured product and eating subject, more than one between an authoritative original and its bastardized imitation. Literary cannibalism, as performed in this and other instances, does not point to originality, authenticity, and legitimacy, but rather introduces a mode of devouring the other that has neither beginning nor end; or rather yet, whose beginnings and ends are abysmal, and whose foundations are corrupt. Andrade's call is not an end in and of itself since Caribbean writers from the 1940s to the present continue to ingest it. For instance, we can identify remnants of "Tupi or not Tupi," in Suzanne Césaire's proclamation that "Martinican poetry will be cannibal or will not be" (*Le Grand Camouflage,* 66). Césaire's sentence, in turn, will be incorporated and transformed by other Antillean authors such as René Ménil, Aimé Césaire, and Maryse Condé. The call for literary cannibalism thus stands in an endless chain of preservation and mutation.

As Renaissance scholar Peter Stallybrass unveiled in his provocative essay "Against Thinking," Hamlet's "To be or not to be" itself lay on an abysmal series of previous texts. Thus the "original" of "Tupi or not Tupi" is similarly compromised. With the help of new electronic databases comparing texts at a vertiginous speed and efficacy, Stallybrass argues that Shakespeare, "deliberately and shamelessly," "appropriated for his own use what he read and heard" ("Against Thinking," 1581).[4] In this light, Andrade's cannibalizing of Shakespeare's text is not the theft of an original but an appropriation of an already secondary and corrupt imitation.

This example of literary consumption challenges two assumptions: that literary cannibalism is a particular fact of the Americas; and that New World citizens are "second" to "first" or primary "Old World" references. Consequently, where is the originality and the particularity of the Brazilian, Caribbean, or American acts of literary cannibalism if its supposed originals are already acts of cannibalism themselves? Can we argue that the colonized—in the guise of Condé's lute-playing Tupis—are secondary if their supposed primary objects are themselves already second? French intellectual Christian Salmon has denounced the unfortunate habit of placing postcolonial writers in the position of imitators. This "age-old suspicion, often associated with postcolonial writer and *métis* literatures, challenges not only the authenticity of these texts, but also the very possibility for the 'ex-colonized,' of possessing an 'original' and 'authentic' identity" (Salmon, 43). Indeed, the so-called "ex-colonized" have often been portrayed as imitators at best and plagiarists at worst, as frequent literary examples[5] and even actual trials of indictments of plagiarism of postcolonial or minority writers have indicated. While Condé seems to be taking this sin of secondariness for granted when she claims "we have to admit that we're just Tupis playing the lute," she is actually revoking this assumption with her characteristic irony and cleverness. While apparently claiming that the lute-playing Tupi imitates European lyricism, Condé's allusion to the lute turns the notion of originality on its head since the early Renaissance instrument is, after all, an off-shoot of the Persian, Turkish, and Arabic *al'ud.* The lute, therefore, is not a mother but an offspring, not an original, but a derivative.

Therefore, Andrade and Condé not only question the validity of the original object, but also of the very notion of originality. They challenge the secondariness of literary cannibalism since any text is always already cannibal, always already feeding on other texts and discourses. Literary cannibalism therefore sets in motion a model of devouring that follows an endlessly circular and reciprocal movement, rather than a unidirectional arrow of linear devouring.[6] This model does not respond to structures such as that of the biological food chain in which sea mammals eat big fish that eat little fish that eat zooplankton. In the cannibal model, I eat you, you eat me, and I eat you back, endlessly. The model of literary cannibalism, based on the fallacy of legitimacy, defies hierarchies or easy classification, and undermines clear limits between the other and the self, the original and the secondary precisely at the moment in which the image of the "cannibal" is created to consolidate these differences. Let me recall, as I discussed in the introduction of this book, that the figure of the cannibal was created to represent an absolute otherness, aimed at consolidating the limits of the European self.

Thinking generally about "phallogocentric" cultures, Jacques Derrida reflects on a similar mode of subject formation—or rather subject disintegration—in which categories of being such as the living and the nonliving, the human and the animal, the animal and the vegetal, are at best problematic categories in that, metonymically or metaphorically, all eat each other: "The question is no longer to know whether it is "good" or "nice" ["bon ou bien"] to eat the other and which other. We eat it anyway and it eats us. So-called non-anthropophagic cultures practice a symbolic anthropophagy and even build the sublimity of their morals, their politics, and their laws on this very anthropophagy" ("Il faut bien manger," 295–96). Derrida's model of a generalized and reciprocal eating of the other emerges from a reflection on categories, of living and nonliving, human, plant, and animal. Similarly, the same could be argued about texts put in contact in the practice of literary cannibalism. In this practice defying the legitimacy of the original, like in Derrida's model, emerges an ethics that defies notions of authority, originality, and strict borders between texts and authors. Obviously we should keep in mind that pushing the logic of literary cannibalism to its extreme and denying all textual authority and intellectual property in any situation would lead to devastating and absurd situations, and ultimately to the end of thinking.[7]

Hence, it is crucial to define precisely what is meant by literary cannibalism. It is a strategy of discourse produced within a specific situation, that of a colonial, postcolonial, or minority author writing from a forced and imagined position of secondariness vis-à-vis a so-called first-world or primary position. The practice carries a particular cultural significance when used by writers who belong to what I have termed the "cannibal zone,"[8] that is, the zone in which people have been systematically imagined as cannibals according to their geographical location (Americas, Africa, insularity, borders of the "known" world on

Renaissance maps) or ethnicity and race (Tupis, Caribs, Africans). Literary cannibalism uses specific tools and techniques such as the excision of segments of texts from a mostly European canon to incorporate them into a new textual body with the effort to keep these incorporations as such visible. These textual ingestions include the characteristics of performativity (a text that does what it says) and irony (a text that points to its own gesture with a critical distance). Finally, the act of literary cannibalism is driven by a specific intent—revenge, justice, reappropriation, even homage—and sealed by an ethical contract with the reader. When performing acts of literary cannibalism, writers do not fool the reader into thinking that the consumed text is their own, such as in acts of plagiarism. Rather, the writers wink at their readers, who become their partners in irony. Indeed, it would be ludicrous to confuse Andrade's "Tupi or not Tupi," which satisfies all the definitions of literary cannibalism that I have just listed, with an act of plagiarism. Nonetheless, the line between legitimate acts of literary cannibalism and dishonest forms of plagiarism is not always as clear, as recent examples of "cannibal" literary texts put on trial and charged with intellectual property theft have shown.[9]

If literary cannibalism cannot always be clearly separated from other forms of literary borrowing, honest or dishonest, it also sometimes resists being grounded in the particularity of the New World "cannibal zone." Indeed, the question of originality and theft emerged with the establishment of the idea of single authorship in Europe after the Renaissance. Thus literary cannibalism is closely tied to European notions of textual authority. Moreover, the argument could be made that there is nothing new, nothing original, in the practice of literary cannibalism, and that Andrade and his followers just gave a new name to an old and tried European practice.[10]

Moreover, "cannibal zone" itself is not restricted to the Americas. European Dada artists Daniel Spoerri and Francis Picabia, among others, have used the term "cannibalism" to describe their artistic project. While the artistic cannibalism practiced by these Dadaists certainly demonstrates an aesthetic edge, we could nonetheless say that it lacks contextual teeth.[11] The Swiss-Romanian artist Spoerri, creator of the Zurich-based exhibit "Le Dîner Cannibale" in 1970,[12] for instance, does not belong to a national or ethnic community that has been systematically portrayed as cannibal. Switzerland and Romania are certainly outside the "cannibal zone."[13] Thus the "cannibal" gestures of a

Spoerri, a Tzara, or a Picabia lose a certain contextual and political edge.[14] In brief, reclaiming the trope of the cannibal for French, Swiss, or Romanian artists does not come with the same historical or discursive baggage as for Andrade, Condé, or Césaire, who represent people who have been portrayed as cannibals, or as Fanon puts it, who carry the "cannibal gene" that pseudoscientific discourse has charged them with: "At the start of my history that others have fabricated for me, the pedestal of cannibalism was given pride of place so that I wouldn't forget. They inscribed on my chromosomes certain genes of various thickness representing cannibalism. Next to the *sex linked*, they discovered the *racial linked*. Science should be ashamed of itself" (*Black Skin,* 100, emphasis in original).

This cultural particularity, which responds to debasing stereotypes of cultural colonialism, has implications for the ethics of the cannibal gesture. It alters the notion of shame and guilt that Stallybrass associates with European plagiarism—in Shakespeare's case, for instance. Indeed, the simple question is the following: Is a writer—colonized, postcolonial, or descendant of slaves—guilty of ingesting a text that exploits discursively her or his community? Is robbing the robber a theft punishable by law or, instead, an ethical act of reappropriation? Césaire's and Condé's respective practices of literary cannibalism will help us reflect on these ethical and political questions. Both authors present literary cannibalism as a necessary stage of revenge and justice. Yet both also eventually move away from the confrontational mode of devouring the other to the more fertile exchange of *eating with* the other, or *feeding* the other in return.

Suzanne Césaire's Discrete Cannibalism

"Fulguration" is the term that best encapsulates Suzanne Césaire's writings. The Martinican author wrote a total of seven essays published in the Martinican journal *Tropiques* between 1941 and 1945,[15] in addition to a play for a local actors' group in Fort-de-France. The 1955 play—inspired by Lafcadio Hearn's *Youma* and entitled *Aurore de la liberté*—is nowhere to be found.[16] The fulgurating nature of Césaire's writing, which surged with speed and intensity, immediately to be followed by a perpetual silence, could easily be explained by the author's life circumstances: her obligations as a literature professor at the Lycée Schoelcher of Fort-de-France, her role as the mother of six, her decision to leave her husband and family, her exile in Paris, and her premature death in 1966 of a brain tumor at the age of fifty. Nonetheless, as in the case of Arthur Rimbaud's similar abrupt silence, life circumstances fail to account fully for the end of Césaire's writing. Guadeloupean writer Daniel Maximin, who wrote the preface to Césaire's newly collected works,[17] wonders whether the writer's silence could not be explained by the very nature of her writings: "The secret of Suzanne Césaire's silence, which came so quickly, might be explained by the fact that the cannibal fire of her writings consumed her whole self . . . burning of its own capacity of refusal and involvement of body and soul, gone where writing could no longer follow" (Maximin, 21). Maximin's insightful explanation illuminates the violent characteristics of her writing, in which she threw herself fully, and which consumed her entirely in return. The image of "cannibal fire" alludes to a total form of consumption in the etymological sense of "con-sumare," or "taking in completely." *Webster's* defines consumption as destruction "by separating the component parts and annihilating the form of the substance, *as by fire or by eating*" (emphasis mine). Césaire's "cannibal fire" consumes with both abrasive fire and ingesting mouth. While this chapter deals with her consumption of others' texts rather than with her self-consumption, the raw etymological nature of Maximin's notion of consumption will be central to my argument. The image of consumption puts the emphasis on the violence of the act, and on its propensity to annihilate by *separation.*

Suzanne Césaire's consumption should not be confused with "assimilation," a different form of ingestion. In an interview with Euzhan Palcy, Aimé Césaire, in reply to a question about his use of canonical French literary sources, contends that the Caribbean writer "must assimilate in order not to be assimilated."[18] While the notions of "cannibalism" and "assimilation" both evoke acts of eating or being eaten, they have very different structural implications and modes of being-with-the-other. Again, a return to the etymology helps us understand the nature of the beast. The Latin root of the verb *ad-similare* means "to make similar to." The contemporary definitions of the term include "to become like or alike" or "to become absorbed or incorporated" *(Webster's)*. Aimé Césaire's endorsement of assimilation therefore entails the realization that the loss of one's particularity is inevitable in a cultural contact, and that the relationship between self and other leads to impoverishment. While Aimé Césaire's poetry and speeches offer a much more complex practice of literary ingestion than his single comment in the interview,[19] Suzanne goes further in her endorsement of cannibalism in her literary project than Aimé does in his. Aimé Césaire's 1956 speech "Culture et colonisation," delivered at the Premier Congrès des Ecrivains et Artistes Noirs in Paris, provides an elaborate reflection on cultural assimilation. According to him, colonization prevents the "internalization" of external (European) cultural elements by the colonized that would lead to the emergence of a new civilization. In Césaire's pessimistic view, a civilization can only emerge if it does not sense "a foreign element" [un corps étranger] as such, since, through the process of internalizing, this element would cease to be foreign. In the colonial situation, "Foreign elements are thrown upon the [colonized] land while remaining foreign to the colonized. White man's things. White man's business. Things that indigenous people frequent but do not master" ("Culture," 202). Nick Nesbitt astutely reveals the tension in the speech between Césaire's pessimism and his own assimilation of "multiple exterior elements within a single totalizing and unified subject" (*Voicing,* 125) through his copious quoting of Hegel, Malinowski, Nietzsche, and Captain Cook. What Nesbitt calls a "virtuosic assemblage of discourses" and a demonstration of cultural cannibalism (125–26) seem to link Aimé's practice to Suzanne's. However, like his model of failed "civilisation métisse" made of "juxtaposed and unharmonized" cultural traits, Aimé's speech seems to represent a case of undigested assimilation, in which the borrowed—stranded?—cultural elements forcefully contrast with Suzanne's dynamic agglutinative cannibalism.

With assimilation and cannibalism, we are thus faced with two very different modes of eating the other. Literary assimilation remains at a defensive and survival stage and leaves the power structure intact. Assimilation implies the conservation and the adoption of the form of the consumed object and the dissolving of the eater's self; cannibalism implies the violent destruction of the eaten object by the eater. However, as previously discussed, the act of cannibalism is more complex than a simple annihilation of the consumed object since its incorporation also implies its partial conservation.[20] Indeed, in the act of cannibalism, something remains from the original object as it gets absorbed. The eater and the eaten are both paradoxically preserved and changed by the act. The result is a congregated object in which the violence of the act of devouring remains visible. Literary cannibalism also simultaneously entails violence and respect toward the consumed object. Similarly, the sacred practice of what Native American scholar Jack D. Forbes calls "traditional ritualistic 'cannibalism'" consists in "eating a small portion of a dead enemy's flesh in order to gain part of the strength or power of that person or to show respect . . . for that person. (Thus, usually a respected enemy warrior was so used)" (24). This respect and admiration for the ingested object is also evident in Césaire's practice of literary cannibalism.

In her endorsement of literary cannibalism, Suzanne Césaire can be seen as a precursor of Glissant's creolization. Indeed, structurally, cannibalism is to creolization what assimilation is to *métissage,* according to Glissant's terminology. Glissantian creolization shares with cannibalism the visible violence of the original, the agglutination of fragments recognizable as such (as opposed to the dissolving that *métissage* entails), and the resistance of both the ingested object and the ingesting body.[21] In textual cannibalism, as in cultural creolization, the result of the encounter consists of "more than the sum of its original parts." In cannibalism and creolization, this added value is an active agent, and not a redundant or supplemental waste, as in assimilation or *métissage* as I explore below through my reading of Zita Nunes. *Métissage,* like assimilation, flattens the salience of its original parts and impoverishes its result, human or textual. Césaire's product of textual cannibalism, like Glissant's process of creolization, unsettles the objects preceding it in time from a position of originality since the cannibal text, like creolization, can re-mother its origin while keeping visible the shreds of the texts it devoured. While Césaire's cannibalistic practice is mostly textual, structurally it functions like the act of creolization, which could be based on the mixing of bodies, texts, or cultures, as opposed to textual assimilation, which shares its impoverishing effect with sexual *métissage.* Thus Césaire accomplishes a double recasting of the Caribbean self: from assimilated object to agent, from sexual, biological product to discursive writer. More than a gratuitous analogy, the eating metaphor of cannibalism and the sexual reality of *métissage* and racial mixing are strongly intertwined in Césaire's texts. Through cannibalism, Césaire confronts *métissage* as a form of racial exoticism embedded in white sexual desire.

In her seven essays, Césaire offers both a theory and a practice of literary cannibalism, a cannibalism we might call both discreet and discrete; two homonyms that fit her practice perfectly. The quality of being discreet entails being careful about what one does or says. This practice of prudence is not just a good wife's attribute—a quality that French ethnographer Michel Leiris saw lacking in Suzanne Césaire[22]—but also acts as a strategy of survival in the context in which Césaire and her colleagues from *Tropiques* were writing. Indeed, the essays were published under the close scrutiny of the Vichy regime's intelligence bureau. Lieutenant Bayle, the director of censorship, eventually censured *Tropiques* for its subversive nature.[23] Césaire was also writing in the shadow of a very famous husband, who eclipsed her, and of André Breton, otherwise known as the "Pope of Surrealism."[24] Suzanne Césaire used literary cannibalism to subtly undermine the authority and influence of these powerful public figures. Césaire's discreet cannibalism, for instance, provides a surreptitious, yet unflinching, response to the surrealist writer who flattened her into an eroticized, exotic muse. Her discretion adopts the tactic of the cannibal who pretends to befriend its future meal before devouring it.[25] Thus Césaire, the camouflaged woman,[26] in her essay "André Breton, poète," dissimulates the French writer's very demise under an apparently unabashed praise.

Césaire's cannibalism is also discrete in the sense of *discretio* or "separation" as in "discursive discrimination." It involves, like the adjective "discrete," "the action or power of discerning, judgment," "the freedom and authority to make decisions and choices," and "the power to judge and act" *(Webster's)*. It is thus an intellectual practice of separation, division, reordering, and naming that gives her authority over the organization of discourse and knowledge that she takes in. In this sense, cannibalism cannot be confused with imitation. In her "Malaise d'une civilisation," Césaire warns us against the act, or rather the vegetative state, of imitation: "What is so critical is that the desire of imitation . . . has now migrated into the realm of the dreadful secret forces of the unconscious. . . . He does not truly KNOW that he imitates. . . . Similarly, hysterics ignore that they only mimic a disease, but the physician, who cures and delivers them from their morbid symptoms, does know" (*Le Grand camouflage,* emphasis in original, 47–48). Imitation is described as the predicament of a powerless object plagued by a disease. This disease is in the hands of the uncontrollable agents of the unconscious and the therapist. In contrast with the imitator, who does not "KNOW"—Césaire's capital letters evoke a desperate scream—the body of the cannibal does know, takes herself into her own hands, incorporates, discriminates, in order to escape from the interpretation of others and from the plague of assimilation.

In his *Caliban*, Roberto Fernández Retamar reflects on the fictional division that Europeans projected onto native Amerindians in a political mind-frame of "divide et impera."[27] The belligerent Carib and the peaceful Arawak or Taïno appear as the two opposite sides of the Amerindian; on one side of the coin is the cannibal and on the other side—the imitator. For Retamar, the gesture of the cannibal "belongs to the arsenal of politicians of action, those who perform the dirty work," (7) while the *Arauaco* of Columbus's writings is "peaceful, meek, and even timorous and cowardly" (6). In her practice of literary cannibalism, Suzanne Césaire reconciles the two faces of Caribbean subjects by insufflating cannibal strength into their Taïno guise.

A Caribbean Tamar: Césaire and Breton's Dialogue

To pursue Retamar's analogy, critics have written at length on Suzanne Césaire's Taïno predicament; she was evacuated from the battleground of the Negritude terrain dominated by her male counterparts, such as the triumvirate of Aimé Césaire, Léopold Sédar Senghor, and Léon Gontran Damas. Suzanne Césaire was not an isolated case. For instance, women were flagrantly absent from the list of invited speakers at the 1956 "Congress of Black Writers and Artists" in Paris, organized by the literary review *Présence africaine*. Caribbean women writers and "Negritude women," as Sharpley Whiting has called them, have been systematically relegated to the side of the invisible or silenced Taïno by the plain fact of their gender. The work of unearthing Césaire from oblivion and of removing her from her subservient at best, at worst invisible, position has marked the past two decades of criticism.[28] While these analyses are crucial, my own focuses not on Césaire's silencing but instead on her active speech, or on her Carib or cannibal side, if you wish. This section is concerned specifically with her textual cannibalistic relationship with French surrealist and passing poet André Breton.[29] Her cannibalizing of Breton can be seen as an act of revenge against the writer who attempted to cannibalize her, that is, to reduce her intellect and literary production to the image of an exotic beauty, as he famously claimed: "Suzanne Césaire: belle comme la flamme du punch" [Suzanne Césaire: as beautiful as the flame of rum punch] (*Martinique,* 120).

Césaire's radical statement that "Martinican poetry will be cannibal or will not be" in "Misère d'une poésie" (*Le Grand camouflage,* 66) is not only a prophecy gesturing toward the future.[30] Like Andrade's "Tupi or not Tupi," it is a performative statement acting in the moment of the utterance of the sentence. The sentence already performs literary cannibalism as it contains several voices it has incorporated. In Césaire's ultimatum, we can hear Andrade's "Tupi or not Tupi, that is the question," a sentence that is already itself the cannibalizing of Hamlet's famous soliloquy. Additionally, Césaire's sentence adopts the grammatical structure, or skeleton, of Breton's radical aesthetic proclamation that "La beauté sera CONVULSIVE ou ne sera pas" [Beauty will be CONVULSIVE or will not be] (*Nadja,* 190). The condition of Breton's convulsive beauty is that it be "explosante-fixe," a quality that seems to be met by the face of Suzanne Césaire metaphorized by a flame, both fixed in its unity and exploding in its varying intensity. Césaire's incorporation of Breton's sentence is thus a discrete *and* discreet reclaiming of her own image as well, previously devoured by Breton.

Césaire's declaration of poetic independence occupies an ambivalent position toward place, and toward debt and autonomy. As Marie-Agnès Sourieau has pointed out, Césaire restricts her theories in her essays to Martinicans.[31] However, by claiming that Martinican poetry will be cannibal or will not be, Césaire goes beyond Martinique by inserting her thinking into the literary lineage of Brazilian modernists such as Oswald de Andrade.[32] With this move, she aligns her work with an American literary family, inscribes Martinique in an American consciousness, and thereby detaches it from a debt to French literary history. By brandishing the image of the cannibal, she also claims her affiliation with the "cannibal zone" and thereby asserts her Caribbeanness; we recall from the introduction that "cannibal" and *"Cariba"* are inextricably linked. Thus the declaration could be read as "Martinican poetry will be *Caribbean* or will not be." It is paradoxically in her proclamation of being a literary cannibal, in other words, one whose literary production feeds off the texts of others, that Césaire claims not her secondariness but, instead, her Caribbean originality.

Césaire's performative declaration in her works is not an isolated instance of literary cannibalism. Her essays feed on textual shreds from Shakespeare, Frobenius, Nietzsche, or Mallarmé. Her essay entitled "Malaise d'une civilisation" is a barely disguised ingestion of Freud's 1929 *Malaise dans la civilisation* (the French title of *Das Unbehagen in der Kultur* or *Civilization and Its Discontents*). While the question of intertextuality and literary ingestion in Césaire is a rich one that critics have pursued and should continue to pursue, I restrict my reading to her cannibalistic dialogue with Breton because it provides a particularly complex example of intersectionality between literary influence (the mixing of texts) and *métissage* (the mixing of bodies).

French surrealist André Breton arrived in Martinique, his forced port of call, on a journey to the United States in 1941. The freighter *Captain Paul-Lemerle* also transported Jews, intellectuals, artists, and dissenters fleeing the Nazi regime, such as Claude Lévi-Strauss, André Masson, Anna Seghers, and Wilfredo Lam.[33] Breton's three-week stay in Martinique resulted in the publication of the essay "Martinique charmeuse de serpents,"[34] a series of poems,[35] as well as, on a personal level, an intense friendship with Suzanne and Aimé Césaire. In "Martinique," Breton recalls the surrealist stroke of luck that led him to "discover" Aimé Césaire's poetry. While looking for a ribbon for his daughter in a notions store, Breton chanced upon a copy of the first issue of *Tropiques*.[36] The shopkeeper, who happened to be René Ménil's sister,[37] immediately introduced Breton to Aimé Césaire. Soon after, Breton expressed his praise for Césaire's poetry: "The Word of Aimé Césaire, beautiful as the birth of oxygen" (*Martinique,* 126). Breton's praise begins as the realization of a parthogenesis, a poetry whose language is unheard of. However, Breton's praise for the poem's originality is quickly followed by a paternalistic reclaiming of the poem: "I confess that I immediately felt a certain pride in it: what was said there was in no way foreign to me" (120). Aimé Césaire's poetry, which first appears strikingly original, soon moves into the realm of the secondary, the habitual lot of the colonized. Breton, despite acknowledging Césaire's genius, still considers him his heir and genial imitator. But at least Breton recognizes Aimé for his poetic word, while he considers only Suzanne's beauty, even if he was clearly aware of her writings, published in *Tropiques* since April 1941. "Suzanne Césaire: belle comme la flamme du punch" (*Martinique,* 120). Suzanne, in contrast with her husband, is recognized as a muse, not a writer in her own right.[38] She is inscribed in a portrait gallery of Breton's muses such as Nadja whose "beauté explosante-fixe" reminds us of the flame of alcohol of Breton's Martinican muse. J. Michael Dash perspicaciously called the Suzanne Césaire of Breton's fantasy his "tropical Nadja" ("Le Je de l'autre," 85).

The following passage from "Martinique" constitutes the original palimpsest on which will be inscribed the lightly veiled dialogue between Suzanne Césaire and André Breton:

> Our meetings in a bar at night . . . after the high-school lessons that [Aimé Césaire] gave around the main theme of Rimbaud, our meetings on the terrace that the enchanting presence of Suzanne Césaire, as beautiful as the flame of rum punch, perfected, but what's more, an excursion into the deepest depth of the island: I will forever see us leaning from high above to the point of losing us over the abyss of Absalon as if over the very materialization of the crucible in which poetic images are forged when they have earth-shattering strength, without any other markers within the swirling frenzied flora than the huge enigmatic canna flower which is a panting triple heart on the tip of a sword. (121)[39]

The hyperboles and references to loss of control, mystery, and hubris—"enchanting," "in the deepest depth," "earth-shattering," "without markers," "swirling frenzy," "enigmatic"—signal Breton's exotic intoxication.[40] Suzanne appears as an extension of the feverish tropical landscape. Her body blends into the terrace, which in turn merges with the "depths of the land," in a flowing description. Human body, house, landscape, and flora are juxtaposed in a fluid metonymic relation. Metonymy and metaphor at once—by her proximity to the land and by her coincidence with the flame—Suzanne Césaire comes to signify entirely the magical land Breton encounters. She becomes the actualization of Breton's ideal of a "fixed exploding" beauty. She is thus swallowed up both by the tropical landscape and by the surrealist aesthetic image.

The nature of the referent of the "we" dangerously leaning on the balcony is troubling. It is not clear whether it refers to the duet of André and Suzanne or to the trio of André, Aimé, and Suzanne. The symbolic three-hearted flower of the *balisier* (*canna* flower) leads us to think that the "we" leaning above the abyss refers to the threesome. The flower's triple heart panting at the extremity of a spade introduces a highly sexually charged meaning. In this description of sex merging with heart, we can hear Rimbaldian echoes.[41] Rimbaud's poetry, recall, is the subject of Aimé's literature class at the time of the scene. In Breton's delirium, the Martinican landscape and the desire-laden relationship are thus invaded by aesthetic and literary visions.

The androgynous *canna* flower, equipped with spades and receiving cups, signals the sexual ambivalence inhabiting the scene. The evocation of the "creuset" or crucible, a word dear to Breton aesthetically,[42] also clearly evokes in this context the crucible of racial mixing or *métissage* ["la matérialisation du creuset"]. The scene presents a complex amalgam of surrealist aesthetic intensity, unruly sexual desires, androgyny, hypertrophic sexuality, and danger. Césaire will recycle the image of the crucible in her essays written after her encounter with Breton by linking it explicitly to *métissage,* and by raising ethical concerns about the irresponsible attitude of passing white men, avid of exotic beauties, co-initiators of the so-called crucible, but unwilling to admit their own responsibility in the fathering of *métis* children.

The abyss of Breton's scene of Absalon is itself based on an unfathomable referent. While "la forêt d'Absalon" is the name of the site in Martinique where the Césaires brought Breton,[43] other evocations of Absalom come to mind. An obvious referent is the biblical story in which Absalom avenges his sister Tamar by killing his brother Amnôn, David's eldest son, for falling in love with and raping their sister (*King James Bible, Samuel II,* 13). The story of Absalom is first and foremost about sexual transgression and revenge. Moreover, the biblical story is laden with food references. The name "Tamar" itself, meaning "date palm," refers to a sweet, energy-packed, and life-sustaining food. To attract his sister into his room, Amnôn pretends to be sick and requests that she prepare cakes in front of him and feed them to him with her own hands. When Tamar reaches toward him, her brother rejects the food, grabs her, and rapes her. Legitimate gestures of family exchange based on the preparation and sharing of food with the intent of healing are violently evacuated by the transgressive sexual act. The dangerous confusion of eating with sexuality has become a prevalent trope in this book by now. Generally, sexuality confused with the act of eating reduces the object of desire to a consumable commodity. The story of Amnôn and Tamar presents a reverse movement whereby sexuality invades basic modes of hospitality and exchange.

When, in the biblical story, familial rules of transmission are violated, Breton's scene of Absalon presents a violation of the rules of friendship. In the biblical story as well as in Breton's, illicit sex or sexual desire seems to be what is at stake. It is the violation of the rules of marriage that causes Tamar's outrage: "Nay, my brother, do not force me; for no such thing ought to be done in Israel. . . . Now therefore, I pray thee, speak unto the king; for he will not withhold me from thee" (*Samuel II,* 13:12–13). Tamar seems to think genuinely that the problem is the illicit sex, which could be legitimized by the king's approval of their marriage, more than it is incest, which couldn't be ruled out by the union.[44] In Breton's land of Absalom, the illegitimacy of sexual desire, which increases this very desire, is a combination of the taboo of racial mixing and the transgression of the desire for a forbidden woman—a friend's wife.

Importantly for my purpose, Absalom's murder of Amnôn takes place during a feast. Thus revenge, like in the act of cannibalism, is strongly associated with food consumption. Interestingly, if we interpret Breton and Suzanne's relationship as a repetition of Amnôn and Tamar's, the position of Absalom is thus left open for Aimé, the third member of the trio. However, Aimé Césaire remains noticeably silent in the aftermath of the original scene of triple desire.[45] Suzanne, the Caribbean Tamar, is her own avenger. This interpretation goes against the common perception of Suzanne, silenced by her famous husband's formidable work. In this occurrence, Caribbean Tamar acts as the agent who has regained control of her own speech. We could even go as far as to say that Suzanne Césaire occupies at once the position of Tamar—the "raped" victim, the fruit date, the comestible—and that of Absalom the avenger.

The biblical story of Absalom, Tamar, and Amnôn constitutes an undeniable referent for Breton. The characters, two men and a woman among whom forbidden desire circulates, and the object—sexual transgression—inhabit his text as well as the passage from the Second Book of Samuel. While "no such thing ought to be done in Israel," as biblical Tamar comments, the marvelous "land of Martinique," for Breton, lends itself well to similar forbidden desires. Like our typical colonial travelers, Breton experiences in the Tropics a sensory disorder explained, and thus absolved, by the perceived disorder of the place itself, epitomized by the obscene hubris of the *canna* flower.

The name of the Martinican forest also evokes William Faulkner's *Absalom, Absalom!* published in 1936, five years before Breton's journey to Martinique. Faulkner's novel, like the biblical story, deals with the transgression of incestuous desire, doubled by the taboo of racial mixing. It is also the story of a trio—two half-brothers who desire their sister—in which the transgression of miscegenation is stronger than that of incest.[46] Faulkner's version of the myth certainly adds depth to the dangerous Martinican forest of Absalon, and to the cryptic references to the forbidden desire circulating between the three friends: "Je nous reverrai toujours de très haut penchés à nous perdre" [I will for ever see us, leaning from high above to lose ourselves]. The height does not simply refer to the physical elevation of the cliff but also to the dangerous abyss of the relationship formed there. While I am not concerned with exploring the relationship of love or desire that the three friends might have experienced, I am interested in pointing out the barely cryptic messages that Suzanne Césaire saw in Breton's writings. The response to Breton's barely camouflaged desire is one of the main engines of Césaire's literary revenge.

Four months after the April 1941 publication of "Martinique," Breton reiterates his admiration for Suzanne's physical beauty in a poem entitled "Pour Madame."[47] The poem begins with the evocation of the extraordinary beauty of young mixed-race girls ("des petites chabines")[48] and ends with the epitome of this tropical beauty through a description that unmistakably recalls Suzanne's face: "this quest, in the depth of the crucible [creuset], for feminine beauty here much more often accomplished than elsewhere and that never appeared to me more radiant than in that face of white amber and charcoil" (*Tropiques 3*, 1941). The term "crucible" links the evocation of the light-skinned girls to the episode in the forest of Absalon. In this poem, the beauty expressed by the crucible is no longer only the aesthetically successful image of the *Surrealist Manifesto,*[49] but becomes deeply grounded in racial mixing, exemplified by the racial contrasts materialized in the *chabines'* bodies, with their astonishing simultaneous possession of light hair and skin and African features. Breton's final portrait of Suzanne is also defined by an astonishing encounter between "night" and "day," preceded by mathematic evocations of racial measurements: "en vue de quel dosage ultime, de quel équilibre durable entre le jour et la nuit" [what ultimate dosage, what durable equilibrium between day and night]. The human flesh is fragrant and edible: "We search, among these native essences, which is the wood that warms up these beautiful fleshes of prismatic shadows: cocoa tree, coffee tree, vanilla whose printed foliage throw an enduring mystery on the coffee paper bags into which the desire of childhood cuddles." Flesh becomes chocolate, coffee, and vanilla. All senses of the poet—sight, hearing, scent, touch, and taste—are summoned to take in the girls' bodies. Skin adopts the color of the coffee paper bags in which the childlike masculine desire curls up. A young boy's erotic fantasies—albeit expressed by a grown man—are triggered by the erotic description of very young schoolgirls: "And then the school bells scatter to the four corners swarming laughing little shabeens [les chabines rieuses], often with hair lighter than skin." Like the young *chabines*, Suzanne Césaire's beauty is built on aesthetic contrasts. The juxtaposition of the young girls' bodies and Suzanne Césaire's face introduces yet another contrast. Her black hair appears as the negative image of the little girls' blond hair; the singleness of her face contrasts with the multiple images and sound bites evoked by the young *chabines*, disseminated like flower spores. Her face is convoked to create a successful surrealist image whose ideal is the encounter of very different attributes that meet in one single object (*Manifestes,* 31). In Breton's poem, Césaire is a quickly burning flame, consumed by the empire of surrealism and by its emperor.

However, we cannot stop at the observation that Césaire was consumed by Breton, both in his surrealist project and in his erotic desire. Such an interpretation would reduce the writer to a silenced, helpless, and ultimately victimized prey, which she is not. Césaire strikes back, bites back, discreetly, diplomatically, surreptitiously, and camouflaged. In April 1942, a few months after the publication of Breton's "Pour Madame," Martinican intellectual René Ménil also cryptically—yet unmistakably—comments on Suzanne Césaire's vengeful cannibalism toward Breton's gesture and ridicules the passing poet. He alludes to Suzanne Césaire as the "encounter . . . between an ember-complexioned cannibal and chabine" (Ménil, "Laissez passer," 26). We recognize the very words "chabine" and "ember" Breton used to describe "Madame Césaire." By the addition of the word "cannibal" to that of "chabine," Ménil restores to Césaire her warrior strength. Ménil also acts as the missing Absalom evoked above. His text is addressed to an unnamed "colonial friend" whose "sugary heart" ("coeur sucré") might skip a beat in front of the spectacle of the tropics "made for a spectator other than him" (27). The unnamed colonial spectator, feminized by the adjective "sugary" and rendered vulnerable by a weak heart, is clearly André Breton. The tropical spectacle is situated in "a forest near mount pelée," which corresponds to the location of the forest of Absalon. Ménil's language is laden with expressions reminiscent of Breton's style, such as "l'amour absolu," which echoes his *Amour fou.* The dialogue around the abyss of Absalon, in no way restricted to Breton and Suzanne Césaire, circulates in the open, among the members of the intellectual community of *Tropiques*. In this context, Suzanne Césaire's response to the surrealist writer reads like an open book.

In a more explicit and prosaic style than Ménil, Condé also evokes Césaire's resistance to surrealism. In "Unheard Voice," the Guadeloupean writer reads Césaire's short intellectual journey as a clear progression from a dependency upon European thinking to an emancipation achieved in her final essay, "Le grand camouflage." More specifically, Condé defines Césaire as an unconditional admirer of Breton: "Suzanne

Césaire, in her first writings, seemed to be extremely infatuated with the poetry of André Breton and could find no fault with him" ("Unheard Voice," 63). Instead of a belated emancipation, as Condé sees it, I contend that Césaire's resistance to Breton starts from the get-go.

Césaire evokes Breton in four of her seven published essays: explicitly in her October 1941 "André Breton, poète . . ." (*Tropiques,* 3); implicitly in her January 1942 "Misère d'une poésie," (*Tropiques,* 4); explicitly in her October 1943 "Le Surréalisme et nous" (*Tropiques,* 8–9), and indirectly yet unmistakably in her final 1945 "Le Grand camouflage" (*Tropiques,* 13–14). Recall that Breton's texts concerning "Madame Césaire" were published in April 1941 *(Martinique)* and in October 1941 ("Pour Madame"). This chronological information is important to understand that Césaire had indeed read Breton's texts and that they acted as implicit subtexts for her camouflaged response to the surrealist writer.

Césaire's criticism of Breton revolves around seeing ("voyance") and blindness. The gist of her criticism resides in her portrayal of Breton, not as the "seeing" poet he sets himself to be, but rather as the passing traveler blinded by the beauty of Martinican landscapes and women. Césaire unmasks the great surrealist poet, inheritor of the Rimbaldien *voyance,* as a disabled traveler who looks without seeing.[50] In "André Breton, poète . . . ," she describes him as carrying "the dashing of discoveries, the smiling peacefulness of the one who sees" (*Le grand camouflage,* 37). Breton is thus not the one who sees but the one who believes he sees with the self-confidence of a tourist.[51] Césaire's criticism of the minor exotic writer Jean-Antoine Nau in her "Misère d'une poésie" is a barely disguised criticism of Breton:[52] "il passe à côté. Il regarde. Mais il n'a pas 'vu'" [he passes by. He looks. But has not seen] (64). Nau's poetry is described as a "sugar and vanilla literature" (65), epithets that clearly evoke Breton's description of the female Caribbean "flesh" as vanilla. We should also remember that Breton wrote his poems "Some Trembling Pins," on the backs of postcards—the ultimate accessory of the tourist. In his commentary to Breton's *Martinique Snake Charmer,* Franklin Rosemont indicates that the poem "Pour Madame" was written on a picture postcard depicting "people doing the laundry on rocks in the Rivière Madame" (*Martinique,* 111n13). While the last sentence of Césaire's "grand camouflage"—"C'est qu'il fait trop beau, ici, pour y voir" [It's so pretty here things can't be seen]—refers to various forms of blindness, it could very well refer to Breton's blinding by Martinique's and the Martinicans' "natural" beauty. Breton is more specifically blinded by the diffuse sexual desire he feels toward the continuum of Martinican nature, Martinican mixed-race girls, all metaphorized and metonymized by Madame Césaire.

Condé contends that "Suzanne Césaire . . . seemed to be extremely infatuated with André Breton's poetry" ("Unheard Voice," 63). The sexual connotations of the word "infatuation," literally the state of being rendered a fool by "an unreasoning passion or attraction" *(Webster's)*, do indeed permeate Breton and Césaire's texts. However, Césaire, in her powerful retort to Breton, is nobody's fool, despite all appearances. Césaire's essay "André Breton poète. . ." (ellipsis in original) seems to be an unconditional praise of the surrealist writer, as Condé and other critics have read it. However, the ellipsis contained in the title already suggests a mitigation of the apparently unabashed praises that the essay includes. Césaire calls Breton's poetry the "supreme reward of the supreme science of poetry" (*Le Grand camouflage,* 54). The double hyperbole indicates a clearly ironic posture. A few lines down appears another seemingly praiseful moment: "And indeed, Breton inhabits a marvelous land where clouds and stars, winds and tides, trees and beasts, men and universe ploy under his desires" (ibid.). The "marvelous land" Breton inhabits could, on the surface, refer to the surrealist poetic land of unexpected encounters leading to astonishing images. More likely, however, it points to his lack of connection with the land he experiences. Césaire's description evokes the vision of a tourist who is rediscovering the lost image of his childhood books in a "marvelous" tropical landscape.

The marvelous land—its landscape, flora, fauna, and human inhabitants—crumbles under Breton's imperial desire. From its very inception, Césaire's first text on Breton is far from the simple praise it seems to be on the surface. Much of Césaire's praise for Breton cannibalizes words from Breton's writings. Suzanne Césaire's conclusion, "André Breton, le *plus* riche, le *plus* pur" [the richest, the purest] (*Le Grand camouflage,* 62, emphasis in original), echoes Breton's own problematic praise of Aimé Césaire: "I recall my very elementary first reaction at discovering him of the purest of black ["d'un noir si pur"]. . . . And it is a black man who handles French language like no white man can handle it today" (*Martinique,* 121). The evocation of Breton's purity appears as false praise since Suzanne Césaire was a fierce critic of the idea of pure categories.[53] The praise is thus mined both by its ironic tone and by its response to the dubious association of her husband's poetry with the "so pure blackness" of his skin. In this, we recognize the technique of Shakespeare's Caliban of turning the master's words into a curse directed toward the master's discourse: "You taught me language, and my profit on't / Is I know how to curse" (*The Tempest,* act I, scene 2, 368–70). Armed with her Caliban-like strategy, Césaire gets closer to the figure of the cannibal. As Cuban writer Roberto Fernández Retamar explains: "Caliban is Shakespeare's anagram for 'cannibal,' an expression that he had already used to mean 'anthropophagus . . . and that comes in turn from the word carib" (6). The Caliban cannibal Césaire ingests her master's curse in order to regurgitate it in his face.

Césaire's gestures of appropriation allow us to consider her essays—as well as the journal *Tropiques,* which houses them—not just as offshoots of surrealism but also as sites where surrealism gets renewed, transformed, and ultimately surpassed by a process of ingestion and transformation. Caribbean writing gives surrealism a new energy, remothers it. This critical gesture runs countercurrent to decades of criticism, which have portrayed, for instance, Aimé Césaire as the heir of Breton or Cuban painter Wilfredo Lam as the inheritor of Picasso. Franklin Rosemont, for instance, belongs to the long list of critics who see only a unilateral influence from an imperial center to peripheral colonial or postcolonial sites. In his introduction to the American edition of Breton's *Martinique Snake Charmer* (2008), he interprets *Tropiques* as an "all-out surrealist publication" (11). More crucially for us, it is time to acknowledge Césaire as an originator who feeds on surrealism, goes beyond surrealism, while surrealism feeds on her.

In 1943, Césaire defined surrealism as "the tightrope of our hopes" (*Le Grand camouflage,* 83). The metaphorical tightrope allowed for a way to cross a dangerous breach, but it also involved the risk of falling into the abyss. In her later writings, Césaire goes beyond the metaphor of the dangerous ancillary tool. Surrealism becomes instead a nourishing substance. Cannibalism, as we saw, takes only the best of the ingested product. It is a discriminate, discursive, and discrete act of consumption. While cannibalism destroys and annihilates parts of the ingested object, it also creates from and beyond the ingested object. As the Freudian reading of the myth indicates, the sons who devour their father give him a new—sublimated—life and meaning instead of annihilating him.[54] As such, the consumed Breton should be seen as indebted to his devourer, Suzanne, who becomes his new mother.[55] The question of mothering is not to be taken as an empty metaphor. Césaire's practice of cannibalism is indeed embedded in a reflection on sexual desire, reproduction, and racial mixing. Her essays provide a nexus where the complex relationship between cannibalism and *métissage,* colonial hunger for food and sex, coexist in a troubling relation.

Césaire's most direct and anguished response to Breton resides in the following passage, in which she metaphorically, yet unquestionably, strikes her old offender, several years after the offense. Like Absalom, who waits two years before killing Amnôn, the avenger Césaire knows patience: "Cependant les balisiers d'Absalon saignent sur les gouffres et la beauté du paysage tropical monte à la tête des poètes qui passent" [All the while, the canna plants of Absalon bleed on the abyss and the beauty of the tropical landscape intoxicates the passing poets] (*Le Grand camouflage,* 93). Recall that the *canna* plant or "balisier" was for Breton the site of the highly sexualized triple-beating heart, with a spade-like shape. Césaire takes the flower at face value. No longer a symbol of aggressive masculine sexual desire, the plant is reclaimed as a feminine site, an open wound whose blood—of menstruation, of deflowering, of birthing, or of the rape of Tamar—indelibly marks the abyss. Césaire's image takes us back to Absalon *and* to Absalom. More precisely, it brings us back to Tamar's story. After being raped, Tamar covers her head with ashes and rips her brightly colored clothing (*Samuel II,* 13:18–19). Tamar's gestures, which could be seen as expressions of loss and mourning, could also be interpreted, because of their theatrical performance in a public space, as an exteriorization of the rape onto the visible body in order to make the act apparent to her family, and particularly to her brother Absalom. Like Tamar, who waves her colorful rags in the open, Césaire brings the color of a bleeding red to the surface of her writing in order to make the offense apparent to the world, readable as an open text. All the while ("cependant"), Breton is visible in the evocation of the intoxicated passing poet who cannot see the pain and blood of the flower he had so desired, and hurt.

Also notable is the fact that *canna* or *cannaceae* is the Latin name of the bleeding flower in question. While there are no explicit associations between the *canna* flower and the cannibal in Césaire's texts, it is not too far-fetched to imagine that Césaire—like Columbus confused *cariba* and *canis* in a false etymological association—could have associated the "cann-" of "cannaceae" with the "cann-" of "cannibal." This connection, which might be a figment of our imagination, but which is nonetheless close to the spirit of the writer's literary and ethical project, would gender—feminize—the idea of the cannibal by the use of a flower as its emblem. The wounded flower would then strike back, eat back, in a way reminiscent of Césaire's declaration of independence for Caribbean and Tropical women in "Le grand camouflage": "Et quant aux femmes-colibris, aux femmes-fleurs tropicales, aux femmes aux quatre races et aux douzaines de sang, elles n'y sont plus. Ni les balisiers . . . ni les couchers de soleil uniques au monde / Pourtant elles y sont" [As for humming-bird-women, tropical-flower women, four-raced women and dozen-blooded women, they are long gone. . . . Yet they're here] (*Le Grand camouflage,* 86).

Cannibalism and *Métissage*

While Césaire and Breton's palimpsest dialogue illuminates us on the private and intellectual relationship of two individuals, it also acts as a springboard for a general discussion on colonial desire, consumption, and *métissage.* The stakes of their private relationship—romance, infatuation, literary influence—are much higher when the exchange becomes a political commentary and call for action, as clearly expressed in Césaire's final essay, "Le grand camouflage." In the passage quoted below, the figure of Breton as passing poet merges with that of the French civil servant idling on the beach. The interchangeability between the two figures is explained by their common transient nature and by their shared responsibility in—and blindness to—the fact of *métissage*:

> A handful of "Metropolitan civil servants" were sitting on the beach. They were perched there, unconvinced, ready to soar at the first signal. . . . When they bend over the evil Caribbean mirror, they discover a delirious image of themselves. . . . They know that *métis* people have a share in their blood, that they are, like themselves, of Western civilization. Of course, "Metropolitans" ignore color prejudice. But their colored brood instills fear into them, despite exchanged smiles. They did not expect this strange burgeoning of their blood. They might not want to respond to the Caribbean heir who screams and does not scream "my father" [qui crie et ne crie pas "mon père"]. But, one has to account for these astonishing boys, these charming girls. One has to rule over these rambunctious people. (*Le Grand camouflage,* 90)[56]

The civil servants came from metropolitan France to work in the Antilles for a few years.[57] Césaire stages these transient workers on the ambivalent site of the beach. While the beach is considered a site of leisure, idleness, and erotic contemplation by the European travelers, it is invested with memories of shipwrecked slave ships in the Martinican diasporic imagination. The beach, like the tourists it temporarily hosts, is also a site of passage, of transience, of unsettling between land and sea. Interestingly, the French civil servants are turned into birds by the metaphors of being "perched there" and "ready to soar." They become the exotic birds that they had seen in the "native fleshes" they contemplated. The reference to the Europeans' flight alludes both to their transient position in Martinique and to their lack of responsibility.

In contrast with common representations, Césaire throws the civil servants into the same category as the native *békés* or white colonials. The two categories are interchangeable because of their participation in the oppression of the inhabitants of the island and, more specifically, in their shared responsibility as initiators of the sexual act that leads to *métissage*. French civil servants and *békés* alike lust for the *métis* bodies, but they will not acknowledge the *métis* children as part of their inheritance and debt. By implication, tourists, civil servants, and passing poets are all enmeshed in colonial sexual violence. As in the act of cannibalism, the ingested—or in this case the penetrating body—merges with the body of the other and becomes at once conserved ("*métis* people have a share in their blood") and transformed in a result that escapes their control ("a delirious image of themselves," "a strange burgeoning of their blood"). In her accusation, Césaire goes further than dominant interpretations of the violence of *métissage*, which typically limit the responsibility of the violence of a handful of local white planters who sexually coerced women in positions of subservience. Thus, the violence of *métissage* is no longer restricted to the plantation walls and slavery; it becomes the responsibility not only of the French civil servants but also of France and of "Western civilization." Césaire's gesture is politically significant on several levels. First, it removes the firewall that protected France from its responsibility in slavery and colonialism. *Békés* have been used politically as buffers between the enslaved and the colonizing power to carry the responsibility of colonialist violence and exploitation in order to keep intact the image of a French benevolent nation and *Mère-Patrie*. Moreover, Césaire offers a sharp criticism of tourism—sexual or literary—as a significant form of colonial violence, an issue that critics and writers will begin to broach several decades after her death.[58]

In Césaire's essays, the violence of *métissage*, like that of cannibalism, relies on the mixing of bodies. Like cannibalism, *métissage* instills fear ("crainte") in the passing traveler as it mingles the bodies of colonizer and of colonized, of Europeans and "charming exotic" boys and girls. One of the major differences between Césaire's practice of cannibalism and her evocation of *métissage* is that the first acts solely on a metaphorical and discursive level. It is indeed never a question, for instance, of serving Breton's body in a cannibal feast such as in Peter Greenaway's *The Cook, the Thief, His Wife, and Her Lover* or in Nelson Pereira dos Santos's *How Tasty Was My Little Frenchman,* which would be absurd. No, cannibalism remains, within Césaire's text, a devouring of words. By contrast, *métissage* refers to the literal mixing of human bodies. Its results or remainders are constituted by people, not words; hence the centrality of ethical and legal responsibility in Césaire's discussion of *métissage.*

Both *métissage* and cannibalism imply a product, or a supplement, something that the ingesting body in one case, or the pregnant or parturient body in the other, cannot assimilate fully. In her *Cannibal Democracy,* Zita Nunes reflects on the state and functions of the remainder in the use of the metaphor of cannibalism in a New World context.[59] She argues that in nation formation, the act of ingestion always excludes a section of the population, for example, the Africans, in the case of the United States, as inassimilable.[60] She bases her analysis on a monologue drawn from African American writer August Wilson's play *Ma Rainey's Black Bottom,* in which the character Toledo describes history as a common stew. Within this mixture composed of many odds and ends—not unlike the "Common Creole Stew" introduced in chapter 1—Toledo emphasizes the leftovers, that is, what remains uneaten or expelled by the body as waste: "You got some leftovers and you can't do nothing with it. You already making you another history. . . . See we's the leftovers. The colored man is the leftovers" (Wilson, quoted in Nunes, 146–47). Wilson's leftovers resemble the products of *métissage* evoked by Césaire, the *métis* children who constitute the remainders that France cannot assimilate in its national model.[61] The *métis* "unexpected boys" and "charming girls," with their "turbulent" character, trouble the fixed identities of the European travelers and of Western civilization itself: "Cependant, il faut compter avec ces garçons innatendus, ces filles charmantes" (Césaire, *Le Grand camouflage,* 271). The *métis* "leftovers" produced by colonial or touristic desire and by the sexual acts that ensued need to be reingested, incorporated in the "white" identity from which they in part originated. For Césaire, they cannot remain external objects of desire or scrap children hidden from sight; they must be internalized in the European consciousness.

"Il faut compter avec eux," Césaire insists. The meaning of the French expression is multifarious: one has to "take them into account," one has to "account for them," one has to "count with them." The three possible English translations of the phrase point, respectively, to acts of acknowledgment, ethical engagement, and cooperation. The ethical duty Césaire demands, unlike the gesture of violent incorporation of an external object as in the cannibal act of revenge, calls for a reenvisioning of the Western self. The West too must internalize *métissage* and the violence, madness, and disorder it carries.

In Césaire's model, the remainder, the indigestible, the waste, is ultimately not the *métis* child but the greed and excess of colonial violence that led to *métissage* in the first place: "We had to take revenge on the nostalgic hell that vomited on the new world and its islands its devilish adventurers, its galley sailors, its repentants, its utopians" (*Le Grand camouflage,* 269). The allusion to vomiting alludes to a solely destructive and abject act far from the creative act of literary or cultural cannibalism. In this mode of violent *métissage,* in contrast with the cannibalistic mode, the European aggressor becomes the perpetrator. In Césaire's reversal, the monstrosity, the excess, the madness, the disease, is henceforth attributed not to the fierce Carib, to the idle native, or to the wobbly *métis,* but to the colonizer and the exploiter.

Césaire's *métis*, like her literary cannibals, ultimately escape their status of commodified remainders and become actors in the process of naming and creation. In the passage discussed, Césaire renames the *métis* "Antillean": "l'héritier antillais qui crie et ne crie pas 'mon père'" (90). Thus she shifts from the European perception, which casts Caribbean people into a fixed racial category, to an empowering position of ethnicity or putative nationality. The Antillean heir of the passage who "crie et ne crie pas 'mon père'" is above all an agent. Recall that the term *crier* in French, "to scream" or "to shout," is inhabited by a Creole meaning that means both "to create" and "to name." The Antillean child thus, while uttering a scream of revolt, in French, gains the power of naming—in Creole. In this particular case, the Martinican sons and daughters, who are above all Caribbean, gain the fatherly and Adamic power of naming and creating their own father. The child is also endowed with the power of choice since she or he can choose either to claim the father or to reject him as an unwanted residue. In becoming

Antillean, the *métis* moves from the position of being processed and rejected as waste by a colonial position to a position of speaking subject. Césaire's Antillean has nothing left to do with the "national remainder" exposed by Nunes. Instead, the Antillean subject, leaving the racial livery of the *métis* behind, trumpets the birth of a nation whose own remainder would be France or the West, the very "civilization" that created and expelled it in the first place. Césaire's model contains the seeds of an emerging Antillean nationalism. I insist on the word "seeds" since this nationalistic passage, in Césaire's essay, appears to be a necessary phase of communal self-assertion destined to be overcome in a dialectical progression. This moment, like the moment of *négritude* that Sartre has famously described, is meant to "self-destruct . . . a passage, not a destination point; a mean, not an end in itself" ("Orphée noir," ix). What would then constitute the resolution of the dialectical movement?

At the close of "Le grand camouflage," which also constitutes Césaire's final written word and also the last word of *Tropiques,* Césaire goes beyond the violent metaphors of confrontation exposed in the first moment of the dialectics—cannibalism and *métissage.* She also leaves behind the antithesis of a nationalism responding to another to focus instead on the figure of the peasant Martinican man who receives the earth without consuming it: "A peasant who escaped the shivers of the mechanical adventure, leaned on the great mapou tree . . . and felt surging into him, through his naked toes deep in mud, a slow organic growth" (*Le Grand camouflage,* 92). This alternative to Césaire's confrontational modes of being-with-the-other allows us to perceive the act of being-with-the-world as a passive, yet nourishing and fulfilling, state. The Martinican "homme-plante" or "human plant," a figure on which Césaire elaborates elsewhere,[62] "lets himself drift through life, docile, light, unstressed, unrebelled—friendlily, amorously" (70). This passivity is not to be confused with idleness or surrender but, rather, should be understood as an amiable and amorous way of being in the world by receiving it. The balanced practice of feeding each other has replaced the violent mode of eating each other. The act of feeding the other and being fed by it, her, or him opens up a space for a relationship to food and nourishment away from the moments of confrontational cannibalism or violent *métissage.* Césaire's seven essays successfully reconcile the two forcefully separated sides of the Caribbean subject: the warrior and the farmer, the proud *Carib* and the humble *Taïno.*

Cannibalism as Farce: Maryse Condé's Story of the Cannibal Woman

In her 2003 novel *Histoire de la femme cannibale (The Story of the Cannibal Woman)*, Maryse Condé picks up where Suzanne Césaire left off in her "Grand camouflage." If Condé had been an ardent theorist and practitioner of metaphorical and literary cannibalism in her past work,[63] her novel, while pretending to be absolutely cannibal, signals the end of the cannibalistic moment. Condé eventually arrives at a post-cannibalistic literary practice escaping vengeance-based logics. Like Césaire, Condé, after a necessary moment of devouring literary texts to feed her own, seems to have realized that the field of metaphorical cannibalism, as Richard King contends, "does not enhance understanding of the contexts in which individuals and institutions deploy them and does less to effectively challenge or undermine them. . . . [I]t reinstates and reaffirms binaries, and worse, often turns on the same forms of appropriation" (King, 108). Fredric Jameson, referring to Caliban's retort, similarly points to the weakness of such a confrontational stage in his foreword to Retamar's *Caliban*: "Can you do anything but curse in this alien language?" (Jameson in Retamar, x). Literary cannibalism indeed curses in the other's language by ingesting its words and regurgitating them in a new form, and in so doing remains stuck in a dialectical trap.

Condé fights against such stifling cannibalism by exaggerating its presence in her text and thereby disarming it. In her *Story*, the more prevalent the cannibal, the more it disappears. As Michel de Certeau argued about Montaigne's foundational essay "Of Cannibals," "The cannibals slip away from the words and discourses that fix their place. . . . They are not to be found where they are thought. They are never *there*" (Certeau, 70, emphasis in original). Similarly, Condé, by making the cannibal omnipresent, renders it omni-absent, so to speak. *Story* carves out a space for the cannibal where it, or more precisely *she*,[64] is everywhere and nowhere. In brief, in a self-ironic gesture, Condé turns her novel into a farce of cannibalism. By farce, I refer both to the literary genre that uses hyperbole, exaggeration, and extravagant drollery in order to undermine the subject or character it depicts and to the action of culinary stuffing, as in filling a sausage or a tomato with forcemeat or miscellaneous mingled ingredients.[65] The novel's object, cannibalism, because of its own embonpoint and profusion, becomes banal and worthless as a commodity of curiosity and voyeurism.

Cannibalism stuffs up the bones, flesh, and skin of Condé's novel. The title, in a manner reminiscent of the titillating titles of Pineau and Laferrière's novels analyzed in chapter 4—*Chair Piment* and *Comment faire l'amour avec un nègre*—lures the reader into a voyeuristic trap. The title leads the reader to expect the unveiling of the story of a real cannibal woman exhibited by a famous Caribbean writer. Additionally, a cannibal woman is indeed present within the novel in a newspaper clipping of a sensationalistic article from the *Cape Tribune*: "That morning, the news of a dark, horrific event was spread across the front page. A woman was accused of murdering her husband, who had been missing for several weeks. According to her son-in-law, who had become suspicious of the meat packed in plastic bags on the refrigerator's shelves, she had cut him into little pieces and frozen them. Why would be anybody's guess" (Condé, *Story,* 77). As in Certeau's comment, the omnipresent "spread across" cannibal woman slips away as soon as the reader realizes that all evidence of cannibalism is absent from the newspaper clipping, which relies on rumors, wild guesses, and logical fallacies to mount its accusation. The nature of the meat in the freezer is never revealed, nor the actual crime ever proved. The alleged victim has simply "gone missing." This accusation of cannibalism based on remnants of meat is strikingly similar to European accusations of Amerindian and African cannibalism based solely on the observation of the remnants of a meal. As Peter Hulme has argued ("Introduction: The Cannibal Scene," 2), the cannibal act is never observed while it is performed but only in its aftermath. In Condé's novel, even if a few weeks of trial "more or less rule out . . . the argument for cannibalism" (Condé, *Story,* 204), Fiela remains a monstrous cannibal in the eyes of all. Despite the lack of legal evidence, Fiela, the alleged cannibal woman, remains a sign of monstrosity that troubles the stability of the nation itself: "It puts our country to shame" (203). Like the Amerindians who were accused of cannibalism with doubtful after-the-fact evidence and for simply standing in the livery of the dog-headed cynocephalus of Columbus's confusion, Fiela is trapped in a form of situational cannibalism. Regardless of her actions, her name, ethnic, and personal status suffice to place her in the position of the abject outsider.

The name Fiela, closely related to the word *fiel*, "bile" or "gall" in French, evokes the act of digestion and the sentiments of rage and fury associated with liver secretions, according to ancient humoral medical theory. Her name therefore associates her with the domains of digestion, anger, and madness. It strikingly contrasts with her face, which Rosélie, the main protagonist of the novel, describes as "no more diabolic-looking than any other. She even looked quite gentle, almost shy" (Condé, *Story,* 77). Like the Caribbean who bears in its name that of the cannibal, Fiela is determined by her very designation. Additionally, her feminized name, "Fiela," associates cannibalism with femininity, more precisely with femininity gone awry.

Fiela's situational cannibalism is reinforced by her racial and gender status. The color of her skin is proof enough to link her to a "cannibal lineage." The main protagonist, Rosélie, a black woman from Guadeloupe drifting from Cape Town to Johannesburg, imagines that, in her white husband's eyes, she is herself a descendant of cannibals, and that, by the same token of her color, Fiela is, too: "She got the impression she was tarnishing the image of their beloved professor, who spoke English with an inimitable accent and was the embodiment of Old World sophistication. What was the sordid connection between him and this descendant of cannibals? Fiela, Fiela, you see, we are alike" (*Story,* 96). Cannibalism therefore migrates from object to object through multiple channels—historical, pseudohistorical, geographical, ethnic, or racial—like a contaminating disease. This propensity to infect all the objects cannibalism touches reveals its instability as a specifically located and stable concept. Cannibalism is defined by its mobility and thus by its uncertainty. It also often follows a semantic tautology whereby a cannibal is a cannibal because it is a cannibal. Similarly, according to Rosélie or an unnamed narrator,[66] "A black man is always guilty. But of what? Of being black, of course!" (226). Guilt, in the case of cannibalism, as in the case of blackness, acts as its own original cause and explanation in a logical fallacy.

A minor event in Condé's novel offers a notable counterpoint to the evocation of the alleged cannibal woman. While in Paris, Rosélie remembers reading about a Japanese man who had raped, killed, skinned, and taken a few bites out of a Dutch student: "Declared insane, he had been extradited to Japan" (*Story,* 78).[67] The Japanese man, in spite of having ingested parts of his victim, is accused not of cannibalism but of insanity, a disorder readable by the Western rules of psychiatry. He is not projected outside humanity like the cannibal but is deviant within humanity and its laws. While he is banished from French national soil, he is not expelled from the nation altogether. The Japanese man can go back to his own country, in contrast to Fiela, who brings shame to her own nation, and with Rosélie, whose country, Guadeloupe, is unimaginable as such: "You mean you're French? Oh no! I'm from Guadeloupe! Where's that? My God, what a mix-up!" (114). The counterexample of the Japanese man, woman-eater yet clean of the monstrosity of cannibalism, proves with great irony that cannibalism is not factual but situational. Cannibalism amounts to being at the wrong place at the wrong time, and in the wrong skin and gender.

Fiela's lack of actual children further consolidates her diabolic and cannibal side. Her neighbors inform the press that "Fiela terrified them. She never smiled. She had never given birth. Her breasts contained a bile that soiled her clothes during her diabolical suckling. Instead of intestines, her belly writhed with snakes" (204). The two chief causes of terror are Fiela's lack of smile and her lack of children. Her lack of smile excludes her from comforting norms of femininity. Her lack of children signals not an absence but, rather, the presence of a pathological, diabolic, and monstrous reality. Her breasts are not simply dry of milk but are lactating bile; her womb is not empty but is sheltering devilish snakes. The lack of children is thus not simply an absence but is the presence of a threatening pathology.

Rosélie, who is also childless, is similarly associated with insanity. Throughout the novel, Rosélie's artistic creations—she is a painter—function structurally and emotionally as children from her own womb. When she paints, "she [is] inhabited by a happiness, no doubt comparable with that of a woman whose fetus moves in the very depths of her flesh" (*Story,* 117). However, her viewers systematically deem her brood monstrous. After visiting her studio, an acquaintance emits a verdict: "My God, it's Bluebeard's closet!" (123). Rosélie is put in the position of the diabolical blue-bearded hero of Charles Perrault's folktale, turned masculine and monstrous in one stroke. By becoming Bluebeard, she also merges with the figure of Fiela since Bluebeard's previous wives, like Fiela's husband, have mysteriously disappeared. Rosélie's creations occupy the position of Bluebeard's dead wives, found in the man's hidden closet. Therefore, Rosélie's lack of actual children paired with her artistic productivity constitutes a deadly threat to the order of society. Rosélie not only refrains from participating in individual reproduction but also halts the reproduction machine itself since she produces dead wives, dead potential motherhood, according to the analogy with the fairy tale. Rosélie's and Fiela's lack of participation in patterns of human reproduction exclude them in turn from patterns of national reproduction, for which they constitute a threat.

Thus, both Rosélie and Fiela occupy the position of Nunes's remainder. Condé's two female protagonists represent that which cannot be absorbed in a South African nation striving to become pure of shame. Fiela shames "our country," according to one of the voices in the novel. In the folk opinion depicted in Condé's novel, it is not the political past of apartheid that constitutes the shame of the nation, nor the shameful confessions emerging from the "Truth and Reconciliation Commission," but the crime of a singled-out alleged cannibal woman. While all the evils of the country are projected onto the scapegoat Fiela, Rosélie remarks that Pretoria revels in "big speeches about the duty of forgiveness, the need to live together, Truth and Reconciliation," while there is "nothing but tension, hatred, and desire for revenge in this patch of land" (*Story,* 81). Thus, the cannibal woman—whether it is Fiela or Rosélie—becomes the singled-out body onto which the generalized evils of a country are projected. Condé inverts this act of singling-out by generalizing cannibalism.

Scholars such as Richard King have pointed out the risk of generalizing the use of the metaphor of cannibalism to the point that it loses meaning entirely.[68] Condé's novel could, on the surface, present an extreme case of this confusion caused by generalization. However, Condé pilots strategically metaphor mixing in her novel, rather than falling victim to it. Condé purposely confuses cannibalism with various forms of incorporation: literal food ingestion, textual and artistic borrowing, voyeurism, touristic gaze, eroticism, and narcissism, as well as bodily, spiritual, and cultural mixing—mothering, *métissage,* multiculturalism, transmigration, telepathy—and violence and transgression, including misogyny, incest, rape, homosexuality, witchcraft, savagery, and vampirism.[69] In short, everything—nothing—is cannibal.[70]

To develop one particular example, Condé's characters and narrators, countercurrent to the rampant political and social discourse, present motherhood as a disease that eats up the body. Rosélie's mother Rose's pregnancy causes a mysterious "perfidious sickness" (*Story,* 5) in which "grease" consumes her and smothers her operatic voice (5–6). Children portrayed as sharp-teethed vampires take in their mother's flesh and blood instead of mother's milk ("Berline [was] constantly clinging to her breasts despite her twenty-four months and her two rows of incisors," 125). Cannibalism ultimately makes it impossible to distinguish between parents and children, selves and others. Even naming fails in its capacity to individuate the child from her parents. Rosélie is consumed, eaten up by her parents' names since mother Rose and father Elie could not think of naming their daughter with any other name than the combination of their own: Rose and Élie, Rosélie. Naming, like the act of cannibalism, confuses parting and fusion, creation and death.

The theme of children devouring their mother, and of mothers devouring their brood, is far from exceptional in slavery-related works such as in Condé's own *Traversée de la mangrove* or in Toni Morrison's *Beloved.* In the slavery and postslavery context, the mother's belly acts metaphorically and literally as an extension of the plantation. Women's wombs constitute the extension of the reproductive machine of slavery, and children are considered as extended limbs of plantation labor. However, in *Story of the Cannibal Woman,* the slave plantation has ceased to function as a primary reference, and the presence of a gnawing motherhood seems to respond more to feminist claims of incompatibility between motherhood and artistic creativity than to criticisms of slavery. Motherhood and children alike devour mothers in that they seem to halt artistic productivity: singing in Rose's case or painting in Rosélie's. In that, too, Condé seems to have fostered a moment beyond the opposition between the colonizer and the colonized. Cannibalism in *Story* is more about an individual woman striving to assert her artistic originality than about criticism of colonialism (even if colonialism still acts as one among many evils such as racism, tourism, and intellectual arrogance).

The process of artistic creation, however, is not purely emancipatory. Rosélie's relationship with her children-paintings represents a circular narcissistic prison in which the painted object reflects and consumes its creator. This is made clear when Rosélie paints a portrait that she calls "Cannibal Woman": "'Fiela, Is that you? Is this me? Our two faces have merged'" (*Story,* 311). Is Rosélie's artistic process an act of feminine or feminist solidarity or a stifling reflection? A self-birth or a sentence of death? An act of creative regurgitating or a destructive self-ingestion? Meeting the other or self-imprisonment? The cannibal relationship leaves us with an open indecision. Condé's novel closes on the naming of Rosélie's last painting, which is also her first true creation because it is the first that she—not her husband—names: "This time, she knew what her title would be. . . . It had welled up from deep inside her on the crest of a raging tide: *Cannibal Woman*" (311, emphasis in original). The last image of the book, the birth—and death—of the cannibal woman through Rosélie's artistic creation and the naming of her work, also constitutes a *mise en abîme* of the novel itself since Condé's novel and Rosélie's painting share the same name: "Cannibal Woman." The indecision between subjectivity and objectivity, between possession and loss, is thus not only about Rosélie and Fiela but also about Condé and the cannibal woman, or rather between Condé and her novel, *Story of the Cannibal Woman.*

Indeed, the text itself constitutes the true cannibal of the novel. *Story* is not the simple adaptation of a text from the European canon by a "colonized" writer, such as was Condé's own *Windward Heights*, which transposed Emily Brontë's *Wuthering Heights* into the world of the plantation. With *Windward Heights,* Condé had practiced a form of discrete cannibalism by selecting her meal with care for a specific purpose, just as a Tupi would have feasted on the heart of a warrior to gain his strength. The cannibalism of *Story* is omnivorous and bulimic, and so its aim gets lost in this lack of discrimination. The novel is stuffed with references to popular songs, classical music, American television shows, and canonical French, British, American, and Caribbean literatures. Hollywood stars such as Keanu Reeves[71]—who occupies a prominent place in the novel—are eclectically juxtaposed with pan-African heroes such as Bob Marley and Léopold Sédar Senghor. Characters think through miscellaneous songs that run through their head, ventriloquize them, such as Vivaldi's *Stabat Mater* (157), Bizet's *Carmen* (5), Billy Joel's "New York State of Mind" (76), Martinican band Kassav's "Zouk-la, sé sel médikamen nou ni" (79), tunes by "handsome Lenny Kravitz or the Spice Girls" (89), and songs from Cape Verde's diva Cesaria Evora and Algerian Raï star Cheb Mami (109). Omnivorous readers quote Senghor on rhythm (79), Shakespeare's *A Midsummer Night's Dream* (96), consume "the complete works of Charles Dickens, Thomas Hardy," and "begin to tackle William Faulkner" (110). The text is also full of references to previous texts by Condé such as *Celanire Throat-Slashed* (71) and plot ingestions such as that of the main narrative of Condé's first novel, *Heremakhonon,* which is also the story of a Guadeloupean woman "returning" to Africa to search for her ancestors and mend her broken identity. In this case of self-cannibalism, Condé ironically and derisorily devours her own previous text in order to feed her new one. All respect for textual authority—including the author's own—is dismissed.

Such bulimic and omnivorous cultural ingestions seem to produce only waste and excess. As Kathryn Lachman cleverly argued, Condé's *Story of the Cannibal Woman* exemplifies a "poetics of indigestion" since she "incorporates so much foreign material into her narrative that the text simply cannot assimilate it all" (72). In this form of generalized and excessive devouring, the threatening figure of the cannibal becomes inoperative as a category of difference. Condé dismantles the age-old monstrosity of the cannibal by making it commonplace.

Other authors writing in the wake of colonialism have arrived at the same postcannibal moment. Congolese writer Alain Mabanckou in his 2005 novel *Verre Cassé* [Broken Glass] generalizes the practice of literary cannibalism to the absurd and grotesque. The novel is composed entirely of a collection of quotes briefly interrupted by a discreet "original" narrative, if the notion of originality still stands. The fictional writer staged in the text "drinks like a sponge" (Mabanckou, 11). This last note can be understood as both a reference to the writer's constant alcoholic intoxication, but also to his propensity to absorb literary material like a sponge would. This practice of extreme literary borrowing prevents all discourse on literary cannibalism and authority in the wake of colonialism. Thus colonial or former colonial subjects such as Condé's "lute-playing colonized" cease to exist in a state of secondariness since both original and secondary are broken into the pieces of Mabanckou's image of the broken glass. The European, the canonic, the historical precedent lacks distinctiveness. Condé's and Mabanckou's gestures, which respond to what we might call a poetics of broken glass, fragment the previously monolithic categories of the colonial, the colonized, and the postcolonial,[72] and allow us to read texts by African or Caribbean writers away from their relation with the colonial center. Thus, for instance, we can read Condé along with American popular culture, rather than against the French literary canon. The practice of extreme—thus disintegrating—cannibalism leads to a healthy eschatological lack of distinct political and disciplinary categories. As Condé claims, "these categories—Guadeloupean literature, Martinican literature, Haitian literature—will likely disappear. It is time for them to disappear! A time will come when people of the Caribbean will create literature anywhere and everywhere" ("A Conversation," 26).

The dissolution of categories and easy labels does not lead to chaos or a complete lack of positionality. It is negative exceptionality—as expressed by the figure of the cannibal, which defines a section of humanity as less-than-human—that must disappear. It is time to think beyond the terms of the cannibal and the victim, the victorious and the cooked, the trapper and the entrapped, the primary and secondary, the culturally dominant and the awkward *métis*. Maryse Condé, in the company of Suzanne Césaire, Édouard Glissant, Gisèle Pineau, and other "kitchen poets," to use Paule Marshall's words, offers a perspective beyond the confrontational trope of cannibalism. In the works of these authors, literal or metaphorical uses of literature, food, eating, and cooking establish cultural and transcultural relations. They aim not at the dissolution of meaning and authority but at their assertion in a relational model of eating, cooking, writing, and speaking. It is no longer a matter of eating the other, but of eating with the other and of feeding the other. As Derrida asserts: "'Eating well' doesn't primarily mean to take in or to comprehend within oneself, but rather to learn and to feed, to-learn-how-to-feed-the-other. One never eats alone, that's the rule of 'eating well.' It is a law of infinite hospitality" ("Il faut bien manger," 296–97). In order to reach that law of infinite hospitality, and to escape the law of the cannibal, the law of revenge, and the law of hunger, one must be in a position to receive, and to give outside of an economy of control and dependency. In order to "learn-how-to-feed-the-other," one must escape the paralyzing position of needy hunger, whether it is a hunger for body nourishment, autonomous words, or independence.

AFTERWORD

Can Hunger Speak?

My passion for eating, cooking, and forging friendships through the sharing of food, recipes, and time spent in the kitchen undeniably drove this book. Its main source, however, resides in hunger. I was privileged to grow up in food abundance and diversity, yet my immediate family memory offered me a different narrative. My grandparents' and parents' experience of the penuries of World War II and of the poverty of watch-factory workers in the Jura border zones of Wehrmacht-occupied France and buffer Switzerland taught me that food should never be thrown away, nor should it be wasted. The words of my grandmother describing the pleasure of sharing an egg for dinner with my young mother as a welcome distraction from the bread dunked in the *chicory-saccharin-au-lait* still resound in my mind. Hunger was not only central to this project, but formative to who I am as a scholar. My grandmother's and mother's quotidian cooking of potatoes, meat, and bread in an endless recycling of *boulettes, galettes, hâchis, ramequins,* and *Röschtis* until everything was eaten, save for crumbs reserved for birds, taught me a life-long awareness of an economy of food, of an economy of words.

I spent my high school years in boarding school in the Jura town of Pontarlier, where the lugubrious Fort-de-Joux culminated over the clouds. As a teenager, I saw, not to ever forget, the *oubliette* of the aforementioned citadel in which Haitian Revolutionary hero Toussaint Louverture died of cold and hunger. My realization of the injustice and inhumanity of the jailers, my compatriots, and of the gloomy history graven across my native landscape is one of the encounters that brought me to Caribbean literature, surreptitiously. I want to make the many stories of hunger, historical and familial, near and far, communicate with each other, instead of leaving them alone in the silence of the *oubliette*, the silence of shame and forgetfulness. That is why Aimé Césaire speaks also to me when he so lyrically evokes Toussaint's death and claims as his own the dark, cold underground cell: "What is also mine: a small cell in the Jura . . . the snow doubles it with white prison bars / the snow is a white jailor" (*Cahier,* 25). As a scholar of literature, my ethical duty is to acknowledge these stories of hunger and oppression, which are also mine, and to make them speak in relation. But can hunger speak? How can we theoretically speak of absolute hunger, which, by definition, silences the weakened and the dead?

Indeed, extreme hunger is the most stifling form of experience. It turns the living into walking dead; it erases the human face under the all-consuming face of hunger. As Primo Levi famously articulated, the absolute hunger of extermination camps such as Auschwitz not only paralyzed and killed, but also serially processed the differences and the humanity of prisoners by replacing their faces with its own: "We ourselves are hunger, living hunger" (Levi, *Survival,* 74). The mouths of the prisoners become a mechanistic extension of the voracious mouth of the extermination machine, moving with it in unison, deprived of all autonomy. Through this machine made of imbricated mechanical and human parts, hunger speaks: "At every bite [that the mouth of the voracious steam-shovel takes] our mouths also open, our Adam's apples dance up and down" (ibid.).

In his *Cahier,* Césaire evokes a similar figure of the human as living hunger that he calls "the hunger-man" ("l'homme-famine"). When hunger rises from its adjectival position, where it should humanely stay, to become nominal (from "hungry man" to "hunger-man"), it ceases to be a detachable attribute, becomes absolute, and evacuates from the human its ontology. To imitate Fanon, "The starved offers no ontological resistance in the face of hunger" ("The black man offers no ontological resistance in the eyes of the white man," *Black Skin,* 90). The extermination-camp prisoner, the Caribbean subject starved by the machine of slavery and exploitation, is no longer a hungry human being, but starvation itself, for whom hunger becomes a subject, a face, and a voice. Amabelle, the main character of Danticat's *Farming of Bones,* evokes the haunting figure of the "sugar woman," the embodiment of the economic machine of slavery and of the exploitation of Haitian cane workers in the Dominican Republic. The sugar woman is at once sugar, hunger, product of enslaved and exploited bodies, victim, and origin of trauma: "I dream of the sugar woman. Again. . . . Around her face, she wears a shiny silver muzzle. . . . 'Is your face underneath this?' . . . 'This?' She taps her fingers against the muzzle. 'Given to me a long time ago . . . so I'd not eat the sugarcane'" (*Farming of Bones*, 132). The muzzle, animalizing by its diverted use on a human, also erases humanity altogether by obliterating the face under the tool of torture. A muzzle is used to prevent its wearer from biting, emitting sounds, and eating.

And yet, humanity survives. Levi's "living hunger," Césaire's "hunger-man," and Danticat's muzzled "sugar woman" continue to speak despite the defacement and annihilation caused by absolute hunger. The book *If This Is a Man* is the living proof of the survival of humanity and language engulfed into hunger. In Levi's account, words, such as the one describing the most basic staple in the many languages spoken in the camp, thrive: "bread-Brot-Broid-chleb-pain-lechem-keynér" (*Survival,* 39). Words indicate not only humanity through speech but also the richness of human difference through their multilingualism. Césaire's "hunger-man," or rather "hunger-boy," in another passage of *Cahier,* leads us to think that hunger silences all speech, swallows up the voice: "for the swamps of hunger engulfed his voice of starvation" (*Cahier,* 11). Hunger becomes the sole subject using the hunger-boy as its empty vessel. There is nothing to be expected from hunger-boy, Césaire laments, but "a heavy and apathetic hunger / a hunger engulfed in the deepest depths of the Hunger of this famished hill" (12). Hunger with the lower-case, which represents the boy's individual hunger, is itself engulfed in absolute *H*unger.

Yet, like Levi's *If This Is a Man,* Césaire's *Cahier* stands as a monument reasserting humanity in the face of hunger with the most flourishing and luminous language. There is speech growing out of hunger. There is art. Paradoxically, the experience of absolute hunger, precisely that which silences and kills, offers a common space of communication between spaces and texts. In this case, the Shoah and Slavery speak to each other. Hunger does not speak *for* humanity; it fails to turn humans into ventriloquized puppets. Hunger is not, cannot remain, the absolute speaking subject. Humanity speaks despite and through hunger, turning hunger into its own vessel.

We must observe, as we already did in chapter 2, that the vitality of Caribbean intellectuals was never so intense as in the time of food penury called *an tan Wobè* in Martinique during World War II; that the journal *Tropiques* was published under censorship, and under penury of food, paper, and ink; that the experience of hunger in pre- and post-earthquake Haiti could not halt aesthetic production; that it could not stop beauty and humanity from flourishing. One of the most gripping moments of "Our Guernica," Danticat's personal account of the aftermath of the 2010 earthquake, resides in the following image: "Jhon and I spot, past a cardboard sign with a plea for food in the entryway of a makeshift refugee camp, a large white tent with a striking image painted on it: a stunningly beautiful chocolate angel with her face turned up toward an indigo sky as she floats over a pile of muddied corpses" (*Create,* 169). Danticat and her companion Jhon dub this scene "Our Guernica," a name encompassing the heart-wrenching juxtaposition of hunger, death, and devastation with artistic beauty. In so doing, they create an aesthetic network between Haitian art and Cubism under war, making them speak with each other, communicate, and reach out, despite and through hunger. By establishing a link with the Spanish Civil War, they also define the earthquake as the result of political and historical factors, and not as a doom-driven natural disaster.

There is a certain incentive to reach out aesthetically, politically, to the rest of the world when hunger bites, Glissant claims: "We know that hunger makes us see far away. That is, when it is not definite, when it hasn't bulldozed all life around it, and when you still have a few unripe plantains that you stole away from the mariners' greed and that you buried in your backyard to escape requisitions" (*Traité,* 47). While a hunger that does not lead to starvation can stimulate thinking or acting, Glissant's description of the precarious nature of survival also indicates that there is a fine line between the energy stimulated by a bearable hunger and the stifling or even fatal effect hunger would have, should the precarious and dicey supply of unripe fruit fail. We must be ethically aware that while we cannot assimilate the hungry with hunger, we must nonetheless acknowledge the stifling experience of hunger, the use of hunger as weapon of war or tool of economic and political control. Being well fed, having the means of feeding oneself: these are human rights.

Philippe Jonassaint, a beneficiary of a human rights fund for rehabilitation in Haiti, interviewed by Erica Caple James in her book on the politics of intervention in Haiti, expresses the disjunction between the right to speak and the right to eat: "'We can speak, but we can't eat.'" James comments that although "there might be 'democracy,' along with, in theory, the ability to speak freely that democracy ensures, there [is] little 'security.'" She adds that Jonassaint's words repeated a political slogan: "'lapè nan tèt, lapè nan vant' (peace of mind, peace / bread in the belly). The slogan suggests that . . . without ontological security, there would be no end to conflict" (*Democratic Insecurities,* 223). Being kept in a state of physiological hunger maintains human beings in a state of conflict and forces them to experience hunger as enslavement, instead of being able to hunger willingly, and amicably, toward the other.

Once hunger is no longer an urgent need, it can become a desire of reaching out toward the other. When detached from survival, hunger leaves behind the absolute nominal position of Césaire's "hunger-man" and Levi's "living hunger" to function as a verb. It is no longer a matter of "being hungry" or "being hunger," but rather of the ability—for the subject—to "hunger." "To hunger," then, would fit the meanings of the Greek *oregein,* "to stretch," "to reach out toward the other," "to offer," "to aspire," and "to desire" *(Greek–English Lexicon).* As philosopher Juan Manuel Garrido, in the wake of Aristotle, has recently articulated, hunger is more than structural to life. Hunger is life: "Through hunger *[orexis],* living beings are a priori opened to the world. Hunger is the 'transcendent' structure of all living beings" (*On Time,* 41). Garrido invites us to defy traditional modes of conceiving hunger as incorporation and to imagine it instead as a relational form of exchange: "The traditional view of metabolism rests on a similar denial of hunger. Metabolism is never understood as the exchange of matter with the environment, but rather as a process of assimilation, of incorporation to one's own body" (42). A view of metabolism based on a network of exchange and on reaching outward instead of incorporating the other within resonates with Glissant's ethical practices of creolization and Relation, which the Martinican philosopher defines as movements whose "results alter each time the elements that make [them], and, as a result, the relation that emerges from them and that modifies them once again" (*Poétique,* 185–86). While creolization and Relation function as incessant and multicircuited exchanges of matter, *métissage* and cannibalism, as this book has shown, are ruled by the principles of incorporation and assimilation. The theories and practices of creolization and Relation are the ones that respond to liberating hungering or *oregein,* while *métissage* and cannibalism are subject to an economy of need, dependency, survival, and confrontation: hunger. The practitioners of cannibalism (sexual or textual) featured in this book—Suzanne

Césaire, Maryse Condé, Gisèle Pineau, and Dany Laferrière—are also the ones who teach us the limits of cannibalistic thought. Creolization and Relation should then be considered, like Garrido's metabolic model, as an exchange with the world. The authors featured in this book, through their reflections on the culinary, force us to imagine an ethical practice of exchange of matter, a practice of reciprocal and boundless hospitality. I would like to hope that this book as well offers a reading practice based on an economically balanced, ecological, and sustainable exchange; a just reading practice that does not feast or feed on Caribbean texts, but rather reaches out to them, hungers for them, as well as they hunger for one another in relational metabolism.

ACKNOWLEDGMENTS

This book would not be without the network of friends and scholars who have helped along the way by lending an ear, reading chapter drafts, providing references, or brainstorming when the engine stalled. They include Cécile Accilien, Hughes Azérad, Kate Bennett, Jean-Godefroy Bidima, Celia Britton, Bernadette Cailler, Jacqueline Couti, Corrie Cratz, Anny Dominique Curtius, Catherine Dana, Cécile Dolisane, Anne Donadey, John Drabinski, Carla Freeman, Juan Manuel Garrido, Robert Goddard, Ricardo Gutiérrez-Mouat, Kathleen Gyssels, George Handley, Naïma Hachad, Edwin Hill, Deborah Jenson, Benjy Kahan, Ivan Karp, Claire Katz, Cilas Kemedjio, Barbara Ladd, Candace Lang, Jeffrey Lesser, Françoise Lionnet, John Lowe, Elissa Marder, Brinda Mehta, Judith Misrahi-Barak, Lydie Moudileno, Adlai Murdoch, Nick Nesbitt, Domenica Newell-Amato, Karla Oeler, Mylène Priam, Benjamin Reiss, Christine Ristaino, Mireille Rosello, Larry Scherr, Karen Stolley, Allen Tullos, Lucie Viakinnou-Brinson, Katherine Wickhorst, and David Wills. I am also immensely grateful to the writers, artists, and cooks who along the way generously shared about food, creolization, and cultural cannibalism, especially Marie-Célie Agnant, Irène Assiba d'Almeida, Victor Anicet, Prudence Marcelin, Daniel Maximin, Ernest Pépin, and Gisèle Pineau. The anonymous cooks I met in Guadeloupe during the *Fête des Cuisinières: Calalou, matété, chiquetaille, féwòs,* and *migan* are now forever attached to their stories.

The students in my graduate seminars, "Cannibalism in Caribbean Literature," "Eating the Antilles," and "Édouard Glissant," brought to the conversation invaluable insights, vivid intelligence, and a plural disciplinary background, as well as a collective experience made of the threads of life they brought from Haiti, Martinique, Puerto Rico,

Colombia, Mexico, the Bahamas, France, Germany, Poland, Lithuania, Romania, Egypt, Morocco, Algeria, South Africa, Benin, and the United States.

This adventure began many years ago when I plunged simultaneously into the unforgettable teachings of Édouard Glissant and into the creolization of all things musical, culinary, linguistic, and cultural in Baton Rouge and New Orleans. Many thanks as well to my hosts and friends in the Caribbean. In Guadeloupe, I would like particularly to thank Ernest Pépin for taking me on a culinary journey of his country. I am also grateful to his aunt, who rented to me a *case* in her yard and surprised me every day with a bounty of *zananas, zavocats, pamplemousse, pomme-cannelle, corossol, maracuja,* vanilla beans, and aloe vera.

In Martinique, I would like to thank the Curtius family as well as André Claverie, Katia Gottin, William Rolle, Sylvie Sainte-Agathe, and Hanétha Vété-Congolo. Manuel Norvat shared with me his friends, landscapes, and Glissantian memories. I am grateful to Victor and Manou Anicet, who, through the years, have overwhelmed me with their generosity. They taught me the art of proper hammock-rest after a meal; of eating *piment bonda-man-jak* without injuring myself; of cooking the perfect red snapper court-bouillon, and of appreciating a Creole garden. Victor gave me patient lessons in cultural cannibalism and artistic restitution to the people of Martinique.

In Barbados, I want to thank the Goddard family for High Tea at the amazing botanical garden, as well as visual artist Annalee Davies for explaining the aesthetics of *bajan pepper-pot* and the art of sustainability on a family dairy farm. To my travel companions: Cécile Accilien, who marooned in the back of a pickup truck with me in Martinique; Carolette Norwood, who, in Barbados, experimented with 101 ways of cooking flying fish; and Naïma Hachad, who shared with me the teasing *marchandes* of the commune du François in Martinique who told us we could not possibly cook breadfruit without "tails and ears." I also thank the voracious ants that cleaned up all traces of leftovers in my outdoor kitchen in the middle of cane fields in Guadeloupe's Lamentin, and the polyrhythmic bugs and frogs that serenaded my Caribbean nights. I do *not* wish to thank the fierce invisible *yen-yen* who feasted on my blood.

For my creolized culinary experiences elsewhere: to Roger and Pascale de Souza for the very green Trinidadian callaloo in Washington,

D.C.; to Michel Laronde and Anny Curtius for the vegetarian gumbo in Iowa City; to my fast friends Eugène Ebodé and Marie-José Lapierre for the *raclette* and Cameroonian fish stew in Montpellier; to my many Louisiana friends who taught me to make red beans and rice last on down-and-out days and to peel crawfish at a native speed. For Sylvie Glissant, who hosted memorable culinary parties linking one Creole South to the other in Baton Rouge.

Sections of this book were tested on energetic and generous audiences: the Departments of French and Italian at the University of Iowa; Tulane University; the University of Kentucky; the University of Illinois at Urbana-Champaign; and the University of Miami of Ohio in partnership with the College International de Philosophie; the Department of Black Studies at Amherst College; the CIEF in Aix-en-Provence; the SSSL in New Orleans; the "Islands in Between" symposium in Guadeloupe, and the Caribbean Literary Studies Symposium at Morehouse College.

I am grateful for the institutional support and initiatives that Emory University has provided throughout the years. Dean Michael Elliott has been unflinching in his support. Dean Robin Forman has provided intellectual curiosity. The ICIS and Woodruff Research and Travel Funds helped finance several research trips to the Caribbean. The Piedmont Project, the Transforming Community Project, and the Gustafson Seminar "The Ethics of Race" offered valuable interdisciplinary forums. The Fox Center for Humanistic Inquiry, by granting me a senior fellowship, offered me luminous space, a rich intellectual community, and a gentle staff fiercely protective of my time: Keith Anthony, Colette Barlow, and Amy Erbil.

In the late stages of the project, Amy Wilkins offered superior proofreading and editing; Abbey Carrico provided a careful eye for formatting. Nick Nesbitt and the two other readers for the University of Minnesota Press who remained anonymous devoted time and care to the manuscript, and their comments made this book tremendously richer. I also want to thank Richard Morrison and Erin Warholm at the University of Minnesota Press for their sustained support. Cherene Holland, the manuscript editor, was immensely helpful.

On an elemental level, I owe everything to my families. My grandmother and mother have always sprinkled their food with that special spice called love. My father, for as long as I can remember, nourished me with books. My precious children, Zoë Cécile and Nathan Pierre, taught me that milk and books were not incompatible. Peter Wakefield made every day a culinary feast, did much more than his share, provided ancient Greek expertise and emotional support, read all my words, and, in short, allowed me to write. They fill my days with awe.

NOTES

All translations from French, Creole, and Spanish are my own unless reference to an English edition is provided.

Introduction

1. See Lestringant, 43–46.

2. Mimi Sheller, *Consuming the Caribbean,* offers a groundbreaking socioeconomic analysis of the ways in which Caribbean subjects have been "ingested" by the global machines of the conquest and the genocide of Amerindians, the spread of disease, plantation slavery, colonial capitalism, tourism, and sexual exploitation. See Sheller, "Eating Others," 143–73.

3. The term is Patricia Hill-Collins's. These stereotypes "are designed to make racism, sexism, and poverty appear to be natural, normal, and an inevitable part of everyday life" (*Black Feminist Thought,* 68).

4. "Our Role in Haiti's Plight," Guardian.co.uk, Wednesday, January 13, 2010, http://www.guardian.co.uk.

5. The representation of foreign-aid intervention in Haiti as the solution to hunger acts as a correlate to the severing of hunger from its historical and political roots. In her remarkable book on intervention in Haiti, Erica Caple James calls this phenomenon "the tyranny of the gift" (*Democratic Insecurities,* 287–95). Just as Haitian historian Michel-Rolph Trouillot called for an examination of Haitian history beyond "external influences" (*Silencing the Past,* 103), James insists that Haitians "must participate as equal partners in the reconstruction of their nation" (xxiv). To render this active participation of internal agents possible, we must cease to represent the West as both innocent and savior when it comes to hunger.

6. http://www.montraykreyol.org. January 11, 2010.

7. I analyze the political movement in chapter 2.

8. Condé, while she denounces Confiant's violent words, endorses his disappointment with the vote. http://www.montraykreyol.org.

9. See, for instance, Robert Sae, spokesperson of the Martinican "Conseil national des comités populaires," who lucidly analyzes the election results in their full context. http://www.caraibcreolenews.com.

10. On the reclaiming of a "politics of the belly" in Sub-Saharan Africa, see Jean-François Bayard, *L'État en Afrique,* 15.

11. Recipes are important for this book in that they participate in cultural or ethnic creations of Caribbeanness, Creoleness, or provide examples of creolization. For Caribbean, Creole, and African diasporic cookbooks, which contain many precious cultural references, and which often intermingle recipes with personal or historical narratives and illustrations, see Ntozake Shange, *If I Can Cook/You Know God Can,* and Vertamae Smart-Grosvenor, *Vibration Cooking;* Cristine Mackie, *Trade Winds;* Lynn Marie Houston, *Food Culture in the Caribbean;* Annick Marie and Christiane Roy-Camille, *Les meilleures recettes de la cuisine antillaise;* Stéphanie Ovide, *French Caribbean Cuisine,* with a preface by Condé; and Hearn, *Creole Cookbook.*

12. Catherine Bedarida reports that Condé urges Caribbean writers to become cannibal: "Bitten [croqués] by the culture of their respective colonial powers . . . it is now time for them to bite back [mordre en retour]" (*Le Monde,* July 5, 2002). Njeri Githire uses the same metaphor of "biting back" in her compelling essay entitled "Food Politics and the Making of a Nation in Andrea Levy's Works."

13. The "Fête des cuisinières" in Guadeloupe, celebrated annually in mid-August, provides an example of a politically organized and religiously ritualized celebration of the power of—female—cooks.

14. In that sense, the Tropics serve the same function as Edward Saïd's Orientalism: a way to show that "European culture gained in strength and identity by setting itself off against the Orient as a sort of surrogate and underground self" (3).

15. On the influence of climate in the "torrid zone" on physical and moral human characteristics, see Buffon, "Variétés dans l'espèce humaine" (*Œuvres,* 398–400). On the absence of History in the Tropics, see Hegel, *Introduction to the Philosophy of History.* For a discussion of Tropicality or the discourse on the Tropics, see Adam Rothman, "Lafcadio Hearn," 267–68. Natalie Ring argues for the inclusion of the U.S. South in the "Tropical Zone."

16. See Christopher Dunn, *Brutality Garden.*

17. My use of the term "Black Atlantic" is taken from Gilroy, who defines it as "the web of diaspora identities and concerns" whose logic operates "at other levels than those marked by national boundaries" (218). But of course the Black Atlantic is not only "black," but an interwoven network of complex African, East Indian, Asian, European, Amerindian, and inter-Carribbean encounters and traces.

18. Condé contends that "for Suzanne Césaire, the adhesion to Surrealism was complete" ("Unheard Voice," 64).

19. See Brathwaite, "Caribbean Man in Space and Time," Benítez-Rojo, *The Repeating Island,* Glissant, *Poétique de la Relation,* Curtius, *Symbiose d'une mémoire,* and Walcott, "The Sea Is History."

20. For excellent analyses of the politics of hunger in an African American context, see, respectively, Warnes, *Hunger Overcome,* and Witt, *Black Hunger;* for a discussion of the Haitian situation, see also Erica James, *Democratic Insecurities.*

21. Renee Bergan and Mark Schuller, producers; Edwidge Danticat, writer.

22. The supermarket "Carrefour" (equivalent to our Target) and its surrounding mall were built on former plantation land in Guadeloupe's Baie-Mahault. The Casino supermarket in the town of François in Martinique was also built on land owned by the Hayot family, the island's richest family of white landowners.

23. http://www-peda.ac-martinique.fr.

24. Repeated ecological scandals continue to plague the Caribbean. See, for instance, the recent case of the use of the pesticides "Chlordecone" and "Mirex," forbidden in the United States yet widely used in Martinique and Guadeloupe, which have contaminated land and food. See http://www.naturavox.fr.

25. Inverted cripples are those "who lack for nothing, except having one thing in excess." This excessive trait, however, cripples them of all else (quoted in Derrida, *Otobiographies,* 35).

26. I use terms such as "Black," "White," "Western," "French," "colonized," and "enslaved" not because I believe in their stability. These less-than-perfect terms are impassible in the discursive situations that I analyze and in which they are constructed as discrete categories.

27. This book is not concerned with real occurrences of cannibalism in the Americas. As William Arens puts it, what matters is not so much the question of whether cannibalism has existed or not but the fact that "the pervasive anthropological conclusion that it was rampant . . . was based on something less than a rational evidential process" ("Rethinking Anthropophagy," 42).

28. Bachollet, Raymond, et al.

29. The image of the cannibal is rare in visual representations advertising food products. In other representations, though, images of black men or women as cannibals abound. The practice of cannibalism, as Fanon indicates, is not based on observation but on the pseudoscientific link of the act of cannibalism with the biological: "At the start of my history the others have fabricated for me, the pedestal of cannibalism was given pride of place so that I wouldn't forget. They inscribed on my chromosomes certain genes of various thickness representing cannibalism. Next to the *sex linked,* they discovered the *racial linked.* Science should be ashamed of itself!" (*Black Skin,* 100).

30. For an excellent discussion of the "Banania" commercial and of the ethics of representing such images in scholarship, see Donadey, "Y'a bon Banania." Donadey, quoting Rosello, suggests that critics working on these images face the following predicament: "There is no possible innocent reference to a stereotype, and there is no stereotype to denounce until it's quoted" (10).

31. For a historical analysis of the Senegalese *Tirailleur,* see Pap Ndiaye, 129–41.

32. "Poème liminaire: A L.-G. Damas" (*Hosties noires,* 55).

33. Quoted in Anne Girollet, 203. I extend my gratitude to Domenica Newell-Amato for the reference.

34. Chaunu in Lestringant, 18.

35. Madureira indicates that the Amerindian word "Carib" (caraíba) "designates not only the 'warlike tribes of Amazonia and the Antilles, but a shaman or 'prophet' endowed with supernatural powers" (*Cannibal Modernities,* 41). Provocatively,

Madureira derives from this last meaning that, as master of the written word endowed with a special power, the European himself appears as "caraíba" (40).

36. See Lestringant (*Le Cannibale,* 46) for a discussion of the link between the cannibal and the cynocephalus, the Great Khan, and other semantic slippages. Retamar also explains how the term "cannibal," applied to the so-called Caribs, was an important tool of the "divide et impera" method to distinguish the supposed warlike Caribs from the peaceful "Arawaks" (*Caliban,* 6–7). Retamar specifies that the difference between Arawaks and Caribs was not clear-cut, and that both people—if they are indeed two—"suffered jointly one of the greatest ethnocides recorded in history" (7). For a detailed analysis of Columbus's journals as he relates his encounter with the "story" of cannibalism, see Jáuregui, 49.

37. Lestringant explains that "the figure of the savage darkened, in all senses of the term. It is no longer attributed to the light-skinned Brazilian barter partner, but to the Negro as potential slave, movable good at worst, and circus phenomenon at best" (28).

38. The English translations of the "Manifesto antropófago" are limited to the manifesto per se. Andrade's complete anthropophagic writings are available in Portuguese and Spanish only. Since I do not read Portuguese, I am referring to the Spanish version.

39. "Alongside and against these traditions, indigenous peoples and marginalized communities have elaborated nuanced interpretations of the West as cannibalistic. Although by no means universal, it appears to be quite common for non-Western peoples to understand Western individuals or institutions as cannibals" (King, 110).

40. The exploitation of the land and its inhabitants through agricultural or industrial enterprise or tourism constitutes a logical extension of this book's argument. Numerous critics have reflected on this type of consumption of the Caribbean. On tourism, see Strachan, *Paradise and Plantation,* and George Gmelch, *Behind the Smile*. On the power of poetry to "transfigure our environmental imagination" and to bring hope to "our degraded plot of New World soil" (15) and to the disastrous consequences of "settlement, animal husbandry, monocultural plantations, mining" (22), see Handley, *New World Poetics;* and DeLoughrey, Gosson, and Handley, *Caribbean Literature*. See also the works of Native American critic Jack D. Forbes, who interprets the exploitation of land and people alike as actual acts of cannibalism, which he names with the Cree term *wétiko* (*Columbus,* xvi–xvii).

41. For a discussion of cannibalism and the Eucharist, see Lestringant (34) and Kilgour. Consult Prado Bellei on Brazilian *Antropofagia*. For an imagination of the Darwinian primitive scene of the killing and cannibalism of the father by a horde of sons, see Freud, *Totem and Taboo* (175–78).

42. On the topic of "waste" or "remainder" in national and racial constructions, see Zita Nunes, xvi, and chapter 5 of this book.

43. See Rosello's essay on Césaire's appropriation of Baudelaire's words ("One More Sea").

44. See King, "The (Mis)Uses of Cannibalism in Contemporary Cultural Critique."

45. I discuss hunger on the slave plantation in chapter 2.

46. For the French anthropologist, the cooked represents the cultural process of

food transformation that renders it edible, and ultimately technological and human. See "Culinary Triangle," 29.

47. Creoleness or *Créolité* is the term theorized by Confiant, Bernabé, and Chamoiseau in *Éloge de la Créolité.* They define it as the aggregate between elements inherited from African, European, Asian, and Levantine cultures, which converged in the Caribbean. For Glissant, *Créolité* indicates a state while creolization refers to a process. I come back to these notions in the subsequent chapters.

48. Glissant's clearest definitions of *métissage* and creolization can be found in his essay "Métissage et Créolisation." "Creolization diffracts while *métissage* flattens," Glissant summarizes (50). While *métissage* is embedded in a discourse on race, creolization is rooted in a linguistic process. See chapters 1 and 3 for an extended analysis of creolization and chapter 5 for a discussion of *métissage.*

49. See *Totem and Taboo* and *Civilization and Its Discontents.*

50. I am not invoking an actual rape but, rather, the violent reduction of Césaire to a sexual, erotic, and exotic object while ignoring her intellect and literary production.

51. Respectively, in *Physiologie du goût* and "The Culinary Triangle."

1. From Gumbo to Masala

1. Paris: K'a Yéléma Productions, 2009.

2. Manthia Diawara recounts to an interviewer that he asked him to explain his ideas to him as if to a "twelve-year-old child" (quoted in Barlet).

3. By the term Circum-Caribbean, I mean the Antilles as well as geographically or culturally adjacent zones such as Brazil, Guyana, and parts of the United States. The term "Black Atlantic" works imperfectly in this chapter since I demonstrate precisely that African inheritance is a significant but not exclusive player in Glissant's model. I could have simply used the broader term "New World." However, my aim here is to show that Caribbean specificity resonates outside its geographical borders as far as New Orleans, Cayenne, and even Philadelphia.

4. Andrew Warnes exposes and discredits the Western belief that "the skill of writing is superior to that of cooking." This hierarchization of cooking and writing has reduced cooking to "an inartistic functionalism in those cultures forged by the Judeo-Christian separation of the body and soul" (*Hunger Overcome,* 6).

5. Calling texts such as *Tout-monde* or *Traité du Tout-monde* "theoretical" is not as simple. *Tout-monde* bears the subtitle "roman." By theoretical texts, I mean texts that are not as obviously classifiable in the novelist genre as *La Lézarde, Le Quatrième Siècle,* or *La Case du Commandeur.*

6. In Parama Roy's model, "Food and cooking have become . . . the favorite optic . . . to filter questions of national-diasporic filiation and affiliation and their economies of taste and consumption" ("Reading Communities," 476).

7. See Jessica B. Harris's cookbooks *Beyond Gumbo* and *Iron Pots and Wooden Spoons.* For Harris, "The culinary histories of the New World and African cooking . . . are so intermingled that it is almost impossible to separate them" (*Iron Pots,*

xiii). In her rich historical introduction, Harris lists ingredients, utensils, and techniques directly transposed or imported from Africa. These include yams, leafy greens, gourds, cucumbers, roasted and smoked meats, and techniques such as "savoring the pot liquor or water in which vegetables had been cooked" (xvi), and the earthenware pot "canari." Some African dishes such as *ndolé,* the national dish of Cameroon, closely resemble in preparation (stew; slow and long cooking), in ingredients (green leaves, goat meat, fish), and in function (unification) the Caribbean callaloo. I thank Dr. Cécile Dolisane-Ebossè for talking about her national dish with so much passion, and for her explanation of how bitterness has to be "cooked out" of the leaves in order to remove any unpleasant feeling in the community.

8. *Calalou* is the usual Martinican spelling of callaloo. *Soupe-zhabitan* is a country vegetable soup.

9. In the past decade, a dynamic debate as to whether Glissant betrayed his early struggle for Martinican independence and political action marked Glissantian criticism. From the 1950s to the late 1970s, Glissant was particularly active politically. He founded the "Antillo-Guyanese Front" for autonomy with Paul Niger in 1961 and was prohibited from traveling outside metropolitan France in 1962 in retaliation for his anticolonial affiliations and actions. Nesbitt identifies the strong anticolonialist discourse of *Discours antillais* (*Voicing,* 184). Critics such as Hallward and Nesbitt have commented on Glissant's increasing "depolitization" in both his actions and writing. Hallward, for instance, defines *Tout-monde* (1993) as the moment when "Glisssant has moved without reserve to a post-national coherence" (*Absolutely Postcolonial,* 105). Nesbitt identifies Glissant's privileging of the aesthetic over the political since *La Case du Commandeur* (1981), but sees a "recovery" of "political and ethical dimensions" in *Traité du Tout-Monde* (1997) (*Voicing Memory,* 184). Bongie, adopting a "middling approach" to the question (*Friends and Enemies,* 365), offers a more nuanced view by claiming that Glissant moved from his "once trenchant political commitments" to an "increasing hostility" not to politics but to a "politics of hostility" (329). Britton argues, against Hallward, that Glissant's late emphasis on sustainability in Martinique and on a view of "the world as made of cultures rather than nations" ("Globalization," 11) in a globalized world does not preclude political action. For an excellent summary of the debate, see Nesbitt, "Politiques et poétiques."

10. In an interview with Renée Gosson, Martinican writer Raphaël Confiant claims that "98 percent of the products on [Martinique's] supermarket shelves come from Europe and not even from the Caribbean or the U.S." and that Martinique "produce[s] 250,000 tons of garbage per year" ("Cultural and Environmental Assimilation," 145). The Martinican Préfecture comments on the severe and chronic economic imbalance between Martinique and the Métropole. In 2002, Martinique exported goods for 2 billion Euros, while its importation amounted to 12.3 billion. http://www.martinique.pref.gouv.fr.

11. For an analysis of the Martinican economic resistance to the Métropole, see Katherine E. Browne, *Creole Economics*. Browne argues that Martinican "Creole values do indeed shape economic behavior in Martinique" (xii). "Creole economics,"

a parallel, unofficial, clandestine economy, largely based on *débrouillardise*—resourcefulness paired with cunning—allows Martinicans to restrict the control of the Métropole. I should add, however, that this power is limited by the very fact that it works against and within the economic superstructure of France.

12. Françoise Ega, *Le Temps des Madras,* provides a counterexample to the reality Glissant describes. The characters of the novel, as Condé points out, opt for a glorification of the Antillean environment: "The protagonist savors fruits of her land that she prefers to French ones. It is a French apple [une pomme-France], my [father] said, bite into it! Yuck! How dull it tasted. I dropped it on the ground out of disgust" (*La Paroles des femmes*, 59–60).

13. On the Martinican consumers' preference for imported food over local products, see Browne, 17–18.

14. See William Rolle, "Alimentation et dépendance idéologique en Martinique."

15. See Browne, 39.

16. On the topic of food and language, see Celia Britton, "Eating Their Words." Britton compellingly argues that the literal consumption of the Caribbean by Europeans who ingest its "rum, coffee, tobacco, coconuts, fruit, etc." goes hand in hand with the metaphorical treatment of Caribbean novels as palatable products. Economically or ideologically, "in the European imagination, the Caribbean has always been associated with things that you put in your mouth" (15).

17. "One is white above a certain financial level. . . . It is in fact customary in Martinique to dream of a form of salvation that consists of magically turning white. . . . And in another way it is quite easy to see the place that the dialectic of being and having would occupy in a description of this behavior" (*Black Skin,* 44).

18. Hardt and Negri identify "a major shift in global power relations" (*Empire,* 9) in the late twentieth century, marked by the passage from the supremacy of capitalist nation-states to the economic and political dominance of powers located in multinational sites. This globalization "operated by the capitalist imperial machine . . . sets in play mobile and modulating circuits of differentiation and identification" (45).

19. The breadfruit is a large starchy fruit found across the Caribbean. It is often associated with freedom because it offered life sustenance to maroon individuals and communities.

20. See Mintz, *Tasting Food,* 38–42.

21. For an ironic description of the introduction of the breadfruit to the West Indies, see Austin Clarke, *Pig Tails 'n Breadfruit*: "Nobody nowadays don't remember too much about C'pan Bligh except that he is the man who introduce breadfruit into the Wessindies. . . . Appears that the English slave-holders didn't have enough food that was cheap enough and filling enough to feed the slaves with. . . . Being a lover of botany, Cap'n Bligh hit on the breadfruit" (114).

22. See, for instance, Anne Goldman, "I Yam What I Yam"; bell hooks, *Sisters of the Yam;* and Shange, *If I Can Cook,* xi–xii.

23. On Glissant's "identité-racine" vs. "identité rhizome," refer to "L'Errance, l'exil," (*Poétique,* 23–34) and "L'étendue et la filiation" (*Poétique,* 59–75). Glissant's

concept of rhizome derives from Deleuze and Guattari's theorization of the term in *A Thousand Plateaus.*

24. In contrast, a political ecology would have beneficial implications for "populations that are decimated or threatened with disappearance as a people" (*Poétique,* 146).

25. Such an exploitation of food metaphors or association of people with the food they consumed has been termed by Asian-American critics Frank Chin and Sauling Wong "food pornography" (See Mehta, "Bhaji, Curry, and Masala," 355).

26. Barbecue, for instance, is a form of cooking that could be emblematic of the Americas. Andrew Warnes presents it as the forgotten "first" American food. For Warnes, Barbecue has been excluded from discourses of identity construction in the Americas, as well as from menus of restaurants that claim to offer a representative list of food from the Americas, such as the Mitsitam Café at the National Museum of the American Indian in Washington, D.C. (*Savage Barbecue,* 1–3). Barbecue has been the victim of another misrepresentation, that of the European gaze, which "wanted to associate those practices with preexisting ideas of savagery and innocence" (3).

27. In Martinique and Guadeloupe, for instance, the *migan,* a soup made with breadfruit, plantain, salt pork, and greens, could also serve as a metaphor for Caribbeanness.

28. Interestingly, if we follow the presence of the dish, the West Indies extend as far as the East Coast of North America (or vice versa), since pepper-pot is also a famous Philadelphia dish: a survival stew consumed by the Continental Army during the American Revolutionary War. The stew was made of tripe, vegetables, and whatever other ingredients could be found (Dubourcq, 86).

29. "For Haitian people, kalalou is okra . . . but for my sister-in-law, who is from Jamaica, when she says callaloo, it's a different vegetable altogether" ("Dyasporic Appetites," 37).

30. In some Cajun versions, gumbo is made with a dark roux instead of okra. The Creole gumbo is more commonly made with okra. Sometimes roux and okra double up to add a rich thickness.

31. *Le Bouillon d'awara,* Cesar Paes, dir., 1995.

32. Hereafter, I capitalize "Creole Stew" to signify the common denominator of the multiple dishes I discuss.

33. By this I mean the Caribbean not as a discrete geographical area but as the larger cultural area including the coast of Brazil, Guyana, and Louisiana. In short, these are area marked by the Plantation economy and processes of creolization. To this cultural ensemble could be added geographical zones outside the Americas, such as Réunion Island, Mauritius, and the Cape Verde Islands.

34. See Benítez Rojo, *Repeating Island* (1–5), and Brathwaite, "Caribbean Man in Space and Time."

35. Spicy grilled cod served with vinaigrette. See my interview with Prudence Marcelin (Loichot, "'Callaloo Is Sacred'").

36. "It is within the Plantation that the meeting of cultures is most clearly and directly observable" (Glissant, *Poetics,* 74).

37. The origin of callaloo is contested and has been described as coming from Asia or Africa. See my interview with Prudence Marcelin, and see Mintz on the transcontinental travels of ingredients (*Tasting Food,* 38–40).

38. "Since our beginning as a nation, Americans have sought ways to integrate and assimilate newcomer populations within some generalized American culture. . . . Most newcomers have been encouraged to forgo their traditional cultures in order to 'become American'" (Mintz, *Tasting Food,* 112).

39. Gustavo Pérez-Firmat, in the lineage of Fernando Ortiz, comments on a similar link between the agglutinative nature of the *ajiaco* and its propensity to represent cubanness: "As Pérez Firmat notes, the ajiaco is agglutinative but not synthetic. . . . Moreover, it is 'indefinitely replenishable, since new ingredients can be added to the stew as old ones are used up'" (Pérez Firmat, quoted in Bongie, *Islands*, 444).

40. In her discussion of the Barbadian pepper-pot and other "folk stews," Spillers comments on the defiance of liquid and solid categories: "These kinds of stews, which cross their wires between liquid and solid and the delicious blend of this and that might be as close as we come to the concept of execution of Everyman's folk food" (47). Danticat adds: "When you eat kalalou . . . there is a very thin line between cooked and non-cooked" ("Dyasporic Appetites," 37).

41. See Lévi-Strauss, "The Culinary Triangle."

42. For the French philosopher of taste Brillat-Savarin, gastronomy is "the rational knowledge of everything that relates to humankind, as far as food is concerned" (58).

43. In his *Creole Cookbook,* Hearn includes nine different recipes for gumbo, including "Simple Okra Gombo," "Okra with Filé, No 1," "Okra with Filé, No 2," and "Maigre shrimp gombo for lent" (18–22).

44. On the commonalities between food and language, see Roland Barthes's introduction to Brillat-Savarin ("Lecture," 17).

45. Reflecting on the specific Caribbean case of Belize, anthropologist Richard Wilks defines Creole food as a language that unites different ethnic, linguistic, and sociological groups. Creole cooking becomes "a kind of 'lingua franca,' a set of dishes that everyone in the colony understood and ate" (*Home Cooking,* 125).

46. See Danticat, "Dyasporic Appetites." See Gabaccia, *We Are What We Eat*: "Psychologists tell us that food and language are the cultural traits that humans learn first. . . . The food they ate as children forever defines familiarity and comfort" (6).

47. The relationship between food, time, and community building is explored further in chapter 3 on Danticat and Pineau.

48. See my interview with Marcelin.

49. Smart-Grosvenor wittingly explains that vibration cooking is not "cooking with a vibrator" (*Vibration Cooking,* xvi), but rather, cooking without a recipe, cooking with vibrations, rhythms, and improvisation.

50. See chapter 3.

51. "Reading Callaloo, Eating Callaloo," Thirtieth anniversary edition (30.1).

52. We notice the same recycling of masala and addition of masala into itself in India. According to *The Best of India,* tandoori masala is the result of mixing "Shahi masala" ("a zesty combination of several piquant spices") with ground turmeric, ground coriander, red food-coloring powder, and asafetida" (Khanna, 94).

53. I express gratitude to my interlocutor Brinda Mehta for proposing a divergent interpretation of Glissant's use of masala. Mehta reads Glissant's indeterminacy and secrecy toward masala as a tentativeness toward a culture that remains an "inassimilable exotic element in his theories of Relation" (personal discussion). She also points out Glissant's inaccurate translation of "lason" as "dhal" (lentils), whereas it means "garlic" in Hindi. While I agree that the example of masala conserves exotic elements in Glissant's model, his inclusion of the East Indian example in his theory of creolization constitutes nonetheless a step beyond critics such as Brathwaite, who deem East Indians unable of creolization (see note below). On the topic of multiple uses of material or metaphorical masala in film, see Mehta, "Bhaji, Curry, and Masala."

54. See Glissant, "The Novel of the Americas" (*Caribbean,* 144–50) and *Faulkner, Mississippi.*

55. On the cultural and political contribution of East Indians in Trinidad, see also Viranjini Munasinghe, *Callaloo or Tossed Salad.*

56. In the second half of the nineteenth century, "25,000 Indian indentured workers, mostly of Tamil origin, were brought to Martinique. In 1884, they constituted an estimated 15% of the population. 239,000 East Indians were brought to British Guyana, 144,000 to Trinidad." http://www.zananas-martinique.com.

57. On the Indian culinary influence on Pineau's texts, see Mehta, "Culinary Diasporas": "The reference to coconut milk highlights the Indian cultural heritage that survived the journey from India as a form of liquid memory to be creolized with Caribbean impressions. Coconut milk, as an integral part of Southern Indian cooking, flavours and thickens curries, chutneys, and desserts. Its use in Caribbean cooking testifies to the importance of the South Indian Tamil presence in the Antilles" (32).

58. See, for instance, *Chair corail, fragments coolies.*

59. The Indians, for Brathwaite, cannot become part of the nation "because their immigrant equipment is so geared for materialism that their spiritual inputs are/were ritualistic rather than dynamic—a factor which the nature of Indian culture must have something to account for" (63).

60. The concepts of *tout-monde, chaos-monde,* and Relation have grown increasingly interchangeable in Glissant's late thought and increasingly conceptual. Whole-world and chaos-world refer less to the totality of planet-earth than to unpredictable dynamic movements between parts of a whole that human and scientific modes of observations fail to fully comprehend. Whole-world functions like the conceptual dynamic movement of Relation theorized in *Poétique* (183–94) and to the chaos theory of physicists. See *Introduction à une poétique du divers* (82) and "L'Imaginaire des langues" (42–44).

2. Not Just Hunger

1. Published in the daily French newspaper *Le Monde,* February 16, 2009.

2. From December 2008 to February 2009, Guadeloupeans and Martinicans were in upheaval against "la vie chère" (the high cost of living). The protests included marches of more than one hundred thousand people at a time, as well as general strikes that paralyzed the countries. The people were united under the leadership of the autonomist organization LKP, "Lyannaj Kont Pwofitasyon," or "Union Against Profit," led by Élie Domota. The negotiations resulted in wage increases from the French government. The official site of LKP demands not only the right to food but also to epistemic needs: "konstwi on sosyété nèf ki dwet kapab prévwa manjé, édikasyon, konésans, santé, kaz, travay é respé" [building a new society that must be able to oversee eating, education, knowledge, health, housing, work, and respect]. "Matinik se ta nou Matinik se pa ta yo" [Martinique is ours; Martinique is not theirs] was the motto of the strikes in Martinique, adapted from the Guadeloupean slogan, "la Gwadloup cé tan nou—la Gwadloup cé pa ta yo." http://www.lkp-gwa.org.

3. See, for instance, the article in the French daily *Libération,* March 14, 2009. http://www.liberation.fr. (accessed December 8, 2011).

4. In a January 2010 referendum, voters from Martinique and French Guiana rejected a proposal that would have given more political, economic, and cultural autonomy to the French Overseas Departments by a wide margin of 80 percent.

5. In 1944, Césaire wrote: "The Martinican Revolution will be made in the name of bread, naturally . . . but also in the name of air and poetry (which amounts to the same result)" (quoted by Maximin, "Suzanne Césaire," 15).

6. "The raw constitutes the unmarked pole . . . the cooked is a cultural transformation of the raw, whereas the rotted is a natural transformation" ("The Culinary Triangle," 29).

7. Condé, in *La Civilisation du Bossale,* also insists on the necessity to see beyond the historical lack and to acknowledge the creation of a new civilization born out of the disconnections of the Middle Passage and slavery: "In new and radically different conditions, the black Man [l'Homme noir] did not simply repeat what he already knew, like the bee that repeats itself since the Antiquity, but he also created a new form of civilization" (7).

8. The corpus of Caribbean folklore and *orature* in which food plays a crucial role is immense. I decided to restrict my analysis to Chamoiseau's folktales, but I invite readers to consult Lydia Cabrera, *Cuentos Negros de Cuba;* Ina Césaire, *Contes de nuits et de jour aux Antilles;* and Suzanne Comaire, *Sylvain's Contes du pays d'Haïti.*

9. In 1946, Martinicans voted to become a French Overseas Department in a process called Departmentalization.

10. For a comparative reading of Hearn and Chamoiseau's folktales, see my essay "Survie et création." See Suvélor's remarkable structural analysis, "Yé," and Césaire and Ménil's discussion of "Yé" in "Introduction au folklore martiniquais" (*Tropiques,* January 4, 1942, 6–7).

11. Although the American paperback edition is widely available (New York: New Press), the original is out of print; its last edition was published by Hatier in 1995. Note also the distance between the French title, clearly inscribing the tales in a long-ago time *(Au temps de l'antan)* and specifically rooted in Martinique. The American title, in its simplicity, situates the tales in a geographically unmarked Creole zone, more directly in continuity with a Louisiana or New Orleans Creole familiar to the American readership. Linda Coverdale's translation, while it provides a highly readable text, is at times far from the French original. For instance, "Nanie-Rosette et sa bouche douce" [Nanie-Rosette and her sweet/soft/sugary/gourmand mouth] became "Nanie-Rosette the belly-slave." When necessary, I worked from the original text and provided my own translation to conserve crucial linguistic and lexical nuances. I use the abbreviated title *Au temps* when I translate from the French original.

12. See Lewis C. Seifert for a thorough analysis of the position of the storyteller in Chamoiseau's *Folktales*.

13. *Tropiques,* January 4, 1942.

14. Article 22: "Masters will be responsible to provide their slaves, ten year old and above, with a weekly ration of two jars and a half of manioc flour or three cassavas . . . with two pounds of salt beef or three pounds of salt fish" (*Code noir,* 25).

15. Read "in the time of the Admiral Robert," the name of the delegate governor of the Vichy regime in Martinique. The period of blockade and hunger was called "le temps Saurin" in Guadeloupe.

16. For a thorough analysis of hunger in Martinique during World War II and of its consequences in the attitudes of Martinicans several decades later, see Rolle, "Alimentation et dépendance idéologique à la Martinique."

17. Ti-Fonté, a character of *Creole Folktales* whom I will analyze below, presents himself as a master of "the art of survival that his friend famine taught him" (74).

18. For a discussion of the relationship between freedom and food on the Caribbean plantation, see Mintz, "Tasting Food, Tasting Freedom" (*Tasting Food,* 33–49).

19. In the rest of Césaire's poem, sexuality is expressed, or rather repressed, as shame. Humans are desexualized, while the landscape or cityscape bears the stigmas of a shameful sexuality marked by venereal disease: "And this rue Paille, this disgrace / an appendage repulsive as the private parts of the village" (*Notebook,* 10–11).

20. Celia Britton explains that the 1946 departmentalization "brought to Martinique a higher standard of living than that of the independent Caribbean islands, thus providing a further reason not to seek independence" ("Globalization," 6).

21. The number of cars is 370 to 1,000 persons. http://www.populstat.info. According to French government data, the percentage of unemployed in Martinique was 23.5 in November 2003 (vs. 9.6 percent in metropolitan France). http://www.martinique.pref.gouv.fr (accessed November 19, 2011).

22. Because Martinique is not an independent nation but an integral part of the European Union, it is hard to find definitive importation figures. *The Courier* states that "vegetables can be produced locally, but 61 per cent are imported." http://www.acp-eucourier.info. Confiant claims that 98 percent of the goods on the supermarket shelves are imported ("Cultural and Environmental," 145).

23. As subsequent chapters show, autonomous cultural production is overwhelmingly present: see the examples of literature, theater, food, and even economics (*Creole Economics*, 10–11). However, these are expressed within oppressive imported structures: whether in literature published by Gallimard or French literary prizes such as the Renaudot, by the canonical guidelines of the French school system, in the local economy by the presence of multinational tourist resorts, or by economic structures and state funding that fund only a handful of agricultural initiatives.

24. See, for instance, Suzanne Césaire, who reflects on the pain and disconnection that defines the relationship of Martinicans to their land, due in part to the "atrocious conditions of a brutal transplantation on a foreign soil" (*Grand camouflage,* 68). In spite of these disconnections and sufferings, Césaire argues, Martinicans learn to reestablish a livable and even symbiotic relationship to the land by abandoning themselves to it instead of conquering it in a gesture that would be reminiscent of colonial violence (45).

25. See Joseph Zobel, *La Rue Case-Nègre,* for fictional illustrations of the childhood consumption of bad rum (70–72).

26. In 2002, the percentage of Martinicans afflicted with diabetes (85 percent of the diabetics were suffering from type 2 diabetes) was significantly superior to the percentage of diabetics in metropolitan France and in the rest of the world: 9.1 percent of Martinicans suffered from diabetes (vs. 2.9 percent in metropolitan France, 6.3 percent in the United States, 4.3 percent in Cuba, and 2.8 percent worldwide). http://www-peda.ac-martinique.fr (accessed November 17, 2011). Source: OMS (World Health Organization) and Atlasseco (atlas économique mondial), 2002.

27. In this sense, Nanie-Rosette is part and parcel of the Caribbean megamachine, or the "machine of machines" that Antonio Benítez-Rojo describes as an interconnecting whole of working human bodies and a complex ensemble "made up of a naval machine, a military machine, a bureaucratic machine, a commercial machine, an extractive machine . . . that is, an entire huge assemblage of machines which there is no point in continuing to name" (*Repeating Island,* 7).

28. On the association of mulatto women and sugar, see Vera Kutzinski, *Sugar's Secrets.*

29. On the controlling image of the "Breeder," see Hill-Collins, *Black Feminist*, 76–77.

30. For a historical account of the exploitation of Caribbean women's bodies as breeders during slavery, see Barbara Bush, *Slave Women in Caribbean Society,* 133.

31. See Rosello, *Littérature et identité créole,* 113–42, for a through analysis of metaphors of ingestions and vomiting in Césaire's *Cahier.* In contrast with the vomited enslaved bodies, Rosello describes a subversive form of vomiting or regurgitation that expresses "a revolt under the sign of nausea and revulsion" (114–15).

32. While Glissant identifies the maroon as the sole incontestable hero of the Caribbean (*Caribbean*, 104), the popular perception of the maroon is often that of a degraded and marginal being. See Cynthia James, *Maroon Narrative,* which provides a helpful summary of binaries associated with the maroon figure (9).

33. Hearn also attributes Yé's misery to his individual vices: "I té ni toutt défo assou la tè: I té finyan—I té vorace—agoulou pou mié di" [He possessed all earthly vices: he was lazy—he was voracious—or gluttonous, to be more exact].

34. The English version mistranslates the Creole "poux-de-bois," literally "wood-lice," or termites as "beetles."

35. "I mangé encô prinne vett, zicaque, carata—toutt vié ti cochonnerie i cé pé trouvé!—den'ye té glacé kan I rivé kaille-li; a penne si i-té pè di fenme-li fè mangé-a."

36. In the act of "riding," we can read a clear reference to *vaudou* religion in which a *lwa* (or divinity) takes possession of a woman or man by riding on their back. The *lwa* is at the same time within and without the ridden subjects, part of them, controlling them, and freeing them. See Laënnec Hurbon, *Les Mystères du vaudou,* 110.

37. Aloss, diab-là té ka monté assou tab-là, té ka caca a dan toutt mangé a . . . Y té ka di yo: 'Valé ça!' É toutt fanmille-là té ka mô faim té obligé valé zôdi diab-là."

38. See the introduction and chapter 5.

39. "So we may call these people barbarians, in respect to the rules of reason, but not in respect to ourselves, who surpass them in every kind of barbarity" ("Of Cannibals," 156). In "Brodie's Report," Borges's narrator, in a style reminiscent of Montaigne, describes the imaginary people of Mlch's cannibalism as a gesture of conservation of humanity's best features: "They devour the raw flesh of their witch doctors and kings in order to assimilate their virtue to themselves" (*Collected Fictions,* 403).

40. See article 38, 30–31.

41. See the revolutionary figure of Joseph in *Danse sur le volcan,* whose tongue was cut off to punish him for instructing slaves about religion (262) in prerevolutionary St. Domingue: "Joseph . . . forgot his infirmity, opened his mouth to speak and emitted an awful [affreux] and disarticulate [désarticulé] sound" (324). The adjectives "affreux" and "désarticulé" testify to the turning of a great orator's voice into a bestial utterance. The literal cutting of the tongue-organ in Chauvet's texts parallels a smothering of Creole language in the public sphere. The opera singer Minette, in spite of her revolutionary soul and actions, refuses to sing in Creole on stage, asking, "Wasn't the language of African negroes (Creole) the symbol of their degradation?" (289).

42. Early historian of the French Caribbean Moreau de Saint-Méry (1750–1819) trivializes this act: "We know too well that certain Africans easily make themselves choke to death by swallowing their tongue and that this act is justified by frivolous reasons" (78). The trope of choking on one's tongue, and more specifically on one's word, appears in Chamoiseau's novel *Solibo Magnifique,* in which the storyteller dies of an "égorgette de la parole" ("a choking of the word," 218).

43. On this generalized "francisation artificielle," see Glissant, *Discours, 87.* While French is still the language of education and government in Martinique, we should note, however, the increasing institutional or quotidian presence of Creole. See, for instance, the creation of a C.A.P.E.S. (state teachers' examination) in Creole in 2002, the Institut du GEREC, and the increasing presence of Creole on television

shows and in the press and blogs. See the site for the promotion of Creole language and culture, "Potomitan": http://www.potomitan.info.

44. Rolle observes that food is inextricably linked to France in Martinicans' minds. He calls it a "couple France-nourriture" (77). One of Rolle's interviewees stated in the 1980s: "France was your *mère-patrie*, she was your mamma. If your mother doesn't feed you, what do you do?" (86)

45. The RMI (Minimum Income for Insertion) was a state allocation granted to people with limited or no financial resources in metropolitan France and its DOM (Overseas Departments) between 1988 and 2009. The RSA (Revenu de Solidarité Active) replaced it in June 2009. In 2008, 30.8 percent of Martinicans were RMI recipients as opposed to 3 percent in the Metropole. http://www.insee.fr.

46. The Creole garden in Martinique is a private garden that could, in theory, sustain a family and a few neighbors. Glissant describes it as containing "all possible species on such a small tongue of land" (*Tout-Monde,* 471). While the practice of cultivating a Creole garden is common for people who own land, it is not generalized enough to sustain the entire country, nor could it be with the acute erosion of the land and urbanization. In 1982, Rolle was pessimistic about the potentials for sustainability of the Creole garden, which he called "jardin nègre" or "negro garden": "In an economy still dominated by the plantations owned by the *békés* [white planters] the negro garden . . . should be able to produce the totality of resources. Of course, it is impossible" (86). On sustainability initiatives in Martinique, see Eric Prieto, "The Uses of Landscape" (244–46). See Chamoiseau, Glissant, and Bertène Juminer, "Manifeste pour un projet global."

47. According to Mintz, the breadfruit was brought to the Caribbean from Oceania in the late 1700s ("Tasting Food," 39). For Cristine Mackie, it was "first introduced to the West Indies from West Africa in 1792 by Captain Bligh" (17). These conflicting stories about the origins of foodstuffs in the Caribbean exemplify the difficulty of rooting Caribbean food in a specific original land. I thank Elizabeth DeLoughrey, who alerted me to this debatable origin.

48. Louise E. Robbins calls for a closer look at texts by naturalists such as Buffon and social critics who projected into their zoological descriptions current political and ethical debates: "For instance, I believe the proliferation of sympathy towards 'animal slaves' was most likely connected with the widespread critical movement that arose in late eighteenth-century France. Social critics portrayed wild animals as symbols of freedom and independence, contrasting them to the enslaved creatures that lived under a tyrannous regime" (6).

49. Lydia Cabrera's *Afro-Cuban Tales* abounds with speaking animals and stories in which the line between the human and the animal blurs. For an explicit use of the animal to comment on race and power dynamics, see "Bregantino Bregantín," in which Earthworm is "a little white man with fine features; thin, bitter lips" (7).

50. In his 2009 novel *Les neuf consciences de Malfini*, Chamoiseau gives center stage to birds since the novel is focalized through the consciousnesses of a bird of prey and a hummingbird.

51. "[The presence of the bird] also invites skepticism at the authority of the

writer / narrator / storyteller, all the more so if the bird is seen as a sign of authorial self-reference (Chamoiseau's name contains the French word for bird [oiseau])" (228).

52. In *Solibo Magnificent,* for instance, the author, "oiseau de Cham," is projected as a character of his own novel.

53. See, for instance, the grandmother's story about the colorful talking bird in Danticat's *Breath,* 124–26, Condé's character who claims, parroting Saint-John Perse: "I will come back each season with a chatty green bird on my fist" (*Traversée,* 234).

54. Paul Carter discusses the divine character attributed to parrots in Christian iconography (43).

55. We should note, however, the widespread fascination for the parrot regardless of the context. Carter begins his extensive study on the fascination for parrots by pointing out the fact that "everyone has a parrot story to tell" (7). I would like to thank Geoffrey Bennington for an enlightening talk on reading the parrot as "Comparative Literature" at the colloquium "Constellations: Of Comparative Literature and the New Humanities," October 16–18, 2009, Emory University.

56. Louise E. Robbins also comments on the fascination for parrots and for the popularity of parrots as a culinary delicacy in eighteenth-century France (11–12). She indicates that in times of animal protein scarcity, what counted as food was much broader than now: "The line separating food from nonfood was neither distinct nor fixed" (11). I would like to thank Karen Stolley for recommending Robbins's book.

57. See, for instance, the description of the punishment of a slave accused of witchcraft (117–18) in which Labat takes delight in explaining the humiliation and torture he inflicted on the slave: spitting in his face, kicking his head open, covering him with hot pepper before having him attached to the iron and whipped.

58. "The black man has no ontological resistance in the eyes of the white man" (*Black Skin,* 90).

59. The neocolonial curiosity of eating exotic animals is still very much alive. See, for instance, the following company specializing in the sale of snakes, antelopes, and kangaroos: http://www.exoticmeatsales.com.

60. "The future readers of these memoirs will surely be surprised by the fact that we ate birds during Lent. But it should be stated that the Islands missionaries . . . after mature deliberation and consultation with medical doctors, declared that the . . . *diables* [a type of small birds] were meager meat and consequentially could be eaten at all times" (182).

61. See Montaigne, "Des Cannibales," for the description of destroying and conserving the enemy in one's body and community through the act of ritualistic war cannibalism (207).

62. "Break a vase, and the love that reassembles the fragments is stronger than that love which took its symmetry for granted when it was whole. The glue that fits the pieces is the sealing of its original shape" (*Twilight,* 69).

63. See Britton's *Sense of Community* on the importance of community in post-slavery Caribbean contexts. Britton reads Martinican, Guadeloupean, and Haitian

novels through the interpretative grid of French philosopher Jean-Luc Nancy's notion of community.

64. For a thorough discussion of the exchange of goods escaping the channels of the colonial and globalized economy, see Katherine Browne, *Creole Economics.*

65. "This throng which doesn't know how to be a throng," Césaire, *Notebook,* 3.

66. See Stéphanie Ovide, *French Caribbean Cuisine,* 15.

67. Mintz identifies three types of Creole cuisine on the West Indian plantation: 1. "What the slaves learned to eat upon their arrival" (maize, porridge, greens, salt cod, or beef; boiled yam and breadfruit; 2. "What the slaves cooked for themselves" (what the slaves fished, gathered, and trapped, added to the food of the first category); 3. "What slaves cooked for their masters and their families" (large variety of crustaceans, fish, and wild fowl, Creole poultry and meats, starchy food, spices) (45–46).

3. Kitchen Narrative

1. See my interview with Pineau, "Devoured by Writing."

2. The term *banlieue* defines the peripheral space of densely populated areas with subsidized, often precarious, housing developed around French cities in the 1950s. It has become a code word to define the French perception of so-called visible minorities, who are often French citizens. See Mylène Priam for a discussion of the specific situation of Antilleans living in France, whom she calls "national migrants" (112–20). On the ambivalent situation of Guadeloupeans in France, who are French by citizenship and perceived as foreign because of their physical appearance, see Mehta, *Notions of Identity,* 96–99.

3. See Glissant, "Métissage et créolisation."

4. "Time becomes human only when it is articulated in the narrative mode" (*Temps*, 17).

5. Even though Warnes rightly points out that food and literacy have often been seen as antonymic practices, anthropologists and cultural historians have abundantly reflected on cuisine as a crucial element of the building of American culture. Among a wealth of examples, see Mintz, *Tasting Food, Tasting Freedom,* particularly his analyses of U.S. and Caribbean food practices, and Gabaccia, *We Are What We Eat.* Gabaccia demonstrates that American food is inherently Creole, i.e., constantly enriched by immigrant contribution (202–24).

6. On the notion of *Antillanité*, see Glissant, *Caribbean Discourse* and *Poétique de la Relation.* Glissant's *Antillanité* is not limited to Caribbean space; nor does Caribbean space provide a sufficient condition for *Antillanité*. *Antillanité* originates in the enclosed space of the Plantation, but expresses itself in an "open word," or in the process of creative construction from the violent encounter of disparate cultural elements (*Poétique,* 77–89). *Antillanité* is not a geographical and historical entity to be taken for granted, but rather a movement prompted by reconstruction, desire, and imagination (*Discours,* 728).

7. For a comparative discussion of the histories of Haiti and the French Overseas

Departments, see Dash, *The Other America;* Nesbitt, *Voicing Memory;* and Dubois, *A Colony of Citizens.*

8. The word is Lionnet's: "I prefer [the word transcolonial] to the more commonly used 'transnational' or 'postcolonial' since my goal is to stress the spatial dimensions at the heart of the history of colonialism" ("Narrating the Americas," 69). In a parallel move, anthropologist Appadurai elaborates the concept of a "transnation." For him, large groups of immigrants and exiles in the United States produce a "delocalized *transnation*, which retains a special ideological link to a putative place of origin but is otherwise a thoroughly diasporic community" (*Modernity at Large,* 172). Similarly, Danticat's and Pineau's only viable locus is a Caribbean related to the United States and France, where nodes of belonging multiply instead of converge.

9. On the function of the grandmother in the literature of the African diaspora, see Mildren A. Hill-Lubin, who argues that the "Black grandmother" echoes the "revered status, position, responsibility which elders hold in West African societies" (257).

10. By "relation," I allude both to Glissant's theoretical definition of the term as a dynamic link, a relay, and an act of narration (*Poétique,* 183–94) and to Elisa Sobo's "body-in-relation," a basic connection performed by the person who unifies the members of the rural community, the generations of women in her family, and the land and its inhabitants.

11. Spillers argues that, under slavery, "'kinship' loses meaning since property relations can invade it at any given arbitrary moment" (*Black, White, and in Color,* 218).

12. The phrase is also homonymous with "mal de mer," or seasickness.

13. Moreau's 1789 expression is strikingly similar to American physician and abolitionist Benjamin Rush's expression "mal d'estomac," stomach or belly pain, described in his 1787 article "An Account of the Diseases Peculiar to the Negroes in the West Indies, and Which are Produced by Their Slavery" in the *American Museum.* Deborah Jenson summarizes Rush's interpretation of the malady as a "somatoform result of the Middle Passage itself, not a result of poisoning (Jenson, 106).

14. "It is a shame that thoughts of inadequacy and even melancholic feelings lead mothers to ravish the existence of their fruit, even before letting it see the light of day!" (Moreau, 61). While Moreau shows an unusual sensibility to the enslaved mother's plight for his time, he is strangely blind to the fact that slavery could be the explanation of this curious illness.

15. See Sethe's predicament in Morrison's *Beloved* and Barbara Bush's historical account of motherhood in the Caribbean during slavery (*Slave Women,* 83–119).

16. For Mintz, "eating American," rather than being defined by cultural terms, is characterized by the "societal" traits of speed, efficiency, infinite land resources, processed food, and disconnection from nature (106–24).

17. The *marassas* are a central figure in Danticat's *Breath, Eyes, Memory.* For Alfred Métraux, a sharp observer of *vaudun* practices in the 1940s, the *marassas* occupy a privileged position in mysteries and are even more powerful than the *lwas,* or deities (*Le Vaudou,* 129–36).

18. See "Léo Frobénius et le problème des civilisations" and "Malaise d'une civilization," in *Le Grand Camouflage,* 29–40 and 67–75.

19. On the distinction between root and rhizome thought, see Glissant, *Poetics,* 47–62.

20. On the transdiasporic values of the tubercule, see hooks, *Sisters of the Yam,* and Shange, *If I Can Cook.*

21. When commenting on Haiti and Haitians in the novel, I do not conflate a "real" or experienced "Haitianness" with the fictional account provided by Danticat. This note is particularly important in light of the all-too-frequent false interpretations of Danticat's first novel as autobiographical, which led to a controversy in which some fellow Haitian Americans accused the author of giving a degrading portrayal of Haitians (see Mardorossian, 127–28).

22. The *Tonton Macoutes* were members of François Duvalier's private army. The death squad terrorized the Haitian population under his presidency and that of his son Jean-Claude ("Baby Doc").

23. Casey concludes that the veiled references to *Breath*'s "real-life's backdrop" provide a "necessary though not sufficient literary response to the appalling latest chapter in Haiti's horrifyingly emblematic story" (Casey, 525). Nesbitt also reflects on the inherently guilty nature of *Breath,* which builds its commercial popularity (by its commodification through the *Oprah Winfrey Show*) on the painful history of Haiti, and which turned historical sufferance into an aesthetic object (*Voicing Memory,* 207). Contrast this discrete representation with the central representation of political violence in her later novels: *The Farming of Bones, The Dew Breaker,* or *Brother, I'm Dying.*

24. Sophie's last name "Caco" reinforces this idea of belonging to an agrarian political resistance. As Émile Césaire explains, the Cacos "were a Haitian army made up primarily of peasants who fought against the U.S. occupation between 1915 and 1919" (69).

25. A *konbit* is a traditional Haitian method of communal farming.

26. See chapter 2 for an analysis of Aimé Césaire's Martinican Christmas.

27. "The drum is more than a musical instrument, it is also a sacred object and even the tangible shape of a god" (Métraux, 163).

28. On the processes of assimilating Christianity into Afro-Caribbean religions, see Dianne Stewart, *Three Eyes for the Journey;* and Anny Dominique Curtius, *Symbioses d'une mémoire.*

29. On the invisibility, silencing, or systematic association of corpulent bodies with the grotesque in contemporary culture, see Braziel and LeBesco's collection of essays, *Bodies out of Bounds.*

30. See, for instance, Brillat-Savarin on plumpness and beauty (126).

31. Sophie's situation is similar to Kim Chernin's patient in *The Hungry Self*: "'My mother was born in Panama,' she says abruptly one day, 'dark-skinned like me. A big woman, but we didn't think she was fat. Then when we came here . . . right away the four women went off and enrolled themselves in some diet group. . . . I

was fourteen years old. My mother put me on a diet . . . and all this was part of the way she prepared me to become an American'" (5–6).

32. While medical classifications of eating disorders such as bulimia can flatten complex cultural differences, the exclusion of certain ethnic groups from illnesses considered as white and upper class risks the exclusion of Latina, Haitian, or African American girls from medical treatment. The character in Josefina Lopes's *Hungry Woman in Paris,* for instance, contributes to this ethnic exclusion: "I couldn't imagine being Mexican and having an eating disorder. . . . The thought of wasting food in that manner made me want to vomit" (131).

33. The traumatic transmission between mother and child needs to be considered in its full political context. The violence originates in a politically inflected sexual act since Martine's rapist was a *Tonton Macoute* of Duvalier's paramilitary force. Erica Caple James argues that acts of torture such as the political or military rape "can be viewed as relational attacks intended to silence and disempower not only the individual victim but also the social community in which he or she is temporally or spatially embedded" (80).

34. On the link between sugar monoculture and racial injustice, see Vera Kutzinski, *Sugar Secrets,* 9–10.

35. See chapter 4.

36. Pineau, by linking mass infanticide to the legalized death penalty in the state of Kansas, offers a powerful criticism of the American judicial system. Moreover, Guadeloupe is no more a site of transgressive violence than the United States.

37. Glissant, *Discours,* 97.

38. On the relationship between cooking and writing, Moudileno's claims that "the gastronomic discourse implies a different kind of metaphysics. It differs from the meta-literary discourse . . . in that . . . it does not provide an access to a transcendental truth as writing could" (426).

39. An outdoor cooking structure made of bricks and braziers.

40. Mehta highlights the association between the secular habit of eating food and its "spiritual consecration" in Guadeloupe (*Notions of Identity,* 90). Mintz argues that cooks are the holders of power in that they "actually invented a cuisine that the masters . . . could not themselves duplicate" (*Tasting Food,* 47–48). However, the anthropologist also indicates that the cooks' agency is limited by the power structure that reduces them to the position of slave or domestic worker.

41. In her "Reading Communities," Parama Roy analyzes the properties of autobiographical and culinary writing, both particularly successful in creating "feminine genealogies" (486). She argues that the "coupling of the literal and the metaphoric upon which autobiographical writing and culinary syntax are both predicated" (473) establishes links between the present and the past, the private and the national, and the birth land and the place of exile.

42. For an elaborate analysis of *marassas* in Haitian spirituality and its reclaiming in Danticat's novel, see N'Zengou-Tayo (129–34), Chancy (124–28), and Métraux (129–36).

43. The *restavecs,* from the Creole "to stay with," are slave children in the service of Haitian families. See Jean-Robert Cadet's autobiographical account.

44. For Jeffrey Pilcher *(¡Que Vivan los Tamales!),* women cooks participate directly in the construction or "imagination," to use Benedict Anderson's term, of the Mexican nation. Since culinary products are central to nation building, "by proclaiming their culinary patriotism, women have established their claim to citizenship, and thereby gained a basis for political participation" (6). Danticat's novel certainly leads in that direction, since remaining Haitian in exile relies heavily on cooking Haitian. For a more explicit equivalence between food and nation-building, see Shange's *If I Can Cook,* where the author proves by food the existence of an African American nation—in her account of the Fifth of July celebration (6)—and of a transnational diasporic African nation unified by food emblems such as peas and rice, okras, and greens shared by Cubans, Afro-Brazilians, and Charlestonians.

45. As we saw in chapter 1, the minority Hindu culture plays a major role in the process of creolization in the French Antilles. See Mehta, *Diasporic Dislocations,* 106–31.

46. See Mintz for a reading of the diverse human fluxes in the Antilles through his analysis of the origin and travels of Antillean ingredients (38–40).

47. "Négropolitain," a term used by Antilleans living in the Caribbean to define Martinicans and Guadeloupeans living in France, is a pun associating the words "nègre" and "métropolitain."

48. Mehta reflects on Pineau's *Papillon* and *Exil dans la cite* as sites of "expanded Creolization" (25) in which merging West Indian and Maghrebi cuisine creates a transcultural diaspora of the margins away from the cultural "center" of France. See her remarkable essay "Culinary Diasporas," later published as a book chapter in her *Notions of Identity.*

49. See Glissant, *Poétique,* 88.

50. "Don Pedro ran his fingers, from right to left, across the slow ocean portion separating the coast of Guinea from the coast that the cosmographer had named on his map *La mer de lentille . . .* they were lentils like Porto Rico, Hispaniola, Cuba, Jamaica, and down below, Margarita, lentils of gold, silver, pearls, hides, of precious tastes, scents, and tints [lentejas de oro, de plata, de perlas, de corambres, de sabores y olores y colores preciosos]" (*El Mar de la lentejas,* 281).

4. Sexual Traps

1. Lorde's "Uses of the Erotic: The Erotic as Power" foundational essay paved the way for an expression of black women's eroticism independent of both racialist and masculine discourses. Lorde's erotic encompasses a "lifeforce" greater than sexual expression ("our language, our history, our dancing, our loving, our work, our lives" 55), which she sees as diametrically opposed to pornography, its "direct denial . . . for it represents the suppression of true feeling" (54).

2. In this genre, we could also include Laferrière's *Le Goût des jeunes filles, Cette grenade dans la main du jeune nègre est-elle une arme ou un fruit?* and *Vers*

le Sud/Heading South and its 2005 film adaptation by Laurent Cantet; Cameroonian writer Calixthe Beyala's *Comment cuisiner son mari à l'Africaine* or *Femme nue, femme noire,* Condé's *Histoire de la femme cannibale,* Carl Van Vetchen's *Nigger Heaven,* and bell hooks's essay "Selling Hot Pussy."

3. See Freud's *Three Essays on the Theory of Sexuality* and Melanie Klein's "Weaning."

4. While sex is at times motivated by erotic desire, sex and *eros* are often dissociated in the experience of sexuality in general, and more specifically in the context of slavery and postslavery literature. Pornography can be defined more specifically. According to the "Williams Report," pornography is a "representation . . . that combines two features: it has a certain function or intention to arouse its audience sexually, and also has a certain content, explicit representations of sexual material (organs, postures, activity, etc). A work has to have both these functions and this content to be a piece of pornography" (quoted in Jon Ellis, 33). While the 1981 report is problematic in its denial of pornography's aesthetic value, it provides a helpful working definition.

5. *Peau noire,* 89.

6. Rosello defines the stereotype as "a block of cast-iron, [which] forms a whole that cannot be dissolved and whose main purpose is to be repeated endlessly" (*Declining,* 23).

7. See Fanon, *Black Skin,* 93; and Patricia Hill Collins, *Black Feminist Thought,* 67–90.

8. The term "satyr," evoking lasciviousness, seems particularly appropriate for the grotesque representation of black men's hypertrophic sexuality. The satyr, a hybrid of man and goat, blurs the line between the animal and the human.

9. The references to the lasciviousness of black and mixed-race women in white texts are innumerable. See, for instance, Moreau on Saint-Domingue ("The entire being of the mulatto woman is given to sensuality, and the fire that burns in the Goddess's heart will extinguish only with her death"; Moreau, 104); Buffon's evocation of Senegalese, "Jalofe" [Wolof] women ("there are beautiful women among them, save for the color . . . who are extremely versed in love and have a fancy for all men, particularly for white men that they actively seek out"; Buffon, "Variétés dans l'espèce humaine," 361). For a literary history and archeology of the categorization of the *mulatto* woman as sexual temptress, see Doris Garraway, *Libertine Colony.*

10. Among countless examples, see the account of the 1899 lynching and castration of Sam Hose in the town of Newman, Georgia, whose lynching was justified by the placard, "We Must Protect our Southern Women." Hose was lynched as a result of the killing of his master and the alleged rape of his master's wife (even though the woman herself had denied the rape). See Litwack, "Hellhounds," in *Without Sanctuary,* 9–10.

11. On sex tourism in the Caribbean, see Mimi Sheller, *Consuming the Caribbean* (156–66), and Laferrière's collection of stories, *Vers le Sud,* and its film adaptation by Cantet dealing with the sexual exploitation of young boys by North American women tourists.

12. See Maurice Manring, *Slave in a Box,* and Marilyn Kern-Foxworth, *Aunt Jemima, Uncle Ben, and Rastus.*

13. See the introduction.

14. See Wallace Sanders, *Mammy,* and Collins, 73–74.

15. See chapter 2.

16. On the dissociation between sexuality and eroticism in Martinique, see Glissant, *Discours,* 514–19.

17. See Spillers, 203–29, and Bush, 83–119.

18. Cameroonian writer Calixthe Beyala's 2003 novel, *Femme nue, femme noire,* provides an extreme counterexample. It depicts the unbridled sexual adventures of the main protagonist, Irène Fofo, in situations of sadism, torture, incest, and zoophilia. Instead of an exception to the "pudeur immémoriale," the novel could be seen as its logical consequence. "I want to know," the narrator claims, "how women get pregnant because, where I am from, certain words do not exist" (11). Sexual logorrhea naturally responds to sexual aphasia. It should also be noted that Irène's (and Beyala's) "erotic project" is presented as a cure to the political ills of the country: "I deploy treasures of sexual sophistication to annihilate . . . the ills of the black continent—unemployment, recession, war, misery" (78).

19. Until recently, published representations of homoerotic love in Francophone Caribbean literature were scarce. In his 2008 *Our Caribbean,* a collection of homoerotic writing from the greater Caribbean, Thomas Glave claims that homosexuality has been confined to "proscriptions, banishments, ostracism, and, in more than a few cases, extreme violence." While Glave includes twenty-nine writers—from Puerto Rico, Cuba, Barbados, Trinidad, Jamaica, the Bahamas . . . the Haitian poet Assotto Saint is the only writer from the Creolophone/Francophone Caribbean represented in the anthology. There are discreet, yet significant, representations of lesbian amorous relationships in Francophone Caribbean literature. Guadeloupe's Ernest Pépin features a lesbian relationship in his *Cantique des tourterelles.* Condé in *Moi, Tituba* and Danticat in *Breath* give snippets of lesbian love. Pineau's *Morne Câpresse* portrays the lovers Sherryl and Zora, who dream of leaving Guadeloupe for the United States because "over there . . . women can love each-other in the open" (264). For a discussion of lesbian love as a site of peace, see Chancy on Lorde (*Searching,* 123–65). See also Omise'eke Natasha Tinsley, who convincingly argues, in *Thiefing Sugar,* that eroticism between women is often and subtly expressed in Caribbean literature in the specificity of spaces such as "waterways, flora, and earth" (15).

20. "The verb '*coquer*' derives from the word 'cock' or 'rooster,' therefore 'coquer' refers to the power of the rooster in the hen-house. . . . The subversion of [French by Creole] language indicates anti-colonial . . . and anti-dogmatic values that readers from the French Metropole, blinded by their exotic *[doudouistes]* expectations, rarely get. This linguistic unsettling aims at preserving Creole culture . . . and at questioning the legitimacy of French culture" (Couti, "Sexual Edge," 214).

21. Haitian writer Jacques Stephen Alexis's *Espace d'un cillement* provides a clear example of the irruption of the political into the erotic. The narrative of the

reciprocal desire between a Cuban prostitute and a Cuban mechanic who meet in Haiti is systematically interspersed with political events. Sexual acts in scenes of prostitution are embedded in a criticism of American military presence and economic imperialism.

22. See *Alleluia pour une femme jardin, Hadriana dans tous mes rêves,* or *Eros dans un train chinois.*

23. The intertwining of love and death in Bataille goes beyond European cultural specificity. The coincidence of Eros and Thanatos is primarily due to the biological nature of the sexual act that implies the simultaneity of life and death: "Eroticism is the approval of life within and until death" (*L'Érotisme,* 17). Bataille evokes the death of the sperm and ovule caused by the fusion of the two in a new life, an encounter "in which two beings mingle to eventually reach together the point of dissolution" (24). We would be hard-pressed to deny such a coincidence of life and death, continuity and discontinuity, in the Caribbean experience.

24. On the topic of self-exoticism in Antillean literature, see Schon.

25. See, for instance, Du Tertre's reference to a common saying in the colonies: "To beat a negro is to feed him" (480).

26. For a discussion of eroticism in Confiant, Chamoiseau, and Despestre, see Spear, 17–18.

27. On the silencing of female sexuality in Haiti, see Chancy, *Framing Silence,* 104–33. The critic reflects on the strategies to create "a language and a frame of reference through which the Haitian woman can come to represent herself and her sexuality directly" (107).

28. See *Three Essays on the Theory of Sexuality.* For instance: "the kiss . . . between the mucous membrane of the lips of the two people concerned, is held in high sexual esteem among many nations . . . in spite of the fact that the parts of the body involved do not form part of the sexual apparatus but constitute the entrance to the digestive track" (16).

29. The French text has once again been out of print since 2010.

30. *Love, Anger, Madness,* translated by Rose Myriam Réjouis and Val Vinokur, with an introduction by Danticat (New York: Random House Modern Library, 2009).

31. Gilman notes that the emphasis on genitalia in the medical and pseudoscientific discourse "privileged" women's bodies: "In comparison, when one turns to the description of the autopsies of black males from approximately the same period, the absence of any discussion of the male genitalia whatsoever is striking. For example, William Turner, in his three dissections of male blacks in 1878, 1879, and 1896, makes no mention at all of the genitalia" (218).

32. See Clifton Crais and Pamela Scully, *Sara Baartman and the Hottentot Venus.*

33. It is not clear whether "Vieux," or "Old Man," is the protagonist's last name or nickname. Mostly he remains nameless throughout the novel. "Vieux Os" (Ole' Bones) is the family nickname of the autobiographical protagonist in Laferrière's *Pays sans chapeau* (1997), set in Haiti.

34. I thank Benjamin Kahan for pointing me in that direction. *Nigger Heaven* also caused scandal because it portrayed the sexuality of black women and men during the Harlem Renaissance and was written by a white man.

35. Lee's movie, like Laferrière's novel, was criticized by feminists as a degrading representation of black female sexuality. See, for instance, Felly Nkweto Simmons.

36. While white characters are absent from Lee's film, symbolic whiteness is nonetheless imposing. See the scene in which the three men are unhappily united around Nola's Thanksgiving table, and in which one accuses the other of being a "street Negro," to which the attacked responds that these words are not surprising coming from the mouth of someone who favors "turkey whites."

37. "Brand states: 'In a world where Black women's bodies are so sexualized, avoiding the body as sexual is a strategy. I know that not talking about the sexual Black female self at all is as much an anti-colonial strategy as armed struggle. But what a trap" (27).

38. "Trans-American," 867.

39. Trans. David Homel.

40. On the difficulty of translating the word "nègre," which could be transposed in an American context as "black," "negro," or "nigger," see Brent Hayes Edward, *The Practice of Diaspora,* esp. 25–38. Laferrière's title evokes the three possible meanings at once.

41. http://www.amazon.fr (accessed November 2009).

42. Laferrière twists the slave code a bit. The reference to the "nègre" as "meuble" appears in fact in article 44 of the 1685 *Code noir* (32) in slightly less pugnacious language: "Déclarons les esclaves être meubles," the word "slave" (and not "nègre") is used.

43. "Trans-American," 883–86.

44. The reference to the protagonist's Haitian mother is absent from this novel. In contrast, the narrator's mother is a central figure in Laferrière's Haitian narrative *Pays sans chapeau.* It is therefore the "*nègre*" and not the Haitian man who is orphaned.

45. The reference to adoption evokes Fanon's notion of "abandonment." For Fanon, the black man cannot enter a balanced loving relationship because he has been orphaned, "abandoned" "too early" by his mother-culture to the coldness of the French school system or to France (*Black Skin,* 60). He develops the psychiatric condition of "abandonism" or abandonment anxiety, which leads to an insatiable need for affection.

46. See Vergès, "The Family Romance of French Colonialism" (*Monsters,* 1–20).

47. The term "Judeo-Christian" is widely used in the novel, extending the category of whiteness to a large cultural-religious group.

48. Condé's *Histoire* uses a similar strategy. While the text includes the story of an alleged cannibal woman, the novel deprives voyeuristic readers of the gruesome scenes of cannibalism they expect to find from the book's title. The same could be said about Beyala's *Comment cuisiner son mari à l'Africaine,* "How to Cook

One's Husband African-Style" (2000). The novel intermingles the narrative of an African exile in Paris attempting to seduce an African man with the recipes she uses to win him. While the recipes could seem exotic to the French reader, to whom the book is mainly addressed ("Smoked antelope with pistachios," "Boa in banana-leaves," etc.), it fails to offer the recipe for the anticipated dish of the "cooked husband."

49. As I show in chapter 5, Condé's *Histoire* offers a quasi-identical evocation drawn from the South African *Tribune du Cap.*

50. On this point, see Uzoamaka's "The Issue Is Race" (91–108). Fictional texts by black writers mistaken as autobiography are common: see, for instance, Mayotte Capécia's *Je suis martiniquaise,* read by Fanon as an autobiography. Minority writers are particularly prone to this form of critical slippage, as if they were incapable of the critical distance dissociating life from aesthetics.

51. We could also read "manger du chat," "eating cat," as eating the female genitals. This, as well, would be unplanned in the white women's expectations of a hyperphallic black man.

52. See Lesser, *Discontented Diaspora,* 47–57.

53. "Her beautiful pink mouth" (*Comment faire,* 48): "her golden hair, her pink clitoris, her white belly . . . her Anglo-Saxon mouth" (82). The *vagina dentata* or toothed vagina is a common trope evoking the fear or threat of castration in psychoanalysis, folklore, and popular culture.

54. Robert Bernasconi argues that Kant invented the first scientific theory of race (11–35). By calling Kant a pornographer, Laferrière presents racism as the true pornographic discourse whose obscenity satisfies primal human drives. More particularly, racism functions as pornography in the act of lynching, in which the torturing, castration, and dismemberment of the black man is closely linked to the white obsession of portraying him as a sexual beast, as Leon Litwack explains: "To endorse lynching was to dwell on the sexual depravity of the black man, to raise the specter of the black beast seized by uncontrollable, savage, sexual passions that were inherent in the race" (22).

55. See Litwack's account of a lynching in Georgia, where the unmasked spectators were described as enjoying the dismemberment and "barbecuing" of Sam Hose "with unfeigning satisfaction" (9). Litwack adds that the voyeuristic spectacle was "prolonged as long as possible (once for seven hours) for the benefit of the crowd" (13).

56. http://www.chapitre.com.

57. http://www.rfo.fr.

58. www.zananas-martinique.com.

59. The excerpt is a composite of several distinct passages from Pineau's novel.

60. See, for instance, Nina K. Martin's analysis of the soft-core genre in cinema in *Sexy Thrills.*

61. See Hill Collins, *Black Feminist Thought,* and Condé, *La Paroles des femmes.*

62. Cameroonian writer Eugène Ébodé tricks the reader with the same misleading meaning of spice. His song-poem about the inhuman violence of humanity, "Le Fouettateur," is subtitled "poème épicé" (spicy poem), preceding the novel's abrasive violence by the promise of exoticism.

63. See Hearn, "Zhistouè Piment," in which a well-meaning woman advises her destitute neighbor to trade her pimientos for codfish (*Two Years,* 473). Instead of following the advice, the woman keeps all the pimientos, turns them into a stew, and ends up killing her family by feeding them such a huge amount of chili peppers. See also the humoristic Antillean mazurka, "Lari Zabym," in which the heat emanating from an old woman is such that it kills the pimiento bush behind her house ("Chalè a vyé fanm la / tchouyé pié piman la").

64. "I had the sorcerer put on iron shackles after ordering him washed with a pimiento mix, that is a sort of brine with crushed pimientos and squeezed little lemons. This causes a horrible pain to those the whip flayed, but it is a sure remedy against gangrene" (Labat, 118).

65. See my analysis of the nameless woman in *Orphan Narratives,* 48–53.

66. See chapter 3.

67. See Faulkner's *Absalom, Absalom!* Glissant's *La Case du commandeur,* Ellison's *Invisible Man,* and Condé's *Traversée de la Mangrove.*

68. See Garraway, *Libertine Colony,* 284–85.

69. See, for instance, Warner-Vieyra's *Juletane* and Pineau's *L'Espérance-Macadam.*

70. Florence Jurney arrives at a similar conclusion: "Pineau traces the contours of a Caribbean identity that render obsolete the geographic limits of the island and opens up the door to what we could call a 'novel of globalization'" (42–43).

5. Literary Cannibals

1. See "Discursive Cannibalism" in the introduction.

2. I had originally intended to refer to the author by her maiden name—Roussi—in order to mark her independence from her famous husband. However, I ultimately decided to use the name with which she signed her texts in the hope that readers will not automatically default to "Aimé" when the last name "Césaire" is used. I have used the first names "Suzanne" and "Aimé" to avoid confusion in the passages in which both authors appear.

3. The Tupi or Tupinambá people of Brazil have been historically identified as cannibals. See Montaigne and Lestringant.

4. The electronic databases reveal that Shakespeare's famous soliloquy fed on texts by Ralph Lever, Dudley Fenner, Abraham Fraunce, William Perkins, and John Deacon, among others, who all preceded the great British tragedian in their use of "To be or not to be" (Stallybrass, 1581).

5. See Martinican Joseph Zobel, *Rue Case-Nègres,* in which José is wrongly accused of plagiarism by his teacher (270).

6. By this nonlinear interpretation of the *process* of cannibalism, I am not denying the historical trajectory of the *intellectual movement* of "cannibalism," which helps us redefine notions of influence. Luis Madureira, for instance, importantly notes that "anthropophagy reverts the relationship between margin and center, and becomes an antecedent to postmodernism" (Madureira, 50).

7. To put it plainly, it would be absurd for an educator to preach literary cannibalism while warning students against the illegality of plagiarism.

8. See "Food Racism" in the introduction.

9. Alice Randall's *Wind Done Gone* (2001) was put on trial by the estate of Margaret Mitchell. Randall's novel, an African American rewriting of *Gone With the Wind,* is told through the perspective of Cynara, Scarlett's mulatto half-sister, who lives on a Plantation derisorily named "Tata." The case was eventually settled in court with the agreement that Houghton Mifflin would add the following subtitle: "The Wind Done Gone: The unauthorized Parody." What could be interpreted as an act of cultural reclaiming—giving a voice to the silenced stereotypical African American characters Sissy, Mammy, and Pork—was sanctioned by law as intellectual property theft. See Richard Schur, "*The Wind Done Gone* Controversy." The *Wind Done Gone* is far from being an isolated example of postcolonial textual reappropriation. Jean Rhys based her *Wide Sargasso Sea* on Charlotte Brontë's *Jane Eyre,* while Condé transposed the characters of Emily Brontë's *Wuthering Heights* into her 1995 *Windward Heights.*

10. See Hulme for a discussion on the influence of the Dadaist on the Brazilian Modernists ("Introduction," 27).

11. Hulme argues that for Oswald de Andrade "the figure of the cannibal was part of a possible national past, an authentic Brazilian figure which offered the possibility of a defined national tradition, an anti-colonial critique, and a communitarian ideal" (27).

12. On the topic of Spoerri's "Cannibal Feast," the "Manifeste cannibale Dada," and more generally on the aesthetic and philosophical use of food and cannibalism in the European avant-garde, see Cecilia Novero's fascinating *Antidiets of the Avant-Garde.*

13. One could argue that Romania is part of the "vampire zone." But this is another matter altogether.

14. Francis Picabia, author of the "Manifeste cannibale Dada" (1920), presents an interesting case. While the Paris-born author was associated with the European avant-garde, his father was Cuban, and thus could claim a "cannibal" cultural lineage.

15. Césaire's writings were made available in a single volume for the first time by the French publisher Éditions du Seuil in 2009.

16. Anny Curtius questioned Suzanne's daughter Ina as well as actors in the play to locate the document to no avail. The missing play is mentioned by Michel Leiris (*Contacts,* 80).

17. "Suzanne Césaire, fontaine solaire," in *Le grand camouflage* (7–23).

18. The interview is featured in Palcy's documentary *Aimé Césaire: Une voix pour l'histoire.*

19. I am in no way reducing Aimé Césaire's poetic practice to literary assimilation. His poetry is much more fierce than his expressed literary project. See, for instance, his reclaiming of "cannibal glories" and his complex ingestion of Baudelaire's "L'Albatros" in his *Cahier.* On Césaire's ingestion of Baudelaire, see Rosello's essay "One More Sea to Cross."

20. See "Discursive Cannibalism" in the introduction.

21. See Glissant, "Métissage et créolisation," 50–51.

22. As Condé recalls, "Leiris . . . complained of [Césaire's] aggressiveness in putting forward Communist-oriented ideas and did not believe that it went well with her duties as the mother of five children" ("Unheard Voice," 62).

23. See Bayle's denunciation letter and Suzanne Césaire's reply in *Tropiques,* as well as a description of the censorship process in Maximin, 10–14.

24. On the shadowing of Césaire, see Sharpley-Whiting and Jennifer Wilks.

25. Pereira dos Santos's *How Tasty Was My Little Frenchman* portrays the Tupinambá community welcoming a Frenchman as one of its own, feeding him well, giving him a wife, initiating him with rituals before devouring him in a sacrificial mode.

26. In Césaire's "Le grand camouflage," "camouflage" refers to: (1) the beauty of the tropical landscape masking the country's poverty; (2) Césaire's cryptic writing concealing her dissident criticism of the Vichy regime; (3) an apparent praise for Breton covering up a sharp criticism.

27. On this topic, see also Tzvetan Todorov, *Conquest of America,* 148.

28. See Kara M. Rabbitt, Marie-Agnès Sourieau, and Smita Tripathi. Condé presents Césaire as "one of the first intellectuals who tried to piece together the broken fragments of Antillean identity" ("Unheard Voice," 62) and as "the founding mother of all postcolonial critics" (66); Sharpley Whiting contextualizes Césaire in the intellectual history of Negritude; Wilks discusses Césaire's contribution to negritude and surrealism and defines her as a precursor of Caribbeanness, who negotiated "Martinican identity through an American lens" (126). See also Maximin's tribute to Césaire in his *L'Isolé Soleil* (1989) and his preface to her collected works.

29. For a discussion on the relationship between the French surrealists and intellectuals in Martinique and Haiti, see Michael Richardson's "Introduction" to *Refusal of the Shadow.*

30. René Ménil will use her motto again in 1942: "Martinican poetry will be virile. Martinican poetry will be cannibal. Or will not be" (*Tropiques,* 5, 27).

31. While I tend to agree that Césaire is careful not to universalize the particular position of Martinique, she nonetheless inserts her country in a clearly extended Caribbean geography. For instance, "Le grand camouflage" juxtaposes Martinique with the city of Pétionville in Haiti and with the island of Puerto Rico.

32. According to Condé, Césaire was "the first Caribbean writer to acknowledge and rehabilitate the appellation 'cannibal,' once a term of opprobrium, and transform it into a new, noncolonized self. The claim to a cannibal identity forms a part of any poetical self-birth or parthogenesis" ("Unheard Voice," 64). While Condé is right in pointing out the earth-shaking cesairean moment, the term "parthogenesis" seems to isolate Césaire from the discourses that were circulating in the Circum-Atlantic space at the time, such as Brazilian *Antropofagismo.*

33. For accounts of the journey, see Rosemont's introduction to *Martinique Snake Charmer,* 2–4.

34. Breton's "Martinique" was later published as the preface to the 1947 French-English edition of Césaire's *Cahier,* published by Brentano.

35. "Les aiguilles qui tremblent" ("Some Trembling Pins"). The trembling pins allude to the brooches used to secure Martinican women's madras headscarves (see *Martinique,* 109n1).

36. J. Michael Dash dubs this narration a "mysterious adventure in which he is helped by a magical ribbon to transcend the wreckage of Martinique's colonial past and shadows of its Vichy present and pursue the 'noir et magnétique' Aimé Césaire and the tropical Nadja, Suzanne Césaire" ("*Le Je de l'autre,*" 86).

37. René Ménil was a philosophy professor who taught at the lycée Schoelcher in Fort-de-France with the Césaires. He was also a co-founder of *Tropiques* and an important writer, theorist, and commentator, unfortunately much ignored by critics.

38. Ina Césaire rectified Breton's reification of her mother: "Ma mère / belle comme la flamme de sa pensée" [My mother, beautiful as the flame of her intellect] (Ina Césaire in Suzanne Césaire, *Le grand camouflage,* 122).

39. "Nos rencontres, le soir dans un bar . . . à l'issue des cours qu'[Aimé Césaire] donnait au lycée et qui prenait alors pour thème majeur l'oeuvre de Rimbaud, les réunions sur la terrasse qu'achevait d'enchanter la présence de Suzanne Césaire, belle comme la flamme du punch, mais plus encore, une excursion au plus profond de l'île: je nous reverrai toujours de très haut penchés à nous perdre sur le gouffre d'Absalon comme sur la matérialisation même du creuset où s'élabore [*sic*] les images poétiques quand elles sont de force à secouer les mondes, sans autre repère que les remous d'une végétation forcenée que la grande fleur énigmatique du balisier qui est un triple coeur pentelant au bout d'une lance."

40. For an analysis of Breton's tourist vision of Martinique and of his infatuation with the land and the Césaires, see Dash, "Le Je de l'autre," 86–87.

41. "My sad heart drools on the prow" ("The Stolen Heart").

42. See Breton, *L'Amour fou,* 11.

43. Maximin indicates that Lam's 1943 painting *The Jungle* was also inspired by the Martinican forest of Absalon (100). Breton's travel companion to Martinique, the surrealist artist André Masson, also refers to the forest of Absalon, to the balisier, and to Suzanne Césaire in his poem "Antille": "Question the sensitive one she answers no but red in the heart of the vaginal shadow reigns the carnal canna flower—blood congealed in the eminent flower. Spermatic lava that nourished you. . ." (quoted in Suzanne Césaire, *Le Grand Camouflage,* 101). The "sensitive one" is undoubtedly Suzanne Césaire.

44. I extend my gratitude to Jacob L. Wright for clarifying this passage.

45. To my knowledge, Aimé Césaire has left Breton's erotic praises of his wife uncommented upon. In contrast, the couple's friend René Ménil publicly ridiculed Breton's infatuation (see Ménil, "Laissez passer").

46. Bon confronts his half-brother Henry: "So, it is the miscegenation, not the incest, which you can't bear" (*Absalom,* 285).

47. The definitive title will be "Pour Madame Suzanne Césaire."

48. The term *chabin,* or its feminine form, *chabine,* refers to individuals of mixed African and European descent with light complexion and often blond or red hair. Ina Césaire describes her mother as a *chabine*: "My amber-eyed and luminous-gazed mother / With the light complexion of a golden shabeen [chabine dorée] / With a long and slender silhouette / With electric hair that she liked to set free to amuse us" (in Césaire, *Le Grand camouflage,* 122).

49. "Plus les rapports des deux réalités rapprochées seront lointains et justes, plus l'image sera forte" [The more the relationship between two juxtaposed realities will be distant and true, the stronger the image] (Breton quoting Reverdy, *Manifestes,* 31).

50. Rosello argues that Breton and Masson did not see anything in Martinique, where they remained for a very short time. The artists saw Martinique through exoticized artistic and literary representations that were already themselves based on representations (Rosello, "Martinique," 68). Breton named his essay after Douanier Rousseau's painting *La Charmeuse de serpents,* itself inspired by the re-created jungle of the *Jardin des plantes* in Paris and by tourist brochures.

51. Artist and scholar Franklin Rosemont sees things in a different light. For him, Breton was "the opposite of a tourist" ("Introduction," 10) because of his acute consciousness of the horrors of colonialism.

52. Nau, a precursor of symbolism, was a French poet born in San Francisco, who passed through Martinique and Haiti while a sailor.

53. "What is at stake is to transcend the sordid current dichotomies: black-white, European-African, civilized-savage" (*Le Grand camouflage,* 82–83).

54. See Freud's *Totem and Taboo* and my discussion of the text in the introduction.

55. Robin Kelly admits that "[t]he Césaires' impact on Breton was no small matter. It would not be going too far to say that the few weeks he spent in Martinique marked an important turning point not only in his life but also in the history of the international surrealist movement" (quoted in Rosemont, 19).

56. "Il y avait sur la plage quelques 'fonctionnaires métropolitains.' Ils étaient posés là, sans conviction, prêts à s'envoler au premier signal. . . . Quand ils se penchent sur le miroir maléfique de la Caraïbe, ils y voient une image délirante d'eux-mêmes. . . . Ils savent que les métis ont part avec leur sang, qu'ils sont, comme eux, de civilisation occidentale. Il est bien entendu que les 'métropolitains' ignorent le préjugé de couleur. Mais leur descendance colorée les remplit de crainte, malgré les sourires échangés. Ils ne s'attendaient pas à cet étrange bourgeonnement de leur sang. Peut-être voudraient-ils ne pas répondre à l'héritier antillais qui crie et ne crie pas 'mon père.' Cependant, il faut compter avec ces garçons inattendus, ces filles charmantes. Il faut gouverner ces peuples turbulents."

57. The civil servants, nowadays called "Métros" or "Métropolitains," typically stay in Martinique for one to three years. They are usually contrasted with the *Békés*, the local whites of the plantocracy who have been there for many generations.

58. See, for instance, Jamaica Kincaid's *A Small Place,* Mimi Sheller's *Consuming the Caribbean,* and Ian Strachan's *Paradise and Plantation.*

59. "The Remainder Is A Reminder" (Nunes, 145–72).

60. See chapter 1 for a discussion of the position of the "East Indian" as a "remainder" in Martinique or Guadeloupe.

61. While the remainder seems to be a universal component of nation-building, the category occupying that position varies from context to context. The inassimilable *métis* in the French case, for instance, becomes an ideal model of nationalism in Cuba. See Benítez-Rojo, *Repeating Island,* 12.

62. See "Malaise d'une civilisation" (*Le Grand camouflage,* 67–75).

63. Condé's *Windward Heights* illustrates a typical practice of literary cannibalism whereby she ingests Brontë's novel, locates it in the plantation context, and creates something new. See Lionnet, "Narrating the Americas," on this particular case of literary ingestion. On Condé's general practice of cannibalism, see the essays in Broichagen, Lachman, and Simek, *Feasting on Words.*

64. The cannibal is feminized immediately in the novel's title.

65. In a comparable ironic gesture, Novero explains, 1970s food artist Dieter Ross "turned . . . literary works he disliked into sausages" (*Antidiets,* 235). The twenty volumes of Hegel's *Complete Works* were made into "something apparently digestible but, in fact, indigestible because inedible" (ibid.). While Condé's gesture is not quite as literal, she acts in the same spirit.

66. Like the cannibal, the narrative voice in *Histoire* constantly migrates from a defined character to a floating narrator.

67. This story is based on a famous real event. In 1981, Issei Sagawa murdered and ate parts of Renée Hartevelt, a Dutch student. Sagawa was extradited to Japan after being declared insane.

68. See King, "The (Mis)Uses of Cannibalism in Contemporary Cultural Critique."

69. With their sharp canines and blood-sucking habits, the characters of the novel are often closer to vampires than cannibals. The link between cannibalism and vampirism is interesting in that the vampire does not refer historically or discursively to the colonial subject or to the figure of the savage. It is often associated with nobility, as in the famous example of Count Dracula. One could wonder whether through her multiple references to vampirism Condé does not point away from the colonial question or from the cannibal zone.

70. The examples are too numerous to name since they stuff the entire novel. For noteworthy examples, see pages 133 and 204 for the confusion between cannibalism, sorcery, and healing practices. For the mixup between homosexuality and cannibalism, see veiled avowal of Rosélie's husband: "Like a Tupinamba Indian I devoured their liver, their spleen, and their heart. But these bitter feasts left me even more despondent" (*Story,* 153–54). See pages 109–10 for the cannibalistic nature of the consumer of multicultural artwork; 6–7 for voyeurism as cannibalism; and 252 for touristic cannibalism. For the tourist, the Antilles are "an edible fruit plate" and the sexually consumed Caribbean women are acquired in airport stands along with "jars of hot pepper" (*Story,* 165). Cannibalism is a banal object circulating among other colonial creations. See page 245, the postcards and paintings of colonial "types" such as "Algeria—Negro with a Fan; . . . New Guinea—A

Head Hunter; . . . Tupinamba Cannibal Indians at a Feast" (214). Cannibalism becomes colonial junk.

71. The Beirut-born actor's mixed origins—he is of English, Portuguese, Chinese, and Hawaiian descent—might explain his prevalence in Condé's book in which *métissage* and cross-cultural encounters play a major role. Or else, Condé might just be a fan of Reeves.

72. Dawn Fulton similarly argues that by "multiplying the novel's cannibalizing gestures in unpredictable directions, Condé frustrates the postcolonial reader's expectations of finding a heroic self-liberating cannibal and a unilateral condemnation of the West" (*Signs of Descent,* 141). For Rosello, Condé's novel establishes a "post-cannibalistic" moment, which "successfully reworks the difference between colonizer and colonized by remapping it over a . . . continuum between . . . the cannibal and the cannibalized" ("Post-Cannibalism," 49).

BIBLIOGRAPHY

Adisa, Opal Palmer, and Donna Weir-Soley, eds. *Caribbean Erotic: Poetry, Prose, and Essays.* Leeds, UK: Peepal Tree Press, 2010.

Alexis, Jacques Stephen. *L'espace d'un cillement.* Paris: Gallimard, 1959.

Allen, James, Hilton Als, John Lewis, and Leon F. Litwack. *Without Sanctuary: Lynching Photography in America.* Santa Fe: Twin Palms Publishers, 2000.

Anderson, Benedict. *Imagined Communities: Reflections on the Origin and Spread of Nationalism.* London: Verso, 1991.

Andrade, Oswald de. "Cannibalist Manifesto (1928)." Translated by Leslie Bary. *Latin American Literary Review* 19, no. 38 (1991): 38–47.

———. *Escritos Antropófagos.* Translated by Alejandra Laera and Gonzalo Aguilar. Buenos Aires: Ediciones Corregidor, 2001.

Appadurai, Arjun. "Gastro-Politics in Hindu South Asia." *American Ethnologist* 8, no. 3 (August 1981): 494–511.

———. *Modernity at Large: Cultural Dimensions of Globalization.* Minneapolis: University of Minnesota Press, 1996.

Arens, William. "Rethinking Anthropophagy." In Barker, Hulme, and Iversen, 39–62.

Ariès, Paul. "On mange de plus en plus seul." *Le Temps Stratégique* 93 (May–June 2000): 39–45.

Avramescu, Cătălin. *An Intellectual History of Cannibalism.* Translated by Alistair Ian Blyth. Princeton: Princeton University Press, 2009.

Azodo, Ada Uzoamaka. "The Issue Is Race: Gender and Sexuality in Dany Laferrière's North-American Autobiography." *Gender and Sexuality in African Literature and Film.* Edited by Ada Uzoamaka Azodo and Maureen Ngozi Eke, 91–108. Trenton, N.J.: Africa World Press, 2007.

Bachollet, Raymond, et al. *Négripub: L'image des Noirs dans la publicité.* Paris: Somogy, 1987.

Bambara, Toni Cade. *The Salt Eaters.* New York: Vintage Books, 1980.

Barker, Francis, Peter Hulme, and Margaret Iversen, eds. *Cannibalism and the Colonial World.* Cambridge: Cambridge University Press, 1998.

Barlet, Olivier. "Édouard Glissant: Un monde en relation: Première mondiale du film de Manthia Diawara." *Africultures,* July 15, 2010. http://www.africultures.com/php/index.php?nav=article&no=9595 (accessed November 17, 2011).

Barthes, Roland. "Lecture de Brillat-Savarin." In Brillat-Savarin, 7–33.

———. "Toward a Psychosociology of Food Culture." In Counihan and Van Esterik.

Bataille, Georges. *L'Érotisme.* Paris: Les Éditions de Minuit, 1957.

Bayard, Jean-François. *L'État en Afrique: La politique du ventre.* Paris: Fayard, 2006.

Bedarida, Catherine. "Lettres insulaires des Caraïbes." *Le Monde,* July 5, 2002.

Benítez Rojo, Antonio. *El Mar de las lentejas.* Barcelona: Plaza & Janés Editores, 1985.

———. *The Repeating Island: The Caribbean and the Postmodern Perspective.* Translated by James Maraniss. Charlottesville: University of Virginia Press, 1996.

Bergan, Renée, Mark Schuller. *Poto Mitan: Haitian Women, Pillars of the Global Economy.* Directed by Renée Bergan and Mark Schuller. Written by Edwidge Danticat. Tèt Ansanm Productions. Renegade Picture, 2009.

Berglund, Jeff. *Cannibal Fictions: American Explorations of Colonialism, Race, Gender, and Sexuality.* Madison: University of Wisconsin Press, 2006.

Bernabé, Jean, Patrick Chamoiseau, and Raphaël Confiant. *Éloge de la Créolité: In Praise of Creoleness.* Paris: Gallimard, 1993.

Bernasconi, Robert. "Who Invented the Concept of Race? Kant's Role in the Enlightenment Construction of Race." In *Race.* Edited by Robert Bernasconi, 11–35. Malden, Mass.: Blackwell Publishers, 2001.

Berry, Wendell. *The Unsettling of America.* San Francisco: Sierra Club Books, 1977.

Beyala, Calixthe. *Comment cuisiner son mari à l'africaine.* Paris: Livre de Poche, 2002.

———. *Femme nue, femme noire.* Paris: Livre de Poche, 2005.

Bhabha, Homi K. *The Location of Culture.* London: Routledge, 1994.

Bongie, Chris. *Friends and Enemies: The Scribal Politics of Post/Colonial Literature.* Liverpool: Liverpool University Press, 2008.

———. *Islands and Exiles: The Creole Identities of Post/Colonial Literatures.* Stanford: Stanford University Press, 1998.

Bordo, Susan. *Unbearable Weight: Feminism, Western Culture, and the Body.* Berkeley and Los Angeles: University of California Press, 1993.

Borges, Jorge Luís. *Collected Fictions.* New York: Viking, 1998.

Boyce Davies, Carol. "Secrets of Sweetness." In Opal Palmer Adisa and Donna Weir-Soley, 292–301.

Brathwaite, Kamau. "Caribbean Man in Space and Time." *Savacou* 11–12 (1975): 1–11.

———. *Contradictory Omens.* Kingston: Savacou Publications, 1974.

Braziel, Jana Evans. *Artists, Performers, and Black Masculinity in the Haitian Diaspora.* Bloomington: Indiana University Press, 2008.

———. "Trans-American Constructions of Black Masculinity: Dany Laferrière, le Nègre, and the Late Capitalist American Racial Machine-Désirante." *Callaloo* (Summer 2003): 867–900.

Braziel, Jana Evans, and Kathleen LeBesco, eds. *Bodies Out of Bounds: Fatness and Transgression.* Berkeley and Los Angeles: University of California Press, 2001.

Breton, André. *L'amour fou.* Paris: Gallimard, 1953.

———. *Manifestes du surréalisme.* Paris: Gallimard, 1985.

———. *Martinique Snake Charmer.* Translated by David Seaman. Introduction by Franklin Rosemont. Austin: University of Texas Press, 2008.

———. *Nadja.* Paris: Gallimard, 1964.

Brillat-Savarin. *Physiologie du goût.* Edited by Michel Guibert. Paris: Hermann, 1975.

Britton, Celia. "Eating Their Words: The Consumption of French Caribbean Literature." In *ASCALF Yearbook.* Edited by Peter Hawkins, 15–23. Bristol: Association for the Study of Caribbean and African Literature in French, 1996.

———. *Edouard Glissant and Postcolonial Theory: Strategies of Language and Resistance.* Charlottesville: University of Virginia Press, 1999.

———. "Globalization and Political Action in the Works of Édouard Glissant." *Small Axe* 30 (November 2009): 1–11.

———. *The Sense of Community in French Caribbean Fiction.* Liverpool: Liverpool University Press, 2008.

Broichhagen, Vera, Kathryn Lachman, and Nicole Simek, eds. *Feasting on Words: Maryse Condé, Cannibalism, and the Caribbean Text.* Princeton: Program in Latin American Studies, Princeton University, 2006.

Browne, Katherine E. *Creole Economics: Caribbean Cunning under the French Flag.* Austin: University of Texas Press, 2004.

Buffon [Georges-Leclerc, Comte de Buffon]. O*euvres.* Paris: Gallimard, Bibliothèque de la Pléiade, 2007.

Burton, Richard. *La famille coloniale: La Martinique et la mère-patrie.* Paris: L'Harmattan, 1994.

Bush, Barbara. *Slave Women in Caribbean Society, 1650–1838.* Bloomington: Indiana University Press, 1990.

Cabrera, Lydia. *Afro-Cuban Tales: Cuentos negros de Cuba.* Lincoln: University of Nebraska Press, 2004.

Cadet, Jean-Robert. *Restavec: From Haitian Slave Child to Middle-Class American.* Austin: University of Texas Press, 1998.

Cantet Laurent. *Vers le Sud.* Dir. Laurent Cantet, Paris. Celluloid Dreams, 2007. Film.

Capecia, Mayotte. *Je suis martiniquaise.* Paris: Corrêa, 1948.

Casey, Ethan. "Remembering Haiti." *Callaloo* 18, no. 2 (1995): 524–28.

Casteel, Sarah Phillips. *Second Arrivals: Landscape and Belonging in Contemporary Writing of the Americas.* Charlottesville: University of Virginia Press, 2007.

Castro-Klarén, Sara. "A Genealogy for the 'Manifesto antropófago,' or the Struggle between Socrates and the Caraïbe." *Nepantla: Views from the South* 1, no. 2 (2000): 295–322.

Cazenave, Odile. "Erotisme et sexualité dans le roman africain et antillais au féminin." *Notre Librairie: Revue des Littératures du Sud* 151 (July–September 2003): 58–65.

Certeau, Michel de. *Heterologies: Discourse on the Other.* Translated by Brian Massumi. Minneapolis: University of Minnesota Press, 1986.

Césaire, Aimé. *Cahier d'un retour au pays natal.* Paris: Présence africaine, 1983. Translated by Clayton Eshleman and Annette Smith as *Notebook of a Return to the Native Land.* Middletown, Conn.: Wesleyan University Press, 2001.

———. "Culture et colonisation." *Présence africaine* 8–9–10 (June–November 1956): 190–205.

Césaire, Aimé, and René Ménil. "Introduction au folklore martiniquais." *Tropiques 4* (1942): 7–11.

Césaire, Émile. "Charlemagne Péralte and the Cacos." *Revolutionary Freedoms: A History of Survival, Strength, and Imagination in Haiti.* Edited by Cécile Accilien, Jessica Adams, and Elmide Méléance, 67–69. Coconut Creek, Fla.: Caribbean Studies Press, 2006.

Césaire, Ina. *Contes de nuits et de jours aux Antilles.* Paris: Éditions Caribéennes, 1989.

———. "Maman Flore." *Nourritures d'enfance: Souvenirs aigres-doux.* Edited by Claude Danziger, 48–56. Paris: Autrement, 1995.

Césaire, Suzanne. *Le grand camouflage: Écrits de dissidence, 1941–1945.* Paris: Seuil, 2009.

Chamoiseau, Patrick. *Au temps de l'antan: Contes du pays Martinique.* Paris: Hatier, 1988.

———. *Creole Folktales.* Translated by Linda Coverdale. New York: New Press, 1994.

———. *Les neuf consciences du Malfini.* Paris: Gallimard, 2009.

———. *Solibo Magnifique.* Paris: Gallimard, 1988.

Chamoiseau, Patrick, and Raphaël Confiant. *Lettres créoles.* Paris: Gallimard, 1999.

Chamoiseau, Patrick, Gérard Delver, Édouard Glissant, and Bertène Juminer. "Manifeste pour un projet global." *Antilla,* January 14, 2000, 17–19.

Chamoiseau, Patrick, Édouard Glissant, et al. "Manifeste pour les 'produits' de haute nécessité." *Le Monde,* February 16, 2009.

Chancy, Myriam J. A. *Framing Silence: Revolutionary Novels by Haitian Writers.* New Brunswick: Rutgers University Press, 1997.

———. *Searching for Safe Places.* Philadelphia: Temple University Press, 1997.

Chernin, Kim. *The Hungry Self: Women, Eating, and Identity.* New York: Harper Perennial. 1994.

Clarke, Austin. *Pig Tails 'n Breadfruit: A Culinary Memoir.* New York: New Press, 1999.

Le Code noir. Paris: L'Esprit frappeur, 1998.

Collins, Patricia Hill. *Black Feminist Thought: Knowledge, Consciousness, and the Politics of Empowerment.* New York: Routledge, 1991.

Comhaire-Sylvain, Suzanne. *Contes du pays d'Haïti.* Port-au-Prince, 1939.

Condé, Maryse. *La civilisation du Bossale: Réflexions sur la littérature orale de la Guadeloupe et de la Martinique.* Paris: L'Harmattan, 1978.

———. "A Conversation at Princeton." In Broichhagen, Lachman, and Simek, 1–28.

———. *Histoire de la femme cannibale.* Paris: Mercure de France, 2003. Translated by Richard Philcox as *The Story of the Cannibal Woman* (New York: Washington Square Press, 2007).

———. *La parole des femmes.* Paris: L'Harmattan, 1993.

———. *Traversée de la Mangrove.* Paris: Gallimard, 1992.

———. "Unheard Voice: Suzanne Césaire and the Construction of a Caribbean Identity." In *Winds of Change: The Transforming Voices of Caribbean Women Writers and Scholars.* Edited by Adele S. Newson and Linda Strong-Leek, 61–66. New York: Peter Lang, 1998.

———. *Victoire, les saveurs et les mots.* Paris: Mercure de France, 2006.

Confiant, Raphaël. *Dictionnaire du créole martiniquais,* August 13, 2009. http://www.potomitan.info/dictionnaire.

———. *Ravines du devant-jour.* Paris: Haute Enfance, 1994.

Counihan, Carole, and Penny Van Esterik, eds. *Food and Culture: A Reader.* New York: Routledge, 1997.

Couti, Jacqueline. "Sexual Edge: Re-colonization of Black Female Bodies in Caribbean Studies." Ph.D. diss., University of Virginia, 2008.

Crais, Clifton, and Pamela Scully. *Sara Baartman and the Hottentot Venus: A Ghost Story and a Biography.* Princeton: Princeton University Press, 2008.

Croly, D. G., and G. Wakeman. *Miscegenation: The Theory of the Blending of the Races Applied to the American White Man and Negro.* London: Trübner, 1864.

Curtius, Anny Dominique. *Symbioses d'une mémoire: Manifestations religieuses et littératures de la Caraïbe.* Paris: L'Harmattan, 2006.

Damas, Léon-Gontran. *Pigments.* Paris: Présence africaine, 2001.

Danticat, Edwidge. *Breath, Eyes, Memory.* New York: Vintage Books, 1994.

———. *Brother, I'm Dying.* New York: Alfred A. Knopf, 2007.

———. *Create Dangerously: The Immigrant Artist at Work.* Princeton: Princeton University Press, 2010.

———. *The Farming of Bones.* New York: Penguin Books, 1998.

———. *Krik?Krak!* New York: Vintage Books, 1996.

Danticat, Edwidge, and Nancy Mirabal. "Dyasporic Appetites and Longings: An Interview with Edwidge Danticat." *Callaloo* 30, no. 1 (Winter 2007): 26–39.

Dash, J. Michael. "Le Je de l'autre: Surrealist Ethnographers and the Francophone Caribbean." *L'Esprit Créateur* 47, no. 1 (2007): 84–95.

———. "Martinique/Mississippi: Édouard Glissant and Relational Insularity." In *Look Away! The U.S. South in New World Studies.* Edited by Jon Smith and Deborah Cohn, 94–109. Durham: Duke University Press, 2004.

———. *The Other America: Caribbean Literature in a New World Context.* Charlottesville: University Press of Virginia, 1998.

Deleuze, Gilles, and Félix Guattari. *A Thousand Plateaus: Capitalism and Schizophrenia.* Translated by Brian Massumi. Minneapolis: University of Minnesota Press, 1987.

DeLoughrey, Elizabeth, Renée K. Gosson, and George B. Handley, eds. *Caribbean Literature and the Environment: Between Nature and Culture.* Charlottesville: University of Virginia Press, 2005.

Depestre, René. *Le métier à métisser.* Paris: Stock, 1998.

Derrida, Jacques. *La dissémination.* Paris: Seuil, 1972.

———. "Il faut bien manger ou le calcul du sujet," 269–301. *Points de suspension.* Paris: Galilée, 1992.

Desmond, Adrian, and James Moore. *Darwin's Sacred Cause: How a Hatred of Slavery Shaped Darwin's Views on Human Evolution.* Boston: Houghton Mifflin Harcourt, 2009.

Diawara, Manthia. *Édouard Glissant: One World in Relation.* Directed by Mantia Diawara. Paris: K'a Yéléma Productions, 2009.

Donadey, Anne. "'Y'a Bon Banania': Ethics and Cultural Criticism in the Colonial Context." *French Cultural Studies* 11, no. 31 (February 2000): 9–29.

"Données économiques et sociales." *Préfecture de Martinique,* January 2007. http://www.martinique.pref.gouv.fr/pages/ecosocio2.html.

Döring, Tobias, and Markus Heide, eds. *Eating Culture: The Poetics and Politics of Food.* Heidelberg: Carl Winter Universitätsverlag, 2003.

Dracius, Suzanne. "Fantasm Fanm: Women's Wicked Desires." In Opal Palmer Adisa and Donna Weir-Soley, 92–95.

Dubois, Laurent. *A Colony of Citizens: Revolution and Slave Emancipation in the French Caribbean, 1787–1804.* Chapel Hill: University of North Carolina Press, 2004.

Dubourcq, Hilaire. *Benjamin Franklin Book of Recipes.* London: FlyFizzi Publishing, 2004.

Dunn, Christopher. *Brutality Garden: Tropicália and the Emergence of a Brazilian Counterculture.* Chapel Hill: University of North Carolina Press, 2001.

Du Tertre, Jean-Baptiste. *Histoire générale des isles.* Paris: Jacques Langlois, 1654. Microfilm 481.

Ebodé, Eugène. *Le Fouettateur: Poème épicé.* Paris: Vents d'ailleurs, 2006.

Ebroïn, Ary. "Les origines de la cuisine créole." *Antilles* 41 (1989): 178–84.

Edwards, Brent Hayes. *The Practice of Diaspora: Literature, Translation, and the Rise of Black Internationalism.* Cambridge, Mass.: Harvard University Press, 2003.

Ellis, Jon. "On Pornography." *Pornography: Film and Culture.* Edited by Peter Lehman, 25–47. New Brunswick: Rutgers University Press, 2006.

Esteva, Gustavo, and Madhu Suri Prakash. *Grassroots Post-modernism: Remaking the Soil of Cultures.* London: Zed, 1998.

Fanon, Frantz. *Peau noire, masques blancs.* Paris: Seuil, 1952. Translated by Richard Philcox as *Black Skin, White Masks.* New York: Grove Press, 2008.

Firmin, Anténor. *The Equality of Human Races: Positivist Anthropology.* Translated by Asselin Charles. New York: Garland, 2000.

Forbes, Jack D. *Columbus and Other Cannibals: The Wétiko Disease of Exploitation, Imperialism, and Terrorism.* New York: Seven Stories Press, 2008.

Freud, Sigmund. *Civilization and Its Discontents.* New York: W. W. Norton, 1989.

———. *Three Essays on the Theory of Sexuality.* New York: Perseus Books, 2000.

———. *Totem and Taboo.* New York: W. W. Norton, 1989.

Fulton, Dawn. *Signs of Dissent: Maryse Condé and Postcolonial Criticism.* Charlottesville: University of Virginia Press, 2008.

Gabaccia, Donna. *We Are What We Eat: Ethnic Food and the Making of Americans.* Cambridge, Mass.: Harvard University Press, 1998.

Garraway, Doris. *The Libertine Colony: Creolization in the Early French Caribbean.* Durham: Duke University Press, 2005.

Garrido, Juan Manuel. *On Time, Being, and Hunger: Challenging the Traditional Way of Thinking Life.* New York: Fordham University Press, 2012.

Gilman, Sander. "Black Bodies, White Bodies: Toward an Iconography of Female Sexuality in Late Nineteenth-Century Art, Medicine, and Literature." *Critical Inquiry* 12, no. 1 (1985): 204–42.

Gilroy, Paul. *The Black Atlantic: Modernity and Double Consciousness.* Cambridge, Mass.: Harvard University Press, 1992.

———. "Route Work: The Black Atlantic and the Politics of Exile." In *The Postcolonial Question: Common Skies, Divided Horizons.* Edited by Iain Chambers and Lidia Curti, 17–29. New York: Routledge, 1996.

Girollet, Anne. *Victor Schoelcher, abolitionniste et républicain.* Paris: Karthala, 2000.

Githire, Njeri R. "The Empire Bites Back: Food Politics and the Making of a Nation in Andrea Levy's Works." *Callaloo* 33, no. 3 (Summer 2010): 857–73.

Glave, Thomas. *Our Caribbean: A Gathering of Lesbian and Gay Writing from the Antilles.* Durham: Duke University Press, 2008.

Glissant, Édouard. *Caribbean Discourse: Selected Essays.* Translated by Michael J. Dash. Charlottesville: University Press of Virginia, 1989.

———. *Le Discours antillais.* Paris: Seuil, 1981.

———. *Faulkner, Mississippi.* Paris: Gallimard, 1996.

———. *L'Imaginaire des langues: Entretiens avec Lise Gauvin.* Paris: Gallimard, 2010.

———. *Introduction à une poétique du divers.* Paris: Gallimard, 1996.

———. "Métissage et créolisation." In *Discours sur le métissage, identités métisses: En quête d'Ariel.* Edited by Sylvie Kandé, 47–53. Paris: L'Harmattan, 1999.

———. *Poétique de la Relation.* Paris: Gallimard, 1990. Translated by Betsy Wing as *Poetics of Relation.* Ann Arbor: University of Michigan Press, 2000.

———. *La Terre, le feu, l'eau et les vents: Une anthologie de la poésie du Tout-Monde.* Paris: Galaadé, 2010.

———. *Tout-monde.* Paris: Gallimard, 1993.

———. *Traité du tout-monde.* Paris: Gallimard, 1997.

Gmelch, George. *Behind the Smile: The Working Lives of Caribbean Tourism.* Bloomington: Indiana University Press, 2003.

Gobineau, Joseph Arthur comte de. *Essai sur l'inégalité des races humaines.* 2 vols. Paris: Firmin Didot, 1853.

Goldman, Anne. "I Yam What I Yam. " In *De/Colonizing the Subject: The Politics of Gender in Women's Autobiography.* Edited by Sidonie Smith and Julia Watson, 169–95. Minneapolis: University of Minnesota Press, 1992.

Gosson, Renée. "Cultural and Environmental Assimilation in Martinique: An Interview with Raphaël Confiant." In *Caribbean Literature and the Environment: Between Nature and Culture.* Edited by Elizabeth M. DeLoughrey, Renée K. Gosson, and George B. Handley, 143–53. Charlottesville: University of Virginia Press, 2005.

Greek–English Lexicon. Oxford: Clarendon Press, 1968.

Guest, Kristen, ed. *Eating Their Words: Cannibalism and the Boundaries of Cultural Identity.* Albany: State University of New York Press, 2001.

"Guide Vacances Martinique." *Zananas: Le Guide actif et festif de la Martinique.* January 6, 2007. http://www.zananas-martinique.com/immigration-indienne/histoire-2.

Guyer, Sara. "Albeit Eating: Towards an Ethics of Cannibalism." *Angelaki* 2, no. 1 (1995): 63–80.

Haddad, Gérard. *Manger le livre: Rites alimentaires et fonction paternelle.* Paris: Hachette, 1998.

Hallward, Peter. *Absolutely Postcolonial: Writing between the Singular and the Specific.* Manchester: Manchester University Press, 2001.

———. "Our Role in Haiti's Plight." *Guardian,* January 13, 2010.

Handley, George B. *New World Poetics: Nature and the Adamic Imagination of Whitman, Neruda, and Walcott.* Athens: University of Georgia Press, 2007.

Hardt, Michael, and Antonio Negri. *Empire.* Cambridge, Mass.: Harvard University Press, 2000.

Harris, Jessica B. *Beyond Gumbo: Creole Fusion Food from the Atlantic Rim.* New York, Simon and Schuster, 2003.

———. *Iron Pots and Wooden Spoons: Africa's Gifts to New World Cooking.* New York: Atheneum, 1989.

Harrus-Révidi, Gisèle. *Psychanalyse de la gourmandise.* Paris: Payot, 2003.

Hearn, Lafcadio. *American Writings.* New York: The Library of America, 2009.

———. *Creole Cook Book.* New York: Coleman, 1885.

———. *Gombo Zhèbes.* New York: Coleman, 1885.

———. *Two Years in the French West Indies.* New York: Interlinks Books, 2001.

Hill-Lubin, Mildred A. "The Grandmother in African and African-American Literature: A Survivor of the African Extended Family." In *Ngambika: Studies of Women in African Literature.* Edited by Carole Boyce Davies and Anne Adams Graves, 257–70. Trenton, N.J.: Africa World Press, 1990.

Hitchcott, Nicki. "Comment cuisiner son mari à l'africaine: Calixthe Beyala's Recipes for Migrant Identities." *French Cultural Studies* 14, no. 2 (2003): 211–20.

hooks, bell. *Black Looks: Race and Representation.* Boston: South End Press, 1992.

———. *Sisters of the Yam.* Boston: South End Press. 1993.

Houston, Lynn Marie. *Food Culture in the Caribbean.* Westport, Conn.: Greenwood Press, 2005.

Huggan, Graham. "Ghost Stories, Bone Flutes, Cannibal Countermemory." In Barker, Hulme, and Iversen, 110–25.

Hughes, Marvalene. "Soul, Black Women, and Food." In Counihan and Van Esterik, 272–80.

Hulme, Peter. "Introduction: The Cannibal Scene." In Barker, Hulme, and Iversen, 1–38.

Hurbon, Laënnec. *Les mystères du vaudou.* Paris: Gallimard, 1993.

Jaccard, Anny-Claire. "Nourriture, syncrétisme et acculturation." *Syncrétisme et interculturel: De Rome à l'ère postcoloniale: Cultures, littératures, esthétique.* Edited by Jean-Pierre Durix, 31–44. Dijon: Editions Universitaires de Dijon, 1997.

James, Erica Caple. *Democratic Insecurities: Violence, Trauma, and Intervention in Haiti.* Berkeley and Los Angeles: University of California Press, 2010.

James, Cynthia. *The Maroon Narrative.* Portsmouth: Heinemann, 2002.

Jameson, Fredric. "Third-World Literature in the Era of Multinational Capitalism." *Social Text* 15 (Autumn 1986): 65–68.

Jáuregui, Carlos A. *Canibalia: Canibalismo, Calibanismo, Antropofagia Cultural y Consumo en América Latina.* Madrid: Iberoamericana, 2008.

Jenson, Deborah. "The Writing of Disaster in Haiti: Signifying Cataclysm from Slave Revolution to Earth Quake." *Haiti Rising.* Edited by Martin Munro, 103–12. Liverpool: Liverpool University Press, 2010.

Joubert, Jean-Louis. "Présentation." *Notre Librairie* 151 (July–September 2003): 1.

Jurney, Florence. "Transgresser l'insularité: Inscriptions de l'espace antillais dans *Chair Piment* de Gisèle Pineau." *Littéréalité* 16, no. 1 (Spring/Summer 2004): 31–43.

Kern-Foxworth, Marilyn. *Aunt Jemima, Uncle Ben, and Rastus: Blacks in Advertising Yesterday, Today, and Tomorrow.* Westport, Conn.: Praeger, 1994.

Khanna, Balraj. *The Best of India.* San Francisco: Collins Publishers, 1993.

Kilgour, Maggie. *From Communion to Cannibalism: An Anatomy of Metaphors of Incorporation.* Princeton: Princeton University Press, 1990.

King James Bible. New York: Meridian, 1974.

King, Richard. "The (Mis)Uses of Cannibalism in Contemporary Cultural Critique." *Diacritics: A Review of Contemporary Criticism* 30, no. 1 (2000): 106–23.

Klein, Melanie. "Weaning." In *Love, Guilt, and Reparation, and Other Works, 1921–1945,* 290–305. New York: Free Press, 1984.

Kutzinski, Vera. *Sugar's Secrets: Race and the Erotics of Cuban Nationalism.* Charlottesville: University Press of Virginia, 1993.

Labat, Jean-Baptiste. *Voyage aux îles françaises de l'Amérique.* Paris: La découvrance, 2006.

Lachman, Kathryn. "Le cannibalisme au féminin." In Broichhagen, Lachman, and Simek, 71–83.

Laferrière, Dany. *Comment faire l'amour avec un nègre sans se fatiguer.* Paris: Le Serpent à plumes, 1985.

———. *Pays sans chapeau.* Paris: Le Serpent à plumes, 1999.

———. *Vers le Sud.* Paris: Grasset, 2006.

Lamming, George. "Concepts of the Caribbean." *Frontiers of Caribbean Literature in English.* Edited by Frank Birbalsingh. New York: St. Martin's Press, 1996.

Lee, Spike. *She's Gotta Have It.* Directed by Spike Lee. Beverly Hills: Twentieth Century Fox Home Entertainment, 2008. Originally released 1986.

Leiris, Michel. *Contacts de civilisations en Martinique et en Guadeloupe.* Paris: UNESCO–Gallimard, 1955.

Lesser, Jeffrey. *A Discontented Diaspora: Japanese Brazilians and the Meanings of Ethnic Militancy, 1960–1980.* Durham: Duke University Press, 2007.

Lestringant, Frank. *Le Cannibale: Grandeur et décadence.* Preface by Pierre Chaunu. Paris: Perrin, 1994.

Levi, Primo. *Survival in Auschwitz (If This Is a Man).* New York: Summit Books, 1985.

Lévi-Strauss, Claude. "The Culinary Triangle." In Counihan and Van Esterik, 28–35.

———. *The Raw and the Cooked: Introduction to a Science of Mythology.* New York: Harper and Row, 1969.

———. *Tristes tropiques.* New York: Athenaeum, 1974.

Lionnet, Françoise. "Narrating the Americas: Transcolonial *Métissage* and Maryse Condé's *La Migration des cœurs.*" In *Mixing Race, Mixing Culture.* Edited by Monika Kaup and Debra J. Rosenthal, 65–87. Austin: University of Texas Press, 2002.

———. *Postcolonial Representations: Women, Literature, Identity.* Ithaca: Cornell University Press, 1995.

Lionnet, Françoise, and Shu-Mei Shih. *Minor Transnationalism.* Durham: Duke University Press, 2005.

Loichot, Valérie. "'Callaloo Is Sacred': An Interview with Prudence Marcelin." *Callaloo* 30, no. 1 (Winter 2007): 68–69.

———. "'Devoured by Writing': An Interview with Gisèle Pineau." *Callaloo* 30, no. 1 (Winter 2007): 328–37.

———. *Orphan Narratives: The Postplantation Literature of William Faulkner, Édouard Glissant, Toni Morrison, and Saint-John Perse.* Charlottesville: University of Virginia Press, 2007.

———. "'Survie et création': La nourriture dans les contes louisianais et martiniquais." *La Revue Française* 7, University of Kwazulu-Natal (July 1999): 35–45.

Lopes, Josefina. *Hungry Woman in Paris.* New York: Grand Central Publishing, 2009.

Lorde, Audre. "Uses of the Erotic: The Erotic as Power." In *Sister Outsider: Essays and Speeches,* 53–59. New York: The Crossing Press/ Trumansburg, 1984.

———. *Zami: A New Spelling of My Name.* New York: The Crossing Press, 1982.

MacKie, Cristine. *Life and Food in the Caribbean.* Kingston: Randle, 1995.

———. *Trade Winds: Caribbean Cooking.* Bath: Absolute Press, 1996.

Madureira, Luís. *Cannibal Modernities: Postcoloniality and the Avant-Garde in Caribbean and Brazilian Literature.* Charlottesville: University of Virginia Press, 2005.

Manring, Maurice. *Slave in a Box: The Strange Career of Aunt Jemima.* Charlottesville: University Press of Virginia, 1998.

Marcuse, Herbert. *Eros and Civilization: A Philosophical Inquiry into Freud.* Boston: Beacon Press, 1966.

Mardorossian, Karine. *Reclaiming Difference: Caribbean Women Rewrite Postcolonialism.* Chalottesville: University of Virginia Press, 2005.

Marshall, Paule. *Reena and Other Stories.* New York: Feminist Press. 1983.

Martin, Nina K. *Sexy Thrills: Undressing the Erotic Thriller.* Chicago: University of Illinois Press, 2007.

Maximin, Daniel. "Suzanne Césaire, fontaine solaire." In Suzanne Césaire, 7–23.

Mayr, Suzette. "Absent Black Women in Dany Laferrière's *How to Make Love to a Negro.*" *Canadian Literature* 188 (Spring 2006): 31–45.

Mbembe, Achille. *On the Postcolony.* Berkeley and Los Angeles: University of California Press, 2001.

Mehta, Brinda. "Bhaji, Curry, and Masala: Food and/as Identity in Four Films of the Indian Diaspora. *India and the Diasporic Imagination.* Edited by Rita Christian and Judith Misrahi-Barak, 353–72. Montpellier: Presses Universitaires de la Méditerranée, 2011.

———. "Gisèle Pineau, *Un papillon dans la cité* and *L'exil selon Julia.*" *International Journal of Francophone Studies* 8, no. 1 (2005): 23–51.

———. "Indo-Trinidadian Fiction: Female Identity and Creative Cooking." *Alif: Journal of Comparative Poetics* 19 (1999): 151–84.

———. *Notions of Identity, Diaspora, and Gender in Caribbean Women's Writing.* New York: Palgrave Macmillan, 2009.

Ménil, René. "Laissez passer la poésie." *Tropiques 5* (April 1942): 26–27.

Métraux, Alfred. *Le Vaudou haïtien.* Paris: Gallimard, 1958.

Mintz, Sidney. *Tasting Food, Tasting Freedom.* Boston: Beacon Press, 1996.

Montaigne. "Des Cannibales." *Œuvres complètes.* Paris: Gallimard, 1962. 200–213. Translated by Donald Frame as "Of Cannibals." *The Complete Essays of Montaigne.* Stanford: Stanford University Press, 1958.

Montel, Aurélia. *Le Père Labat viendra te prendre.* Paris: Maisonneuve et Larose, 1996.

Moreau de Saint-Méry. *Description topographique, physique, civile, politique et historique de la partie française de l'isle de Saint-Domingue.* Paris: Société française d'histoire d'Outre-Mer, 1984.

Morrison, Toni. *Beloved.* New York: Alfred A. Knopf, 1987.

———. *The Nobel Lecture in Literature.* New York: Alfred A. Knopf, 1993.

Morton, Timothy. *The Poetics of Spice: Romantic Consumerism and the Exotic.* Cambridge: Cambridge University Press, 2000.

Moudileno, Lydie. "La Gastronomie furtive de Maryse Condé." *Romanic Review: Order, Disorder, and Freedom: An Homage to Maryse Condé* 94, nos. 3–4 (May–November 2003): 421–27.

Munasinghe, Viranjini. *Callaloo or Tossed Salad: East Indians and the Cultural Politics of Identity in Trinidad.* Ithaca: Cornell University Press, 2001.

Ndiaye, Pap. *La Condition noire: Essai sur une minorité française*. Paris: Calmann-Lévy, 2008.

Novero, Cecilia. *Antidiets of the Avant-Garde: From Futuristic Cooking to Eat Art*. Minneapolis: University of Minnesota Press, 2010.

Nesbitt, Nick. "Politiques et poétiques: Les errances de l'absolu." In *Entours d'Édouard Glissant*. Edited by Valérie Loichot. *Revue des sciences humaines*, special issue, forthcoming, 2013.

———. *Voicing Memory: History and Subjectivity in French Caribbean Literature*. Charlottesville: University of Virginia Press, 2003.

Nunes, Zita. *Cannibal Democracy: Race and Representation in the Literature of the Americas*. Minneapolis: University of Minnesota Press, 2008.

N'Zengou-Tayo, Marie-José. "Rewriting Folklore: Traditional Beliefs and Popular Culture in Edwidge Danticat's *Breath, Eyes, Memory* and *Krik? Krak!*" *MaComère* 3 (2000): 123–40.

O'Rourke, Dennis. *Cannibal Tours*. Directed by Dennis O'Rourke. Los Angeles: Direct Cinema Limited, 1988.

Ovide, Stéphanie. *French Caribbean Cuisine*. Preface by Maryse Condé. New York: Hippocrene Books, 2002.

Paes, César. *Le Bouillon d'Awara*. Directed by César Paes. San Francisco: California Newsreel, 1995.

Palcy, Euzhan. *Aimé Césaire: Une voix pour l'histoire*. Directed by Euzhan Palcy. San Francisco: California Newsreel, 1994.

Picard, Michel. *Lire le temps*. Paris: Minuit, 1989.

Pilcher, Jeffrey. *¡Que Vivan los Tamales! Food and the Making of Mexican Identity*. Albuquerque: University of New Mexico Press, 1998.

Pineau, Gisèle. *Chair Piment*. Paris: Mercure de France, 2002.

———. *L'Exil selon Julia*. Paris: Stock, 1996.

———. *Morne Câpresse*. Paris: Mercure de France, 2008.

———. *Un Papillon dans la cité*. Paris: Sépia, 1992.

Platon. *Phèdre*. Translated by Léon Robin. Paris: Les Belles lettres, 1994.

Pollan, Michael. *The Omnivore's Dilemma: A Natural History of Four Meals*. London: Penguin Books, 2006.

Poon, Angelia. "Re-Writing the Male Text: Mapping Cultural Spaces in Edwidge Danticat's *Krik? Krak!* and Jamaica Kincaid's *A Small Place*." *Jouvert: A Journal of Postcolonial Studies* 4, no. 2 (2000). http://english.chass.ncsu.edu/jouvert/.

Prado Bellei, Sérgio Luís. "Brazilian Anthropophagy Revisited." In Barker, Hulme, and Iversen, 87–109.

Pratt, Mary Louise. *Imperial Eyes: Travel Writing and Transculturation*. London: Routledge, 1992.

Priam, Mylène. "'Loup y es-tu?' 60 ans de départementalisation." *International Journal of Francophone Studies* 11, no. 1–2 (2008): 107–22.

Prieto, Eric. "The Uses of Landscape: Ecocriticism and Martinican Cultural Theory." In DeLoughrey, Gosson, and Handley, 236–46.

Proust, Marcel. *Swann's Way*. London: Chatto and Windus, 1951.

Quay, Michelange. *Mange, ceci est mon corps*. Directed by Michelange Quay. Paris: Cinéma de Facto, 2007.

Reboux, Paul. *Le Paradis des Antilles françaises*. Paris: Librairie de la Revue Française, 1931.

Retamar, Roberto Fernández. *Caliban and Other Essays*. Minneapolis: University of Minnesota Press, 2000.

Richardson, Michael. "Introduction." *Refusal of the Shadow: Surrealism and the Caribbean*. London: Verso, 1996.

Ricoeur, Paul. *Temps et récit*, vol. 1. Paris: Seuil, 1983.

Riggs, Marlon. *Black Is, Black Ain't: A Personal Journey through Black Identity*. Directed by Marlon Riggs. San Francisco: California Newsreel, 1995.

Ring, Natalie. "Inventing the Tropical South: Race, Region, and the Colonial Model." *Mississippi Quarterly* 56, no. 4 (Autumn 2003): 619–31.

Robbins, Louise E. *Elephant Slaves and Pampered Parrots: Exotic Animals in Eighteenth-Century Paris*. Baltimore: Johns Hopkins University Press, 2002.

Rolle, William. "Alimentation et dépendance idéologique à la Martinique: 'An tan Wobe' (1940–1943)." *Archipelago* 2 (1982): 76–95.

Rosello, Mireille. *Declining the Stereotype: Ethnicity and Representation in French Cultures*. Hanover, N.H.: Dartmouth University Press, 1998.

———. *Littérature et identité créole aux Antilles*. Paris: Karthala, 1992.

———. "Martinique charmeuse de serpents: Changer la vue sous les Tropiques." *L'Esprit Créateur* 36, no. 4 (Winter 1996): 64–75.

———. "One More Sea to Cross: Exile and Intertextuality in Aimé Césaire's *Cahier d'un retour au pays natal*." *Yale French Studies* 83 (1993): 176–95.

———. "Post-Cannibalism in Maryse Condé's *Histoire de la femme cannibale*." In Broichhagen, Lachman, and Simek, 35–49.

Rothman, Adam. "Lafcadio Hearn in New Orleans and the Caribbean." *Atlantic Studies* 5, no. 2 (August 2008): 265–83.

Roy-Camille, Christiane, and Annick Marie. *Les Meilleures recettes de la cuisine antillaise*. Paris: Fleurus, 1999.

Roy, Parama. *Indian Traffic: Identities in Question in Colonial and Postcolonial India*. Berkeley and Los Angeles: University of California Press, 1998.

———. "Reading Communities and Culinary Communities: The Gastropoetics of the South Asian Diaspora." *Positions* 10, no. 2 (2002): 471–502.

Sands, Peter. "Octavia Butler's Chiastic Cannibalistics." *Utopian Studies* 14, no. 1 (2003): 1–14.

Sartre, Jean-Paul. "Orphée noir." *Anthologie de la nouvelle poésie nègre et malgache*. Edited by Léopold Sédar Senghor, ix–xliv. Paris: Presses Universitaires de France, 1948.

Scapp, Ron, and Brian Seitz, eds. *Eating Culture*. Albany: State University of New York Press, 1998.

Schor, Naomi. "Eating and Disorder." *Differences: A Journal of Feminist Cultural Studies* 10, no. 1 (1998): n.p.

Schur, Richard. "*The Wind Done Gone* Controversy: American Studies, Copyright Law, and the Imaginary Domain." *American Studies* 44, no. 1–2 (Spring/Summer 2003): 5–33.

Schwarz-Bart, Simone. "Du fond des casseroles." In *Nouvelles de Guadeloupe,* 75–81. Paris: Miniatures, 2009.

Scott, Helen. *Caribbean Women Writers and Globalization: Fictions of Independence.* Burlington: Ashgate, 2006.

Schon, Nathalie. *L'Auto-exotisme dans les littératures des Antilles françaises.* Paris: Karthala, 2003.

Seifert, Lewis C. "Orality, History, and Creoleness in Chamoiseau's *Creole Folktales.*" *Marvels and Tales* 16, no. 2 (2002) 214–230.

Senghor, Léopold Sédar. *Hosties noires.* Paris: Seuil, 1948.

———. *Œuvre poétique.* Paris: Seuil, 1990.

Shakespeare, William. *The Tempest.* New York: Chelsea House, 1988.

Shange, Ntozake. *A Daughter's Geography.* New York: St. Martin's Press, 1991.

———. *If I Can Cook/You Know God Can.* Boston: Beacon Press, 1998.

Sheller, Mimi. *Consuming the Caribbean: From Arawaks to Zombies.* London: Routledge, 2003.

Simmonds, Felly Nkweto. "'She's Gotta Have It': The Representation of Black Female Sexuality on Film." *Feminist Review* 29 (Summer 1988): 10–22.

Smart-Grosvenor, Vertamae. *Vibration Cooking; or, The Travel Notes of a Geechee Girl.* New York: Ballantine Books, 1992.

Smith, Eric. "Pandering Caribbean Spice." *Journal of Commonwealth Literature* 39, no. 3 (2004): 5–24.

Sobo, Elisa. "The Sweetness of Fat, Health, Procreation, and Sociability in Rural Jamaica." In Counihan and Van Esterik, 256–71.

Spillers, Hortense. *Black, White, and in Color: Essays on American Literature and Culture.* Chicago: University of Chicago Press, 2003.

Stallybrass, Peter. "Against Thinking." *PMLA* 122, no. 5 (October 2007): 1580–87.

Stewart, Dianne M. *Three Eyes for the Journey: African Dimensions of the Jamaican Religious Experience.* New York: Oxford University Press, 2005.

Strachan, Ian Gregory. *Paradise and Plantation: Tourism and Culture in the Anglophone Caribbean.* Charlottesville: University of Virginia Press, 2002.

Suvélor, Roland. "Yé et les malédictions de la faim." *Acoma* 3 (1972): 52–70.

Taylor, Lelia. "Callaloo Anyone?" *Callaloo* 1 (1976): 1–2.

Tinsley, Omise'eke Natasha. *Thiefing Sugar: Eroticism between Women in Caribbean Literature.* Durham: Duke University Press, 2010.

Tomich, Dale. *Slavery in the Circuit of Sugar: Martinique and the World Economy, 1830–1948.* Baltimore: Johns Hopkins University Press, 1990.

Torabully, Khal. *Chair corail, fragments coolies.* Paris: Ibis Rouge, 2000.

Trinh Min Ha. *Woman, Native, Other: Writing Postcoloniality and Feminism.* Bloomington: Indiana University Press, 1989.

Trouillot, Michel-Rolph. *Silencing the Past: Power and the Production of History.* Boston: Beacon Press, 1995.

VanVechten, Carl. *Nigger Heaven.* New York: Avon, 1951.

Vergès, Françoise. *Monsters and Revolutionaries: Colonial Family Romance and Métissage.* Durham: Duke University Press, 1999.

Vété-Congolo, Hanétha. "Love and Lovemaking in French Caribbean Women's Writing: Kettly Mars, Nicole Cage-Florentiny, and Suzanne Dracius." In Opal Palmer Adisa and Donna Weir-Soley, 302–23.

Vieux-Chauvet, Marie. *Amour, Colère, Folie.* Paris: Maisonneuve et Larose/Emina Soleil, 2005.

———. *Danse sur le volcan.* Paris: Plon, 1957.

Walcott, Derek. *What the Twilight Says.* New York: Farrar, Straus and Giroux, 1998.

Wallace Sanders, Kimberly. *Mammy: A Century of Race, Gender, and Southern Memory.* Ann Arbor: University of Michigan Press, 2008.

Warnes, Andrew. *Hunger Overcome: Food and Resistance in Twentieth-Century African American Literature.* Athens: University of Georgia Press, 2004.

———. *Savage Barbecue: Race, Culture, and the Invention of Americ's First Food.* Athens: University of Georgia Press, 2008.

Webster's New World Dictionary of the American Language. New York: World, 1957.

Wey-Gómez, Nicolás. "Cannibalism as Defacement: Columbus's Account of the Fourth Voyage." *Journal of Hispanic Philology* 16, no. 2 (1992): 195–208.

Whitman, Walt. *Complete Poetry and Selected Prose.* Boston: Houghton Mifflin, 1959.

Wideman, John Edgar. *The Island: Martinique.* Washington, D.C.: National Geographic, 2003.

Wiegman, Robyn. "The Anatomy of Lynching." *Journal of the History of Sexuality* 3, no. 3 (January 1993): 445–67.

Wilks, Jennifer. *Race, Gender, and Comparative Black Modernism: Suzanne Lacascade, Marita Bronner, Suzanne Césaire, Dorothy West.* Baton Rouge: Louisiana State University Press, 2008.

Wilks, Richard. *Home Cooking in the Global Village: Caribbean Food from Buccaneers to Ecotourists.* Oxford: Berg Publishers, 2006.

Wilson, Elizabeth. "Island and Journey as Metaphor." In *Out of the Kumbla.* Edited by Carole Boyce Davies and Elaine Savory Fido, 45–57. Trenton, N.J.: Africa World Press, 1990.

Wilson, Peter. *Crab Antics: The Social Anthropology of the English-Speaking Negro Societies in the Caribbean.* New Haven: Yale University Press, 1973.

Witt, Doris. *Black Hunger: Food and the Politics of U.S. Identity.* New York: Oxford University Press, 1999.

Zobel, Joseph. *La Rue Case-Nègres.* Paris: Présence africaine, 1974.

INDEX

VALÉRIE LOICHOT is associate professor of French and English at Emory University, where she also serves as core faculty in comparative literature. She is the author of *Orphan Narratives: The Postplantation Literature of Faulkner, Glissant, Morrison, and Saint-John Perse* and of numerous essays on Caribbean literature and culture, American literature, and creolization theory.